WITHDRAWN BY THE
UNIVERSITY OF MICHIGAN

Greek Romans and Roman Greeks

Aarhus Studies in Mediterranean Antiquity (ASMA)

III

ASMA is a series which will be published approximately once a year by The Centre for the Study of Antiquity, University of Aarhus, Denmark.

The Centre is a network of cooperating departments: Greek and Latin, Classical Archaeology, History, and the Faculty of Theology. The objective of the series is to advance interdisciplinary studies of Antiquity by publishing articles, e.g., conference papers, or independent monographs, which among other things reflect the current activities of the centre.

Greek Romans and Roman Greeks

Studies in Cultural Interaction

Edited by Erik Nis Ostenfeld

with the assistance of

Karin Blomqvist and Lisa Nevett

AARHUS UNIVERSITY PRESS

GREEK ROMANS AND ROMAN GREEKS

Copyright: Aarhus University Press 2002
Cover design by Jørgen Sparre
Illustration: Marble bust of the Roman emperor Hadrian.
Ny Carlsberg Glyptotek, Copenhagen, cat. 681, I.N. 777.
Photo: Jo Selsing
Printed in Denmark at the Narayana Press, Gylling
ISBN 87 7288 796 6

AARHUS UNIVERSITY PRESS

Langelandsgade 177
DK-8200 Aarhus N
Fax (+45) 89 42 53 80
www.unipress.dk

73 Lime Walk
Headington, Oxford OX3 7AD
Fax (+44) 1865 750 079

Box 511
Oakville, CT 06779
Fax (+1) 860 945 9468

Published with financial support from
The Danish Research Council for the Humanities
The Aarhus University Research Foundation
Kungliga Humanistiska Vetenskapssamfundet i Lund

Preface

This third volume of Aarhus Studies in Mediterranean Antiquity contains a series of papers given at a conference entitled *Greek Romans or Roman Greeks? Interaction, confrontation and Cultural Responses in the first three Centuries of the Roman Empire,* held in Lund, Sweden from 25-28 June, 1998.

A number of distinguished scholars from different countries took part in this conference which was organised as a joint venture between Klassiska Institutionen, University of Lund, Sweden, and the Center for the Study of Antiquity at Aarhus University, Denmark. As her part of the enterprise, Dr Karin Blomqvist of Lund took responsibility for organising the conference in Lund while the publication of the acts was committed to Dr Erik Ostenfeld of Aarhus. This division of work meant that the financial burden of the project was divided so that Lund provided support for the conference itself, whilst Aarhus covered most of the publication expenses. In this regard I should like on the behalf of the organisers to extend our warmest thanks for financial support to the Danish Research Council for the Humanities, Aarhus University Research Foundation and Kungliga Humanistiska Vetenskapssamfundet i Lund.

The purpose of the conference was to explore the intercultural aspects of a period where the Roman Empire expanded while Greek culture was experiencing a new heyday. This occasioned both tension and fertile inspiration, mirrored in the various ramifications of contemporary culture. Accordingly, the conference focussed on widely diverse disciplines such as philology, epigraphy, archaeology, history, the history of ideas and the history of literature. The conference provided a most useful forum for the exchange of ideas between scholars from various fields dealing with a crucial multicultural period, both different from and similar to our own time. The title has been slightly modified to *Greek Romans and Roman Greeks* to clearly accommodate the fact that the contributors deal with both Romans who 'became' Greek and Greeks who 'became' Roman.

Finally, I would like to thank Dr Karin Blomqvist and Dr Lisa Nevett who most helpfully assisted in the editing of this volume. Also thanks are due to Lisa Irene Hau who kindly prepared the indices and to Sanne Lind Hansen and Mary Lund of Aarhus University Press for their patient support throughout the publishing process.

Aarhus, Jan. 2002   E.O.

Contents

Erik Nis Ostenfeld and Karin Blomqvist
Introduction   9

Archaeological Studies

Helène Whittaker
1   Some Reflections on the Temple to the Goddess Roma and Augustus on the Acropolis at Athens   25

Arja Karivieri
2   Just one of the Boys – Hadrian in the Company of Zeus, Dionysus and Theseus   40

Jakob Munk Højte
3   Cultural Interchange? The Case of Honorary Statues in Greece   55

Renée Forsell
4   The Argolid Countryside in the Roman Period   64

Kalle Korhonen
5   Three Cases of Greek/Latin Imbalance in Roman Syracuse   70

Lisa Nevett
6   Continuity and Change in Greek Households under Roman Rule: The Role of Women in the Domestic Context   81

Philology, History and History of Ideas

Luigi Senzasono
7   Some Influences of Greek Poetry in the first Choral Song of Seneca's *Phaedra* (274-357)   101

Anne Malling Eriksen
8   Redefining *Virtus* – the Settings of Virtue in the Works of Velleius Paterculus and Lucan   111

Philip A. Stadter
9   Plutarch's Lives and Their Roman Readers   123

Contents

Frances B. Titchener
10 Plutarch and Roman(ized) Athens — *136*

Victor Castellani
11 Plutarch's 'Roman' Women — *142*

R. Anthony Kugler
12 The Ox, the Crow, and the Orator:
    Image, Allegory, and Motive in Dio Chrysostom's
    Second Tarsian Oration (*Oration* 34) — *156*

Ewen Bowie
13 Hadrian and Greek Poetry — *172*

Jaap-Jan Flinterman
14 The Self-portrait of an Antonine Orator:
    Aristides, *Or.* 2.429 ff. — *198*

Anthon Xenophontov
15 Polyaenus: A Greek Writer as a Job-seeker in the Roman World — *212*

Paolo Desideri
16 The Meaning of Greek Historiography of the Roman Imperial Age — *216*

Sophie Lalanne
17 Hellenism and Romanization:
    A Comparison between the Greek Novels
    and the Tale of Psyche in Apuleius' *Metamorphoses* — *225*

Joseph Geiger
18 Language, Culture and Identity in Ancient Palestine — *233*

Abbreviations — *247*

Text editions used — *249*

General Bibliography — *250*

Notes on Contributors — *273*

Index rerum — *275*

Index nominum — *278*

Index locorum — *283*

Introduction

by Erik Nis Ostenfeld and Karin Blomqvist

In its first three centuries the Roman Empire expanded politically at the same time that Greek culture was having its second heyday in what since Antiquity has been called the Second Sophistic. This created tensions as well as fruitful impulses, which were mirrored in different branches of cultural life. This third volume of *Aarhus Studies in Mediterranean Antiquity* (ASMA III) explores the intercultural aspects of that thriving period.

The book is a collection of papers from a conference, 'Greek Romans or Roman Greeks? Interaction, confrontation and cultural responses in the first three centuries of the Roman Empire', held in Lund in 1998 and sponsored jointly by the Center for the Study of Antiquity, University of Aarhus, Denmark and the University of Lund, Sweden. It assembled an international team of scholars from the fields of philology, history of ideas, literature, epigraphy, archaeology and history.

The material culture of the period is illuminated by papers on honorary statues in Achaea, settlements in the Argolis, the Acropolis at Athens, Syracusan epitaphs and Greek houses in general. The gallery of literary personalities dealt with extends from Velleius Paterculus to Heliodorus but centers around authors active in the Second Century. The emphasis is on Greek writers. Thus three essays deal with Plutarch, others with Dio Chrysostom, Aristides, Polyaenus and Greek novelists. The Latin side is represented by Seneca, Lucan and Apuleius. Interestingly, Hadrian hovers somewhere in between.

***

Helène Whittaker von Hofsten in 'Some reflections on the Temple to the Goddess Roma and Augustus on the Acropolis at Athens' argues for a dating of the Temple to Augustus and Roma on the Acropolis after 10 BC in connection with Gaius' visit to Athens and sees the cult of Roma and Augustus in the context of Rome's attempts to equate their campaigns against the Parthians with the wars between the Greeks and Persians. Whittaker takes up the much-debated question about the dating of Monopteros on the Acropolis in Athens. The issue is an important one, since it concerns the Romanization of Athens in the Augustan age. By way of studying texts and monuments of the era, the author suggests a new dating of the monument in question. This has a bearing on the whole debate on how early the Romanization of Athens, and thus of Greece, began, and on how far it went.

Arja Karivieri in a paper entitled 'Just one of the Boys – Hadrian in the Company of Zeus, Dionysus and Theseus' deals with the ideological background for the rebuilding of Athens in the second century AD planned and financed by Hadrian. The main source here is by Pausanias, whose description of Athenian monuments offers a general frame for the analysis of the buildings and other monuments and of their role in the imperial and religious policy of Hadrian. Another important source is Plutarch whose *Parallel Lives* gives a comparison between the founders of Athens and Rome, Theseus and Romulus. The buildings, statues and other known monuments of this period are discussed, and comparisons are made to ancient sources and to the monuments that were built by other Roman emperors and which were utilized by Hadrian in his imperial propaganda. A special emphasis is given to the arch of Hadrian, the temple of Zeus, and to the rebuilding of the *scaenae frons* in the theatre of Dionysos. The motivation for starting this building programme in Athens was to spread the idea of Hadrian as the ruler of Rome and the new founder of (the Roman) Athens, with the help of Theseus and Romulus. For this purpose he used a cuirassed statue of himself in the Agora, with a representation of Athena standing on the back of the wolf that nurtured Romulus and Remus. In the Arch he was assimilated with Theseus, the first founder of Athens. He also gave himself a divine status by association with Zeus, or Dionysus, son of Zeus.

Jakob Munk Højte in his paper 'Cultural Interchange? The case of Honorary Statues in Greece' deals with the honours that Greek Cities could bestow on foreigners. He focuses on honorific statues given to Romans in the province of Achaea, with particular focus on the dedicatory inscriptions on the statue bases, of which there remain almost 300 (apart from those relating to the imperial family) from the two first centuries of the principate. Although the inscriptions were still in Greek, the way names and titles were recorded conformed with Roman practices. While the Hellenistic rulers invested in large Panhellenic sanctuaries, Roman influence in the late Republic is seen by Højte as the possible explanation for the spread of these statues.

Renée Forsell's paper on 'The Argolid Countryside in the Roman Period' studies settlement patterns and a single bath and a villa and concludes that the land was owned by absentee landlords and that the population was not exposed to much of Roman culture. In the first centuries of the Roman Empire, the Argolid countryside was definitely Roman backwater. With Methana as an exception, the Argolid countryside retained the sleepy existence that started in the late Hellenistic period. There are signs of shifts in land holding: the land now belonged to absentee landowners and the money extracted was probably more often put into buildings in the towns like Argos and Hermione or the sanctuary of Epidaurus than invested back into the soil of the land. There is, however, nothing to suggest that the owners were Romans. Comparing the Argolid with the prosperous western parts of the Peloponnesus, in which we know that the Romans had interests (Patras for instance was a Roman colony), and where the settlement patterns display distinct parallels with those revealed by surveys in Italy, Renee Forsell draws the conclusion that the poverty of the Argolid countryside shows a lack of Roman interest in the region.

Kalle Korhonen in 'Three Cases of Greek/Latin Imbalance in Roman Syracuse' examines the sociolinguistic aspects of three groups of Syracusan epitaphs from early imperial period to the 6th century. They reflect an increasing Romanization.

The purpose of this paper is to examine the use of Greek and Latin in certain groups of written material in Roman Syracuse. The investigation has been focused on three groups of funerary inscriptions: those of the early imperial period from the whole city, those from the catacomb of Vigna Cassia, and inscriptions from late Antiquity and the beginning of the Middle ages. Korhonen applies sociolinguistic methods on this material, with interesting results.

As funerary inscriptions belong to a relatively formal domain of language use, the language was not chosen arbitrarily but with attention to the conventions of the family or reference group to which the family belonged. As regards the early imperial period, Greek was often used even when Latin would have been expected. For a local notable of the first centuries AD, Greek remained an appreciated cultural language. Trying to describe the situation in sociolinguistic terms, one could say that in the domain of funerary epigraphy, neither Greek nor Latin was the high variant; instead, the distinction between high and low depended on the linguistic form. There were other means, too, which could be used in showing a higher social position, namely the form of the monument.

In Vigna Cassia, the question is whether the proportion of Greek and Latin epitaphs reflects the proportion of the language groups therein. The answer is affirmative, but with a certain reservation, for Greek may have been chosen for the sake of convenience in communication.

Lisa Nevett's paper 'Continuity and Change in Greek Households under Roman Rule: The Role of Women in the Domestic Context' looks at the extent to which individual households were changed by Roman control, especially it looks at attitudes to women. Literary sources suggest that women's roles may have changed rapidly during the first century BC to first century AD, but evidence is scarce and it is difficult to establish to what extent statements made by different authors are reliable. Nevett therefore focuses on archaeological evidence for Greek housing, which offers direct evidence of patterns of social behaviour in individual households. In houses across the Greek world there are three changes which take place in spatial organisation: (i) changes in patterns of circulation which make it easier to enter the house and to move between rooms, (ii) changes in the use of the court from a domestic area to an area aimed at display, (iii) the appearance of a Campanian type *atrium* with a central *impluvium*, in a minority of houses. Together these changes suggest that corresponding changes took place in underlying patterns of social behaviour. In particular, the opening up of the domestic environment implies a relaxation of the restrictions placed on women during the Classical and earlier Hellenistic periods. The extent to which these changes can be interpreted as evidence of 'Romanization' is difficult to gauge – especially since Roman houses themselves are so diverse and our knowledge of them so dominated by the (probably unrepresentative) houses fra Campania. Nonetheless, these developments are in keeping with the broader trajectory of social change taking place from the later Hellenistic period onwards and attested in a variety of different sources, which suggest that in some respects attitudes to women may already have been changing prior to the arrival of the Romans. This emphasis on the role of pre-existing Greek culture in creating the culture of Roman Greece is in agreement with archaeological models of Romanization, which have stressed the role of indigenous cultures in the changes which accompanied Roman political control.

Luigi Senzasono in his 'Some Influences of Greek Poetry in the first Choral Song of Seneca's *Phaedra* (274-357)' argues that Greek influence at several levels shows that an author of this time could consciously and unconsciously use Greek models to display a decorous literary craft rather than as an inspiration to genuine creation of something new. Senzasono finds Greek influences from a microstructural level at a microstructural level in Seneca (Hes. *Th.*, Eur. *Hipp.*, *Alc.*, Archil., Homer, Mosch.), from a macrostructural level at a microstructural level in Seneca (Ap. Rh. 3.112-66), Greek influences from a microstructural level at a macrostructural level in Seneca (e.g. Eur. *Hipp.* 530 and 1-6) and finally, influences from a macrostructural level at a macrostructural level in Seneca (Soph. *Ant.* 781-800). Senzasono finds that Seneca is *inter alia* more intellectual than poetical, or more rhetorical, artificial and exaggerated, and that the concentration and intensity of the model is diluted in e.g. a paratactic sequence of images. The only positive aspect Senzasono finds in Seneca is a skill in amalgamating the Greek suggestions in a composition unified by the motive of love and by a paratactic structure. The poem is thus 'an attempt of lyrical synthesis, pursued by a cerebral and refined art, foreboding the dramatic action that is about to be developed'.

Anne Malling Eriksen in her contribution 'Redefining *Virtus* – the Settings of Virtue in the works of Velleius Paterculus and Lucan' examines the vocabularies of virtue in Velleius Paterculus' *Historia Romana* and Lucan's *Bellum Civile*, and suggests that we should not judge Roman literature of the post-Augustan age by literary standards alone, but appreciate it as exemplifying Roman self-reflection and conceptual development. The late Republic had already seen two features nearly collide, namely that of the general Hellenization process and that of the reinforcement of traditional Roman values and virtues. In the early Principate these features seemingly co-exist, and the works of Velleius Paterculus and Lucan are, in particular, examples of their interaction. The paper concentrates on the vocabulary employed by both authors in describing the relationship between a Roman army general and his soldiers, the backbone of the Roman Empire. Velleius Paterculus' prime concern is Tiberius, whom he clearly wishes to describe in moral terms suitable for a contemporary Roman hero. Lucan, on the other hand, lavishly employs all the traditional virtues in describing his soldiers, but at the same time does so with such apparent disgust and disbelief that the whole spirit of Roman tradition dissipates. Being a soldier, and willing to sacrifice oneself or one's fellow soldiers for the sake of the Roman Empire is no longer an honourable goal.

Philip A. Stadter in his essay 'Plutarch's Lives and their Roman Readers' asks Who was the initial audience for Plutarch's *Parallel Lives*, and how did Plutarch want to influence them? Stadter argues that Plutarch, contrarily to what has previously been claimed, did not write for a purely Greek audience, but hoped to influence Romans prominent in the imperial administration, including the senators and consulars among his own friends. The *Lives* were dedicated to Sosius Senecio, who was a consular, general and close associate of Trajan. Plutarch's practice of explaining Roman institutions reflects the Greek desire for linguistic purity and Plutarch's own literary technique, and does not indicate a primarily Greek audience.

Plutarch's position is that of philosopher-adviser to a statesman. However, in the *Lives* he is counselling not one man but the élite class of the Roman

Empire, and in particular those who held most power, the senators and the Emperor himself.

Tiberius Gracchus, in particular, would have provided a useful lesson for the Emperor Trajan, for example.

Frances Titchener in 'Plutarch and Roman(ized) Athens' tries to get an idea of Plutarch's own opinion of Romans in general from his decision to stay in Chaeronea. Why did Plutarch, who seemed to be thriving in Rome, decide to move to a backwards little town in Greece? In her article, Titchener attempts to answer this question. Plutarch, a pragmatist, was very careful not to display his own opinions about Rome and the Romans, although he could be very negative about certain Roman individuals. His decision to live his life in Chaeronea may provide a key to his underlying feelings. Allegedly, his reasons for staying there was that Chaeronea was such a small town that even the absence of one single citizen would be noticed. The author of this paper, however, discerns several other possible reasons than this.

Plutarch was not in favour of big towns, especially not Rome. He did not wish to compete in the international area more than necessary, and to embark on a political life could be dangerous to the health. Besides, Plutarch's lack of confidence in Latin may have made it difficult to use the libraries and other intellectual resources that would compensate for the noisy and expensive life in Rome. Even Athens may have seemed too big, and thus expensive, bureaucratic, crowded, impersonal, and even dangerous.

However, Plutarch stresses the positive rather than the negative reasons for choosing Chaeronea. He seems to have sincerely thought that living in a big city was not a necessary prerogative for a virtuous and happy life. By the end of the millennium, the empire was so huge and well-connected that there was little need to live in Rome to be a creative writer anymore.

Victor Castellani in his essay 'Plutarch's "Roman" Women' defends the view that Plutarch when developing his theory of powerful widowed mothers in the *Lives* comprehended the Roman *matrona/materfamilias* as no different from the Greek or Hellenized Italian women he knew personally or from Greek literature, and hence distorted her legal and personal relationships with father and brothers, husband and sons. Castellani counts 11 Roman lives in which significant mothers appear. However, Plutarch does no attend to family-factional affiliations and their role in family *consilia*. Roman mothers then, like Greek mothers, offer personal and emotional exhortation but are not seen as mediums of power in their own right. Moreover, Castellani ascertains that for 13 Romans of the *Lives*, their wives made a difference. However, the frequency of divorce and the practice of several marriages with quite young women and consequently many widows resulted in a great number of self-reliant, self-conscious women of which Plutarch is almost silent. The legends of the Sabine Women and of Coriolanus show how Plutarch de-Romanized Roman women. The Sabine women in Plutarch's life of Romulus are pathetic, lacking the 'manly' and deliberate, and indeed political, argumentation referred to by Dionysius of Halicarnassus and Livy. Similarly in Plutarch's life of Coriolanus the mission of his wife and mother is private, unpolitical and irrational (moved by divine inspiration).

R. Anthony Kugler's contribution is entitled: 'The Ox, the Crow, and the Orator: Image, Allegory, and Motive in Dio Chrysostom's Second Tarsian Oration (Oration 34)'. In this oration, one of two (of those preserved) which were delivered in the city of Tarsus, Dio of Prusa, commonly called Dio Chrysostom, introduces two intriguing images, the fable of the ox and the crow in chapters five and six and the boxing metaphor of chapters twelve and thirteen. As Kugler shows in his analysis, these images bear meaningfully on the project of self-characterisation that Dio undertakes in this speech.

Kugler argues that the tale of the ox and the crow serves as a paradigm for the speech as a whole; it is a carefully crafted summary of the orator's mission in Tarsus and of the various means of persuasion available to him to ensure its success. In comparing himself to a prophetic crow and his audience to an ox-rider brought to grief by that crow, Dio underscores the seriousness of his message by symbolising the disastrous consequences of ignoring him. The fact, moreover, that the crow possesses power over others as well as god-given knowledge extends the range of Dio's oratorical *persona*, transforming him from a mere announcer of the divine to an enforcer of it.

The boxing metaphor of chapters twelve and thirteen refines this picture. This, too, is a threat, for it suggests, through the ominous figure of the referee, that Tarsus is subject to a temporal power with the strength and resolve to punish it for its disruptions of the political status quo. This could be none other than Rome. Together, then, the two figures present Dio as a mediator and messenger for both the gods, who punish those who misbehave, and the Romans, who punish those who disobey. The implication of this dual role is clear: moral misbehaviour and political disobedience are equivalent.

Does Dio actually believe this? His position, in the uneasy intersection between ruler and ruled, offers considerable opportunity for profitable fence-sitting. To his primary audience, the Tarsians before him, Dio presents himself as a solicitous Samaritan whose only concern is to steer them away from the problems that have dogged them in the past. To his secondary audience, the Romans, he is a stern disciplinarian, using his fame and prestige to bring an annoyingly vocal and free spirited city to heel. Yet there can be little doubt as to where Dio locates his own interests along this continuum: namely alongside those of the occupying Romans. Only thus is the tone of his remarks, at once threatening and paternalistic, explicable.

The orator transforms himself from a mere transformer to an enforcer of the divine will. And the divine will, at least in this case, equates with the Roman imperial will.

Ewen Bowie in his article 'Hadrian and Greek Poetry' explores the literary tastes and preferences of Hadrian in Latin and particularly Greek poetry as well as Hadrian's own compositions and some of the poems composed by his friends or ministers. Hadrian seemed to have preferred Antimachus over Homer and admired Archilochus and Parthenius for whom he wrote sepulchral epigrams. Moreover, Hadrian composed a mixed bag (called *Catachannae*) of short polymetric compositions in imitation of Antimachus. Bowie thinks these may have been satirical or just diverse verses, containing epitaphs and other epigrams, possibly a bilingual collection. Other poems by Hadrian belong to a collection *Anathemata*. Here we find a dedicatory poem to Zeus Kasius, on Trajan's behalf in AD 114, a dedicatory hendecasyllabic epigram to Eros after a bear-hunt, an epitaph in Latin on the memorial of his horse Borysthenes, and possibly an epitaph in choliambics for the prince Amazaspus who died on a Parthian campaign. Bowie considers the Latin 'farewell to life' poem spurious. He ends with a discussion of two poems in Greek by friends where the impact of Hadrian's own interests is felt: an altar poem by Vestinus tentatively dated Athens AD 131/2, the addressee being Hadrian, and a dedicatory epigram to Artemis by Arrian (the historian according to Bowie) apparently intertextually connected with the abovementioned poem to Zeus Kasius, dated ca. 124/5. Vestinus was a Westener writing in Greek and Arrian, as an author writing in Greek, advanced to high posts in the Roman administration. Hence they, and Hadrian, would have had difficulty in telling whether they were Greek or Roman.

Jaap-Jan Flinterman's contribution 'The Self-portrait of an Antonine Orator: Aristides *Or.* 2.429ff.' focuses on the inconsistency between Aristides' Isocratean conception of oratory as set out in *Or.* 2, *To Plato: In Defence of Oratory* on the one hand, and, presented in the same speech (dated after 145 AD), the self-portrait of the Antonine orator as an unpractical belles-lettres man at a time where political necessities had divested deliberative oratory of any practical function. Flinterman finds a parallel in Philostratus' *Vitae Sophistarum* and argues that sophistic oratory was, paradoxically, helped not hampered by its lack of practical use. In support of this argument he adduces modern social theory (Veblen's theory of the leisure class and Bourdieu's theory of practice). However, Flinterman finds a similar inconsistency in *Or. 3, To Plato: In Defence of the Four* where Aristides both proposes yearly prayers for the appearance of a new Themistocles and recognizes the pointlessness of such a wish in the contemporary situation. Flinterman's aim is to use Aristides' Platonic orations as evidence for the self-awareness of imperial sophists and for the mentality and ideology of the social elite in the Greek-speaking provinces of the Roman empire. The examples from Aristides are meant to demonstrate contradictions and anomalies involved in constructing and expressing Greek elite identity under Roman rule.

Anthon Xenophontov in his 'Polyaenus: A Greek Writer as a Job-seeker in the Roman World' takes a look at a surviving work, the *Strategica,* of a less known author of the time of the Second Sophistic. What is interesting, in this connection, is the self-presentation of Polyaenus and thus in general the self-promotion of Greek intellectuals in the Roman Empire. Xenophontov asks if the author, Polyaenus, was an ambitious careerist or just an unlucky person awaiting his chance in life? The answer is sought not only in the scanty information about his life but in an examination of his own writings. His principal work, the *Strategica* in eight books, was dedicated to the emperors Marcus Aurelius and Lucius Verus. Although published late in life, in a hurry, and in appearance a conventional military treatise (an anthology of stratagems) it reveals a deeper level of meaning to those readers familiar with sophistic debate. Thus Polyaenus unfolds a concept for the ideal *strategos* of whatever race or nationality, modelled on the person of Odysseus. As examples of followers of this ideal he gives Agesilaus, Alexander, Hannibal, Caesar and others, thus inviting contemporary heads of state to similar imitation. The examples are taken from the past, according to Xenophontov, not to embarrass contemporary readers by contemporary disasters which are only hinted at by analogies and anedotes. The underlying message, according to Xenophontov, is to warn the authorities in Rome against the eastern enemies and offer (Macedonian) advice of how to cope with them and thus to rank with the heroes of the past. And the intention of course is to promote the author's own status. Xenophontov assumes that Polyaenus was not alone in such an attempt at furthering his own career, though he was not cynically exploiting Roman tastes.

Paolo Desideri in a contribution entitled 'The Meaning of Greek Historiography of the Roman Imperial Age' surveys 'the most impressive group of ancient historians of one and the same period', Greek historiographical literature of the second century AD, to find a key to Greek mentality and political ideology in the late Roman Empire. Beginning with Plutarch, who considers his biographies *historia*, it is noted that he deals not only with the examples of the distant past but also with almost contemporary events. Appian's *Historia Romana* is divided into geographical sections, intended to show how the Romans took possession of the several parts of their empire. History is here in the service of geography, and the last (lost or never written) book was designed to show the present military force of the Romans. The *Historia* also included books on imperial conquests and thus had a contemporary outlook. Arrian's principal historical work was the *Anabasis*, but he is the author also of *Bithyniaka* and of *Parthika* in 17 books ending with Trajan's war (fragments only are preserved). Again we see ethnographical interests combined with contemporary political and military history. Cassius Dio too wrote a *Historia Romana* but his point of departure was contemporary history. Herodian's eight books from the death of Marcus Aurelius to the accession of Gordian deal with contemporary events: the dignity of the present as a proper subject is stressed.

Desideri asks what makes this group of historians a group? It is not just that they *qua* Greeks can look at the Roman experience from outside (cf. Bodin). There were other (Roman, now lost) historians as well, and it is not because of their career that they are interested in Roman administration. Rather they felt as much Roman as Greek. Byzantium was the New Rome and they were part of the Rome Empire. A tendency that originated in the third century BC and developed by Dionysius of Halicarnassus culminated in Plutarch who provided the ideology that Greeks and Romans were almost the same people with the same moral, political, religious and cultural values and with the same history. The Greeks naturally took pride in their cultural heritage but had to be selective with it in public and political appearances. Greek identity was more moral and cultural than political. Just as the Italian communities after the social war had two fatherlands, one by nature and one by adoption, so the Greeks had two fatherlands. But the Greeks were able to incorporate their conquerors and preserve their cultural identity. And they succeeded in reconciling this with acceptance of a new 'Roman' political identity. This is clear from their recalling of the ancient glories side by side with the telling of contemporary events. The Greeks did not have to give up their civilization and identity, and Appian and particularly Cassius Dio even created the idea of a Hellenistic rather than Roman Empire. For some time there were in fact no Roman historians.

Sophie Lalanne's original contribution: 'Hellénisme et romanisation: le cas des romans grecs et du conte de Psyché dans les *Métamorphoses* d'Apulée' has been translated specifically for this volume. The author deals with the different treatment accorded the same model (Psyché) by Greek and Latin authors.

Apuleius is inspired by Milesian narratives, but the Greek novelists from Chariton to Heliodor undergo a remarkable development of taste in the direction of the spectacular and macabre due to the Romanization of the imperial Greek society.

Lalanne analyses five Hellenistic novels and their reflection of contemporary society: *Chaereas and Callirhoë* by Chariton, *Ephesiaca* by Xenophon of Ephesus, *Daphnis and Chloe* by Longus, *Leucippe and Cleitophon* by Achilles Tatius and *Aethiopica* by Heliodorus, which are then compared to Apuleius' *Metamorphoses*.

These five novels, almost contemporary but of different cultural settings, reveal several traits in common and may be said to follow one single narrative model. They all describe the love between two young people, who are separated and must undergo a series of hardships before they can overcome the obstacles and marry. These hardships actually mean a form of *paideia*, which leads the two lovers to a higher status than before, morally and socially. Without exception the principal characters belong to the aristocracy; their virtues and moral upstanding help them to achieve their goals, and the tribulations that they undergo form them for their coming role as members of the élite.

However, there are certain interesting differences between these novels. From Chariton to Heliodorus one can trace a considerable development which can partly be explained by the Romanization of Greek society in the Roman Empire. For instance, the taste of Latin authors – the spectacular, even the macabre and bizarre – influences the Greek authors to an increasing degree. This is reflected and confirmed in a comparative study of the Roman author Apuleius, who was clearly influenced by the Greek narratives, especially the Milesian, in his writing of *Metamorphoses*. However, the fact that he preferred certain narrative features and motifs to others, is worthy of attention, for the tests that the heroine has to undergo reveal an imagination belonging to the Roman world.

Thus, 'Hellenism' and 'Romanization' reveal two cultures, of which the former appears in the universal frame of reference, whereas the latter is defined by the narrative strategy, i.e., the transformation process which the actors undergo during their trials.

Finally, Joseph Geiger in his essay 'Language, Culture and Identity in Ancient Palestine' looks at ethnic, religious and linguistic identities in Ancient Palestine. When discussing the questions of confrontation or interaction in the Roman world, one should not forget those who were neither Greeks, nor Romans, but who identified themselves as belonging to quite a different people. Few peoples have been so well documented in Antiquity as the Jews.

And traditionally, the history of the Jews in Antiquity has been seen as one of confrontation. Historians like Tacitus and Josephus have recorded several tales of a small but fierceful people, persistently resisting the attempts of foreign masters to impose new ideas upon them. In his contribution, Joseph Geiger approaches the question of cultural identity in ancient Palestine not only by way of a survey of literary texts ranging from poetry and historiography to the gospels, but also of other kinds of documentation. The contradictory cultural self-presentation Paul gives of himself is analysed and commented as are the criteria Meleager uses for identification of a person's cultural or linguistic belonging. Geiger gathers the evidence available in Josephus on the self-presentation of King Herod, who is seen to have been both a Hellenized ruler and in many aspects a surprisingly much Romanized Roman citizen. Among other things this is seen in the fact that King Herod sent his sons to Rome – not to Athens or an other centre of education – for their education and to learn to speak and write Latin. Judging from the documents found in the desert, people felt no need to emphasize ethnic, cultural or religious identity.

Geiger's survey demonstrates how the identity of both an individual and a group is of fluctuating importance and changing depending on the context – sometimes it was to expressly draw a line between 'us' and 'them', be they Greeks, Romans or Jews, and sometimes not. Further aspects of the complex identity of an individual or a group could be emphasized according to the specific need of the situation (witness the case of Paul).

***

In conclusion, it may be said that archaeological evidence shows that among the Greeks there was an adaptation of inscriptions to Roman practices but that – perhaps not surprisingly – the general (rural) population was not exposed to Roman culture. Moreover, the relaxation of restrictions on women generally predates the arrival of the Romans. At the literary level, the Greeks in the period considered were becoming increasingly self-confident and self-conscious. They tried to understand the Romans, and some, e.g. novelists, also imitated Romans, not entirely succesfully, and others even felt a coincidence of interests with the Romans. More often, however, the Greeks just tried to take advantage of the power that controlled them. In any case, they did not give up their civilization and identity, but rather reinterpreted the Roman power in Greek terms: e.g. as a Hellenistic Empire. Some uneasiness is of course felt in straddling the ideal self-confidence and the reality of politics.

On the other hand, the Roman Administration was actively promoting its ideological campaign of Rome and the emperor as the Saviour of the civilized world, particularly in Athens and the building programme there. The Roman writers of course acknowledged the greatness of the Greek models in various genres but, according to the contributors, the use they are put to differs: either merely for decoration or display (Seneca) or in imitation of the Greeks in a kind of (bilingual) hobby (Hadrian) or more professionally as models (Apuleius).

Somewhat apart, but completing the picture and with interesting general implications, stands a study on the ethnic, religious and linguistic identity of the Jews in Ancient Palestine. According to ancient historians the Jews stubbornly resisted foreign control. However, we learn how complex and fluctuating individual or group identity can be even in this case.

* The above introductory remarks are based on abstracts provided by the contributors.

ARCHAEOLOGICAL STUDIES

CHAPTER 1

Some Reflections on the Temple to the Goddess Roma and Augustus on the Acropolis at Athens

Helène Whittaker

The temple to Roma and Augustus on the Acropolis at Athens is not mentioned in any ancient literary source. Pausanias, for instance, the most detailed source on the Acropolis, after describing the shrine of Zeus Polieus and the rituals connected with it, goes directly on to a description of the Parthenon omitting any mention of the shrine to Augustus and Roma which stood between the two. The identification of a cult to Augustus and Roma on the Acropolis at Athens has been made through the dedicatory inscription of the temple which had been inscribed on one of the epistyle blocks.[1] The dedicatory inscription records that the *demos* dedicated the temple to the Goddess Roma and Augustus Caesar when Pammenes was hoplite general and priest of the Goddess Roma and Augustus *Soter*, Megiste priestess of Athena Polias and Areos *Archon*.

A number of building fragments have been found and an almost complete reconstruction of the temple is possible (Fig. 1). The temple is a round building with nine outer columns of the Ionic order. The diameter is somewhat greater than eight metres. The roof was most likely conical and the building was probably some nine metres high. No traces of interior walls have been recovered and it is therefore uncertain whether there was a cella or whether the building was an open colonnade.[2]

The building fragments from the temple which have been recovered have been associated with the remains of a foundation platform just to the east of the Parthenon in which area the dedicatory inscription was also found. Although there has been some controversy over the precise location of the temple, it seems most probable that the location to the east of the Parthenon is correct (Figs. 2-3).[3]

The location of the temple on the Acropolis in itself indicates a clear association between the cult of Roma and Augustus and the centre of Athenian political and religious life.⁴ Furthermore, the temple is situated more or less on the same axis as the Parthenon. It is also visually connected with the Erechtheion in that the Ionic columns and details of external decoration are copied from it. Moreover, the shrine to Zeus Polieus lay just to the north of the temple. It seems therefore that there was a deliberate desire to associate the new cult of the Roman ruler with the most important Athenian state cults on the Acropolis and to proclaim ties with the political past of Athens.

The closest architectural parallel in Greece to the temple, is the Philippeion at Olympia which, according to Pausanias, contained chryselephantine statues of Philip II of Macedonia's family and has been seen as a monument whose purpose was to glorify the royal Macedonian family. Although on a larger scale, it was, like the temple to Roma and Augustus in Athens, a round structure with Ionic columns.⁵ It has further been argued that the Philippeion established the *tholos* or round building as a suitable type of structure for honouring rulers and that buildings with a circular plan were accordingly considered appropriate for monuments of the Imperial Cult in Greece.⁶ A function connected with the Imperial Cult has been suggested for other round buildings in Greece. Pausanias mentions a temple containing statues of Roman emperors in the Marmaria area at Delphi. Although the identification is not absolutely certain, it is most likely that the temple to the Roman emperors mentioned by Pausanias is to be identified with the *tholos*.⁷ Pausanias also mentions that a round building near the agora at Elis was dedicated to the Imperial cult.⁸ It has, however, also been suggested that the round plan of the temple to Roma and Augustus in Athens reflected the temple of Vesta in the Forum at Rome.

Although, as mentioned, the dedicatory inscription of the temple is preserved, and the names of the *archon*, the priestess of Athena Polias, and the hoplite general who was also priest of the Goddess Roma and Augustus are mentioned in the inscription, it has not been possible to date the temple precisely. Nothing is known about Areos, the *archon* mentioned, but his archonship must fall either before 17 BC or after 11 BC as the names of the *archon*s in the intervening period are known. Pammenes, mentioned as hoplite general, is a much less shadowy figure, but his career stretched over a long period of time. He is estimated to have been born during the 50's and his public career to have begun in the year 24/23. He was also a lifelong priest of Apollo on Delos, perhaps from 17 BC, and is known from as late as 5 AD.⁹ Accordingly, a date before 17 BC and after 11 BC are both possible for the construction of the temple to Roma and Augustus on the Acropolis at Athens. Since the dedicatory inscription mentions the emperor as σεβαστός, the Greek translation of Augustus, it can also be ascertained that the temple must date to after 27 BC. Most scholars have preferred the earlier date, between 27 and 17 BC. Paul

Fig. 1. Fragments of the Temple to the Goddess Roma and Augustus at the Athenian Acropolis. (Photo by the author)

Graindor and John Travlos have suggested a date close to 27 BC seeing the temple as part of the reconciliation between the Athenians and Augustus after Actium, while Heidi Hänlein-Schäfer, Michael Hoff, and Paola Baldassari have preferred to connect the monument with Augustus' visit to Athens in 19 BC.[10]

However, if one separates cult from temple, the most probable date for the institution of the cult would seem to be the year 29 BC. There is evidence that various types of honours, including altars, statues and periodic sacrifices, were accorded to Octavian by many cities in the years immediately following the battle of Actium.[11] In the winter of 30/29 BC, as Cassius Dio tells us in a well-known passage, Octavian permitted cults of himself in conjunction with the Goddess Roma to be established at Pergamon and Nicomedia.[12]

The Acropolis had, in the Hellenistic period, been the centre of extravagant honours conferred on important foreigners. Antonius had been honoured as the New Dionysos in Athens, and Plutarch in his *Life of Antonius* mentions that colossal statues of Eumenes II and Attalos II, which had stood on the Acropolis, had been reinscribed with the name of Antonius, while Cassius Dio records that statues of Antonius and Cleopatra in the guise of gods had stood on the

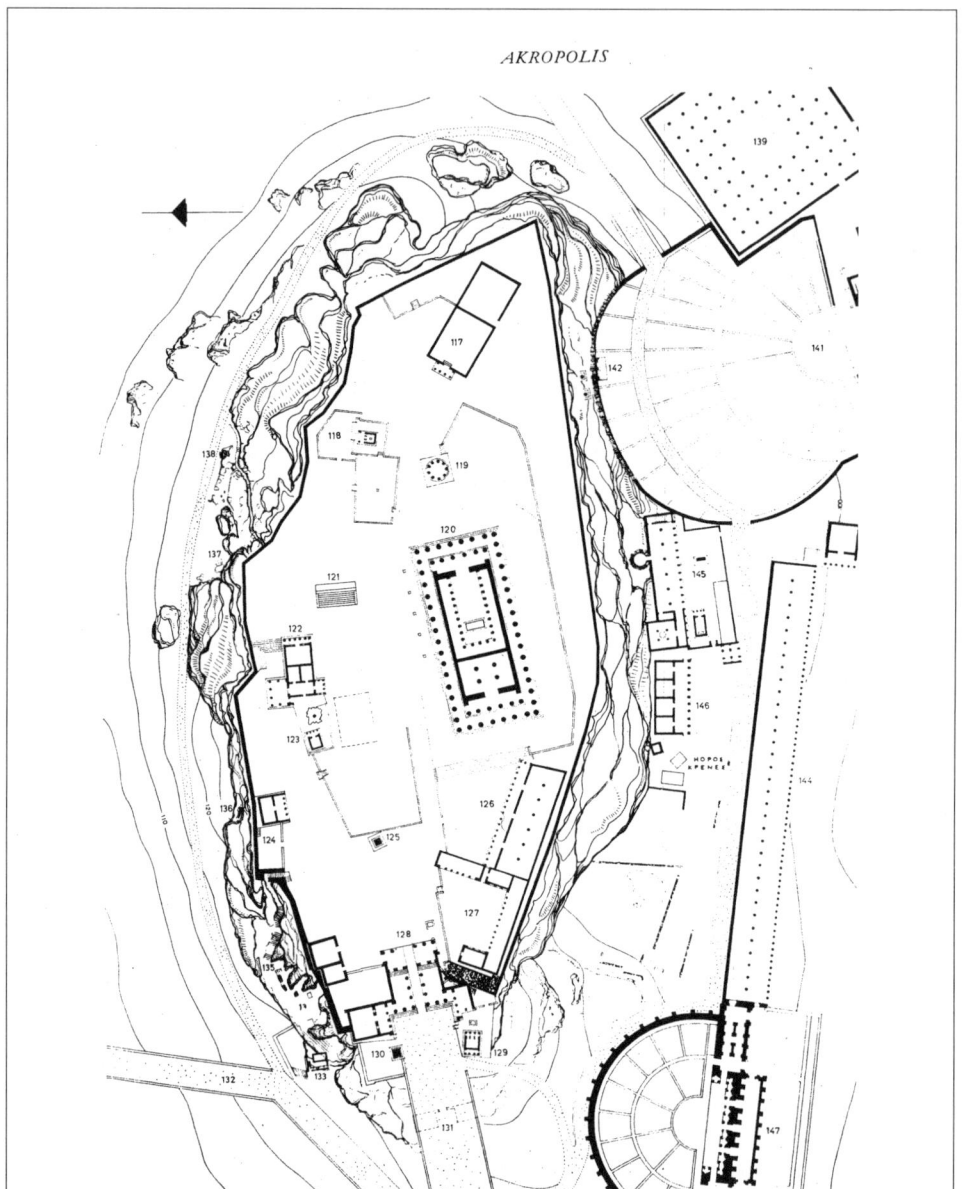

Fig. 2. The Athenian Akropolis. (after Travlos 1971, fig. 71)

Acropolis prior to the battle of Actium.[13] It seems hard to believe that the Athenians did not seek to offer comparable honours to Octavian, and that they offered him additional honours in the form of cult does not seem improbable, in particular after Octavian himself had taken the initiative by permitting divine

Fig. 3. Monuments of the northeastern corner of the Parthenon with the temple of Roma and Augustus. (after Travlos 1971, fig. 624)

worship of himself and the Goddess Roma to the provinces of Asia and Bithynia. Although there is no positive evidence, it is possible that Augustus may have visited Athens in 29 BC on his return from the East when he passed through Greece.[14] In any case, it seems very likely that the Athenians took the opportunity offered by Octavian's presence in Greece to imitate the example of the cities of Asia Minor and to approach him with an offer of cult.

Reasons for the Athenians particularly wishing to honour Octavian are not hard to find. Sulla's siege of Athens and the succeeding devastation were within living memory and the signs of it were still evident.[15] Gratitude towards Octavian because he had not exacted vengeance for their support of

Antonius, as well as the wish to give concrete expression to promises of future loyalty, would have been the motivation behind an offer of divine honours and the institution of a cult.

Moreover, the mention in the dedicatory inscription of the temple of a priest of the Goddess Roma and Augustus would in fact seem to indicate that a cult with a priesthood was already in existence before the temple was dedicated. The assumption then that the Athenians had instituted a cult to Octavian and the Goddess Roma centred on the Acropolis, before the temple itself was dedicated, is perhaps not overly speculative.

Although the cult of Octavian and the Goddess Roma may have been an entirely new cult institution, it is also possible to speculate that a cult of the Goddess Roma may already have existed on the Acropolis before being associated with that of Octavian.[16] Epigraphic evidence shows that the cult of Roma had been established at Athens at least by the year 150 BC. There is no evidence which could indicate the occasion for its institution, but it may have been established already at the beginning of the second century BC, or possibly in 167 BC, after the battle of Pydna.[17] Evidence from elsewhere in Greece indicates that cults of Roma were often connected with the centre of a city's political life, and in general Roma was often incorporated into pre-existing cults.[18] As has been pointed out by Ronald Mellor cults of Roma in the Republican period were often associated with cults of Zeus.[19] Even if there is no evidence which indicates where the cult of Roma may have been located in Athens, an early cult of the Goddess Roma in the vicinity of the shrine to Zeus Polieus on the Acropolis would seem a plausible hypothesis. A connection between the patron goddess of Athens and Roma was made on Athenian coinage. Roma appears on Athenian coins from around the year 90 BC, and in the depictions on coins she is closely similar in appearance to Athena.[20] The manner of her depiction is perhaps also an indication that her cult was closely associated with the most important Athenian state cults on the Acropolis.

An incident which occurred in the winter of 21 BC recounted by Cassius Dio is possibly to be associated with the presence of a cult of Augustus on the Acropolis. Augustus, who visited Greece in that year, imposed certain sanctions on Athens. Cassius Dio records that some people believed that the support of Athens for Antonius was the reason for Augustus' anger, but that the Athenians themselves thought that the reason was that a statue of Athena, which stood on the Acropolis facing east, turned to the west, spitting blood, an episode which could only be interpreted as being intended to convey a clear demonstration of divine anger towards Rome.[21] The incident described by Cassius Dio has been associated by Glen Bowersock with a passage in Plutarch which states that Augustus was once so angry with the Athenians that he declined to visit Athens and instead passed the winter on Aegina.[22]

As has been recognised, it is unlikely that Augustus should wish to express his anger towards the Athenians for their support of Antonius as late as 21 BC and the reason for Augustus' anger must have been the incident with the statue of Athena on the Acropolis. Michael Hoff has suggested that the incident represents an example of wide-spread civil discontent and anti-Roman sentiment at Athens and that it is unlikely that the sanctions were imposed as a response to a single incident.[23] Hoff suggests also that the incident took place while Augustus was in Athens. However, neither Plutarch nor Cassius Dio affirm this and Plutarch rather implies that Augustus had been planning to visit Athens, but changed his mind and took up residence on Aegina from where he wrote to the Athenians so that there should be no doubt about his anger towards them.[24] Rather, it will have been the expectation of Augustus' visit to Athens which provoked the outburst of anti-Augustan feeling. Plutarch also implies that Augustus saw the incident as a personal insult rather than as an expression of anti-Roman feeling in general.

Public statues which are struck by lightning or behave in peculiar ways, bleeding, sweating or even frowning, were common forms of prodigy generally associated with death or defeat.[25] For instance, before the Battle of Actium, a statue of Antonius which had stood next to a statue of Jupiter on the Alban Mount spat out a great amount of blood, clearly foretelling, according to Cassius Dio, the death of Antonius after his defeat in the coming battle.[26] Since, as Suetonius records, Augustus was extremely superstitious, it is not unlikely that he saw the incident with the Athena statue as a bad omen.[27] The incident can perhaps be seen in the light of events in Athens some years earlier. Plutarch records that, on the eve of the battle of Actium, a figure of Dionysos which was part of a Gigantomachy on the Acropolis was toppled into the theatre below by heavy winds and that the previously mentioned colossal statues of the Attalids, which had been reinscribed with Antonius' name, were thrown to the ground. Cassius Dio also records that the statues of Antonius and Cleopatra in the guise of gods were struck by lightning and fell into the theatre.[28] These incidents are narrated by Plutarch and Cassius Dio as portents foretelling the outcome of the Battle of Actium, but it would seem fairly clear that they demonstrate that not all of Athens was loyal to Antonius. The statues involved in portents which were unfavourable to Antonius had associations with Antonius' pretensions to divinity and the significance of the figure of Dionysos is explicitly explained by Plutarch with reference to Antonius' identification with the god. It seems possible that certain Athenians may have chosen to manifest opposition to Augustus in a similar way and that the incident with the Athena statue is to be interpreted as an attack on the presence of a cult to the Roman ruler on the Acropolis.

The question can also be raised whether there may not be some connection between anti-Roman or anti-Augustan feelings in Athens and recent events at Rome. Rome at the beginning of 21 BC is described by Cassius Dio as being in a state of lawlessness, a situation which may not have been completely under control at the time of the Athenian incident.[29] Furthermore a plot to assassinate Augustus had been discovered in 23/22 BC.[30] It seems possible that within the empire the position of Augustus may at times have been perceived as unstable and that this may have inspired acts of opposition. Cassius Dio also reports outbreaks of anti-Roman feelings at Cyzicus and in Syria the following year.[31] The riots at Rome could therefore have inspired anti-Augustan feelings at Athens in the time before the planned visit of the Emperor. The two reasons for Augustus' anger are stated by Cassius Dio as alternatives, but it is possible that they are related, and that the incident with the Athena statue indicates that anti-Augustan feelings were still prevalent among some Athenians who had supported Antonius.[32]

Although, as I have tried to show, there would seem to be good reasons for supposing that an early cult of Roma and Augustus was instituted on the Acropolis, the date of the construction of the temple building cannot be decided with any certainty. It is possible that the decision to construct a temple, which was not completed until after 27 BC, was made at the same time that the cult was established. The temples at Pergamon and Nicomedia had been promised in 29 BC and construction may have started soon after.[33] The temple at Nicomedia is known only from depictions on coins which date to the reign of Hadrian, but at Pergamon epigraphic evidence indicates that construction of the temple had been started by 27 BC, although it may not have been dedicated until some years later. If, as suggested, Athens was emulating the example given by the cities of Asia Minor, then it is likely that a decision to build a temple was made at the same time that the cult was established. We also know that a temple to Roma and Augustus at Mytilene was constructed in 27 BC in connection with the institution of a cult which included priests, monthly sacrifices and games, and that the temple at Xanthos had been built before that date.[34]

As previously mentioned, the year 19 BC has been suggested as a plausible date for the construction of the temple. In that year Augustus visited Athens on his return from the East and Michael Hoff and Paola Baldassarri see it as likely that Augustus' diplomatic victory over the Parthians provided the occasion for a reconciliation between Athens and Augustus. Michael Hoff suggests that the cult and temple were established as a sign of gratitude to Augustus for providing funds for the building of the Roman Agora as well as to placate Augustus after the incident with the Athena statue on the Acropolis and commemorate the re-establishment of good relations between Augustus and Athens.[35]

Although most commentators have preferred a date before 17 BC, a case can also be made for dating the construction of the temple to the period after the year 11 BC. Objections have been made on the grounds of the titulature of the dedicatory inscription.[36] In the year 12 BC Augustus was elected Pontifex Maximus. The Greek translation ἀρχιερεὺς μέγιστος occurs in the preserved remains of the temple to Roma and Augustus at Mylasa and could therefore be expected in the dedicatory inscription of the temple in Athens if it had been constructed after 12 BC.[37] However, the dedicatory inscription of the temple at Pola, which must be dated to after 2 BC since Augustus is given the title *pater patriae*, does not, on the other hand, include the title Pontifex Maximus.[38] Other types of dedications show that in the Greek East the use of titles is erratic, so that the absence of the title ἀρχιερεὺς μέγιστος on the temple to Roma and Augustus does not seem to be a decisive factor in determining a date for its construction.[39] A date after the year 11 BC should therefore also be considered possible.

In the dedicatory inscription of the temple, Pammenes the hoplite general is termed priest of Roma and Augustus on the Acropolis. The words ἐπ' ἀκροπόλει have generally been taken to signify the existence of another cult to Augustus, either alone or with Roma, located elsewhere at Athens. Furthermore, inscriptions on seats in the theatre of Dionysos indicate that there were at least two priests of the Imperial Cult in Athens in the Augustan period, one of Augustus and Roma and one of Augustus alone.[40] Evidence from elsewhere in the Empire shows that major centres of emperor worship were often in or bordered on the agora and could be located either in buildings which were adapted or in new establishments.[41] A number of altars to Augustus have been found in Athens. Most of them have been found in the vicinity of the Agora or the Roman Agora and it is a plausible assumption that they should be connected with a cult place in that area.[42]

In the Agora itself, a two-roomed annex, which was built as an extension on the Stoa of Zeus Eleutherios, has been associated with the worship of Augustus and other members of the Imperial family and possibly also with Roma. There is no direct evidence that the annex was constructed to house the Imperial Cult and the conclusions as to its purpose have been based mainly on the cultic association between Zeus and Augustus attested from many places in the Empire. The annex, however, was not constructed until late in the Augustan period or even after the death of Augustus.[43]

A more plausible candidate as a major centre of the Imperial Cult in the lower city would seem to be the Roman Agora.[44] In essence, the Roman Agora is a porticoed enclosure and it can be compared to building complexes at Alexandria, Antioch and Cyrene which have been identified as Caesarea or Sebasteia, that is as centres of Emperor worship.[45] Finds from the area provide some further evidence for the presence of the Imperial cult in the Roman Agora. A slightly over life-sized head of Augustus was found in the market and a statue of Augustus' adopted son Lucius had been set on the pediment of the West Gate, above the dedicatory inscription which dedicated the market to Athena.[46] The initial decision to build a new market-place was probably made in 51 BC when Julius Caesar promised funds for its construction, but it seems little or no construction took place at that time. Renewed construction of the Roman Agora started probably in 19 BC and the new market area was completed and dedicated in 10 BC at the earliest, and probably not much later.[47] There would seem to be good reasons for suggesting that a major centre of the Imperial Cult may have been localised in the Roman Agora and that it should be identified with the centre of a cult to Augustus in the lower city implied by the dedication of the temple on the Acropolis. If this can be accepted as a plausible hypothesis then it should also be proposed that the temple to Roma and Augustus on the Acropolis was not dedicated until after the Roman Agora had been dedicated.

As previously mentioned, it has been suggested that there was some connection between the temple to Roma and Augustus at Athens and the temple to Vesta in the Roman Forum. This was first suggested by Paul Graindor and has been accepted as likely by Ronald Mellor.[48] Both Graindor and Mellor believe that the temple should be dated to some time in the 20's. If, however, the temple on the Acropolis is to be seen as a reflection of the temple of Vesta in Rome, then a date after 12 BC when Augustus was elected Pontifex Maximus would seem to be the more likely. The office of Pontifex Maximus traditionally had a close connection with the cult of Vesta, and after his election Augustus established a shrine to Vesta with an altar and a statue within his house on the Palatine.[49] Augustus himself attached great importance to the office of Pontifex Maximus as is evident from the *Res Gestae*, and Glen Bowersock has argued that the processional frieze on the Ara Pacis represents the procession of the imperial family on the day that Augustus became Pontifex Maximus.[50] That the Athenians were aware of the importance to Augustus of the priesthood is indicated by dedications of what were probably statues, set up by the Athenians in the sanctuaries to Apollo at Delos and Delphi, which commemorate Augustus as Pontifex Maximus.[51]

Supporting evidence for a connection between the architectural form of the temple of Vesta in Rome and the temple to Roma and Augustus at Athens has been seen in an inscription on a seat in the theatre of Dionysos which mentions a priestess of the cults of Hestia on the Acropolis and of Livia and Iulia.[52] The establishment of cults of Livia and Iulia must certainly date to before 2 BC when Iulia was banished, and the most likely occasion for the institution of a cult to Augustus' wife and daughter in conjunction with a cult of Hestia would seem to be in connection with honours given to Augustus himself as Pontifex Maximus.

There is no direct evidence for an earlier cult of Hestia on the Acropolis at Athens, and therefore Mellor saw it as likely that the inscription which honoured Livia and Iulia in conjunction with Hestia was a new cult, which was associated with the already existing cult of the Roman ruler and would therefore probably have had its seat in the temple to Roma and Augustus. However, Plato in the *Laws* mentions the institution of cults to Hestia, Zeus, and Athena on the Acropolis of his ideal city.[53] The religion of the Platonic *polis* reflects traditional *polis* religion and it seems arguable that in the official cult of the Greek *polis* a cult of Hestia was often associated with cults of Zeus and Athena as protectors of the polis. It is therefore possible that there was an important cult of Hestia on the Acropolis at Athens, in which the cults of Livia and Iulia were incorporated, even if there is no corroborating archaeological or epigraphic evidence. Since it is uncertain whether this cult was localised within the temple to Roma and Augustus, the existence of a cult to Livia and Iulia associated with Hestia is perhaps doubtful evidence for a connection between the temple to Roma and Augustus on the Athenian Acropolis and the temple to Vesta in the Roman Forum.

Sometime around the year 2 BC, when Gaius Caesar, the grandson and adoptive son of Augustus, was sent on a journey to the East in order to undertake negotiations with the Parthians, can be suggested as a plausible date for the dedication of the temple. In Rome, as Ovid demonstrates, his mission was conceived as a campaign of revenge against the Parthians. The temple to Mars Ultor in the Forum of Augustus was dedicated in 2 BC and the dedication should be seen in connection with Rome's campaigns against the Parthians.[54] In Rome Gaius had been associated with Mars before his departure. Gaius' journey to the East was also coloured by Rome's propaganda effort to present herself as the successor of Athens as the champion of freedom by placing Roman campaigns against the Parthians on the same level as the wars between the Greeks and Persians. The assimilation of Rome's dealings with the Parthians to the Persian Wars was made very explicit when the Battle of Salamis was re-enacted in a magnificent *naumachia* which was staged on the Tiber, before the departure of Gaius for the East.[55] Ronald Syme has called the *naumachia* a piece of pageantry which advertised Rome as the champion of Hellas against the Orient and Glen Bowersock has emphasised that its propaganda message was directed mainly towards the Greeks.[56] Gaius visited Athens on his way to the East, and that the Athenians were sensitive to propaganda directed from Rome would seem to be clear from an inscription which honours Gaius as the new Ares.[57] Sometime towards the end of the first century BC, a fifth century temple of Ares was transplanted from the countryside in Attica into the Athenian Agora.[58] The most convincing explanation for the relocation of the temple of Ares is that it was intended as an Athenian counterpart to the dedication of the temple to Mars Ultor at Rome, thereby establishing an explicit link between Roman religion and official Athenian cult.[59] Pausanias mentions that statues of Aphrodite stood within the temple along with those of Ares.[60] The significance of Mars and Venus in the Augustan period as the ancestors of the Roman people and the Julian family has been discussed by Paul Zanker, and a statue of Venus stood in the temple of Mars Ultor next to that of Mars.[61] One could speculate that the temple to Ares in the Athenian Agora was rededicated during Gaius' visit.

Accordingly, it would seem a possibility worth consideration that the temple to Roma and Augustus on the Acropolis should be associated with Gaius' visit and that it may have been constructed as a response to Roman propaganda which associated their campaigns against the Parthians with the wars between the Athenians and Persians. The location of the temple directly in front of the Parthenon can be seen in the context of the enormous symbolic significance of the Athenian victory over Persia. The Parthenon in itself was seen by later Greeks as a votive offering for the Athenian victory over the Persians at Marathon and Salamis, as a passage in Demosthenes demonstrates.[62] Although it is perhaps debatable whether there was originally any propagandistic intent, in the Hellenistic and Roman periods the themes from mythological battles depicted on the metopes of the Parthenon were certainly considered as an allegory over the Persian defeat.[63] Dedications by Alexander after Granikos, and the Attalids after their victory over the Galatians, alluded to the Athenian victory and reinforced the significance of the Parthenon as a symbol of victory over eastern barbarians.

It can therefore be suggested that the construction of the temple to the Roman ruler was intended to exploit the Persian Wars symbolism given by the location of the cult in the vicinity of the Parthenon, and the temple to Roma and Augustus can be seen as a statement of the Athenians' or certain influential Athenians' willingness to accept the Romans in their role as defenders of freedom against the East.

In conclusion, although verification is not possible without further archaeological or epigraphic evidence, and other suggestions cannot be excluded, it can be argued that the most likely occasion for the decision to construct the temple to Roma and Augustus on the Acropolis at Athens was in connection with the visit of Gaius to Athens.

Notes

1. *IG* II² 3173; [Ὁ] Δῆμος Θεᾷ Ῥώμῃ καὶ Σ[εβασ]τῷ Καίσαρι Στρα[τηγ]οῦντος ἐπὶ τ[οὺ]ς Ὁπλίτας Παμμένους τοῦ Ζήνωνος Μαραθωνίου ἱερέως Θεᾶς Ῥώμης καὶ Σεβαστοῦ Σωτῆρος ἐπ᾽ Ἀκροπόλει ἐπὶ ἱερείας Ἀθηνᾶς Πολιάδος Μεγίστης τῆς Ἀσκληπίδου Ἁλαιέως Θυγατρὸς ἐπὶ ἄρχοντος Ἀρήου τ[οῦ] Δωρίωνος Παιανιέως.
2. Travlos 1989, 494; Binder 1967, 19. If there was a cella, it may have been constructed of brick or wood. Pausanias mentions that the cella of the Philippeion at Olympia was made of burnt brick. As stone wall-blocks from the cella walls have been preserved, Pausanias is clearly wrong in this case, but it has been suggested that the walls may have been painted in imitation of brick work (Grobel-Miller 1973, 191. See also Arafat 1996, 51-52).
3. Cf. Hoff 1996, 185-86, n. 5; Baldassari 1995, 72-73; Shear Jr. 1981, 363. See Binder 1967, 31-33, 45-47, for arguments against the present location of the temple. Hänlein-Schäfer 1985, 157-58 follows Binder.
4. Cf. Zanker 1988, 298; Arafat 1996, 124-25.
5. Paus. 5.20.9-10; Grobel Miller 1973, 189-217.
6. Tzavella-Evjen 1985, 315; Roux 1965, 51; Roux 1992, 191-95.
7. Fingarette 1970, 403; le Roy 1977, 247-71; Roux 1965, 37-53; Roux 1992, 191.
8. Paus. 6.24.10.
9. Geagan 1992, 29-44.
10. Graindor 1927, 30-31; Travlos 1989, 494; Hänlein-Schäfer 1985, 159; Hoff 1989b, 5-6; Hoff 1994, 110; Hoff 1996, 193; Baldassarri 1995, 73.
11. Millar 1984, 37-60; Benjamin & Raubitschek 1959.
12. Dio Cass. 51.20, 6-7.
13. Plut.*Vit.Ant*. 60.5-6; Dio Cass. 50.15.2.
14. Cf. Bowersock 1964, 121.
15. Hoff 1997, 42-43.
16. Price 1984, 43, believes that many of the cults of Augustus and Roma were new cults rather than the extension of pre-existing cults to Roma alone. Cf. Fayer 1976, 17-18.
17. Mellor 1975, 101-2; Fayer 1976, 61-62.
18. Mellor 1975, 129; Fayer 1976, 81.
19. Mellor 1975, 129.
20. Mellor 1975, 147.
21. Dio Cass. 54.7.3.
22. Plut. *Mor*. 207F; Bowersock 1964, 120-21; Bowersock 1987, 298-99. See also Arafat 1996, 122-23. For a different view of this episode see: Rich 1990, 180; Schmalz 1996, 384-86. It has not been possible to ascertain which Athena statue was involved. Certainly it was not the Athena Promachos, which already stood facing west and moreover, being perhaps 10 m high, would have been too heavy to shift. Baldassari 1995, 73 has suggested that it may have been the Athena Parthenos. However, the image of the Athena Parthenos spitting blood with her face turned towards the

wall as an expression of divine anger and political discontent seems to me at any rate to be less than compelling. The Athena Polias seems equally unlikely. Robertson 1996, 47 argues unconvincingly that it must have been the statue of Athena Hygieia which stood at the west entrance to the Acropolis.

23. Hoff 1989a, 267-76. See also Geagan 1984, 379.
24. Cf. Bowersock 1987, 298.
25. Cf. Pelling 1988, 265; Bowersock 1987, 294-98; Rich 1990, 12.
26. Dio Cass. 50.8,6. Other examples in Dio Cassius are 51.17.5; 55.1.1.
27. Suet. *Aug*.92.
28. Pelling 1988, 265; Hölscher 1985, 126-27; Habicht 1990, 572; Habicht 1994, 158; Mossman 1991, 112-13.
29. Dio Cass. 54.6,1-5.
30. Dio Cass. 54.3.4-7; Vell. Pat.2.91.2. Syme 1939, 333-34; Raaflaub & Samons II 1990, 425-26.
31. Dio Cass. 54.7.6.
32. As well as documenting the existence of anti-Roman or specifically anti-Augustan sentiment at Athens, the incident probably also reflects the existence of factions within the Athenian population either between the people and an upper class which was supported by Rome or between rival aristocratic groups as discussed by Bowersock 1961, 112-18 for Sparta and elsewhere in Achaia; see also Bowersock 1965, 101-11; Bowersock 1987, 298-99.
33. Hänlein-Schäfer 1985, 164-68; Mellor 1975, 140-42.
34. Hänlein-Schäfer 1985, 179-80, 197; Mellor 1975, 140.
35. Hoff 1989b, 6; Hoff 1996, 193; Baldassari 1995, 80-83 even suggests that since the Roman standards had been recovered from the Parthians while Augustus was in the East and may therefore have accompanied him on his return to Rome and thus passed through Athens, a connection is possibly to be seen between the round form of the temple and a small circular temple which was depicted on coins minted in Spain and at Ephesos in the year 19/18 BC. The legend on the coins reads 'Martis Ultoris' and within the temple a statue of Mars with Roman standards is depicted in some variants, while in other cases the standards alone are shown. The temple may represent the temple to Mars Ultor on the Capitol, mentioned by Dio Cassius which Augustus ordered to be built so as to house the standards recovered from the Parthians (54.8,3). It would seem doubtful whether this temple was ever built. Cf. Simpson 1977, 91-93; Fishwick 1984, 265-66.
36. Hänlein-Schäfer 1985, 159; Baldassarri 1995, 73.
37. Hänlein-Schäfer 1985, 177-79.
38. Hänlein-Schäfer 1985, 149-52.
39. Likewise, no great significance should be attributed to the fact that Pammenes is not mentioned as lifelong priest of Delian Apollo or that priest of Drusus, an office which was associated with that of the *archon* after 9 BC, is not mentioned in the titulature of the *archon* (cf. Geagan 1967, 8). It should be taken into consideration that a limited amount of space was available for the inscription and one might note that θεοῦ υἱῷ was not included in the titulature of Augustus.

40. *IG* II² 5114; *IG* II² 5034.
41. Walker 1997, 68; Hänlein-Schäfer 1985, 31-32; Price 1984, 136-46; Alcock 1993, 181.
42. Benjamin & Raubitschek 1959.
43. Thompson 1966, 171-87.
44. Benjamin & Raubitschek 1959, 85; Shear Jr. 1981, 359-60; Hoff 1994, 112; Hoff 1996, 195.
45. Sjöqvist 1954, 86-108.
46. Furthermore, an inscription which is now lost, but which may have come from the Roman Agora reads Ὁ Δῆμος... Καίσαρος Αὐγούστου Θεοῦ Ἀρχηγέτου Σωτῆρος (Hoff 1994, 100).
47. Hoff 1989b, 6.
48. Graindor 1927, 154-55; Mellor 1975, 139.
49. Fishwick 1993, 88.
50. *Res Gestae* 7; Bowersock 1990, 380-94.
51. Mavrojannis 1995, 86; Bousquet 1961, 88-90; Oliver 1983, 99.
52. *IG* II² 5097.
53. Pl. *Leg.* 745b, 821d.
54. Ov. *Ars Am.* I.177-82; Hollis 1977, 65-73; Syme 1978, 8-9, 31; Bowersock 1984, 171.
55. *Res Gestae* 23; Ov. *Ars Am.* I.171-72; Dio Cass. 55.10.7.
56. Syme 1984, 912-36; Bowersock 1984, 174-75; See also: Spawforth 1994, 233-47.
57. *IG* II² 3250; Romer 1978, 201-2, n. 35.
58. Dinsmoor 1940, 1-52; Holland McAllister 1959, 1-64; Camp 1992, 184-86.
59. Bowersock 1984, 173; see also Alcock 1993, 173. Walker 1997, 72, however, would rather see the transplantation of the temple of Ares to the Agora in connection with Augustus' program of moral reform, which encompassed the regeneration of temples and shrines, while Spawforth 1997, 186-88 would connect it with the initiative of Agrippa and the building of Agrippa's Odeion.
60. Paus.1.8.4.
61. Ov. *Tr.* 2, 296; Zanker 1988, 195-201.
62. Dem. 22.13.
63. Kiilerich 1990, 129; Stewart 1990, 150-51, 154 believes that the subject matter of the metopes was deliberately chosen to illustrate the theme of hybris/nemesis, East/West, barbarism/civilisation.

CHAPTER 2

Just One of the Boys
Hadrian in the Company of Zeus, Dionysus and Theseus

Arja Karivieri

The aim of this paper is to analyze the ideological background for the rebuilding of Athens in the second century AD that was financed and planned by the Emperor Hadrian. The main source for this study is provided by Pausanias, whose description of Athenian monuments offers a general frame for the analysis of the buildings and other monuments and for their role in the imperial and religious policy of Hadrian. Another important source is Plutarch whose *Parallel Lives* gives a comparison between the founders of Athens and Rome, Theseus and Romulus, a comparison that was utilized by Hadrian in his propaganda.

In this study, special emphasis is given to the arch of Hadrian and to the rebuilding of the *scaenae frons* in the Theatre of Dionysus, both of which are seen as important features in the city-plan of Hadrian, with definite propagandistic values. Hadrian emphasized his role as the Emperor of Rome, the new founder of Athens and the founder of the Panhellenic union, with the help of specially chosen architectural features, sculptural decoration and statues. He knew how to utilize very effectively the imperial cult created by Augustus, and he even developed it further. While Augustus had been associated with Zeus[1] and Claudius with Apollo Patroös,[2] Hadrian became associated with Zeus, Dionysus and Theseus in Athens.

1. Hadrian and Athens

To cut a long story short, Hadrian was a philhellene who admired the Greek culture and did his best to be accepted and admired by the Greeks.[3] He was deeply engaged in the affairs of Greece and he visited Greece three times when he was emperor (AD 124/5, 128/9, 131/2). He was especially fond of Athens, and he was initiated into the Eleusinian mysteries as early as AD

112/3, i.e., before he became emperor. Hadrian later attended the Eleusinian mysteries every time he was in Greece, in AD 128 together with Antinous.[4]

Hadrian used a lot of energy to raise Athens to a special position in the Roman Empire. He made Athens into the capital of the Panhellenic union,[5] emphasizing in this way the role of Athens as the cultural capital of the Roman Empire. The embellishment of Athens was the cornerstone of Hadrian's policy of involvement in the provinces, which also had an impact on religious life in the provinces.[6]

Pausanias tells us that Hadrian's benefactions in Greece and to 'barbarians' elsewhere were recorded in the Pantheon of Athens that he commissioned (1.5.5; 1.18.9), which further confirms Athens' position in Hadrian's policy. A great many of Hadrian's buildings and good works in Athens were concentrated in the Olympieion area near the river Ilissos. The chryselephantine statue of Zeus in the Olympieion, the large temple of Olympian Zeus which Hadrian dedicated, is depicted as comparable to the Colossi at Rhodes and at Rome (1.18.6). This image of Zeus gives an association with Hadrian who was called the son of Zeus in an Athenian inscription.[7] As the statue was chryselephantine, it recalled the cult statue of Zeus in the temple of Zeus at Olympia and the statue of Athena in the Parthenon, both made by Pheidias, the admired sculptor of the classical period. In both temples, Pausanias saw statues of Hadrian (1.24.7; 5.12.6). K.W. Arafat states that by reviving the use of a chryselephantine cult statue, Hadrian could call attention to the temple and thereby to himself by using the archaic custom of combining ivory and gold in the cult statues.[8]

Pausanias lists other Hadrianic buildings near the Olympieion: a temple of Kronos and Rhea, father and mother of Zeus, and a precinct of Olympian Earth, Gaia, both emphasizing the importance of the area. Other known Hadrianic constructions in Athens were: a gymnasium with one hundred columns of Libyan marble, the temple of Hera Panhellenia and Zeus Panhellenios, a famous construction of Phrygian marble where books were preserved (the so-called Library of Hadrian), and the sanctuary of all the gods (1.18.9).[9] The localities of the gymnasium and the temple of all the gods have been under discussion for a long time: the latter has been placed in the Olympieion area, or identified with the partially excavated large Hadrianic building on Odos Adrianou, which the excavator Dontas identified as the Pantheon,[10] but Spawforth and Walker say is the meeting place of the members of the Panhellenion.[11]

Hadrian instituted three new agonistic festivals at Athens: the Panhellenia, the Olympieia, and the Hadrianeia. Further, he raised the profile of the Panathenaia: it was elevated to an equal status with the other three festivals.[12] Hadrian raised Athens to be on a par with the other great athletic centres,

Delphi, Isthmia, Nemea and Olympia, emphasizing Athens' role even in this respect, not only as the centre of the Panhellenion.[13] The Panathenaia were originally founded by Theseus in honour of the unification of Attica. As Theseus was the first founder of Panathenaia, Hadrian was the second founder. Hadrian was also the *agonothetes* of the Panathenaia in AD 124/5.[14]

2. Hadrian and the Greek gods

Hadrian's connection to Greek culture and religion was accentuated by giving him a special role in Greek mythology. He was not only worshipped as a Roman emperor in the imperial cult, but also he was associated with the Greek gods, especially Zeus and Dionysus. Hadrian's connection with the Olympian gods was shown by placing statues of Hadrian in the most important temples in Greece, as well as placing statues and other representations of Hadrian at other important spots in the cities, not to mention through the construction of all the religious buildings and monuments that were built during this period.

In Athens, Hadrian was usually associated with Zeus, using the epithets Olympios, Eleutherios and Panhellenios. Hadrian received the epithet 'Olympios' in AD 128/9 and was even called 'Hadrianos Zeus Olympios',[15] and after his death he received the epithet 'Panhellenios'.[16] In Athens he did not receive the epithet 'Eleutherios', but he was called 'the son of Zeus Eleutherios' in an inscription from the Acropolis.[17] Thus, Hadrian was associated with the Olympian gods as being the son of Zeus, a Panhellenic god. Arafat suggests that as Hadrian is honoured as the son of Zeus Eleutherios, by extension, Hadrian would be the brother of Athena.[18]

Not only did Hadrian identify himself with heroes and gods: he utilized self-promotion when he was presented as an inheritor of the legacy of antiquity.[19] Therefore, he concentrated his interests not only on Athens and Olympia: with the help of the imperial cult, Hadrian benefitted from the close association with other long-established religious centres such as Delphi, as he was offered the cult titles 'Pythios' and 'neos Pythios' by the Achaean League in AD 126.[20]

3. Hadrian and Dionysus

Especially interesting to our study is the documented connection of Hadrian with Dionysus in Asia Minor. For example, the initiates of Dionysus at Ephesos put up a statue of Hadrian as Dionysus.[21] In Side, the Imperial Mysteries – *Agon Mystikos* – that Hadrian himself started, were celebrated in honour of Dionysus, Demeter and the Emperor.[22] Similarly, Hadrian was included in the ceremonies of *Agon Mystikos* at Ankyra as *neos Dionysos* jointly with Dionysus:[23] the Roman emperor was associated with Dionysus, becoming the New Dionysus. Fikret Yegül has suggested that a special architectural setting was created in the Eastern provinces for the purposes of imperial propaganda: the architectural imagery invested in the *scaenae frons* of the Roman theatre could have been adopted for the decoration of the large hall constructions dedicated to the imperial cult, both including a comparable ideological content associating Dionysus and the Roman emperor as the New Dionysus.[24]

When Hadrian was in Athens for the first time, around the year AD 111, he was invited to become an Athenian citizen, and later on he was elected *archon eponymos*. Furthermore, the city of Athens honoured Hadrian with a statue in the Theatre of Dionysus, which is a conspicuous occurrence.[25] As Hadrian was *archon eponymos*, one of his duties was to regulate the Great Dionysia, the festival celebrated in honour of Dionysus Eleuthereus. This festival included dramatic performances in the presence of the statue of Dionysus that the ephebes had carried to the theatre from the Temple of Dionysus after the sacrifices.

When Hadrian came back to Athens as emperor in AD 124/5, he presided as *agonothetes* in March of AD 125 at the Great Dionysia,[26] and possibly, but not certainly, once more in AD 132.[27] Hadrian's arrival was celebrated in many ways. As David Geagan has put it: 'A new era was reckoned from Hadrian's arrival [i.e., AD 124/5], and Boedromion, the month in which he arrived, was made the first month of the Attic year'.[28] The council of the Areopagos, the council of the 600 and the *demos* honoured Hadrian with a series of twelve statues in the *cuneii* of the Theatre of Dionysus.[29] The statues were supervised by the members of the twelve Athenian tribes. As there were thirteen *cuneii*, the central, or the seventh place was occupied by the statue that had been dedicated to Hadrian during his archonship in Athens.[30]

On a front-row seat in the Theatre of Dionysus, Hadrian has received the epithet 'Eleuthereus' in an inscription, which is the only instance in Athens where Hadrian is associated with Dionysus.[31] The text reads: '(seat) of the priest of *Hadrianos Eleutheraios*'. Michael Maass has pointed out that in Athens Hadrian was associated with Zeus in the Olympieion, but in the Sanctuary of Dionysus Eleuthereus he was associated with Dionysus.[32] Roman emperors had been associated with Zeus before Hadrian's time, and the association of the emperor with Dionysus also occurs earlier: Nero was associated with Dionysus in an inscription found in the Theatre of Dionysus at Athens, commemorating the restoration of the theatre in the time of Nero.[33]

Fig. 1. Theatre of Dionysos: the orchestra and the so-called Phaidros bema with the reliefs from the Hadrianic scaenae frons. (Photo by the author)

4. The reliefs on the Theatre of Dionysus

Hadrian not only participated as *agonothetes* in the Great Dionysia, but also restored the theatre and built a monumental *scaenae frons* with relief decoration. When the *scaenae frons* of the theatre was decorated with reliefs, what could have been more appropriate than to associate the emperor in the reliefs with Dionysus and the empress with Ariadne, the spouse of the god? Hadrian was already associated with Dionysus in the inscription on the front-row seat, and honoured with thirteen statues in the theatre. Therefore, the iconographic association with Dionysus would suit his policy well.

The association of Hadrian with Dionysus in the Theatre of Dionysus in Athens would have been the peak of the development when Hadrian was legitimized as the New Dionysus in the centre of the cult of the wine-god. According to my interpretation, the reliefs from the Hadrianic *scaenae frons* (Figs. 1-5) allude to Hadrian as Dionysus, the son of Zeus, and to Sabina as Ariadne, including the scene of the wedding of Hadrian/Dionysus and Sabina/Ariadne[34] in the presence of Tyche in Slab III (Fig. 4). The female figure in the wedding scene of Slab III is commonly identified as the Basilinna, the wife of the *archon* Basileus, performing in the ritual marriage with Dionysus,[35] but

Fig. 2. The Hadrianic scaenae frons: *Slabs I (left) and II (right). Slab I: The Birth of Dionysos. Slab II: Dionysos' Gift of the Vine to Man. (Photo by the author, courtesy of the First Ephoria of Prehistoric and Classical Antiquities, Athens)*

I do not find this interpretation convincing. A further proof for the identification of the bride as Ariadne/Sabina is a portrait head in the National Museum of Athens (EM 3058), which Aikaterine Despoine has identified as belonging to the goddess holding a *cornucopia* in Slab III, in her opinion representing Demeter.[36] In my view, this partly damaged head, that is decorated with a diadem and a veil covering the back of the head, fits better with Dionysus' bride. The reason for this is that the veil seems to continue diagonally towards the chest to cover the shoulders. The mantle of the figure at the far right, on the contrary, falls directly on the shoulder. Furthermore, the head with the veil resembles very closely a portrait statue of Sabina from Perge, with a similar coiffure, diadem and veil, dated by Carandini to the year AD 129.[37]

I suggest that the series of four reliefs culminates in the relief to the right, the representation of the enthronement of Dionysus, depicting Dionysus/Hadrian sitting on a throne,[38] next to his spouse Ariadne/Sabina[39] (Fig. 5). To the left of Ariadne, clearly separated from Dionysus and Ariadne by the pose of the figure, is a half-naked male figure who probably represents Theseus, the founder of Athens, as several scholars have suggested.[40] The first person on the left is a female figure holding a *cornucopia*, plausibly Tyche who was depicted in Slab III as the witness to the wedding of Dionysus and Ariadne.

Fig. 3. Slab II (centre): Dionysos' Gift of the Vine to Man. (Photo by the author, courtesy of the First Ephoria of Prehistoric and Classical Antiquities, Athens)

In Slab IV (Fig. 5), Tyche is placed beside Theseus, which to me seems to stress the importance of the legend of Theseus, the legendary founder of Athens, and his connection with Dionysus and Ariadne. Theseus was the one who, on his way from Knossos to Athens, abandoned his fiancée Ariadne on the island of Naxos. Ariadne, the daughter of king Minos, helped Theseus to kill the Minotaur in the labyrinth of Knossos. Ariadne fell in love with Theseus and Theseus took her with him when he fled from Knossos. Theseus, however, abandoned Ariadne on the island of Naxos where Dionysus found her and took her as his spouse. As Pausanias records, this particular scene was depicted in the paintings decorating the Sanctuary of Dionysus (1.20.3), and must have been familiar to the Athenians: while Ariadne is asleep, Theseus sails away and Dionysus comes to take Ariadne away.

Thus, the relief scene in Slab IV could point to the deceit of Theseus. Theseus had abandoned Ariadne, he had turned his back on Ariadne – in my view, the sculptor could have alluded to this part of the legend in Ariadne's movement towards Dionysus, her spouse. This scene can show the connection between Theseus and Dionysus via Ariadne, and the scene simultaneously suggests the connection between Theseus and Hadrian as Dionysus with the help of Ariadne, who could have been associated with Sabina. Here, Hadrian

Fig. 4. Slab III (centre): The Wedding of Dionysos and Ariadne. (Photo by the author, courtesy of the First Ephoria of Prehistoric and Classical Antiquities, Athens)

could have utilized the faults of Theseus to emphasize the assimilation of himself with Dionysus, the god who saved Ariadne. It was important to Hadrian to be associated with Dionysus in the Theatre of Dionysus, as he could be seen as the saviour and the god who gave the knowledge of wine-making to man in Attica, as represented in the second relief, Slab II (Fig. 3).

Hadrian was assimilated with Dionysus in these reliefs. He is the New Dionysus, the new founder of Athens, who also became a new Eponymous hero. He is Dionysus, the son of Zeus. Zeus is represented in Slab I of the relief series (Fig. 2) as a seated figure witnessing the birth of Dionysus. As Slab I alludes to the birth of Athena depicted in the east pediment of the Parthenon, situated just above the Theatre of Dionysus on the Acropolis, Slab IV (Fig. 5) includes, above and behind the seated Dionysus, a depiction of the Acropolis rock, on top of which can be discerned columns of the south flank of the Parthenon, giving another allusion to Athena.[41] Another allusion to the temples on the Acropolis is given by the figures of Tyche and Ariadne in Slabs III and IV (Figs. 4 and 5). Both figures are *peplophoroi*, recalling the late-fifth century BC Erechtheum caryatids.[42] It should also be remembered that copies of the Caryatids decorated the Canopeum in Villa Adriana in Tivoli.

Slab I (Fig. 2) gives an allusion to the Sanctuary of Zeus at Olympia by re-

Fig. 5. Slab IV: The Enthronement of Dionysos. (Photo by the author, courtesy of the First Ephoria of Prehistoric and Classical Antiquities, Athens)

presenting the birth of Dionysus with a copy of the famous Praxitelean statue of Hermes and Dionysus, and, as Mary Sturgeon suggested, the figure of Zeus alludes to the seated figure of Zeus in the east pediment of the Parthenon.[43] Both Slab I and Slab IV give an allusion to the Parthenon, where a statue of Hadrian was the only statue in the cella apart from the statue of Athena Parthenos (*Paus*. 1. 24.7). Hadrian's divine birth as the New Dionysus, as miraculous as the birth of Athena, as well as his connection, as Dionysus, with his sister Athena, and with the father of the gods, Zeus: all these associations could be derived from the iconography of this series of reliefs.

It should be emphasized that the statue of Hadrian in the Parthenon beside the cult statue of Athena was the only statue of a Roman emperor there. Furthermore, a statue of Hadrian, next to one of Trajan, Hadrian's adoptive father, had been placed in the temple of Zeus at Olympia (Paus. 5.12.6).[44] In Athens, his popularity as emperor is also attested by the fact that there are more altars dedicated to the Emperor Hadrian than to any other Roman emperor.[45] As is clearly reflected in his text, Pausanias refers to Hadrian more often than to any other emperor, giving a favourable description of Hadrian and his activities in Greece as a whole.[46]

5. The arch of Hadrian

Modern scholars have been puzzled by the fact that Pausanias does not mention the arch of Hadrian (Fig. 6), an important element in Hadrianic Athens.[47] The arch was deliberately oriented on the line of an ancient processional route which led to the Olympieion precinct, avoiding the line of the Themistoclean wall.[48] The orientation and placement of the arch is important in Hadrian's city plan. It should be remembered that visitors coming to the centre of the Panhellenic cult of Zeus went through the arch and could read the inscription on the arch on their way, as did Hadrian when he entered the sanctuary on the occasion of the dedication of the temple of Zeus in AD 131/132. The arch was placed strategically so that persons coming from the Agora went through the arch and could read the text on the west,[49] traditionally translated as: 'This is Athens the ancient city of Theseus', and returning to the centre from the Olympieion they could read the text on the east side:[50] 'This is the city of Hadrian and not of Theseus'.

The arch has usually been interpreted as a boundary marker between the city of Hadrian and the city of Theseus, as is made explicit by the inscriptions on each side of it. Alison Adams has suggested that the inscription on the west should be translated: 'This is Athens the former city of Theseus', which should mean that the city of Hadrian replaced the city of Theseus.[51] Even though Arafat does not accept the conclusion drawn by Adams, I find it highly persuasive, since the visitors leaving the Olympieion precinct, on their way towards the Acropolis, saw the inscription on the east side of the arch, which underscores that the city belongs to Hadrian, *not* Theseus: i.e., the city that earlier belonged to Theseus, is now the city of Hadrian.

These inscriptions are connected very distinctively to the legend of Theseus. When Theseus founded the Panathenaia, he set up a pillar on the Isthmus as a territorial marker, bearing the inscriptions 'Here is not the Peloponnese, but Ionia', and 'Here is the Peloponnese, not Ionia'. This part of the legend is told by Plutarch (*Thes.* 25.3), which shows how well-known these sentences were in Hadrian's time. Finally, Herodes Atticus, the exceptionally wealthy aristocrat from Athens bears witness to this evident association between Theseus and Hadrian. Herodes played at being emperor by being a generous benefactor in Greece and especially in Athens, where he rebuilt the stadium and erected a grand music hall in the memory of his dead wife Regilla. Herodes repaired temples and dedicated new cult statues to show his generosity, and his works make specific allusions and parallels to those of Hadrian. On his estate at Marathon, an arch preserves two inscriptions directly imitating the ones on the arch of Hadrian at Athens:

Fig. 6. The arch of Hadrian. (Photo by the author)

> The Gate of Eternal Harmony. The Place you enter is Regilla's
> The Gate of Eternal Harmony. The Place you enter is Herodes'

A third inscription on a pillar of the gate is translated as follows: 'Happy is he who has built a new city calling it Regilla's by name'.[52] These inscriptions echo the claims in Hadrian's arch in Athens, where Hadrian is presented as the new founder of Athens, complementing, if not replacing Theseus, the first founder of Athens. Thus, Hadrian was clearly associating himself with Theseus.

6. Hadrian, Athens and Rome

We can also recall the cuirassed statue of Hadrian in the Agora that was placed beside the statue of Zeus Eleutherios in front of the Stoa of Zeus, where there was a hall for the imperial cult built in the reign of Augustus or slightly later.[53] The cuirassed statue of Hadrian preserves a representation of Athena standing on the back of the wolf who nurtured Romulus and Remus. Homer Thompson and Theodor Leslie Shear Sr.[54] have pointed out that this scene connects Athens directly with Rome, suggesting that Athens is superior to Rome, but at the same time needs the support of Rome. Athena is flanked by two winged Victories emphasizing the importance of Athens. This statue shows Hadrian's relation to both Athens and Rome.[55]

As is well known, Plutarch compared Theseus and Romulus in his *Parallel Lives*, which shows the importance of this comparison in its time. In this cuirassed statue Hadrian is connected with these two legendary figures, and the two cities these figures represent: Athens and Rome. Hadrian is the new founder of Athens after Theseus, and, at the same time, the new founder of Rome after Romulus and Augustus.

Thus, to sum up: Hadrian utilized architecture and figurative arts in a deliberate way in his imperial propaganda. Hadrian was assimilated with Theseus in the monumental arch, as the second founder of Athens. Hadrian was alluded to as Zeus in the Olympieion in several inscriptions by giving him the epithets generally used for Zeus. On the Acropolis, he is addressed as the son of Zeus. In Asia Minor, Hadrian was assimilated with Dionysus as the New Dionysus. In Athens, Hadrian was associated with Dionysus, the son of Zeus, in the Theatre of Dionysus, in an inscription of one of the front-row seats and in the relief decoration of the *scaenae frons*. As Plutarch compares the founders of Athens and Rome, Theseus and Romulus, Hadrian utilizes the comparison between Theseus and himself in his imperial policy. He is the ruler of Rome and the new founder of Athens. He is the one who has created the new Athens with the help of Theseus and Romulus, the new Roman Athens.

Notes

* I would like to thank Prof. Eva Rystedt and Dr. Carole Gillis for suggesting improvements to an earlier draft of this paper, and the participants of the conference for comments which have improved this paper significantly. I am also indebted to Dr. Gillis for improving my English. Of course, I am responsible for the remaining shortcomings caused by later additions.

1. Augustus was honoured as Zeus Boulaios in Eleusis (Clinton 1997, 166-67).
2. *IG* II², 3274. Cf. Clinton 1997, 169, and 179, note 53. See also Shear 1981, 363; Walker 1997, 69, and Spawforth 1997, 193-94.
3. For a recent discussion, ancient sources and general bibliography, see Calandra 1996 and Birley 1997.
4. Clinton 1989, 56-58; Birley 1997, 175-77, 215-16. Cf. Clinton 1997, 174-76, for the 'Athenianization' of Eleusis that was begun under Hadrian and completed by Marcus Aurelius; see also Alcock 1997, 5.
5. See especially Spawforth and Walker 1985.
6. Yegül 1982, 28; Price 1984, 67-68; Arafat 1996, 160.
7. Raubitschek 1945, 131-32.
8. Arafat 1996, 174.
9. Cf. Karivieri 1994, especially pp. 89-105.
10. Dontas 1968; Dontas 1969a; Dontas 1969b.
11. Spawforth and Walker 1985, 97-98.
12. Spawforth and Walker 1985, 90-91; Spawforth 1989, 194; Arafat 1996, 164-65.
13. Arafat 1996, 165. According to Anthony Birley, these festivals attracted not only athletes for competions, but also poets, musicians and orators, and spectators from all over the Greek part of the empire (Birley 1997, 266).
14. Kyle 1987, 24-25.
15. Benjamin 1963, 59-60.
16. Benjamin 1963, 72-73, note 47.
17. *IG* II², 3311, 3312, 3314, 3321, 3322; cf. Raubitscheck 1945, 130-31, where the author suggests that 'Zeus Eleutherius' recalls Trajan; Benjamin 1963, 58; Arafat 1996, 163; Calandra 1996, 88, note 29.
18. Arafat 1996, 163.
19. Arafat 1996, 162.
20. Benjamin 1963, 57-58; Arafat 1996, 162.
21. Price 1984, 118; Arafat 1996, 161.
22. Nollé 1986, 204-6; Nollé 1990, 258, fig. 18, 98; Karivieri 1994, 101.
23. *IGR* III, 209 = *SEG* VI, 58-59; Birley 1997, 83.
24. Yegül 1982, 26-27; Karivieri 1994, 101.
25. *IG* II², 3286 (Benjamin 1963, 83, no. 1). See Birley 1997, 64.
26. *HA Hadr.* 13.1; Dio Cass. 69.16.1; *IG* II², 3287; Birley 1997, 182.
27. See Birley 1997, 264, and 351, note 18.
28. Geagan 1979, 392.
29. *IG* II², 3287; Benjamin 1963, 83, nos. 2-5; Geagan 1979, 392; Willers 1990, 50.
30. Geagan 1979, 392.
31. Maass 1972, 116-17; *IG* II² 5035 III 253 – H II c: ἱερέως Ἁδριανοῦ Ἐλευθεραίως (*iereos Adrianou Eleutheraios*). Maass suggests that the *alpha* and *iota*-combination in the word *Eleutheraios* is an archaistic form for *epsilon*. Arafat has wrongly interpreted the epithet as referring to the epithet 'Eleutherios' of Zeus (Arafat 1996, 163).
32. Maass 1972, 116-17.

33. *IG* II², 3182; Geagan 1997, 26.
34. Vase paintings offer several comparisons for the scene with Dionysus and Ariadne, often attended by Satyrs, Maenads and Eros (see *LIMC*, III, 1-2: Dionysus, nos. 708-79). The black-figured vases from the 6th century BC have preserved many representations of Dionysus and Ariadne standing as in Slab III, but in the black-figured paintings Dionysus is always bearded, wearing a *himation* and a *chiton*, usually holding a horn or a *kantharos*, and Ariadne holds sometimes a wreath in her hand (*LIMC*, III, vol. 1, 482, and vol. 2, 381-82: Dionysus, nos. 708-13). Nos. 714-17 (*LIMC*, III, vol. 1, 482-83, and vol. 2, 382: Dionysus) show Ariadne whose head is covered by a veil, in. no. 714 she gives a wreath to Dionysus.
35. See Sturgeon 1977, 39-41.
36. Despoine 1988, 70-72, pl. 14, figs. 1-4.
37. Carandini 1969, 167-68, no. 29, figs. 138-39, 143, and pl. X, figs. xxxv and xxxvi.
38. For the seated Dionysus in monumental sculpture, see *LIMC*, III, vol. 1, 438-39, and vol. 2, 311: Dionysus, nos. 141, 142, and especially no. 143 from Delos.
39. Red-figured vases from the Late Classical period give comparisons for Dionysus and Ariadne as represented in Slab IV; for the seated Dionysus and the standing Ariadne, see *LIMC*, III, vol. 1, 484, and vol. 2, 384: Dionysus, nos. 731-34. Dionysus is depicted holding his *thyrsos* in the left hand and, in one instance (no. 733), a *kantharos* in his right. No. 733, a vase from Athens, shows Ariadne half-naked, standing on the right side of Dionysus (as in Slab IV in the Theatre of Dionysus), and holding a *thyrsos* in her right hand. The pose of Ariadne in this vase painting resembles Ariadne's pose in Slab IV, where the top part of Ariadne's *thyrsos* can be seen above her left elbow and the end of her staff behind Dionysus' foot. No. 742 with both Ariadne and Dionysus seated show Dionysus in a similar pose as in Slab IV, with the *thyrsos* in his left hand and the *kantharos* in the right hand (*LIMC*, III, vol. 1, 485, and vol. 2, 386).
40. See Sturgeon 1977, 41-43, and note 40; Despoine 1988, 73 and note 7.
41. Sturgeon 1977, 34, 41.
42. Sturgeon 1977, 40-41, notes 35 and 36, for more references and different interpretations; Sturgeon gives as other comparisons Eirene of Kephisodotos from the mid-4th century BC, and representations of Demeter from the Classical period; see also Despoine 1988, where Tyche and Ariadne are identified as Demeter and Kore.
43. Sturgeon 1977, 33-35.
44. Arafat 1996, 157, 163, 185.
45. For the altars, see Benjamin 1963; Price 1984, 69, 216; Willers 1990, 66; Arafat 1996, 159.
46. Arafat 1996, 210.
47. See Adams 1989; Willers 1990, 72-85.
48. Travlos 1971, 253; Spawforth and Walker 1985, 93; Arafat 1996, 179.
49. *IG* II², 5185 A (III 401): Αἵδ' εἰσ' Ἀθῆναι Θησέως ἡ πρὶν πόλις.
50. *IG* II², 5185 B (III 402): Αἵδ' εἰσ' Ἀδριανοῦ καὶ οὔχι Θησέως πόλις.
51. Adams 1989, 11.

52. Tobin 1991, 113-19; Arafat 1996, 200.
53. Thompson 1966; Clinton 1997, 168, 174; Spawforth 1997, 186, 193; Walker 1997, 69, and fig. 2.
54. Shear 1933, 181; Thompson 1987, 14.
55. Arafat 1996, 166-67.

CHAPTER 3

Cultural Interchange?
The Case of Honorary Statues in Greece

Jakob Munk Højte

1. Introduction

The Greek cities had a variety of honours that they could bestow upon foreigners for services rendered or in expectation of future services. The honours were primarily the erection of honorific statues, awards of proxeny status, crowns, honorific titles and cult foundation. This paper will focus on only one of these – the honorific statues. This was the type of honour most frequently given to Romans in Greece and consequently the one that was most likely to change as a result of the growing Roman influence. Just as in antiquity when they were the most prominent expression of foreign influence in Greece, honorific statues constitute the most visible aspect of the honorary system as seen from an archaeological point of view. This is clear at the sanctuary of Amphiaraios at Oropos, where the terrace behind the main altar is filled with statues – most of them of foreigners (Fig. 1).

While honorary statues and portraits have been studied intensively, the dedicatory inscriptions from the statue bases that carried the statues remain largely ignored. One of the few studies that has been made concerns the statue bases of Romans and Italians in Greece until the time of the principate of Augustus.[1] For this group of honourees, Payne's catalogue of inscriptions is used throughout. All other inscriptions used are part of a catalogue under preparation containing all statue bases for Hellenistic kings and Roman emperors in the Greek and Roman world. However, the present selection is geographically limited to the area of the Roman province of Achaea.[2]

Statue bases come in such great number that they constitute a large enough sample to be used as statistical material. By studying them in this way, they can provide information beyond what can be achieved by looking at each inscription separately. This is especially true with regard to changes through

Fig. 1. Oropos, Amphiareion. General view of the north-western part of the sanctuary. (Photo by the author)

time and differences between separate groups of inscriptions within the collective body of evidence, for example between different localities or between different categories of honourees.

2. Reservations

The use of epigraphical testimony as statistical material brings with it certain limitations, which must be taken into consideration. Naturally, all figures are approximations; a statue base could have been missed, and for a number of inscriptions it is questionable whether they belong to statue bases or to other types of monuments, such as altars or buildings. These minor variations occur at random and do not effect the conclusions drawn from the material as a whole. Caution is necessary, however, if the figures involved are very small.

More problematic is the question of whether the preserved statue bases constitute a representative sample of the statues originally set up. At least three aspects must be considered:

Geography: Different conditions of preservation prevail at different sites. Delos remains almost intact because of its early abandonment, whereas other sites

Fig. 2. Oropos, Amphiareion. Statue base for Gn. Calpurnius Piso (IG VII, 268). Superscription on an older monument. (Photo by the author)

are practically unknown because of continuous occupation or lack of excavation. Thus, the number of inscriptions actually found at a particular site does not necessarily reflect its importance in antiquity.

Chronology: Historical events can considerably alter the evidence from a location. In Athens the bases for statues of 16 Hellenistic kings and 25 Romans are preserved from the first century BC, but only 3 bases are preserved from the second century. Considering our knowledge of second century Athens this ratio seems very unlikely.

Category of honouree: Not all groups of honourees stood the same chance of having their image and inscription preserved for posterity. This is probably most true of the Hellenistic kings; their prestigious monuments were easy prey for local authorities who were eager to save public funds when the power-balance shifted in favor of Rome. For example in Oropos many of the statue bases have been reused. In their present form they are dedications to Roman magistrates and generals of the late Republic, but originally many of them were probably dedications to Hellenistic kings of the third and second century (Fig. 2).

Date	Proxenies/year	Statues/year
260-200 BC	0,5	0
200-189 BC	1,5	1
189-146 BC	0,25	0,5
146-88 BC	0,2	1
88-82 BC	0,5	3
82-62 BC	0,25	2
62-50 BC	0,25	2
50-44 BC	0,3	6
44-31 BC	0,3	1,5
31-27 BC	0,3	3

Fig. 3. Proxenies and statues to Romans and Italians in Greece. Based on Payne 1984, 358.

Despite the imperfection of the material the statue bases comprise the most valuable source for our understanding of this important aspect of the Greek honorary system, but when comparing between different groups within the material it is necessary to consider carefully how the parameters mentioned above influence the result. It is problematic, for example, to compare the number of statue bases for Hellenistic kings and Roman emperors directly, but it is possible to compare the number of sites where they appear in relation to the number of bases.

3. Scale

In the earliest period of Roman involvement in Greece, the most frequent honour given to Romans was the proxeny,[3] but early in the second century BC statues become more common (Fig. 3). This change seems to have been prompted by the honourees, who did not find the proxeny status as attractive. The Roman institution of patronage in many ways replaced the proxeny for transactions between Rome and Greece.[4] Such patronage appears in inscriptions from the mid-second century.

Around 250 bases of statues of Romans are preserved until the time of Augustus. In the two first centuries of the principate imperial statue bases number almost 300, and if the emperor's family is included the figure almost doubles.

The number of statues of Roman magistrates in Greece increases towards the end of the Republic (Fig. 3); this increase is also noticeable in the number of statues of local Greeks.⁵ The rise continues in most places all through the first and into the second century AD as a kind of inflation in the honorary system. The most reasonable explanation for this phenomenon is the waning independence of the Greek city-states.⁶ The Hellenistic kings gave large donations to cities in order to have their portraits erected. Good relations with the generals of the late Republic and the emperors were of vital importance to the city's very existence, and they were therefore by definition worthy of a statue. This devaluation of the highest respect a city could show a benefactor was soon followed in all ranks of society, and modest contributions had to be awarded with a statue.

4. Formula

The wording of the inscriptions from statue bases conforms to a simple pattern and contains only the most important information. Seldom do we find bases with inscriptions such as those known from copies of decrees in which the circumstances of the erection of the statue is described in great detail.

In both Greek and Latin inscriptions two elements are always present – the name of the honouree with patronymicon and the name of the dedicator. To this may be added a few other pieces of information; rarely the reason and time of the statue's erection, more often the honorific titles and public offices of the honouree.

In the Greek inscriptions the honouree's name always takes the accusative case. Only in imperial times in areas under heavy Roman influence do inscriptions occur with the emperor's name in the dative case. The name of the honouree in the accusative was also used for the earliest Latin inscriptions in Greece. These are for the most part bilingual with the Latin inscription first and the majority of them were erected for and by Roman citizens living or trading on Delos. Only in one documented instance before Augustus did a city in Achaea demean itself to honour a foreigner in a language other than Greek.⁷

The number of preserved statue bases in Italy with inscriptions in Latin before the first century BC is extremely small, and tracing their evolution is difficult. It seems likely, however, that early in the second century traditional *elogia* were replaced by dedicatory inscriptions under influence from Greek practices. By the first century BC, Latin inscriptions use the dative case for the name of the honouree as seen from the inscriptions from statue bases for Sulla in Italy.⁸ Under the empire influences run the opposite way, and bilingual inscriptions can occasionally have the name of the honouree in the dative case in both Greek and Latin. On the other hand, the Greeks were quick to bring the inscriptions into line with the Roman manner of recording name and title. Early in the second century υἱός as the equivalent of *filius* was added and the patronymicon no longer followed the *praenomen* but the *nomen*.[9]

The order in which the dedicator and the honouree appear in Greek inscriptions is dependent on their mutual relationship. The superior of the two, whether factual or fictional, takes first place. This is clearly illustrated by the inscriptions involving Hellenistic kings as honourees as well as dedicators. Whenever private citizens erected a statue of a king they put the name of the king prior to their own; when a king from one of the major kingdoms put up statues of lesser kings or one his generals, he would place his own name first. Public bodies generally appear before the name of the honouree.

Latin inscriptions, on the other hand, give the honouree first rank. In a number of bilingual inscriptions for Romans in Greece, the influence from the Latin inscription is seen in the Greek equivalent. Hence the name of the honouree is at the beginning of the inscription even in the case of public dedicators, where the reverse order would have been expected; this influence does not seem to extend to mono-lingual inscriptions.

In the Augustan age, many inscriptions show 'classicizing' tendencies in which private dedicators disappear and the dedicator again heads the inscription. In addition, the honorific titles and public offices that abound in Caesarian inscriptions are almost completely missing from the inscriptions for Augustus. Only from the time of Caligula does it become normal to put the emperor's name first even in the case of public donations.

5. Dedicators

Throughout the period in question, the primary statue donors were Greek administrative bodies, but there were also, especially in the second century BC, many statues being set up by private individuals (Fig. 4-6). After the Mithridatic war, however, these become less numerous, and by the end of the first century BC they have largely disappeared. For the statues of Hellenistic kings, this could be explained by the fact that they almost entirely derive from Athens, where the Council and the People always had tight control over erection of statues. However, the same is true for statues of Romans and for statues of Augustus, which originate from many different Greek cities and consequently it cannot be a mere coincidence. Whether the same holds true for statues of local Greeks has so far not been tested on a large body of evidence, but it seems probable that it does.

Why private dedicators disappear, is not easily explained. Could it be that the act of dedicating honorary statues had become of such vital interest to the cities that it was far too important to be left to private individuals; or could it be that they were put off by the idea of wasting money on statues of persons who might be next on the proscription list?

After the reign of Tiberius, the private individuals reappear among the dedicators of imperial statues in Achaea. Initially it seems to be mainly people who owed their prosperity directly to the emperor, but later many statues are erected on behalf of the cities under a system much like the *summa honoraria* known especially from Italy and North-Africa. It is now the municipal elite, who, as a munificence to their city, pay for statues of the emperors and might even in return have their own image set up some place in the city.

6. Geographic distribution

As mentioned earlier, determining the original geographical distribution of the honorary statues is very difficult due to the varying conditions of preservation at different localities. What can be done with a more accurate result is a comparison of the distribution pattern for different groups of honourees.

Four localities clearly account for far more statue bases than the others; these are Delos, Athens, Olympia and Delphi. For the Hellenistic kings these make up 83% of the total number of statue bases, whereas the figure for Romans in the Republican age is 65%. During the two first centuries of the Principate the number drops to 44% (Athens alone accounts for 33%) and Corinth emerges as a new centre for erecting statues. This could indicate that the Panhellenic sanctuaries might not have been considered as important by the Romans as they had been by the Hellenistic kings. The distribution is also much wider for statues of Romans than it is for the Hellenistic kings. Statue bases for Hellenistic kings appear at only 14 different localities, whereas the number of sites with statue bases for Romans until the time of Augustus is 31.[10] The trend is continued in the distribution pattern of the statue bases for the Roman emperors. In the period from Augustus to Commodus, bases are known from 59 different localities throughout the province of Achaea. Thus, the showcases of rivalry between the Hellenistic kings in the Panhellenic sanctuaries that are characteristic of the third and second century BC are superseded by a situation in which every Greek city wanted to have images of their Roman benefactors.

The kings disappear from the scene in mainland Greece at quite an early date. Although there are still a substantial number of dedications being made in the first century BC (Fig. 4), the figure conceals the fact that after the Mithridatic wars only Athens found it worthwhile to set up statues of the kings.

	4th cent. BC	3rd cent. BC	2nd cent. BC	1st cent. BC
Public	0	13	8	17
Private	3	10	14	2

Fig. 4. Dedicators of statues of Hellenistic kings.

	260-146 BC	146-88 BC	88-50 BC	50-27 BC
Public	24	30	39	61
Private	6	24	16	4

Fig. 5. Dedicators of statues of Romans and Italians.

	Augustus	Nero	Trajan	M. Aurelius
Public	14	4	10	10
Private	3	4	11	6

Fig. 6. Dedicators of statues of Roman emperors.

7. Conclusion

The transformation of the Roman dedicatory practice in the third and second century BC was a result of Greek influence, but the Roman presence in Greece also had an impact on Greek honorary tradition.

Of lasting importance is the shift towards the honorary statue as the most common award for benefactions in Greece. The scale at which this section of the honorary system came to work can be attributed to Roman pressure in the late Republic. The dedicatory inscriptions retain much of their original Greek character, but they had to be adapted to a Roman world. Greek continued to be the preferred language, even for statue bases for foreigners, but the way names and titles were recorded was brought in line with Latin practices.

Roman preferences are most clearly seen in the distribution pattern of the statues. Whereas the large Panhellenic sanctuaries had been the focal point for the Hellenistic rulers, the Romans were far more interested a wider geographical distribution of their portrait statues.

Notes

1. Payne 1984. For practical reasons Romans and Italians will be referred to here simply as Romans.
2. Still, a complete list of all inscriptions involved is too extensive to be included here.
3. In this respect there was no difference between Romans and other foreigners in Greece.
4. Payne 1984, 352-55.
5. Although not within the province of Achaea, Cos is a very well documented example. Höghammer 1993, 109, table 6.
6. Höghammer 1993, 64.
7. *CIL* I/2, 692. M. Minucius Rufus. According to *CIL* the Greek and Latin texts do not belong to the same monument, but the two dedications are probably contemporary.
8. *CIL* I/2, 720; 721; 722; 723; 724; 2508.
9. Payne 1984, 352-53.
10. This is not simply because there are more surviving bases for statues of Romans.

CHAPTER 4

The Argolid Countryside in the Roman Period

Renée Forsell

From the written sources we know about the Argolid being visited by emperors, such as Nero and Hadrian (Pausanias 2.17.6). Inscriptions tell us that the towns and the large sanctuaries were of interest to prominent Roman citizens.[1] However, the aim of this paper is to try to find out if the attention of the Romans in the Argolid during the first centuries AD was only directed towards these well-known places or if they also had an interest in the countryside.

Evidence of Roman presence consists of two kinds which are not necessarily incompatible. The first is based on an economic interest shown through the acquisition of land. We may find an indication of this by studying the fluctuating countryside settlement pattern of which information can be obtained through the results of landscape survey investigations. Luckily, in the Argolid, three such projects have taken place and been published, namely, the American Argolid Exploration Project, which investigated large parts of the Southern Argolid,[2] the British Methana Survey,[3] and the Swedish Berbati-Limnes Archaeological Survey.[4] The results of these surveys show that there is various evidence implying changes in land holding, such as a significant drop in site numbers, instability in site occupation, an overall loss in small sites associated with independent landholders, site sizes tending to increase, and the survival or foundation of these larger sites when most rural sites disappear. This last feature could indicate either a preference or need for a nucleated settlement pattern, or the presence of a new dominant élite landowning stratum in the countryside.[5] It does not mean, however, that the new owners had to be Romans; it could just as well mean that the land had changed owners among the Greeks themselves.

The second topic on which to focus is the search for signs of an élite living in the countryside. This kind of information is given by surveys as well as other archaeological investigations. The surface surveys have found some sites with material wealth, such as fragments of marble, mosaics and finds of sculpture. This is taken to represent a new or continued presence of wealthy

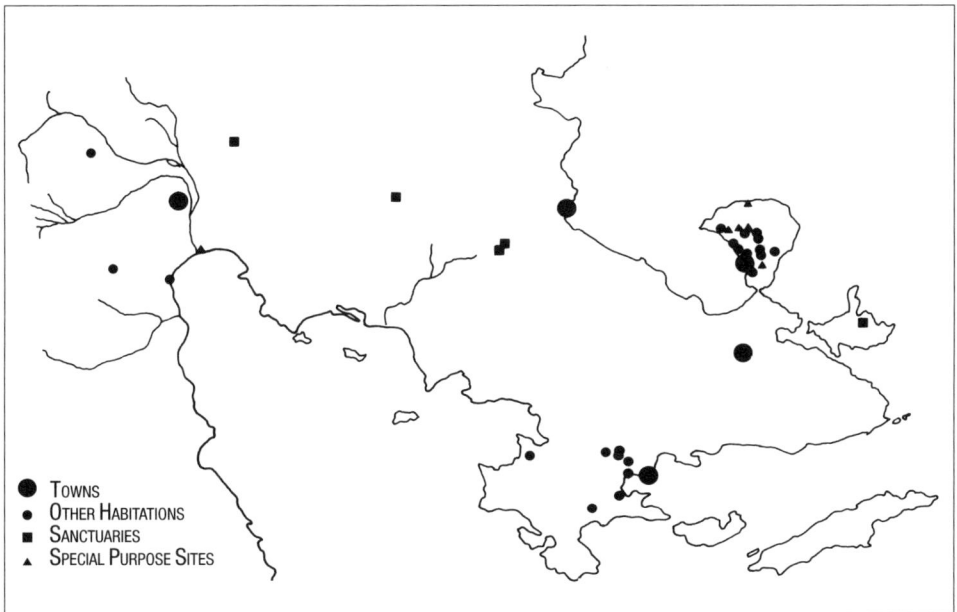

Map of the Argolid with Roman sites.

proprietors in the countryside. The appearance of villa establishments and other types of monumental structures, for instance baths or tombs, signals an increasing social stratification in the countryside.[6]

1. The site pattern in the Argolid as it is shown through the archaeological surveys

The authors of the time, such as Strabo and Pausanias, speak of a 'deserted land'. This description of Greece has been much discussed lately but archaeological investigations have shown that this was not altogether true. Actually, the surveys conducted in Laconia, Messenia, Patras and Pylos show a picture of intense population and prosperity in the countryside.[7] In the Argolid, as well as in Nemea, Boeotia and Keos, the overall settlement pattern of the countryside does, however, show a significant drop in site numbers in the Late Hellenistic and Early Roman periods, but the land was far from deserted.[8]

Some 183 Roman sites have been identified in the Argolid. Of these only about 50 belong to the Early Roman period.[9] Disregarding the towns and the sanctuaries we shall concentrate on the remaining 38 sites as being of interest for this study. The reason why Early Roman sites are so few when compared to the number from later periods may be that many of these sites have never been registered. This in turn may be a consequence of the fact that the dating of the sites was often dependent on the presence of imported red-glazed pottery. It would seem, however, that this pottery has seldom spread beyond the towns and coastal sites, and is therefore lacking in the inland territories.

In the Berbati valley no find-spot could with certainty be dated to the early phase of the Roman Empire, although some activity was noticed. In fact all the sites had disappeared already in the Late Hellenistic period.[10] We must therefore turn to Southern Argolid and Methana for a study of the rural settlement pattern. Some differences can be detected between the two areas, although the general trend is the same. In Southern Argolid the site loss was at its greatest already around the middle of the third century BC. Later on, in the first centuries AD, a rather stable but low site frequency pattern is shown.[11] Only six sites remain from the Hellenistic or earlier periods, while two new Early Roman sites appear. The new sites are both considered to have been small farmsteads.[12] Not until the fourth century do we find a real change and a large increase in site numbers.[13] All Early Roman sites except one are located not far from the city of Ermioni.

More than half of the Argolid rural sites are located at Methana. The site loss there starts later and belongs mainly to the Early Roman period when, according to the surveyors, the greatest site loss on Methana since the Middle Bronze Age takes place.[14] The Methana sites are, although seldom located on the coast, oriented westwards, and most are within travelling distance from the ancient city of Methana. In the second century they tend to spread further east.[15] Of the new sites three were farmsteads, one a hut or shelter and four were most likely agricultural sites.[16] Although small, they were still considerably larger than the Southern Argolid sites. The new sites at Methana, as well as in Southern Argolid, are all located on land not far from previous occupation, and no new soil seems to have been broken in districts not already cultivated.

It is obvious that fewer people lived on the land. The reasons for this have been disputed but, at least for Southern Argolid, a decrease in population has been suggested. Contrary to this it could of course be argued that people had moved from the countryside to live in the town. But as the town of Halieis is abandoned sometime around 280 BC, this does not seem likely.[17] Pollen analyses have shown that some land must have been left uncultivated. In particular, the slopes where grain used to grow between the olive trees would have been abandoned, while the lowlands were still attractive for continued cultivation.[18] A switch from intensive farming to extensive growing of cereals and a continued use of the existing olive trees, along with an increase in the importance of herding, are explanations given by Jameson and Runnels. They also suggest that most of the land was now divided into larger estates which made less use of labour, and that these estates were owned by people living in town.[19]

Although there are signs of change in land-holding in Southern Argolid, this trend can be attributed mainly to the Late Hellenistic period. Judging from the countryside settlement patterns I would suggest that no significant changes in land holding are apparent in the first two centuries AD.

Methana on the other hand shows a different pattern and other explanations are argued, in line with those given for Keos, where a similar settlement pattern is shown.[20] A shift from small to larger units owned by absentee landlords seems the most likely explanation. In support of this theory the remote location, the fine building technique, and the expensive pressing equipment, in combination with the poor quality pottery at some of the Methana farms suggest establishments run by tenants or slaves.[21] The new, purely agricultural, sites are other indicators of larger estates as these would not have been needed on a small farm. On many of the sites, including those at high altitude, pressing equipment for the processing of wine and olive oil was found.[22] The olives obviously still played an important role in the agrarian economy. Landlords would also have left large areas for grazing. An additional effect of this would have been that the land was kept safe from exploitation by the small holders.[23] The reduction in coastal sites may be explained by the pirate raids.[24]

2. Signs of élite living in the Argolid countryside

As stated earlier, other remains that may give an indication of the Roman impact on the countryside are those that reveal élite landowners, for instance the existence of villas and other monumental structures, such as tombs and baths.

Starting with the villas, except for a possible *villa rustica* at Methana,[25] all those identified and dated seem to belong to the Late Roman period. Obviously it was not fashionable in the Early Roman period to build luxurious residences on the Argolid country estates.

Other monumental structures of the period are equally hard to find. There were no reports of tombs that were not connected with the towns. Baths were found at Kiveri, Ligourio, Asine and Berbati, but the first have not as yet been dated and the three others are all of a later date.[26]

Once again we have to turn to Methana for evidence of the Early Roman period. At MS 57, at Ayios Nikolaos, a bath was located. It is of Flavian date, the second half of the first century AD. The building takes advantage of the hot springs in the area and has no apparent cold water source. The surveyors think this is the bath mentioned by Pausanias, and described by him as being without frigidarium (Pausanias 2.34.1). The bath is suggested to have been built by a local patron, and is one of the few signs of the presence of a local élite in the Methana countryside.[27]

3. Conclusion

This brief survey shows that in the first centuries of the Roman Empire the Argolid countryside was definitely a Roman backwater. With Methana as an exception, the Argolid countryside retained the sleepy existence that started in the Late Hellenistic period. There are signs of shifts in land-holding: the land now belonged mainly to absentee landowners and the money extracted was probably more often put into building in towns like Argos and Hermione, or the sanctuary at Epidauros, than invested back into the soil. But there is nothing to suggest that the owners were Romans.

If we compare the Argolid with the prosperous western parts of the Peloponnese, where we know there was a Roman interest (Patras for instance, being a Roman colony), and where the settlement patterns are more consistent with those revealed by surveys in Italy, I would like to suggest that the poverty of the Argolid countryside indicates a lack of Roman interest in the region.

As it was not yet fashionable for the upper classes of the time to have country estates in the Argolid, where they came to visit and live in style, the poor tenant or farmer who lived in the country and worked the land, did not notice much of Roman culture and was just as Greek as he had always been.

Notes

* This paper is a preliminary report of facts that will be presented and discussed in my forthcoming doctoral thesis on the Roman Argolid. I would like to thank Dr. Arja Karivieri, Ms. Anita Lennerstedt, Dr. Charlotte Malmgren, Prof. Eva Rystedt and Dr. Ann-Louise Schallin for useful advise and help with this paper.

1. The most well-known is the Roman senator Sex. Julius Maior Antoninus Pythodoros who erected and restored many buildings at the Epidaurian Sanctuaries: *IG* IV^2 88, 454, 514, 684; from Poros an inscription tells us that a Roman *rhethor* made a dedication to Asclepios *IG* IV 847.
2. Jameson, Runnels & van Andel 1994.
3. Mee & Forbes 1997.
4. Wells 1996.
5. The following points are summarised versions of the indicators for change in land holding presented by S.E. Alcock in Alcock 1993, 71f.
6. Alcock 1993, 72.

7. Shipley 1996, 272 fig. 27.7; Lazenby & Hope Simpson 1972, 91; Petropoulos & Rizakis 1994, 199-205; Davis et al. 1997, 455-74.
8. Wright et al. 1990, 617; Bintliff & Snodgrass 1985, 145-47; Cherry, Davis & Mantzourani 1991, 331-33.
9. The Early Roman period, as discussed here, covers approximately the time of the second half of the first century BC and the first two centuries AD.
10. Penttinen 1996, 281; Forsell 1996, 336f.
11. Jameson, Runnels & van Andel 1994, 394.
12. Only the sites that were definitely assigned to the Early Roman period are considered here. They are nos. C31, E36, E49, E56, E60, E61, E67. Another 20 possible sites were noted during the survey, (Runnels & Munn 1994, 471, 492, 496, 498f, 502f.).
13. Jameson, Runnels & van Andel 1994, 401.
14. Bowden & Gill 1997, 77.
15. Bowden & Gill 1997, 80f.
16. C.B. Mee et al. 1997, 118-210: farmsteads 109 (MS109), 170f. (MS211), 173 (MS218), the hut or shelter 159 (MS118), agricultural sites 157-159 (MSS114-117).
17. Jameson, Runnels & van Andel 1994, 395.
18. Jameson, Runnels & van Andel 1994, 398.
19. Jameson, Runnels & van Andel 1994, 399.
20. Bowden & Gill 1997, 80; Cherry, Davis & Mantzourani 1991, 331-33.
21. That is sites MS109 and MS211. Foxhall 1990, 109; Mee et al. 1991, 226f.; Bowden & Gill 1997, 81f.; Mee et al. 1997, 155, 170f.
22. Foxhall 1997, 262-64.
23. Bowden & Gill 1997, 81.
24. Bowden & Gill 1997, 80.
25. The afore mentioned MS211 that might be a farm or a *villa rustica*, supra n. 21.
26. Krystalli & Papachristodoulou 1967, 179; Kritzas 1972, 215-18; Höghammar 1984, 79-106; Forsell 1996, 337.
27. Bowden & Gill 1997, 78, 81.

CHAPTER 5

Three Cases of Greek/Latin Imbalance in Roman Syracuse

Kalle Korhonen

1. Introduction

The purpose of this paper is to examine the use of Greek and Latin in certain groups of epigraphic material from Roman Syracuse. The material consists of three groups of funerary inscriptions, first, those of the early Imperial period from the whole city, second, those from the catacomb of Vigna Cassia, and third, the epitaphs that belong to the transition between Antiquity and the Middle Ages, found in the area of Villa Landolina. I will be looking for phenomena of contact and interference and will try to determine the way in which we should interpret certain imbalances present in the material.

The presence of Latin in Syracuse properly begins with the settlement of a colony by Augustus, which must have caused a change in the population structure. On the level of the written sources, however, the traces of colonists are not numerous. The general nature of the epigraphic material is quite different from that of the big cities in Italy or in the younger provinces, because inscriptions which document municipal life are almost completely lacking. Among almost 1300 published inscriptions from Roman Syracuse, the majority, 80%, are in Greek, but the handful of honorary and building inscriptions are mostly in Latin.[1] In this paper, I will concentrate on the rich material of funerary inscriptions, which raises interesting questions concerning language use.

As inscribed tombstones belong to a relatively formal domain of language use, the language choice in them does not tend to be arbitrary. Their language was chosen with attention to the conventions of the family or of the reference group to which the family belonged, because the language choice was not regulated by laws in this period. It is not reasonable to assume *a priori* that the home language of the family was chosen, because, in a bilingual city, the prestige of the languages had an important effect on this choice, too. But was

Syracuse a bilingual city? The lack of bilingual funerary inscriptions in Syracuse is remarkable: even if the term 'bilingual' is used in the widest sense, i.e., an inscription that contains a Greek and a Latin part, regardless of whether one part should be the translation of the other, this term can still be applied in only one uncertain case.[2] It is also interesting that there are no texts written in the alphabet of the other language, something that is abundant in Rome. This will be one of the problems discussed.

2. Epitaphs of the early Imperial period

As I mentioned, the presence of a Latin-speaking population should begin to leave traces in the early Imperial period when the Roman colony was founded. First, some words on dating. Dating a Greek funerary inscription from Syracuse is not easy in general, but fortunately we often know the archaeological context and do not have to rely solely on palaeographic, onomastic or other criteria.[3] Furthermore, it was first in Imperial times that the material became more abundant, and it is only in few instances that the dating of an inscription remains completely uncertain. However, within the periods 'early Imperial' and 'late Imperial – Christian' the dating often remains vague.

Here, I would like to point out some features which can throw light on the contact between the Greek and the Latin epigraphic cultures in Syracuse. The first of these concerns the persons mentioned in the inscriptions. The late hellenistic funerary inscriptions from Syracuse indicate only the name of the deceased person in the nominative or genitive form, sometimes with filiation.[4] The persons who have set up the inscription, i.e., the dedicators of the epitaph, are not recorded. Their names remain absent from the Greek inscriptions throughout the Roman period. This characteristic connects Syracuse with some regions of the Greek East, say, Greece proper, Syria and Egypt, where it was customary to omit the names of the dedicators.[5] But in two other important cities of Eastern Sicily, especially in Catania, and to some extent in Messina, the names of these are often recorded.[6]

The problem with Catania and Messina is the scanty material available from the pre-Roman period. On the basis of this material it is difficult to determine whether the recording of dedicators' names was introduced during the Roman period, or whether it was the continuation of an older tradition. In Naples, the mentioning of dedicators seems to have been introduced during the Imperial period.[7] In Syracuse, the form 'Name$_1$ in dative (+ attribute) + Name$_2$ in nominative' (or reversed order) is seldom used, even in cases in which it is necessary to mention two persons in the same epitaph and there is a relationship between these two.[8] There is, in fact, only one small and distinct group of epitaphs in which a form of this kind is attested.⁹ In the Latin texts, the dedicators are often mentioned.

As a result, we can say that Syracusan epigraphic culture does not change in this respect during Roman Imperial times. Another feature which separates the Greek funerary inscriptions of Syracuse from those of Catania and Messina, is the use of the phrase Θεοῖς Καταχθονίοις. Borrowed from Latin epigraphy (= *Dis Manibus*) during the Imperial period, it often stands at the beginning of Greek epitaphs, either entire or abbreviated ΘΚ. This feature is rare in Syracuse.

Now I shall turn to the idiosyncratic features of Syracusan epigraphy. The Greek epitaphs of the early Roman period contain examples of an expression that is very common everywhere in the Greek world, namely '[Name in the vocative] χρηστὲ/-ὰ/-ὴ χαῖρε.'[10] However, another laudatory epithet is soon added, and the resulting pair, χρηστὸς καὶ ἄμεμπτος, becomes the characteristic feature of epitaphs from eastern Sicily. These can be in the acclamatory form '[Name in the vocative] χρηστὲ (-ὰ/-ὴ) καὶ ἄμεμπτε χαῖρε.', in some cases followed by the age, or in the indicative form, in which the age is always recorded: '[Name in the nominative] χρηστὸς (-ὰ/-ὴ) καὶ ἄμεμπτος ἔζησεν ἔτη κτλ'. The expression seems to have originated in Syracuse, where it is especially attested, appearing in more than 50% of the relevant material.[11] It was also in use elsewhere in south-eastern Sicily, and in Catania.[12] An inscription containing this pair of attributes can in almost every case be classified as pagan, even though some exceptions are known.[13] The pair is very rare outside Sicily, and can indicate the Sicilian origin of the dedicator or of the epitaph.[14] When burials in the catacombs begin, the use of this particular pair of epithets normally ends.

In the Latin funerary inscriptions of the early Imperial period, the following form can be used: 'Name (vocative) *pie/-a, salve* (or *have*)', sometimes with an indication of age.[15] In Latin inscriptions from elsewhere, the type of acclamation with the final *salve* or *(h)ave* is attested mainly in the late Republican – early Imperial period, in the form 'Name (nominative) (or vocative), *salve*.'[16] Furthermore, the epithet *pius -a* is not at all uncommon. But the combination 'Name (vocative) *pie/-a, salve*' is only attested in Syracuse, Catania and Centuripe,[17] and in the period before ca. 150.[18] It has been suggested that the Latin phrase shows the influence of the Greek tradition.[19] *Pie salve* corresponds in form exactly to χρηστὲ χαῖρε, but not in content, as χρηστός does not mean *pius*. The Latin for χρηστός would be *commodus* or *utilis*; the Greek for *pius* was εὐσεβής.[20] Anyway, it seems reasonably clear to me that the Latin epigraphic culture has been influenced by the Greek here. The Latin-writing persons have not translated the phrase, but used an attribute more familiar to them. On the other hand, there is no Latin phrase that would correspond to χρηστὸς καὶ ἄμεμπτος. The reason may be that contact between the epigraphic cultures was stronger at an earlier period, but questions of prestige may also have played a part.

There are, in fact, some examples of influence in the opposite direction. An interesting example of this is IG 14.45,[21] Βουλκακία / Τερεντία, / εὐσεβὴς / καὶ ἀγαθή, / ἔζησεν ἔτη / μ'. There is another text with εὐσεβῆ χαῖρ[ε-].[22] Vulcacia Terentia seems to have been a woman of some wealth,[23] and a plausible explanation for the phraseology of her epitaph may be the need for distinction. After all, χρηστὸς καὶ ἄμεμπτος is attested in even the most modest epitaphs of the pre-Christian period: it seems that anybody who could afford an inscribed gravestone could also afford one with χρηστὸς καὶ ἄμεμπτος. Furthermore, εὐσεβὴς καὶ ἀγαθή translates the Latin pair of epithets *pia et bona* and is rare in Greek epigraphy.[24]

But if Vulcacia Terentia's family wanted distinction, why did they not use Latin in her epitaph? As far as I can see, the answer to this question is in the prestige factor of Greek and Latin in different kinds of written documents. For a local notable of the first centuries AD, Greek remained an appreciated cultural language, which could be used in funerary epigrams, as well as in prose epitaphs. Trying to describe the situation in sociolinguistic terms, one could, at this phase, say that in the domain of funerary epigraphy, neither Greek nor Latin was the H(igh) variant, but the distinction between H(igh) and L(ow) depended on the linguistic form. There were other means, too, which could be used in showing a higher social position, namely the form of the monument.

3. Vigna Cassia

The cemetery area known as Vigna Cassia (or 'ex Vigna Cassia') includes catacomb A ('Catacomb of Marcia') and the catacomb of S. Diego ('Cimitero Maggiore') which are interconnected, as well as the adjacent catacomb of S. Maria Gesù. The catacomb of S. Maria Gesù, the use of which began in the early third century, is the oldest of the three; S. Diego was opened around 250; and the catacomb of Marcia, approximately half a century later.[25]

Soon after the burials in the catacombs began, Christianity was generally adopted, and some changes took place in the style of the funerary inscriptions. However, the dedicators remained absent from the epitaphs,[26] and family relations were seldom expressed. The attributes given to the deceased changed: the pair χρηστὸς καὶ ἄμεμπτος was replaced by ὁ / ἡ καλῆς μνήμης or ὁ / ἡ μακαρίας μνήμης, but the epithets were not used as frequently as before. The epitaphs normally consist of the following elements:

(A) the name of the deceased in nominative case, possibly with attributes;
(B) the phrase ἐνθάδε κεῖται which practically always indicates Christian context in the prose epitaphs of Syracuse;
(C) the indication of age;
(D) the date of death (often with the verb τελευτᾶν).[27]

A sentence consisting of A and B is a very common composition, and ABC, ABD and ABCD are well attested (with variable order of A and B). A variant focuses on the date of death; in it, the verb 'to die' begins the whole epitaph, and the noun phrase containing the name follows before the date. There are two other significant types, but they are much less common than those consisting of the elements listed above.[28]

The Greek-Latin imbalance reaches its peak in the catacombs of Vigna Cassia. There, the inscriptions number approximately 300, out of which twenty are in Latin (7%).[29] The inscriptions which contain only the name of the deceased are common. These names have been carved on the plaster near the grave or on marble plates. Even if the graffiti generally lack christograms and other Christian symbols which are more common on the marble plates,[30] their use continues in all of the cemeteries. Therefore they seem to have been the alternative of the lowest or poorest social stratum who still could afford a written epitaph. This lower social class begins only now to be represented in funerary inscriptions.[31] Earlier, it had been necessary to buy at least an inscribed marble plate from a stonecutter to produce a permanent funerary inscription, even if χρηστὸς καὶ ἄμεμπτος was included in the price. Now, instead of using marble, which had to be imported, and a professional stonecutter, one could resort to someone who was able to write a name on wet plaster. In Vigna Cassia, the Latin texts are very rare in the group of the name-only epitaphs.[32] Two explanations can be given for this: 1) that in the early period, Greek was used in the catacomb regardless of the mother tongue of the deceased; the few Latin texts would be explained as epitaphs of foreigners; 2) that Greek was the language of more than 90% of the deceased, and every family used the mother tongue of its members in epitaphs. But is it even possible for us to show that one or the other theory is correct?

In Rome, the proportion of Greek texts was highest among the earliest Christian inscriptions. A fundamental reason for the extensive use of Greek is that it could be used as the in-group language in catacombs, whereas the cemeteries of the early Imperial times were under the open sky, in a much more public space. There, it was more convenient to use the common out-group language, Latin, in prose epitaphs.[33] In Syracuse, the situation in early Imperial times was different, and it has been discussed above. In the catacomb burials, however, the circumstances in the two cities may have been more similar, with language choice based on in-group preferences.

One way of approaching the issue is through onomastics. We can look at the distribution of Greek and Latin names in the various groups of epitaphs. In Christian inscriptions, the people in the more Latin-speaking areas tend to use Latin names, and Greek names are in a minority.[34] Compared with the cities of the Greek East, the proportion of Latin names in Early Christian inscriptions is greater in Syracuse. There are about 55 graffiti epitaphs from Vigna Cassia, and the language of the name can be determined in 45 cases. The largest group are the texts from the Marcia catacomb, where about three-fifths of the names are in Latin, but in other parts of the catacomb, Greek names are more common than Latin. While in the catacomb as a whole Greek names are only slightly in the majority, in the marble slab group from Vigna Cassia Greek names are quite clearly in the majority.[35] Indeed, Latin names seem to become more common during the third century in this group of epitaphs. This may be due to the increasing number of Latin speakers, who possibly had to use the services of persons writing in Greek, as there were no Latin writers available.[36] It can be noted, however, that among the rare cases of filiation, some parents with Greek names have given their children one of the Latin names that had spread from North Africa to the other parts of the Mediterranean during the Christian era.[37] A similar phenomenon, namely that parents with Greek *cognomina* tend to give Latin *cognomina* to their children, is attested in Rome and in Ostia in earlier Imperial times.[38] There, prestige factors were certainly relevant, and they must have played a role in Syracuse, too, but they had a small influence on the language choice in epitaphs.

In sum, we have in Vigna Cassia an interplay of too many factors with unknown significance. The question I posed was 'does the proportion of Greek and Latin epitaphs reflect the proportion of the language groups buried therein?' The answer is affirmative, but only to a certain extent, as Greek may have been chosen for the sake of convenience in communication.

4. Villa Landolina

The inscriptions found in the 1940s excavations of the hypogeic tombs in Villa Landolina, where the Museum of Syracuse is now located, were a surprising discovery. The late Roman inscriptions of Syracuse had, so far, been mostly in Greek, and this was a group of Latin funerary inscriptions of persons with almost exclusively Latin names, carved with large letters on extensive limestone plates.[39] An earlier hypogeum was used for their graves, which were cut into the floor of the tomb chamber. Epitaphs which belong to a similar type had been found earlier in the vicinity and elsewhere in the city.[40]

Earlier, A. Ferrua had estimated that the actual linguistic Romanization of Eastern Sicily took place from the 6th century on, when the Latin-speaking elite was replaced by Greeks from the East, and became part of the common people.[41] When these texts were found, he felt that this theory was further corroborated.[42] This was a curious theory, based on what actually followed rather than on any reasonable sociological reasoning. Another, more prudent interpretation was given by S. Borsari who, referring to the peculiarity of the diction and the limited area of findings, argued that the persons mentioned were a group of Latin speakers distinct from the rest of the Syracusan population.[43] Ferrua and Manganaro referred to the absence of Greek inscriptions from the same period. Here, we run into the common problem of this field of studies: the general level of literacy. Are there any possibilities for us to know how common it has been, in a given period, to include a written epitaph next to a grave? One could simply say that the Greek-speaking parts of the population were not able to purchase a written epitaph, or had given up the habit of using a written epitaph. It is important to look at the rest of the written material from the same period.

No study has presented any specific criteria for dating the inscriptions from Villa Landolina. Therefore, the datings given vary greatly: Manganaro proposes the ostrogothic period (last quarter of the 5th century – 535); Bernabò Brea, the 6th century;[44] A. Silvagni, 'per i caratteri paleografici e stilistici', considered 7th century more probable than 6th;[45] Ferrua went even further, and suggested 'secolo VIII circa', when publishing an apparently similar Syracusan text.[46] Here, the great differences from the earlier tradition seem to be the reason for the late dating.[47] It is true that the stonecutting is very different from the other Syracusan inscriptions, but some parallels can be found elsewhere. The writing material has had an effect on the handwriting, making the letters wider than usual, because a lot of space was available.[48] It seems to me that even if the letter forms are not very consistent, two hands can be distinguished: the more experienced 'hand A', with straight lines and *apices* in the letters,[49] and the less practised 'hand B'.[50] In determining the overall dating, many factors can be relevant: all the inscriptions have *A*'s with the broken bar; the *D*'s of hand A are slightly triangular, of the type that is common in the 6th century. The *V*'s in the Villa Landolina inscriptions are always capital. Giving an accurate dating is beyond my competence, but 8th century seems improbable,[51] and 6th or 7th century more likely.

The funerary formulae attested are (1) '(cross) + *memoria* + [name in genitive] + [profession etc.]' (nn. 1, 3, 4, 6, 9); (2) '(cross) *hic e*[*st* (?)] + [name in uncertain case] + [profession]' (n. 2); (3) '(cross) + *sepultura* + [name in genitive]' (n. 5).⁵² None of these is attested outside Syracuse in Sicily. Type (1) seems to have been especially common in the area of Mauretania Caesariensis from the 3rd century on.⁵³ However, it is attested also in the catacomb of S. Giovanni.⁵⁴ Furthermore, an example of a Greek counterpart has survived; it may come from S. Giovanni, as well.⁵⁵ The stones in S. Giovanni clearly belong to the catacomb context, as they are smaller marble or limestone plates and, in physical appearance, similar to the other inscriptions there. The use of large slabs of local limestone in the hypogea might mean that the availability of marble had diminished. Because of this, the period immediately before the Byzantine conquest might be a good guess, when trade connections to the east may have been weaker than before and afterwards. In any case, during this period it was easier to find slabs of limestone than slabs of marble to cover an entire tomb.

In my view, the point made by Borsari is valid. I think that the proper interpretation of the Villa Landolina inscriptions from the point of view of linguistic balance is that they are the epitaphs of a certain Latin-speaking group, who probably had emigrated from North Africa. Most of the Syracusan cemeteries which were in use during this period have only left us with material which does not belong to the study of literacy, and this has often been forgotten when the linguistic conditions have been discussed. The number of Latin speakers in Syracuse very probably had increased, but what was more important, the level of literacy had fallen, and funerary epitaphs had become more rare.

Notes

* I am grateful to Dr. R. Amato and Dr. A. Curcio of the Soprintendenza per i beni archeologici, Syracuse, and especially to Dr. M. Sgarlata of the Ispettorato per le catacombe della Sicilia Orientale, Syracuse, for permission to study the archival and epigraphic material in Syracuse. My thanks are also due to Dr. Shane Butler who revised my English.

1. For a good recent discussion of the public language use in this city, see Wilson 1990, 316. The problematic *SEG* 43.634 must be added to the documents. The numbers given here are my counts. All dates are AD.
2. The bilingual text: Ferrua 1989, 67 n. 260: [E]ΠΙΤΥΓΧΑ/ΝΟC ΑΒΕ (from the catacomb of S. Maria Gesù, datable to the 3rd century).
3. In *IG* 14 the uncertain cases are few, and the later publications are better documented. We cannot be sure of the origin of many inscriptions which came to the museum of Syracuse before the directorship of P. Orsi, which began in 1888; the origin is either unknown, or the old inventory gives false information.

4. The most important cemetery with inscriptions datable to the Hellenistic period is the one published by P. Orsi in *NSc* 1892, 354-65.
5. See, e. g., Kajanto 1963a, 18.
6. For Catania, see Ferrua 1941, 172; for Messina, *IG* 14.411, 414, and *NSc* 1942, 82-84.
7. Compare the epitaphs in Leiwo 1994, 60-86, 117-18 with ibid. 104-9.
8. Illuminating examples are *IG* 14.116 (corrected reading by Ferrua 1989, 45 n. 165): Τύνβος Εὐτυχίωνος ἀγορασία. ἔνθα κῖτε Ἰρήνα, ἡ σύνβιος αὐτοῦ, and *IG* 14.177 (corrected by Ferrua 1989, 47 n. 176): Ἐνθάδε κῖτε Τιμόθιος κὲ Ἰρήνα, ἡ τούτου σύνβιος, ἅμα καὶ Κρισκωνία, ἡ τούτων ποθητή, ζήσασα ἔτη πλῖον ἔλατον εἴκοσι, both from S. Giovanni.
9. *IG* 14.34 cf. Ferrua 1941, 197. It was found by the 18th-century archaeologist C. Gaetani in the vicinity of three other inscriptions that are also very particular in Syracuse, *IG* 14.23, 35 and 44. See Gaetani, in Schiavo 1756, part 5, 15; 60-62 and in Sgarlata 1993 [1996], 163.
10. *NSc* 1912, 299 (i) = 1915, 203 (ii); cf. Ferrua 1941, 214 n. 91; Agnello 1950, 64 n. 24.
11. The material consists of the pagan Greek funerary inscriptions from Syracuse, excluding the fragments of which it is impossible to say whether they had the pair of attributes or not.
12. E. g. *IG* 14.226 cf. Ferrua 1941, 198 (Akrai); *NSc* 1907, 485 (Modica); *SEG* 26.1117 (Rosolini); *NSc* 1912, 363 (Ragusa); the epitaph published by F. Cordano, 'Iscrizioni dal territorio di Palagonia e Mineo', in *XI Congresso internazionale di Epigrafia greca e latina. Atti* 1, Rome 1999, 681-82 (Mineo); *IG* 14.254 (Licodia); *IG* 14.255a (S. Croce Camerina); *IG* 14.510, *NSc* 1915, 216 and *SEG* 44.762 (Catania).
13. This criterion has been studied by Ferrua 1941, 180-210; cf. Ferrua 1974, 431-32. For the pair in the Christian context cf. Ferrua 1941, 202 n. 75; Theodule χρηστιανὴ καὶ ἄμεμπ[τ]ος (Ferrua 1941, 205, fig. 38); and the dated epitaph from the vicinity of Modica (year 396 or 402, *SEG* 36.852).
14. As far as I know, it is attested in Rome twice, in *IGUR* 794 and in the Christian *ICUR* 17227 (= *IG* 14.1639). (Note that *IGUR* 646 is not from Rome, but from Syracuse, namely *IG* 14.36, republished by Ferrua 1941, 186, 198.) A difficult case is *SEG* 26.1855 (Egypt?).
15. *CIL* 10.7129, 8314 and 8315; *EE* 8.694; *NSc* 1901, 344 (*piissime, salve* with long I in pIIssIme); *NSc* 1915, 206; *NSc* 1920, 317 fig. 10 (*pia, have*).
16. Cf. Kajanto 1963a, 17-18. From Syracuse: Manganaro 1962, 499 n. 72; *NSc* 1901, 337; *NSc* 1912, 298 fig. 8.
17. Catania: *CIL* 10.7082; Centuripe: *CIL* 10.7010 (*pius salve*). Note the curious *CIL* 10.7064 = *IG* 14.472 (see n. 20 below).
18. I doubt F. Sinn's dating of *CIL* 10.8314 as 'Hadrianisch (?)' (Sinn 1987, 221 n. 535), but will not go into detail here. *NSc* 1915, 206 is a more difficult case.
19. This was argued (with reference to *EE* VIII 694) by G. Forni (1980, 960 n. 29).
20. To take an example from epigraphy, in *CIL* 10.7064 = *IG* 14.472 (origin uncertain, but attributed to Catania with reason), in which the word *Pius* is translated with Εὐσεβής.
21. Its surviving fragments are *IG* 14.59a (identified by Ferrua, 1940, 276-77) and Orsi

1918, 611 fig. 206. It has not been identified previously, but it was found in the area where *IG* 14.45 was last seen, and it is very probably a fragment of lines 1-2 of that inscription. (Note that *CIL* 10.7173 with an analogous wording is not from Sicily, see Ferrua 1940, 278).
22. Gentili 1961, 21 n. 3.
23. The arguments for this are 1) her name; 2) her monument as described by authors of the early modern age, cited in *IG*; 3) the fine lettering in the epitaph.
24. Tod 1951, 185-86.
25. See Agnello 1958, 69-75.
26. The exceptions are: *SEG* 4.3, possibly also Agnello 1963, 82 (cf. Ferrua 1989, 63 n. 241), Ferrua 1989, 66 n. 254 and 84 n. 332.
27. See also Ferrua 1941, 210-43.
28. They are the τόπος type (τόπος followed by the name in genitive, meaning 'N's grave'), and the μνήσθητι type, a wish that God would remember the dead person.
29. The numbers are my own counts. I have excluded the texts which probably do not originally belong to the catacomb.
30. Christian symbols are seldom used in the graffiti, but feature in about one-third of the marble inscriptions. The position of the painted epitaphs is not clear in the arrangement. They are a minority, and often contain a cross which precedes the name of the deceased. They may have represented a more luxurious alternative than a simple marble plate.
31. This explanation was tentatively suggested and refuted for the city of Rome by J. Kaimio (1979, 172).
32. They are Führer 1897, 103 [773] n. 1 and Agnello 1956, 53 and 60.
33. Kaimio 1979, 173-74.
34. See Kajanto 1963b, 57-59.
35. Their distribution in the different sections of the catacomb is difficult (this concerns particularly the texts published in *IG*), which is why I treat them here as a whole.
36. B. Pace's suggestion (Pace 1949, 255-56), that the use of Greek was due to historical and religious reasons, is not plausible.
37. The examples are not from Vigna Cassia, but from the catacomb of S. Giovanni: *IG* 14.88: father *Eusebius*, son *Bonifatius*; *IG* 14.177 (cf. Ferrua 1989, 47 n. 176): father *Timotheus*, mother *Irena*, daughter *Cresconia*, written Κρισ-. Compare also *IG* 14.156 (father *Hesperianus*, daughter *Urbica*).
38. See Solin 1971, 133-35.
39. *NSc* 1947, 189-91 nn. 1-6 and 9 (Latin); n. 7 (Greek letters, but illegible) = *AE* 1951, 175-179; corrections: Ferrua 1989, 89-90 nn. 344-348; Manganaro 1993, 584-87, photos in 565-67 (figs. 23-27).
40. *NSc* 1907, 777 n. 43 (cf. Ferrua 1989, 31 n. 93a) and Ferrua 1989, 31 n. 93 (*NSc* 1907, 776 nn. 41 + 42) were found in the vicinity. Compare *CIL* 10.7169 and 7185 (cf. Ferrua 1989, 92 n. 358 and 93 n. 361).
41. Ferrua 1942, 214-15.

42. See Ferrua 1946-47, 238. He was supported by Manganaro 1993, 554, 584-87; cf. also the comment of the editor, L. Bernabò Brea, in *NSc* 1947, 192.
43. Borsari 1963, 14 n. 18.
44. *NSc* 1947, 191.
45. Silvagni 1950, 221.
46. Ferrua 1946-47, 238 n. 49 from the suburb of S. Lucia.
47. Cf. Manganaro 1993, 587: 'una rottura nella tradizione funeraria delle famiglie siracusane'.
48. An example of a similarly wide lettering is *AE* 1977, 204, dated in 506, from Cimitile in Campania.
49. This is the stonecutter of the inscriptions nn. 3 and 5. Note also the form of *D* and the small *O*'s.
50. Nn. 1, 2, 9 and possibly 6. See the forms of *M*, the big upper parts of *P* and *R*, the wide *V*'s. N. 4 may also be written by this person, as the *apices* have not been used in it; the *A* in n. 4 is different.
51. See the tables of Gray 1948, 47-48, 56, 61-64, 80-81.
52. The professions are *carpentarius*, possibly *praeceptor*, *medicus* and *figulus*.
53. See Février 1964, 124.
54. *NSc* 1895, 492 n. 185; Griesheimer 1996, 120-21 n. 5. *CIL* 10.7181 (cf. Ferrua 1989, 188) belongs to the group of large limestone plates, see Agnello 1960, 32 n. 28.
55. *NSc* 1893, 298 n. 76 (cf. Ferrua 1989, 18 n. 27): + Μνιμῖον [---] / τα Θεοδο[ρ--- / οδόρου [---] (small limestone block, size 19 x 15 cm [Orsi, *NSc*]). It has been published many times among the inscriptions from S. Giovanni, because of the information given by the unreliable old inventory of the Syracuse museum (see n. 3 above).

CHAPTER 6

Continuity and Change in Greek Households Under Roman Rule:
The Role of Women in the Domestic Context

Lisa Nevett

1. Introduction

Research on Roman Greece has tended to concentrate on literary texts or on major works of art and architecture, examining the identities which wealthier Greeks under Roman rule explicitly created for themselves in the public sphere. In this contribution I shift the focus onto private life, addressing the question of 'Greek Romans or Roman Greeks?' by looking at whether the desire to preserve a distinctive Greek identity, apparent from many of these studies, also affected the home lives of individual families.

The information about family life which can be gleaned from the texts of this period is limited. Nevertheless, one issue which does emerge from Roman authors is a contrast between Roman women and their contemporary Greek counterparts in the degree to which they are said to have participated in social life. Cornelius Nepos, for example, compares the Roman custom of allowing wives to appear in public with that of the Greeks, who he says only allow their wives to appear in front of relatives (Nep. *Vitae* Pr. 6-7). According to Vitruvius the Greek house itself is designed differently from the houses of Romans, providing suites for guests and for men's banquets, which are separate from the *gynaeconitis* where he says the women of the household sit with the wool workers (Vitr. *De Arch.* 6.7.2). Vitruvius also comments on the fact that Greek women do not customarily accompany their husbands at dinner, implying that this is different from normal Roman practice (ibid. 6.7.4). (The context may, however, imply that he is talking about the past, rather than the present). Vitruvius' view of the Greek house is supported in an aside made by the later, Greek writer, Plutarch. Plutarch mentions the *gunaikonitis* along with the *andronitis*, associating the two areas with women and men respectively, although he offers no further indication of how each was used (Plut. *Mor.*

145B). Elsewhere, however, he indicates that Greek women were able to socialise relatively freely, recommending that newly-married husbands allow their wives to share their husbands' friends (id. 140D). He may have followed this advice himself, since he comments on the esteem which his friends have for his own wife, whom they seem to have met (id. 609 C-D).

The attitude which seems to underlie the comments of Nepos and Vitruvius suggests the preservation of ideals represented in the Athenian legal speeches of the fourth century BC, which imply that the female relatives of citizens were largely confined to the domestic sphere and did not appear before unrelated men (see, for example Gould 1980, 47). Plutarch, writing a century or so later than Nepos and Vitruvius, and from a Greek perspective, seems to assume patterns of behaviour among the Greeks of his own time which are rather different. The implication may be that Nepos and Vitruvius failed to grasp what was common practice amongst contemporary Greeks and instead are reflecting the ideals expressed in earlier literature. But it is also possible that the social lives of women, and therefore the organisation of the whole domestic sphere, underwent substantial change during this period. Nevertheless, the evidence is not abundant and it is unclear to what extent the views presented are influenced by the cultural perspectives and literary genres of the individual authors. The aim of this paper is to use the fuller evidence provided by archaeological material, in order to explore the extent and nature of changes taking place in women's roles within Greek households, following the introduction of Roman rule.

This topic is particularly suited to archaeological investigation because gender relations seem to have played a major role in the organisation of Greek houses during the Classical and Hellenistic periods, and this is visible in the organisation of the houses themselves. Traditionally, scholars have thought of Classical houses as having been divided into two different areas in which male and female family members had their own separate living quarters (for example Walker 1983 *passim*; Pomeroy 1994, 295). Although detailed examination of the archaeological evidence confirms the importance of gender relations in shaping Classical and early Hellenistic households, it does suggest a rather more complex pattern of social behaviour.[1] This needs to be outlined briefly as a basis against which to compare the patterns of organisation found in houses of Roman date.

Between the late-fifth and late-third centuries the domestic environment seems to have been shaped by a desire to control interaction between family members and outsiders, and this can be seen in a number of architectural features. Contact between the household and the outside world was limited: exterior windows seem to have been small and high; in general, only a single entrance to the house was provided from the street and various techniques were used to screen the entrance from the remainder of the house, preventing the interior from being visible when the door was open. Internally, the pattern of communication between rooms would have enabled movement through the house to be monitored: space was organised around a single area, an open court, which gave access to the majority of the rooms individually. Wide street doors and ruts show that in some settlements wheeled traffic was brought into the court from the street, indicating that the court played a role in provisioning the household. In addition, where detailed information is available about the distribution of artefacts,[2] equipment used in domestic chores, such as weaving apparatus, braziers and cooking pots, have been found in and around the court, suggesting that this space was used by women in the course of their domestic duties. The court thus seems to have been central to domestic production.

Architectural evidence shows that a specialised room, the *andron*, was often provided for entertaining guests. This was a decorated chamber which was separated from the remainder of the house using a closeable door and sometimes also an anteroom. In the largest houses, several *andrones* of different sizes were provided, arranged around their own separate court which was often a decorated peristyle. In such cases access to the house remained limited to a single street entrance giving on to the peristyle, and the domestic quarters could only be entered from here. This development seems to have offered a means by which the house could be used for an increasingly wide range of social gatherings, while at the same time the integrity of the domestic areas – and presumably the women within them – was maintained. Through time there seems to have been a tendency to build such houses on an increasingly large scale, with the peristyle and surrounding dining rooms becoming more ostentatious. Current evidence indicates that domestic space was laid out in this manner in Greek cities over an area which stretched from Asia Minor to Southern Italy and from northern Greece to North Africa.

2. Greek Households under Roman Rule

Greek houses of Roman date which have been preserved and excavated in their entirety, and which therefore offer a complete picture of domestic organisation, are relatively scarce. There is also a lack of instances in which the distribution of artefacts can be examined in order to give a detailed picture of how different areas of the house were used. Nevertheless, by relying on architectural evidence and looking at a variety of different settlements, it is possible to begin to identify the kinds of changes taking place in domestic organisation between the Hellenistic and Roman periods. These suggest that there were corresponding changes in the patterns of social behaviour which were perceived as acceptable. By detecting similar patterns over a wide geographical area, it becomes possible to distinguish broad trends from local variations.

Three major developments can be detected, either singly or in combination, over a range of Greek communities. These are, firstly, a change in patterns of circulation; secondly, a change in the use of the court; and thirdly, the appearance of a space which has been interpreted as an *atrium*, with a central *impluvium*. Together these developments suggest that during the early years of Roman rule Greek households underwent significant changes in the organisation of domestic social life, including a transformation in the status and activities of their female members.

Changes in patterns of circulation

Two differences can be identified in the patterns of circulation in Greek houses of Roman date as compared with houses of the Classical and earlier Hellenistic periods. They are, firstly, the creation of an additional entrance or entrances onto the street, facilitating movement in and out of the house, and secondly, a change in the organisation of interior space, so that more rooms could be entered independently of the court and there was often more than one way in which to reach an individual room. Both of these developments point to an opening up of the domestic environment in relation to the world outside. This would have made monitoring social contact between different members of the household, and between the household and the outside world, less easy, implying that the activities of women must have become less restricted. A couple of examples will serve to illustrate these trends.[3]

At Kassope, in Epiros, this development shows up clearly in the alterations made to existing fourth century houses, which continued to be occupied following the Roman invasion and the partial destruction of the city in 168 BC, and were finally abandoned in the later first century BC (Dakaris 1989, 38-58; Hoepfner 1994, 156-158). Published phased plans of three houses (houses 1, 3 and 5) (Hoepfner 1994, Figs. 151 and 155) demonstrate the way in which the houses were adapted over that time. In their original, fourth-century form, interior space was divided into an outer area, comprising a dining room and store, and an inner area which seems likely to have been used for domestic activities. In common with other houses of this date, access from the street was limited to a single entrance. The view between the street door and the domestic quarters was obscured by positioning the route to the rear part of the house so that it was not aligned with the outside door, thereby preserving the privacy of the inner area.

By the later second century BC these houses had already undergone considerable adaptation which the excavators link with an episode of Roman

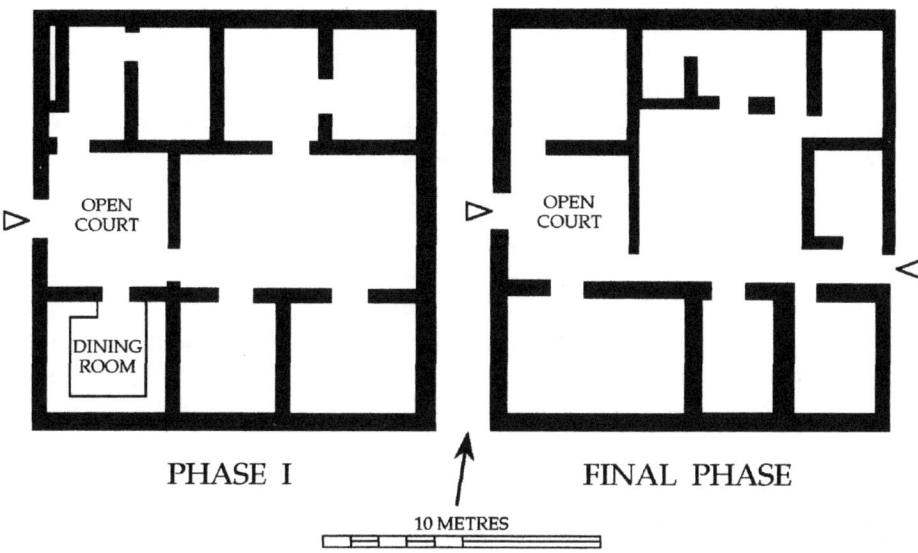

Fig. 1. Kassope: house 5, phase 1 (fourth century BC) and final phase (first century BC). (adapted from Hoepfner and Schwandner 1994, fig. 151)

reorganisation and rebuilding (Hoepfner 1994, 156). At this time some of the houses were expanded in size, taking over land from their neighbours. Patterns of circulation became more complex, and rooms were often now entered in series rather than individually from a central space. A second street entrance was usually also provided. An example is house 5, which, as in its first phase, seems to have been organised around two separate areas (Fig. 1). Nevertheless, a significant difference is that the two separate street entrances would have enabled the occupants of each area to come and go as they pleased, without having to pass through the other section of the house. As a consequence, it would have been less easy to monitor movement around the house or to control contact with the outside world. The implications are that the activities of female members of the household became freer and that social contact was less restricted.

Further examples are provided by a group of houses at Morgantina in Sicily, which are also Hellenistic structures continuing in occupation following the advent of Roman control. Morgantina was sacked by the Romans in 211 BC but was not destroyed until the mid-first century. The city was occupied by a mix of residents of Punic, Greek and later, Spanish descent, but in its material culture it is the Greek influence which is clearly dominant from the fifth century to the late Hellenistic period (Tsakirgis 1995, 126, 131, 139). The houses have yet to be published in full, but preliminary information

(Tsakirgis 1988; Tsakirgis 1995) suggests that they followed the pattern of organisation of the larger houses from Greece at that time, with a single street entrance and circulation patterns within the house organised so that they could have been closely monitored. As at Kassope, later alterations seem to have opened up the house, implying a relaxation of the former requirements for privacy and a corresponding increase in the freedom of individual occupants.

In one instance, the House of the Official (Stillwell 1963, 166-68; Sjöqvist 1964, 144; Tsakirgis 1988, 210-28), these changes can be studied in detail through published evidence (Fig. 2). The house was in use, with substantial modification, down to the end of the first century BC In its first phase a single street door was positioned at right angles to the main axis of the house and prevented the interior from being visible from the street outside, even when the door was open. Space was organised around two courts: to the south was a partial peristyle in which a variety of ornamental architectural fragments were found, and this gave access to two different dining rooms. To the north an undecorated court, furnished with a well and surrounded by smaller rooms, presumably provided space for domestic activities. Broadly speaking, the rooms tended to radiate from central spaces, rather than interconnecting, and it is important that movement between the two parts of the house was restricted by being channelled through the entrance area and the corridor beyond. This would have meant that contact between the occupants of the domestic areas and the more public court could have been closely monitored.

In its final state, the house of the official was split into two separate units. The mosaic decoration in both halves suggests that they were both domestic, accommodating two different household units, with the northernmost rooms also housing a potter's workshop during the second century BC. The main vestibule was subdivided by a new wall providing two separate entrances, one for each half of the building. In some respects the southern section of the house remained unchanged, but one important development which did take place was the creation of a second entrance, leading directly into the colonnaded court. As at Kassope, this suggests that access was less strictly controlled than in the earlier phase. It also seems that privacy for the occupants was less important, since there is no evidence that any visual barrier was erected to block the view into the house when the door was open.[4]

The northern unit shows a somewhat different pattern of organisation, but suggests a similar relaxation of requirements for privacy: a single entrance led to a southern peristyle, while further rooms opened off a second large space to the north (Fig. 2). Superficially this arrangement resembles some earlier Greek houses in that it consists of two clusters of rooms with only a single street door. Nevertheless, in those earlier houses, including the first phase of

Continuity and Change in Greek Households Under Roman Rule

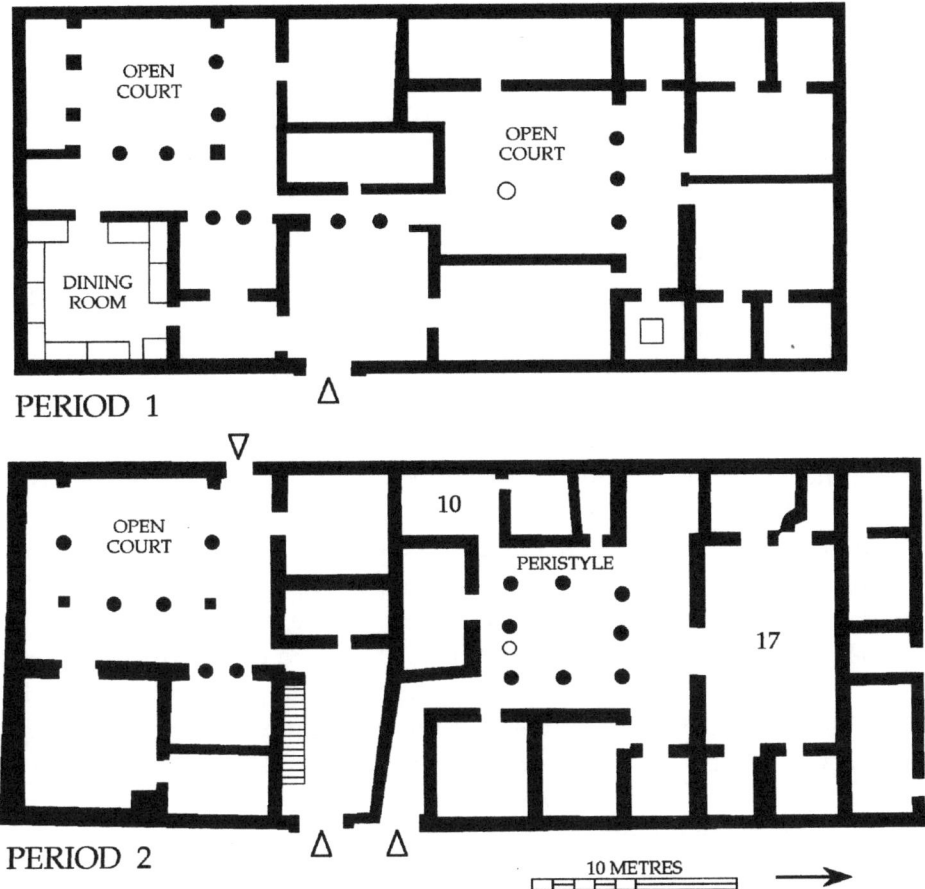

Fig. 2. Morgantina: house of the official. (adapted from Stillwell 1963, fig. 11)

the House of the Official itself, there seems to have been a difference in the functions of the two courts. A plain inner court gave access to the service rooms and domestic apartments, and, together with its surrounding porticoes, was probably used for household chores during warm weather. In contrast, however, in this later phase the remains of pottery and food debris in rooms 10 and 11 suggest that domestic chores were carried out in the outer section of the house, rather than in the inner, more private area around room 17. This placement of the cooking area close to the street door is in keeping with the apparent relaxation of the desire for privacy for the domestic areas of the house, already suggested.[5]

In sum, in these houses as a group, the creation of additional doors to the exterior and the lack of visual barriers to prevent the court being viewed from the outside suggest that conventions about contact between members of the household and outsiders became more relaxed, so that there was less need to control access to the house from the street (and, conversely, access to the outside world by members of the household). The tendency for the organisation of interior space to become less centripetal would also have meant that movement between the different rooms was less closely controlled and that contact between different members of the household, or, more probably, household members and visitors, would have been freer. All of these changes are likely to have increased the freedom of female members of the household. The proximity of the domestic areas to the entrance may also have meant an increase in contact between female household members and visitors.

Changes in the use of the court
During the Classical and Hellenistic periods, the courts of single courtyard houses provided relatively simple spaces for domestic activities, which had to be shared with visitors, presumably by scheduling different uses at different times of day. By the Roman period, however, the emphasis had shifted so that in many single courtyard houses the court came to be more elaborately decorated. This change in the use of the court is illustrated by an Athenian house from the northwest shoulder of the Areopagos (Thompson and Whycherley 1972, 184-85) (Fig. 3).[6] Athens came under Roman control during the mid-first century BC, and this early Roman structure is one of several dwellings of Roman date which have come to light in and around the Agora. Here, the single central space takes the form of a peristyle which has at its centre a garden with a well and an ornamental pool. A low wall running between the columns would have restricted entry to the central area to an entrance on the southeast side. The prominence and space given to the garden, which dominates this large central space, suggests that priorities had changed: the former productive use of the court now seems to have been less important and the symbolic function had come to dominate, although in practical terms the colonnades of the peristyle, particularly on the northeast and southwest sides, may have offered some space for domestic activities. Unlike the houses from Kassope and Morgantina, this structure seems to have had only a single street entrance, which led directly into the court from the southwest side. In contrast with comparable houses from earlier periods, however, there is no obvious means of screening the doorway from the rest of the house, reinforcing the suggestion that by this period the desire for privacy was no longer as strong.

A similar ornamental use of the space provided by a single courtyard is attested at Delos. The large numbers of houses which have been excavated here (see, for example, Plassart 1916, Chamonard 1922, Bruneau *et al.* 1970) make it impossible to do justice to the site in a short discussion. In addition,

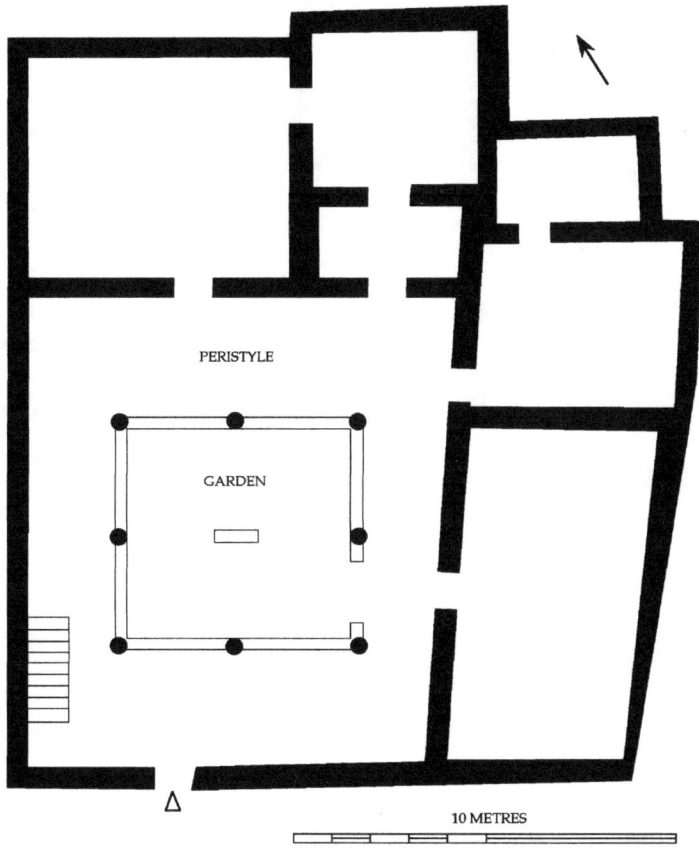

Fig. 3. Athens: house from the north shoulder of the Areopagus. (after Thompson and Whycherly 1972, fig. 46)

the cosmopolitan character of the population after the mid-second century BC makes it difficult to evaluate the houses as evidence of the pattern of a Greek population. Nevertheless, it is useful to consider the houses in the context of the other sites discussed here. In these houses the court was frequently a decorative peristyle. The central space and porticoes together often had mosaic floors, painted wall plaster, elaborate architectural mouldings and sculpted reliefs. In the larger houses the centre of the court was frequently occupied by a pool (sometimes referred to as an *impluvium*: for example, Chamonard 1922, 113; Kreeb 1985, 48 n.18) or fountain. Sculpted figures, often life-size or larger, have sometimes been found in the court and surrounding porticoes. Occasionally there is evidence here, as at Athens, to suggest that some form of barrier was erected between the columns, closing off the central area (Bruneau 1978, 125-34).

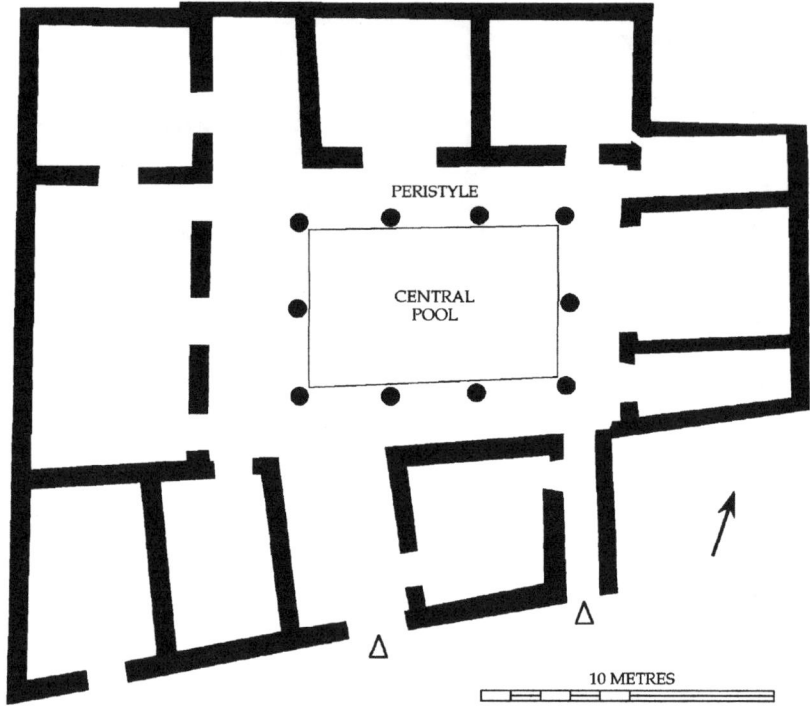

Fig. 4. Delos: house of Dionysos, final phase. (after Chamonard 1924)

An illustration of the way in which these different elements were organised is the maison du Dionysos, a large structure in the theatre quarter (Chamonard 1906, 486-562; Chamonard 1922, 58-59; Kreeb 1988, 29-33 and 252-61). In the final phase of occupation (Fig. 4), the substantial peristyle had at its centre a shallow pool with an elaborate mosaic floor depicting Dionysos and a tiger (Chamonard 1922, 132-33). In the surrounding porticoes a variety of sculpture was displayed, including figures of Poseidon, Cybele, and, by the entrance corridor, fragments of a sculpted frieze (Kreeb 1988, 30-33).

The attention paid to the decoration of the peristyle in these houses, and in particular to the use of the central area for ornamental features such as pools, suggests that a major role of the court was to display the wealth and status of the householder to visitors. Presumably the presence of water features and sculpture in the central area of the court would have prevented this area being used for some domestic activities and craft production. (This, together with the narrow width of the door, also suggests that wheeled traffic would not have been brought into the court as had been the practice in some Greek houses in previous centuries.) Whether the number of sculptures and other objects in the porticoes was also sufficient to prevent these areas from being used for activities such as weaving or food preparation is less clear. The width of the porticoes suggests that they could have been used in this manner, although on the basis of his study of the decorative elements, Kreeb suggests that they did not play a major role as a living space for the family (Kreeb 1988, 80). Many of these houses (including the house of Dionysos) adopted the kinds of circulation patterns described above, including the use of multiple street entrances. In addition, it seems that not only was privacy not sought, but also, that a lack of privacy was on occasion actively exploited: in one instance it has been suggested that sculpture was deliberately positioned in the court so that it was visible from the street when the door was open (Kreeb 1985, 52).

In sum, major changes seem to have taken place in the way in which space was used in these houses, involving a switch in emphasis away from the use of the court as a space for domestic activities, towards its use as a decorative area. The extent to which this would have precluded completely the use of the surrounding porticoes for domestic tasks is unknown, and may have varied between houses, but in many cases the creation of a central pool would have taken up a substantial area. This trend towards an increasing amount of decoration in the courts of single courtyard houses may be part of a tendency towards increasing elaboration of the domestic environment, which is already seen in Greek double-courtyard houses as early as the fourth century BC (Nevett 1995, 374-79; Nevett 1999, esp. 107-14). Nevertheless, its appearance in connection with single courtyard houses points towards to significant changes both in patterns of use and in social priorities.

The appearance of an atrium

Related to the shift in the emphasis of the court from a more functional to a more representational space, is the identification of *atria* in Greek houses of Roman date at some sites. (Such identifications conflict with the statement of Vitruvius that *atriis Graeci quia non utuntur, neque aedificant*: 'Greeks do not use *atria*, so they do not build them': *De Arch*. 6.7.1.) This is an important issue to explore since it implies some degree of Roman influence on the architecture, and perhaps also the life-style, of the occupants of such houses.

The canonical Roman *atrium* is usually defined as a space with an inward-sloping roof, which is open at the centre and has a decorative pool or *impluvium* beneath to catch rainwater. In practice, however, distinguishing the *atrium* from a more open court or peristyle is not straightforward.[7] In many instances there is insufficient evidence to suggest the extent or nature of the roofing, so that identification seems to rely mainly on the presence of a central pool. In assessing the significance of these spaces in behavioural terms it is important to look at these areas in the context of a whole house, and not just in isolation.

The most striking examples of Greek *atrium* houses are those of the extensive Hellenistic and Roman quarter at Agrigento (ancient Akragas) in Sicily (Jones and Gardner 1906; Gabrici 1925, 425-37; Wilson 1990, 114-19; summarised in Hollegaard Olsen 1995, 217-24). Despite the fact that Sicily was annexed in the third century BC there is little sign that Roman culture was widely adopted until at least the late Republic (Wilson 1990, 35), and at Agrigento itself the population seems to have retained elements of Greek culture, including the use of Greek epitaphs, well beyond this date (see Korhonen, this volume). The houses of this quarter are originally late Hellenistic, but they incorporate substantial modifications of Roman Imperial date (Wilson 1990, 114-15). The sequence of alterations is difficult to reconstruct until the houses are fully published, and there is also evidence that the stratigraphy was disturbed by post-depositional factors (Gabrici 1925, 433). Nevertheless, some inferences may be made on architectural grounds.

The example published in the most detail, the house of the tetrastyle *atrium* (Gabrici 1925, 428-37; Wilson 1990, 115-16), began life as an *atrium*-peristyle house before being combined with the house of the peristyle to its south (Fig. 5). The entrance was on the west side, opening directly into the *atrium* (Gabrici 1925, 429). From here the house seems to have presented a symmetrical vista, a characteristic rarely found among Greek houses. A central opening led through a double row of rooms, which Wilson likens to the double-*tablinum* arrangement at Pompeii (Wilson 1990, 115). Beyond lay the peristyle. In a late phase a low wall was constructed between the columns, creating a separate space at the centre in a manner comparable to the Athenian house discussed above. A suite comprising kitchen, bathroom and latrine was entered from this peristyle.

It is unfortunate that to date no complete assemblage of finds from the different rooms of these houses has been published, so that the use of space is difficult to investigate in detail. The best that can be done currently is to draw upon the Pompeian evidence as a parallel. Pompeian *atria* are normally characterised as lavishly decorated, formal spaces which were used by the master of the house for the reception of clients during the morning *salutatio*; the peristyle, on the other hand, has been viewed as a more private and secluded space to which he could withdraw with friends, to dine in the surrounding rooms (for example: Wallace-Hadrill 1994, 47-51). Recent detailed analysis of the architecture of a sample of *atrium*-peristyle houses together with the objects found in them, shows that this model may over-simplify the pattern of domestic activity (Allison 1992, *passim*; summarised in Allison 1997). In reality, although the *atrium* was sometimes decorated and contained marble furniture and other fittings, an equally important function seems to have been storage of items which were associated with a variety of different domestic

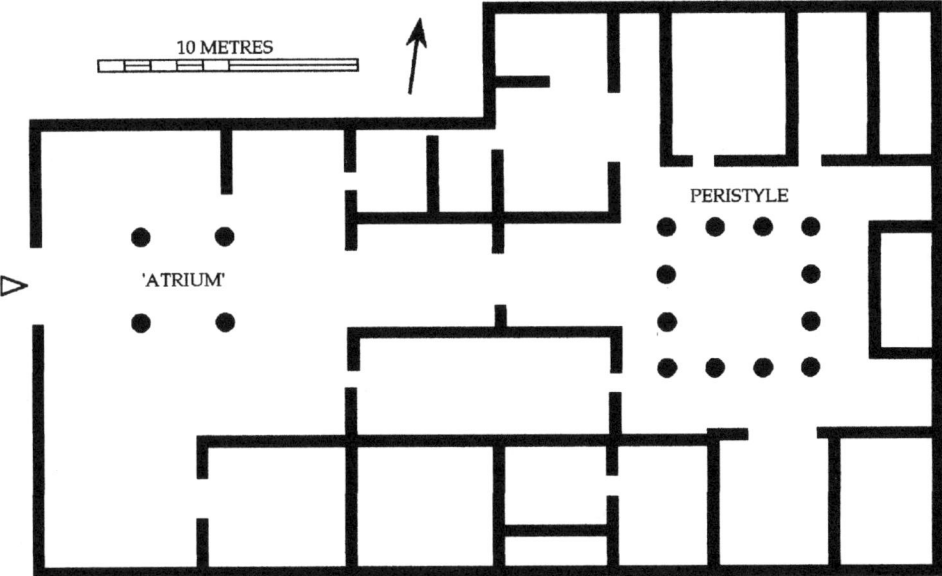

Fig. 5. Agrigento: house of the tetrastyle atrium, earlier phase. (adapted from Wilson 1990, fig. 103 and Gabrici 1925, fig. 5)

activities such as weaving, cookery and craft production, and which were found in cupboards and chests around the walls (Allison 1997, 334). The majority of decorative architectural features and luxury items were located in and around the rear peristyle, although here, too, there was also some storage of a similar range of objects used for domestic activities (ibid. 339-41). The implications of these patterns at Pompeii are that, although there is an architectural division between the area around the *atrium* and that around the peristyle, the mixed nature of the finds in virtually every area of the house suggests that there was relatively little over-all specialisation in the kinds of activities carried out in the different rooms. There may therefore have been ittle attempt to separate the area used for domestic activities from that entered by guests (ibid. 351f; pace Dickmann 1997, who looks only at the architecture and not at the finds which indicate how these spaces were actually used).

At Pompeii, then, it seems that the *atrium* may have fulfilled a range of functions similar to those of the court in the Classical and Hellenistic Greek single courtyard houses, combining reception of visitors with a variety of domestic activities.[8] An important consideration, however, is that activities may have been scheduled so that the *atrium* served as a space for the use of the household at particular times, and as a reception area at others. This would agree with literary evidence which suggests that clients were welcomed into the domus at specific hours in the day (Laurence 1994, 125). The formal similarity between the *atrium*-peristyle houses of Pompeii and those of Agrigento suggests a common architectural influence. Without detailed study of the finds from Agrigento it is obviously impossible to be sure that the Roman modes of behaviour, as documented at Pompeii, were taken up along with the architectural style. If this were the case, then the pattern of use was very different from that found in the earlier Greek double courtyard houses, which are the nearest parallel in terms of layout. This contrast would have clear implications in terms of social relations: visitors would have been permitted to enter a much greater proportion of the house, and distinctions between the two genders and between outsiders and family members are unlikely to have played as major a role in shaping the domestic environment. There was probably therefore a fundamentally different attitude to women from that seen in previous centuries in Greek communities, and this is in harmony with the changes in circulation patterns and in the use of the court, which are discussed above.

The resemblance of the houses at Agrigento to the Pompeian *atrium* houses is striking, perhaps because of the geographical proximity of the two areas. Atrium houses have also been identified in Greece itself, but in most cases they are incomplete, so that it is not possible to evaluate the over-all patterns of spatial organisation and circulation.[9] Only at Agrigento does current evidence show that the houses bear a strong resemblance to the *atrium* houses of Campania. Elsewhere, identification often seems to rest on the presence of a pool or *impluvium*, but the occurrence of such features in peristyles as well as in Pompeian type atria, makes this unreliable as a sole criterion for identification.

3. Conclusion

Having explored some of the evidence, I want to conclude by returning to the question raised in my introduction: to what extent were the traditional patterns of domestic activity, which involved the separation of guests from female family members, maintained in Greek cities during the Roman period, and what light does this shed on the question of whether the occupants of these houses were 'Greek Romans or Roman Greeks'? Given the nature of the evidence currently available, these are clearly preliminary findings, and more evidence is needed in order to assess securely, and in more detail, the significance of the developments identified here. Nevertheless, it does appear that the conservatism evident in some areas of public life during this period was not present in the private sphere. Instead, there were substantial changes in the way in which domestic activities were organised, implying that the social conventions which governed the behaviour of the families occupying these houses were different from those which had structured the lives of their predecessors. By the Roman period the distinctions between the two sexes and between family members and outsiders no longer seem to have dominated the domestic environment to the same extent. Instead, the opening up of the house to the world outside suggests that female family members would have been less restricted in their movements and would have had greater autonomy. Such a finding is in keeping with the conclusions being drawn about the status of women on the basis of other sources of evidence. For example, epigraphic evidence suggests that in Asia Minor women began to enter the public sphere as benefactors during the second century BC (Van Bremen 1996, 11-40), when the cultural and political influence of Rome in the area was increasing. Similarly, on the island of Kos in the early years of Roman rule, women began to be represented in the public sphere in statues whch were set up in public places (Höghammar 1997, 129-32).[10]

The conclusion that the roles of women, and therefore the social life of households in general, changed during this period, raises a further question: to what extent did these changes represent a move towards a more 'Romanised' pattern of domestic life? Comparison of the Roman houses found in Greece with those from elsewhere in the Empire is not straightforward. The *atrium* houses of Pompeii and the surrounding area have sometimes been viewed as 'typical' of Early Imperial Roman housing. Nevertheless, this is to some extent the result of their good state of preservation, rather than because they are representative: recent work has shown that even within the Italian peninsula itself, the organisation of domestic space is very variable (George 1997, *passim*). There is therefore no single canonical Roman house with which to compare our Roman Greek examples. More work needs to be done in order to clarify the factors underlying this variability, but it seems likely that a combination of influences is responsible, including the local climate and also the pre-existing architectural and social traditions. This suggests that even if changing norms of social behaviour were influenced by Roman *mores*, those influences were mediated through a pattern of domestic organisation which was uniquely Greek, and this might go some way to explaining why a Greek like Plutarch still seems to have had difficulty fully understanding Roman attitudes to women (as argued by Castellani, this volume).

Such an emphasis on the role of Greek culture is supported by other types of evidence (for example the dedications used on dedicatory statues examined by Højte in this volume) and also by the longer term trends visible within the evidence of housing itself. During the Classical, and especially the Hellenistic period, the largest houses provided increasing amounts of decorated space for entertaining visitors, which in some instances included an entire court with adjoining rooms. Nevertheless, an important difference between these and the houses of Roman Greece is that in the later houses less attention seems to have been paid to providing a separate area in which domestic tasks could be carried out, away from these decorated rooms. The integration of the domestic areas and those used for entertaining therefore seems to be a new development, which may have been stimulated by increasing Roman cultural influence. This would support the notion that the form of the Greek house under Roman rule resulted from a combination of the influence of Roman patterns of social behaviour with pre-existing Greek architectural traditions. Such a fusion would fit in with more general models being suggested in the context of the Western Empire, where the concept of Romanization is being replaced by the image of a dialectical process in which elements of indigenous cultures are combined with imported traits, to create fresh and distinctive patterns of activity and material surroundings (for example, Woolf 1997).

Notes

* I would like to thank the other participants at the conference, especially Kerstin Höghammar, for their comments: their interest in the gender issues involved have led to my developing this aspect of the original spoken paper. I would also like to thank the conference organisers, especially Karin Blomqvist, for their hospitality and for making the conference such a stimulating and enjoyable experience. My travel to Lund was supported by the Research Committee of the Faculty of Arts at the Open University.

1. For full discussion and detailed evaluation of the evidence see Nevett 1999 *passim*, which is the basis for the summary presented below.
2. The principal sources are Olynthos (Robinson 1929 to 1952) and Halieis (Ault 1994).
3. Other instances of Greek houses which include both of these characteristics are found in the Roman phases at: Thera, including house B6 (Hiller von Gaertringen *et al.* 1899, 252-54; iid. 1904, 137-91) and the house above the sanctuary of the Egyptian gods (Hiller von Gaertringen 1904, 137-91); Delos, in a minority of houses, such as the maison du Dionysos (discussed below), maison des dauphins (Chamonard 1924, 404-10) and maison des comédiens (Bruneau *et al.* 1970, 11-41).
4. The published evidence for at least one further house at Morgantina suggests that two street doors were in use during the latest phase of occupation, see the house of the arched cistern (Stillwell 1961 279-80; Sjöqvist 1962, 138-140; Tsakirgis 1988, 125-51).
5. If the excavators' general remarks about the distribution of activities are accurate, a similar pattern seems to have been found in the final phase of house 33 at Priene (Wiegand and Schraeder 1904, 297-300).

6. This feature is also found elsewhere, for example in house B6 on Thera (Hiller von Gaertringen *et al.* 1899, 252-54; iid. 1904, 137-91) and a house at Phillippi (Lazaridis, 1973, 33). The remains of pools or *impluvia* are also widely reported in preliminary accounts relating to (mainly incomplete) Roman houses from different areas of Greece: for example Athens (Papastolou 1980), Kozani (Karamitrou-Mentesidi 1982), Gytheion (Spyropoulos 1983), and Sparta (Spyropoulos 1980).
7. See, for example, Etienne's attempts to identify each in the context of the Roman houses at Volubilis in North Africa: Etienne 1960, especially 118-20. Compare Wallace-Hadrill's reconsideration of the Pompeian *atrium* as an architectural category (Wallace-Hadrill 1997).
8. This is not intended to imply that Greek models played a role in the development of the *atrium* house in Italy. Rather, in both contexts, the courtyard as an open space was used for a variety of tasks in common with courtyard houses in many other cultural contexts.
9. For example, Corinth (Shear 1930, *passim*), Phillippi (Collart 1937, 357), Patras (Papakostou 1980). A complete house, which includes a central space with pool and a garden at the rear, has been excavated at Eleusina (Kourouniotis 1936); unfortunately, the pattern of communication cannot be assessed in detail as evidence for some of the doorways is missing, but the house lacks the symmetrical layout found at Agrigento.
10. I am very grateful to Kerstin Höghammar for pointing this out to me at the conference and for sending me references.

PHILOLOGY, HISTORY AND HISTORY OF IDEAS

CHAPTER 7

Some Influences of Greek Poetry
on the first Choral Song of Senecas's *Phaedra* (274-357)

Luigi Senzasono

There are several kinds of Greek influence in the first choral song of Seneca's *Phaedra*; therefore we will deal with them by dividing their whole into classes so as to get a certain order.

1. Influences from a microstructural level in the Greek text at a microstructural level in Seneca's choral song

The first line of the choral song: *Diva non miti generata ponto* (ed. Herrmann), 'Goddess born of ungentle sea' joins together two motives of Greek poetry: Aphrodite's birth from the sea, that justifies the popular etymology of the name of the goddess, and the stormy character of the sea itself. The first motive appears for the first time in Hes. *Theog.* 188-98 (ed. West), and we may not exclude the suggestion of Eur. *Hipp.* 415 and 522 (ed. Barrett), where the marine attribute appears in the vocative as here.[1] The second motive is in Homer and Hesiod. In Homer, among the formular epithets of the sea, there is δυσπέμφελος (cf. e.g. *Il.* 16. 748, ed. Mazon) and equally in Hes. *Theog.* 440 and *Erg.* 618 (ed. West) (in this case an attribute of navigation); it means, whatever etymology one accepts,[2] 'stormy', 'difficult to cross'. In *Theog.* 131 we find likewise ἀτρύγετον πέλαγος […] οἴδματι θυῖον, 'the fruitless deep with his raging swell'. Thus Seneca has unified the marine origin of Venus, connected with fecundity, namely with an erotic principle (we must not forget that she was created from Uranus' semen spread in the sea, as it is clear from the *Theogony*) and the stormy character of the sea itself, to stress that the principle of love and generation is connected with the violence of passion. However, the nature of this synthesis, in its plain statement, appears more intellectual than poetical; no development of imagery arises from the initial line and the marine attribute of mercilessness has the form of a *litotes*, but there is no emotion that requires an attenuating expression.

Another influence at a microstructural level may be found in v. 2 with the expression *geminus Cupido*, 'dual Cupid', that has been explained in different ways,[3] but becomes clear only in the light of the probable Greek source, Eur. *Hipp*. 348; there, the nurse answers Phaedra, who asks what is love (v. 347): Ἥδιστον, ὦ παῖ, ταὐτὸν ἀλγεινόν θ' ἅμα. (ed. Barrett), 'The sweetest thing, my child – the bitterest too.'[4] Phaedra's question is an expedient to dodge the immediate revelation of her passion; so the nurse's reply must be considered in this highly dramatic context that flows into the painful confession of her mistress; there the contrast between sweetness and suffering, characteristic of love in the nurse's opinion, really makes sense: she will attempt to ensure her mistress satisfaction and to deliver her from pain. In Seneca's choral song the duality (*geminus*) of Cupid has this meaning and may have no different one, because another sense would not become the text. The adjective, however, arouses no poetical echo, whichever interpretation we choose. If we explain it on the basis of *Hipp*. 348, the antithetical duality of Euripides' line does not emerge from the whole choral song, that, after the initial lines (274-78), is monodically inspired only by the ruinous and painful strength and the irresistible power of Cupid, not by this duality. An influence of the adverb ἅμα is possible in the v. 276 *impotens flammis* simul *et sagittis*, 'Flame violent and in arrows'; but here too there is no real contrast, because both flames and arrows are images of sorrow and destruction defining the monothematic character of the whole choral song.

Another influence very close to Euripides may be Sapphic: γλυκύπικρον ἀμάχανον ὄρπετον, 'the bitter-sweet, irresistible creature' (130. 2. *PLF* Lobel-Page). The compound adjective attributed to Eros indicates an opposition very similar to the Euripidean one, that most probably recalls it, but we should not exclude a direct influence of Sappho on Seneca.[5] Sappho's adjective, bearing in itself the antithetical duality of love sentiment, may have been translated into the faint *geminus*, that reduces the antithesis to a dry quantitative element; this may be explained by the inadequate propensity of Latin in compound epithet use.[6] We may suspect an influence of Hellenistic poetry that multiplies in a graceful manner the figure of Eros (cf. e.g. Theocr. 7. 96, ed. Gow), but at a secondary level, since here Cupid is dual, so there is a more precise quantitative determination.

Another influence may be in 291-92: *senibusque fessis-rursus extinctos renovat calores*, 'in tired age – rekindles the extinguished blaze'. This recalls a fragment of Archilochus (48 West),[7] where the sole part we may read (not without uncertainty) talks about a woman (or women) with hair and breast perfumed so that an old man should have fallen in love with her (or them). Seneca is far from the spontaneous immediacy peculiar to Archilochus: in his text all is explanatory and merely denotative, the adjective *fessis*, the adverb *rursus*, the participle *extinctos*; quite different is the expression ὡς ἂν καὶ γέρων ἠράσσατο, 'that even an old man would have loved her (or "them")' that portrays the violence in progress in the state of mind.

Another case of the possible influence of a Greek poet is to be seen in 296-98, where Apollo is portrayed in the act of serving Admetus; it is an enunciation that merely denotes what it means: *Thessali Phoebus pecoris magister-egit armentum positoque plectro-impari tauros calamo vocavit*, 'Thessalia's herdsman Phoebus – Drove cattle, placed lyre aside – And summoned bullocks with scaled reeds'. The expression that depicts the grazing god perhaps develops: ἐβουφόρβουν, 'I tended cattle', Eur. *Alc.* 8 (ed. Conacher) with which Apollo summarizes his service in the drama, and *Alc.* 573-74: μηλονόμας γενέσθαι, 'to serve as shepherd', with which the god is qualified in the first strophe of the second *stasimon*. This strophe opens with the apostrophe to the hospitable house of Admetus, where Apollo deigned to live. The musical characteristic of the god is indicated only with the epithet εὐλύρας (v. 570), 'famed singer (sweet player) to the lyre', more graceful than the flat and heavy enunciation of the act of placing the plectrum aside to summon the oxen with the pipe. The attribute of the shepherd's pipe is indicated with the expression συρίζων ποιμνίτας ὑμεναίους (vv. 576-77), 'playing pastoral mating-songs', which evokes merry wedding songs, quite different from that prosaic call to the herd. Moreover Euripides' Apollo lives in a bucolic landscape of pastures and mountain slopes absent in the dry hint of Seneca and the picture is extended to the antistrophe, that depicts a herd of wild animals charmed by the god's music in a fanciful amplification which lets us feel even more the poetical poorness of Seneca's passage. Another influence is in v. 300: *ipse qui caelum nebulasque ducit*, 'He who controls the sky and the clouds'.[8] Of course we think of νεφεληγερέτα, 'cloud-gatherer', an epithet of Zeus in Homer. Here, as in the possible Sapphic influence in v.2, the image comprised in the Greek compound adjective may not be kept in the form of the original text, but whereas in the former case Seneca resorts to the substitution of a single word, inadequate to render the qualitative antithesis of the Greek text, here we find the translation of the magnificent Homeric epithet into a periphrasis; there is indeed a cosmic amplification in the idea of dominion over the sky, but also a loss of concentration and expressive intensity in the whole Latin sentence compared to the Greek adjective.

Likewise the charm of the Hellenistic models gets lost: vv. 303-8 evoke the myth of Jupiter abductor of Europa. In v. 304 (*virginum stravit sua terga ludo*, 'he spread his back for virgin's play') it is easy to recognize a reminiscence of Mosch. 2. 99-100.[9] The different context implies a different tone. In the Hellenistic poem the gracefulness of the portrayal clearly prevails: the exchange of caresses between the bull and the girl, the sweet bellow, like a sound of flute (vv. 93-98), precede the narrative movement that perhaps has stimulated Seneca. In Seneca the Hellenistic element (καί οἱ πλατὺ δείκνυε νῶτον, 'and he beckoned her with a look to his great wide back' ed. Bühler) is inserted in a context where the bullock shows a ferocious look (v. 303: *fronte nunc torva petulans invencus*, 'ferocious-browed lusting bull'); this contrasts with the graceful depiction of the following line; however it produces no genuine opposition of dramatic tone. Also the allusive grace of δείκνυε gets lost in the material platitude of Seneca's text (*stravit*). So the following lines, that portray the sea-crossing of the bullock, attempt to bestow a dramatic intonation on imagery (307-8 *pectore adverso domuit profundum – pro sua vector timidus rapina*, 'he breasted the deep and tamed it, – fearful for the cargo he'd raped'); but neither here there is an out and out contrast nor a genuine lyrical connection with the preceding lines (305-6: *perque fraternos nova regna fluctus – ungula lentos imitante remos*, 'and through strange realms, his brother's waves, – his hoofs employed like pliant oars'). Moreover let us consider only v. 306 and compare it with v. 115 of the Greek idyll: χηλαῖς ἀβρέκτοισιν ἐπ' εὐρέα κύματα βαίνων, 'faring over the wide waves with hooves as unharmed of the water'. The exquisite image of the bull which crosses the sea without dipping is surely more stylish and spontaneous than that of the bullock imitating with his hoofs the motion of oars, a cold explanation of vision.

Another passage where a precise influence appears is v. 316: *dum tremunt axes graviore curru*, 'as axles tremble beneath the chariot's weight'. The line brings us back to Hom. *Il.* 5. 837-39.[10] In the Homeric passage, as is the epic rule, the representation seems to be formed by itself in the narrative objectifying course: Athena is boarding Diomed's chariot, the axle groans intensely under the weight because the chariot is carrying a tremendous goddess and a very strong man. In the choral song 'day returns, late-dawned, as axles tremble beneath the chariot's weight'. Seneca's image has an ornamental function, inspired by a kind of mannerism, in the portrayal of the heavenly journey, far from the vigorous Homeric realism. Undoubtedly the chariot trembles because Apollo, not Diana, drives it,[11] but the mythologic reason does not affect the aesthetic meaning of the image.

2. Influences from a macrostructural level in the Greek text at a microstructural level in Seneca's choral song

Some passages of the *Argonautica*, extended enough in their far-reaching narrative rhythm, may have influenced single lines or words of the opening part of the choral song. V. 277 (*iste lascivus puer et renidens*, 'this lascivious, smiling boy') concentrates in an essential form, but without real poetical development, some traits we may find in Apoll. Rhod. 3. 112-66 (ed. Fränkel). In this passage Aphrodite looks for Eros in order to persuade him to wound Medea and catches him playing knucklebones with Ganymede. The anger of Ganymede when defeated is opposed to the exultation of the winner (v. 124: κεχόλωτο δὲ καγχαλόωντι, 'and he was angered by the loud laughter of Eros').[12] Earlier Eros' joy and gracefulness have already been stressed with the 'sweet blush' glowing in his cheeks (vv. 121-22: γλυκερὸς δέ οἱ ἀμφὶ παρειὰς – χροιῇ θάλλεν ἔρευθος, 'and on the bloom of his cheeks a sweet blush was glowing'). The address itself of Aphrodite to Eros stresses his playful character and his smiling bearing: Τίπτ' ἐπιμειδιάᾳς; 'Why dost thou smile?' (v. 129) are the first words addressed to Eros by the goddess. These elements flow together into the adjective *lascivus et renidens*, 'lascivious and smiling', but the whole bearing of Eros while he is playing in the text of the *Argonautica* is comprised in the theme expressed by them. Thus v. 278 of Seneca's choral song recalls Apoll. Rhod. 3. 278-84, where Eros strikes Medea. The narrative process of the throw, that takes up seven hexameters in Apollonius' passage, is reduced here to a Sapphic hendecasyllable (*tela quam certo moderatur arcu*, 'How he aims his shafts from the unerring bow'), where the emotional linguistic function introduced with *quam* seems to be a rhetorical expedient, rather outward, artificial and exaggerated, to revive the expression at a tonal level.

3. Influences from a microstructural level in the Greek text at a macrostructural level in Seneca's choral song

The union of the image of flames with that of arrows (v. 276: *impotens flammis simul et sagittis*, 'flame violent and in arrows') may be inspired by Apoll. Rhod. 3. 286-87: βέλος δ' ἐνεδαίετο κούρῃ – νέρθεν ὑπὸ κραδίῃ φλογὶ εἴκελον, and the bolt burnt deep down in the maiden's heart, like a flame'. Here the image of the dart is transfigured into that of a flame both by the verb and by the comparison which strengthens the expressive function of the verb. By contrast Seneca simply puts either attribute of the god near each other in a faded enunciation; indeed he uses the Greek narrative model to depict Cupid's power in an abridged and emblematic form; but this is only the announcement of the theme which, in its development, will take up the whole extent of the choral song. In a different way v. 280 recalls Apoll. Rhod. 3. 296: αἴθετο λάθρῃ, '(Love) burnt secretly' with a diluted expression (*igne furtivo populante venas*, 'as hidden fire ravages veins')[13] whereas the sentence of the Greek text seals in a swift, incisive and essential manner the simile that precedes it (vv. 291-95), resuming the image of burning present in vv. 286-87; perhaps the adjective *furtivus* refers also to κρυπταδίη, attributed to love by Homer. *Il.* 6. 161) and by Mimnermus (1.3 West),[14] amalgamated with a Sapphic suggestion (31. 10.

PLF Lobel – Page: χρῷ πῦρ ὑπαδεδρόμηκεν, 'a fire has stolen beneath my flesh').

There is also a microstructure from Euripides similar to Apollonius' image of 3. 286-87 for the association of fire and dart that may have influenced *Phaedr.* 276: in *Hipp.* 530-34 we read: οὔτε γὰρ πυρὸς οὔτ' – ἄστρων ὑπέρτερον βέλος – οἶον τὸ τᾶς Ἀφροδίτας – ἴησιν ἐκ χερῶν – Ἔρως ὁ Διὸς παῖς, 'for never so hotly the flame-spears dart, – nor so fleet are the star-shot arrows of light, – as the shaft from thy fingers that speeds its flight – as flame of the Love-queen's bolts fierce-burning, – o Eros, the child of Zeus who art!' However, both the motive of Euripides, that concentrates the view of the god's might in the short double comparison of cosmic vastness, and that of Apollonius, are diluted and repeated by Seneca in a manifold imagery (vv. 276, 278, 284, 335, where the image of the dart appears; vv. 276, 280, 291, 293, 309, 330, 337, 338, 355, where the image of the fire appears). The quantitative accumulation, though it varies the theme, multiplies it with an imagery that spins out the simple concentration of both Greek poets; Seneca seems anxious to bestow on the image of the fire the dignity of a *Leitmotiv*, but without real inspiration, inner lyrical necessity and intensity of expression.

The beginning itself of Euripides' *Hippolytus*, where Aphrodite comes forward stating with an impressive plainness the cosmic extent of her fame and her corresponding power (vv. 1-6), most probably has got a development throughout Seneca's choral song, which sings of the universal might of love by using mythical and naturalistic examples. Here also what we have said above is valid: a motive, enunciated in a simple and concentrated form in a Greek text, is diluted by a paratactical amplification without any rule of inner development. So Euripides concentrates in vv. 3-4 the sense of geographic universality of Aphrodite's power, whereas Seneca, in vv. 285-90, dilutes this theme.

Likewise the motive of cosmic dominion of love and of its presence in the different elements of nature appears more than once in Greek poetry.[15] Plutarch in *Amat.* 760 D quotes the verse of an unknown poet that portrays a man head over heels in love as πῦρ καὶ θάλασσαν καὶ πνοὰς τὰς αἰθέρος – περᾶν ἕτοιμος (Nauck, *TGF*, p. 917, Adesp. 408 = Kannicht – Snell, 2, p. 120), 'ready to cross fire and sea, the air itself'; this text may have influenced vv. 331-38: here too Seneca develops the Greek motive by diluting it with an imagery where the simple and impressive immediacy of the Greek text gets lost. Moreover vv. 335-38, that portray Cupid's might in the depth of the sea and among birds, recalls a Sophoclean fragment (Nauck, *TGF*, p. 329, *Inc. fab.*, fragm. 855,9 = Radt 4, p. 590, fragm. 941,9): Cypris εἰσέρχεται μὲν ἰχθύων πλωτῷ γένει, 'visits the swimming race of fish' and *loc.cit.* 11: νωμᾷ δ' ἐν οἰωνοῖσι τοὐκείνης πτερόν, 'she directs her wing among birds'. But the simple and natural depiction of the goddess of love penetrating into the world of swimming fish becomes more precious and intricate in the portrayal of the Nereids who feel Cupid's darts in deep sea-water and cannot quench its flames by it; while the vivid image of Aphrodite's wing being waved among birds is converted into a banal, merely denotative line: *ignes sentit genus aligerum* (v. 338), 'winged creatures feel his fires'.[16]

4. Influences from a macrostructural level in the Greek text at a macrostructural level in Seneca's choral song

The sentiment of the cosmic almightiness of love that takes up the whole choral song leads us back to the third *stasimon* of Sophocles' *Antigone* (vv. 781-800) (ed. Pearson).[17] It is the song the chorus strikes up for the love of Haemon. In this poem, especially in vv. 781-90 (the first strophe), we find the theme of Eros' universal power, as throughout Seneca's choral song. Especially in this case, by the comparison of two poetical macrostructures, we may observe how Seneca dilutes in a sequence of mythical and naturalistic examples the intensity and the pathos of the Sophoclean choral song: in this a series of relative clauses depends on the vocative that opens the poem, then there is a transition from the second person of the first independent clause (vv. 785 ff. φοιτᾷς δ' ὑπερπόντιος etc., 'thou roamest over the sea') to the third person through a short sequence of three sentences. In the antistrophe the second person appears again (vv. 791-94: σὺ καὶ...σὺ καὶ..., 'tis thou... tis thou...'), but the third person comes back to objectify Eros' might in a definitive form (vv. 795-800): νικᾷ δ' ἐναργὴς βλεφάρων ἵμερος εὐλέκτρου – νύμφας etc, 'victorius is the lovekindling light from the eyes of the fair bride'). This whole movement forms a compact framework. Seneca by contrast proceeds from the invocation to Venus (v. 274) to the theme of Cupid's power through a relative clause (vv. 275-76). This only suffices to weaken the sentiment of love's omnipotence by dividing it between two personages. The examples of this omnipotence are too many and generally have no strong formal concentration: they are arranged through the whole choral song in a paratactic sequence that might have no end.[18] Let us consider vv. 330-56: Cupid's power spares no living being anywhere; this is the meaning of all those images. Let us compare them with *Ant.* 785-90: six short lines suffice to evoke the mighty spatial expansion of Eros, the universality of his power, which neither gods nor men can escape, and the intensity of a might that eventually leads to madness. By contrast Seneca scatters and dispels what the Greek poet compresses, and stresses it with the intellectualistic emphasis of his imagery. The same observation is valid for a comparison with the first *stasimon* of Euripides' *Hippolytus*; the overall influence of it on Seneca's choral song in the sense of love's universality seems less notable than that of Sophocles' choral song, though the former is more similar to Seneca's choral song in the portrayal of love as a harmful might: cf. *Hipp.* 535-64, where the mythical examples, although they are different from those of Seneca's choral song, have this meaning. Here too there is a much better concentration than in Seneca's lines: in fact Euripides in vv. 545-62 judges it adequate to evoke in a terse form and in an intensely dramatic tone the myth of Iole's abduction among flames and death hymns and Semele's death in giving birth to Dionysus.

5. Conclusion

The various influences of Greek poetry on Seneca's choral song, sometimes of a topical nature, suffice to let us understand that he has consciously used (perhaps in certain cases nearly unconsciously) other texts in order to compose a poem that is a specimen of decorous literary craft rather than of genuine poetry. It would seem, therefore, that this learned poet of Latin literature, ripe and advanced of age, regarded models as something to be re-echoed or transformed, rather than as a stimulus for the genuine creation of an original world of art.[19] The only positive aspect we may find here is a skill in amalgamating the Greek suggestions in a composition unified by the motive of love at a thematic level and by a paratactical structure (λέξις εἰρομένη) at a corresponding stylistic level. Thus the poem appears to be an attempt of lyrical synthesis, pursued by a cerebral and refined art, foreboding the dramatic action that is about to be developed.[20]

Notes

1. Phaedra invokes Aphrodite with an epithet of this kind (δέσποινα ποντία Κύπρι, v. 415) in a moment of dramatic intensity, while she is deprecating the behaviour of women who pretend to be virtuous. The nurse invokes the goddess with the same expression (v. 522) in order to obtain her help for her work on behalf of Phaedra. For the dramatic situation in the former case and for the solemnity of the crucial moment in the latter, the epithet recalling the birth, but also the extent and the fearfulness of Aphrodite's might, is used in the nick of time and is more effective than in Seneca, where it does not even have the ironic function claimed by Boyle 1987, 21.
2. Most likely the epithet evokes the swelling of the sea: cf. πέμφιξ, πομφός, πομφόλυξ (Frisk I 1960, s.v.). But Frisk, cautious as usual, qualifies it as an 'expressives Wort ohne sichere Etymologie'. Undoubtedly its basic meaning is felt by Hesiod with a negative connotation: cf *Erg.* 722, where it is attributed to man, surely in the sense of 'rude', 'insociable'. As for the litotes *non miti*, it is transformed in v. 334 into the

synthetic form *immitis*, directly attributed to the *puer*; perhaps there is an influence of Apoll. Rhod. 3. 297 and 1078: οὖλος Ἔρως.

3. Here an influence of Plat., *Symp.* 180 C 6 ff. is unlikely, because there the contrast is between ideal (heavenly) and sensual (popular) Love; undoubtedly this duality does not appear throughout the choral song. We must not exclude, though it is improbable, an influence of Plat. *Phaedr.* 255 D 8-E 1, where Socrates speaks of *anteros*, a reflected image of *eros*; on the contrary we consider unacceptable V. Ussani's interpretation of *geminus* as 'companion', held as 'geniale, preziosa' by Giomini 1955, AD loc.; Seneca attributes the epithet *geminus* to Cupid also in *Oed.* 500, but it is impossible to infer such a meaning from this passage, even less from v. 477, where it is attributed to the cart of the constellation. Moreover elsewhere *geminus* never has this meaning, but sometimes the sense of 'alike', 'similar', 'equal'.

4. Euripides' line quoted e.g. by Grimal 1965, AD loc., has a counterpart in Eur. Fr. 875 – Nauck: ὦ Κύπρι, ὡς ἡδεῖα καὶ μοχθηρὸς εἶ.

5. Seneca, as is well-known, holds lyric poets in very little esteem: cf. *Ep.* 49.5 (ed. Préchac). In his tragedies, however, we may find some influences of them, especially in lyrical passages as this; tragedy is a poetic genre, quite different from epistle or moral treatise. Besides, silence on lyrical poetry is indeed a sign of contempt, not necessarily of ignorance as Mazzoli seems to think (1970, 169). The citation of Cicero, who affirms to have no time to read lyric poets *(Ep.* 49, loc.cit.), must not be taken literally, but as an emblematic and paradoxic statement supported by the authority of an esteemed man preparing the following condemnation of dialecticians.

6. Catullus, in fact, resolves Sappho's adjective into a circumlocution in 68.18: *quae dulcem curis miscet amaritiem* (ed. Ellis), attributed to Venus.

7. Mazzoli, op. cit., 169 affirms that Seneca 'agli elegiaci e ai giambografi non dedica alcun cenno'; however, cf. n. 5. Perhaps here we may find also an influence of Anacr. 13 (5) Gentili: the old poet falls in love with a girl, who condemns his hoary hair. Maybe Seneca recalled also Hom., *Il.* 3. 156-60, where the old Trojans admire and praise Helen's beauty.

8. Among the Mss. E reads *fecit* accepted by Grimal (op. cit., ad loc.), who asserts that A has corrected with *ducit*; the Homeric epithet is for him a reason to accept the reading *fecit*, but the contrary is true, because the Homeric influence in a poetic passage like this and others in Seneca's tragedies is very natural. Moreover Grimal observes that the idea of Jove as a 'creator' *(fecit)* of sky and, generally, of world, is familiar to the Roman thought of that age, imbued with Stoicism. But the whole of ancient thought denies a divine creation of the world out of nothing. Likewise the possible influence of Cleanthes' prayer to Jove on the reading *ducit* of A, as Kunst thinks (1924, ad loc.), is a wrong argument; also in this case the contrary is true: undoubtedly Seneca had a great familiarity with Stoic texts, especially with the most known and important ones, and perhaps here remembered Cleanthes' hymn.

9. Grimal, op. cit., ad loc. quotes Moschus' passage.

10. Kunst, op. cit., ad loc. and Grimal, op. cit., ad loc. quote the Homeric passage.
11. Cf. Boyle, op. cit., ad loc.
12. The verb καγχαλάω, indicating a delight expressed in laughter and generally in deep joy, returns in Apoll. Rhod. 3. 286, there too attributed to Eros, who is leaving Aeetes' court, glad about his work.
13. We judge genuine vv. 279-80, omitted by A. For the question of authenticity, rejected by Bothe, Leo, Richter, Moricca and Giardina, cf. Giomini, op. cit., ad loc.
14. Cf. nn. 5 and 7. Of course the meaning of the adjective is 'hidden', 'secret', as in Mimnermus, not 'illicit' 'adulterous', as in Homer. For the adjective *furtivo* a mediation of Verg. Aen. 4. 171 is likely; so for *igne* of Aen. 4. 66 (ed. Perret).
15. This motive is a *topos*: besides the instances cited by us, cf. Jebb 1928, Part III, *The Antigone,* n. ad 785 f.; add Aesch., fr. 44 Radt; Eur., fr. 941 Nauck, *Hipp.* 447-50; fr. 431 Nauck quoted by Jebb and by Moricca 1915, 161 is ascribed by some to Sophocles, by others to Euripides.
16. We accept, as most editors, the reading *caeruleus undis grex* of A instead of *pervius undis rex* of E in v. 336; for the arguments cf. Giomini, op. cit., ad loc.
17. Cf. n. 15.
18. It is that kind of λέξις that Aristotle has called εἰρομένη: cf. *Rhet.* 1409 A 28-35; it is this, more than lack of a 'coherent structure', the main characteristic of 'the lengthy catalogue of love in the domain of men, gods and animals' (cf. Coffey and Mayer 1990, 21). We find a better concentration in vv. 184-94, where Phaedra evokes Cupid's might that does not even spare gods.
19. Here we abstain from a judgement on the influences of Latin poetry; we suppose, however, that the analysis would lead to the same conclusions. For the general problem of the importance of the influences of Latin literature and generally of Roman themes on Seneca's tragedies, see Tarrant, 1995, 215-30. This scholar tends to overrate the importance of the Roman influences and of the Roman themes, whereas the Greek ones are sometimes important and numerous, as in this choral song. For the *Phaedra* in particular see Segal 1986, passim, especially 3-28.
20. Both in the lyric prologue pronounced by Hippolytus and in the dialogue between Phaedra and the nurse which forms the first act the terms of the drama are only stated. If this tragedy had a regular structure, the chorus entry (*parodos*) should be arranged between the prologue and the first act, but, as F.J. Miller observes (1960, I, 557): 'The technical chorus entry is entirely lacking in this play'. Therefore 'still its presence is in no way manifested until the end of this interview [scil. between Phaedra and the nurse]'. Indeed, after the prelude of the action consisting of the prologue and the first act, the lyric on love's omnipotence forebodes the real dramatic development.

CHAPTER 8

Redefining *Virtus*
The Settings of Virtue in the Works of Velleius Paterculus and Lucan

Anne Malling Eriksen

It is a general conception that the Golden Age of Augustus was followed by a so-called Silver Age as far as both statesmanship and literature were concerned.[1] Augustus had left behind a gigantic empire; Virgil, Horace, and Livy, a gigantic literature. It is inevitable that such greatness should be followed by an age of disappointment, perhaps captured best in Suet. *Tib.* 59.1, where Suetonius claims to quote contemporaries of the Tiberian age saying:

> *Aurea mutasti Saturni saecula, Caesar [Tiberius];*
> *Incolumi nam te ferrea semper erunt.*
>
> You, O Caesar, have altered the golden ages of Saturn;
> For while you are alive, iron they ever will be.

But how could it be otherwise? Indeed, based on the testimonies of both Tacitus and Suetonius, whom scholars even today tend to treat as important sources on whatever subject the two gentlemen chose to embark, tradition has it that the Tiberian age and the decades that followed were but a dark middle age somewhere in between Cicero and the Second Sophistic. The emperors were severely disabled, and literature – however ingenious the discourse of Seneca and the satire of Persius – failed to cure them.

However, neither its lack of political resonance, nor its lack of supreme literary artistry, can justify our neglect of the fact that the surviving literature from this period is still a unique example of Roman self-reflexion and conceptual development. In other words, we cannot snub this period, if we wish to generalize about developments in Roman literature and wonder at apparent changes to the Roman spirit.

By examining Velleius Paterculus' *Historia Romana* and Lucan's epic poem,

Bellum Civile, I seek to demonstrate how the collapse of traditional Roman concepts of virtue after Augustus was contemplated by two such utterly diverse authors, both announcing the need for a redefinition of *the individual* in the Roman Empire. Caution, of course, is of the essence when dealing with any kind of conceptual concordance in classical literature, hence the focus on a single line of thought in the sequel, namely that of the relationship between a Roman general and his soldiers. Traditionally, the *virtus* of the army in unison with the wisdom of the Senate were held to be the prime constituents of the Roman Empire.[2] This delicate *concordia* depended exclusively on the *pietas* of the general towards the Roman people – i.e. his readiness to submit himself and his army to the authority of the Senate – as well as on the *fides* of the soldiers towards the general, which basically meant their trusting him to observe his *pietas*.[3]

In the late Republic, however, Cicero's employment – if not invention – of the term *humanitas* describing the duties and virtues of the Roman 'gentleman' produced a conceptual development of paramount importance.[4] As Cato the Censor had tried before, Cicero stood up to the various challenges to *Romanitas* offered by different branches of *paideia*, and was ever so careful in his attempts at synchronising Greek ideas and Roman ideals, before introducing either to his audience. Although this may have been done to cultivate Roman tradition as represented in the *mos maiorum*, it nonetheless, at the same time, provided an impressive platform for *the individual* – whose space in Latin literature had hitherto been more or less confined to poetry and satire.[5]

Unfortunately, this innovative project was undermined by ideological chaos on the political scene: The whole vocabulary of Roman values and virtues could not but collapse, when Romans came to employ their *virtus* against other Romans in The Civil War, as a result of powerful individuals repeatedly betraying *pietas* and thus shaking the delicate balance between political and military force in the Republic. To restore faith in the Republic and its ability to re-establish a long lost *concordia*, Augustus and his contemporaries worked hard to make visible the destined grandeur of the Roman Empire.[6]

Thus, in post-Ciceronian literature, *the individual* became an ambivalent creature; on the one hand, he is the prime cause of civil war, solely because of his excess of ambition.[7] On the other, he is the hero: Only he alone can exterminate those 'seeds of greed' and thereby secure the future of the Roman people by killing his dark twin, as did Romulus.[8] But even the hero must pay the price for being an individual: To secure his own position he must erase all distracting – and therefore latently disturbing – characteristics of his own person, hence the sterile solidity in the busts and statues of Augustus and Tiberius, as opposed to the abundance of personal features in late Republican portraits.[9] And likewise in literature: The grand design of the Augustan Principate provided no room for philosophical or religious ideas intruding on the *mos maiorum*. Nor were the likes of Seneca at this point allowed to indirectly question the inner *pax* and moral *concordia* of the Princeps.

Still, a gradual – but crucial – change of terminology took place in imperial public relations at some point between Augustus and Tiberius. From the archaeological evidence, in this case coins issued during their reigns, it seems clear in what terms the Princeps wanted the people to contemplate him. As Julius Caesar before him had tried to do, Augustus smoothed over the settlements of his reign with coins advertising the *SPQR*, battles fought and won, the *Clupeus Virtutis*, and several different images of *Victoria*: The promised destiny of the Roman Empire was at hand, and was closely connected with the renewed respect for ancestral customs and virtues.[10] Tiberius, however, issued coins praising *clementia* and *moderatio*, both of which were certainly genuine Roman virtues, but which were also at the same time much more in keeping with traditionally Greek, moral ideals, such as σωφροσύνη or, more generally, ἀρετή, than with the idea of an ever-expanding *Imperium Romanum*.[11]

It is the same conceptual shift we find in Velleius Paterculus' *Historia Romana*, in the vocabulary employed in describing the Caesars, but mainly Tiberius, as generals of the Roman army, all of whom Velleius Paterculus clearly wishes to describe in terms suitable for contemporary Roman heroes. After having carefully demonstrated the bond of *pietas* between Tiberius and Rome as well as the *fides* of his soldiers, Velleius Paterculus omits to dwell further upon traditional virtues such as the *virtus* of the army and the quest for *gloria* which accompanies it. Instead he devotes himself to personal characteristics such as *clementia*, *moderatio*, and even *humanitas*.[12] Granted that Velleius Paterculus must have read Livy, but also granted that he very often disagrees with him, Tiberius is in fact allowed to transgress the boundaries of the Livian hero and become *an individual*. That Velleius Paterculus was in fact well aware of this, becomes clear when he makes a point out of the 'checklist' which Tiberius goes through when preparing for a battle. In Livy, the drive would always be the *virtus* of the army – the aspiration for *gloria* and the willingness to die but never surrender – and those always to be consulted before a battle were, of course, the gods.[13] However, according to Velleius Paterculus, Tiberius does not contemplate such a multitude of factors:

Nihil in hoc tanto bello, nihil in Germania aut videre maius aut mirari magis potui, quam quod imperatori numquam adeo ulla opportuna visa est victoriae occasio, quam damno amissi pensaret militis semperque visum est gloriosissimum, quod esset tutissimum, et ante conscientiae quam famae consultum nec umquam consilia ducis iudicio exercitus, sed exercitus providentia ducis rectus est.[14]

Nothing in the course of this great war, nothing in the campaigns in Germany, came under my observation that was greater, or that aroused my admiration more, than these traits of its general; no chance of winning a victory ever seemed to him timely, which he would have to purchase by the sacrifice of his soldiers; the safest course was always regarded by him as the best; he consulted his conscience first and [only] then his reputation, and, finally, the plans of the commander were never governed by the opinion of the army, but rather the army by the wisdom of its leader.

Two important points are made in this statement, and both counter the ideals of traditional, Roman warfare as described in *Ab urbe condita libri*: Where in Livy an abundance of young Roman soldiers are being sacrificed – more or less willingly – for the sake of discipline or victory, Tiberius sets *conscientia* over *victoria*.[15] Furthermore, in Livy, the *virtus* of the entire army will be in vain, if Fate and the gods do not approve its aim; for Tiberius, the determinant factor is neither the aim of *virtus* nor the approval of the gods; again he sets *conscientia* first and consults not the gods, but his own brain.[16] His prime goal – as opposed to Roman tradition – is not to surpass the greatness of his ancestors through *honos* and *gloria*; it is not to trick his troops into self-sacrifice with fiery speeches – to *movere et flectere*. Instead, the true *virtus* of Tiberius lies in his calm *moderatio* and his ability to think *pro et contra*, thus succeeding in both saving the Roman Empire, and saving the lives of his soldiers as well.[17]

However, neither *moderatio* nor *clementia* can in full describe the kindness and devotion with which Tiberius looks after his soldiers and personally cares for those falling ill. Instead Velleius Paterculus employs the term *humanitas* and says:

O rem dictu non eminentem, sed solida veraque virtute atque utilitate maximam, experientia suavissimam, humanitate singularem! Per omne belli Germanici Pannonicique tempus nemo e nobis gradumve nostrum aut praecedentibus aut sequentibus imbecillus fuit, cuius salus ac valetudo non ita sustentaretur Caesaris cura, tamquam distractissimus ille tantorum onerum mole huic uni negotio vacaret animus. Erat desiderantibus paratum iunctum vehiculum, lectica eius publicata, cuius usum cum alii tum ego sensi; iam medici, iam apparatus cibi, iam in hoc solum uni portatum instrumentum balinei nullius non succurrit valetudini; [...][18]

And now for a detail which in the telling may lack grandeur, but is most important by reason of the true and substantial personal qualities it reveals and also of its practical service – a thing most pleasant as an experience and remarkable for the kindness it displayed. Throughout the whole period of the German and Pannonian war there was not one of us, or of those either above or below our rank, who fell ill without having his health and welfare looked after by Caesar with as much solicitude indeed as though this were the chief occupation of his mind, preoccupied though he was by his heavy responsibilities. There was a horsed vehicle ready for those who needed it, his own litter was at the disposal of all, and I, among others, have enjoyed its use. Now his physicians, now his kitchen, and now his bathing equipment, brought for this one purpose for himself alone, ministered to the comfort of all who were sick.

Whether or not this story is in fact true, it is clearly Velleius Paterculus' intention to prove the degree of closeness and respect between Tiberius and his soldiers. Where in Rome the title of *Pater Patriae* is yet another mark of distinction to raise the Princeps above the Senate, to the soldiers Tiberius in fact *acts* the *Pater*, both in carefully contemplating safe strategies before sending the sons of Rome into battle, and also in nursing them in camp with an attention bordering on intimacy. In acting the *Pater* to his soldiers, Tiberius furthermore displays a remarkable degree of *clementia* as far as discipline is concerned. However Spartan his own conduct, he always shows great forbearance on those who fail to follow his example:

[...] *non sequentibus disciplinam, quatenus exemplo non nocebatur, ignovit; admonitio frequens, interdum et castigatio, vindicta tamen rarissima, agebatque medium plurima dissimulantis, aliqua inhibentis.*[19]

Of those who did not imitate his own stern discipline he took no notice, in so far as no harmful precedent was thereby created. He often admonished, sometimes gave verbal reproof, but rarely punishment, and pursued the moderate course of pretending in most cases not to see things, and of administering only occasionally a reprimand.

It is the exact opposite kind of army leader we find in Lucan's *Bellum Civile*, which was written during the reign of Nero. Contrary to the Tiberius created by Velleius Paterculus, Lucan's Julius Caesar is a bloodthirsty monster, who never treats his soldiers as equals, and who – even though he fears them – never ceases to insult them.[20] Not even during an attempted mutiny, where a soldier confronts him saying:

> *Rheni mihi Caesar in undis*
> *Dux erat, hic socius; facinus, quos inquinat, aequat.*[21]

> Though Caesar was my general on the banks of the Rhine,
> he is my comrade here; crime levels those whom it pollutes.

To which Julius Caesar but answers:

> [...] *numquam sic cura deorum*
> *Se premet, ut vestrae morti vestraeque saluti*
> *Fata vacent; procerum motus haec cuncta secuntur:*
> *Humanum paucis vivit genus.*[22]

> Providence will never stoop so low that fate can attend to the life
> and death of such as you. All these events depend upon the
> actions of the leaders; it is for the sake of a few that mankind
> in general lives.

Although Velleius Paterculus and Lucan obviously approach Roman history from opposite directions – to the former, Caesar is the name of a modest hero, to the latter that of a cruel egoist – they both represent a conceptual movement away from the traditional setting of Roman virtues, whether that be on the battlefield of Livy, or in the hexameters of Virgil. In Lucan, the triad of – *virtus, pietas* and *fides* is equally present in either faction of the Roman army, only it is accompanied by the soldiers either despairing of their own future, or feeling the shame of their own wickedness in committing such crimes against their country.[23]

Indeed, when Virgil in *The Aeneid* lets Aeneas flee from the burning city of Troy carrying his father on his own shoulders together with the religious statuettes, the *Penates*, and at the same time leading his young son by the hand, it is not because Aeneas is just another Hellenic hero; no, at that point he is no less than *mos maiorum* in action.[24] The soldiers of Lucan, however, have been long separated from their fathers and sons, hence desperate, as they are about to sacrifice their own lives, wish it to be a truly honourable deed:

> *Abscidit nostrae multum fors invida laudi,*
> *Quod non cum senibus capti natisque tenemur.*
> *Indomitos sciat esse viros timeatque furentes*
> *Et morti faciles animos et gaudeat hostis*
> *Non plures haesisse rates. Temptare parabunt*
> *Foederibus turpique volent corrumpere vita.*
> *O utinam, quo plus habeat mors unica famae,*
> *Promittant veniam, iubeant sperare salutem,*
> *Ne nos, cum calido fodiemus viscera ferro,*
> *Desperasse putent. Magna virtute merendum est,*
> *Caesar ut amissis inter tot milia paucis*
> *Hoc damnum cladermque vocet.*[25]

> Grudging Fortune has subtracted much from our glory, inasmuch as
> we are not held prisoners together with our old men and little ones.
> But let the foe learn that our men are unconquerable; let him dread
> the mad courage that welcomes death; and let him thank his stars
> that only one of the rafts stuck fast. They will try to tempt us with
> terms of peace, and will seek to bribe us by the offer of dishon-
> ourable life. I wish that they would promise pardon and encourage

> us to hope for life; for so our matchless death would gain greater
> renown, and they would not think, when they see us pierce our
> vitals with the warm steel, that we have abandoned hope. It requires
> a mighty deed of valour to make Caesar, when he loses a few men
> out of so many thousands, call it a disaster and a defeat.

As is the case with the traditional Roman virtues, so too, the nature of man has literally degenerated in Lucan. The soldiers not only bond in crime, they also, like animals, immediately react to the smell of blood. However intelligently Julius Caesar plans his battles and the action of his soldiers – as did Velleius Paterculus' Tiberius – he is still nothing but the merciless leader of a pack of beasts.[26] The difference between the army of Velleius Paterculus and that of Lucan culminates, when Lucan lets the soldiers of Caesar – bonded as they are in crime and wickedness – jostle for the privileges of victory similar to those so readily bestowed upon Tiberius' sick soldiers in Velleius Paterculus:

> […] *Capit inpia plebes*
> *Caespite patricio somnos, stratumque cubile*
> *Regibus infandus miles premit, inque parentum*
> *Inque toris fratrum posuerunt membra nocentes.*
> *Quos agitat vaesana quies, somnique furentes*
> *Thessalicam miseris versant in pectore pugnam.*
> *Invigilat cunctis saevum scelus, armaque tota*
> *Mente agitant, capuloque manus absente moventur.*[27]

> Base-born and bloodstained, they slept on the turf piled for patricians; the infamous rank and file lay down on couches prepared for kings; and the guilty rested their limbs where their fathers and brothers had slept. But a night of madness disturbed their rest, and frenzied dreams kept the battle of Pharsalia ever before their tortured minds. Their pitiless crime is awake in every heart, their whole mind is busy with battle, and their hands that grasp no hilt are never still.

Just as there is nothing virtuous about victory in Lucan, so there is nothing grand in dying for the sake of Julius Caesar: Dead soldiers are lives utterly wasted.[28] The molested corpses sprawled all over Lucan's poem are remnants of an age of powerful lies, lies about the gods taking an interest in the lives of humans, lies about the relativity of justice, and finally lies meant to enslave the Roman people under powerful dynasts.[29] Having already stated that:

> *Namque omnes voces, per quas iam tempore tanto*
> *Mentimur dominis, haec primum repperit aetas,*
> *[...]*[30]

For that age invented all the lying titles that we have used so long to our masters.

Lucan finally ventures to declare that:

> *[...] mortalia nulli*
> *Sunt curata deo. Cladis tamen huius habemus*
> *Vindictam, quantam terris dare numina fas est:*
> *Bella pares superis facient civilia divos;*
> *Fulminibus manes radiisque ornabit et astris*
> *Inque deum templis iurabit Roma per umbras.*[31]

> Man's destiny has never been watched over by any god. Yet for this disaster we have revenge, so far as gods may give satisfaction to mortals: civil war shall make dead Caesars the peers of gods above; and Rome shall deck out dead men with thunderbolts and haloes and constellations, and in the temples of the gods shall swear by ghosts.

Likewise, Lucan clearly despises the whole vocabulary of *virtus* and *pietas* because they, too, are lying titles; applied by excessively ambitious masters to glorify their own vanity and engage their soldiers in meaningless slaughter. Indeed, his Roman soldiers – however beastly – cannot but touch the reader, when in Book 5, seemingly sated with blood and temporarily unwilling to go on fighting, they plead to Julius Caesar:

> *Quaeris terraque marique*
> *His ferrum iugulis, animasque effundere viles*
> *Quolibet hoste paras: partem tibi Gallia nostri*
> *Eripuit, partem duris Hispania bellis,*
> *Pars iacet Hesperia, totoque exercitus orbe*
> *Te vincente perit.*[32]

> You search over land and sea for swords to pierce our hearts, and you are ready to spill our worthless lives by the hand of any foe. Some of us were snatched from you by Gaul, others by the hard campaigns in Spain; others lie in Italy; all over the world you are victorious and your soldiers die.

And Lucan lets them continue on behalf of any Roman citizen:

> [...] *iam respice canos,*
> *Invalidasque manus et inanes cerne lacertos.*
> *Usus abit vitae, bellis consumpsimus aevum:*
> *Ad mortem dimitte senes.* [...]
> *Quid velut ignaros ad quae portenta paremur*
> *Spe trahis;* [...][33]

> Consider at last our grey hairs; behold our enfeebled hands and wasted arms. We have lost the enjoyment of life, we have spent all our days fighting. Now that we are old, disband us to die [...] Why do you lure us on with promises, as if we did not know the horrors of which we are to be the instruments?

Whereupon Lucan intervenes, himself addressing Caesar:

> *Non pudet, heu! Caesar, soli tibi bella placere*
> *Iam manibus damnata tuis?*[34]

> Do you not blush, Caesar, that you alone find pleasure in war which your instruments have already condemned?

But Caesar does not blush, instead he answers without hesitation:

> [...] *Procumbite terra*
> *Infidumque caput feriendaque tendite colla.*
> *Et tu, quo solo stabunt iam robore castra,*
> *Tiro rudis, specta poenas et disce ferire,*
> *Disce mori.*[35]

> Down with you upon the ground, and stretch out for the axe your traitorous heads and necks! And you raw recruits, who alone will form the backbone of the army in the future, watch their execution, and learn how to slay and to be slain.

A better example of Roman self-reflexion is hard to find; being a soldier, and being willing to sacrifice oneself or one's fellow soldiers for the sake of the Roman Empire is no longer an honourable goal, in that *virtus* and *gloria* are either absent, or, even worse: they are reduced to subtle lies in the hands of scoundrels. Both the surprisingly humane conduct of Tiberius in Velleius

Paterculus' *Historia Romana*, and the vocabulary employed in describing his foremost virtues already suggest an overturn of the traditional set of personal virtues and values, accompanied by an uncommonly firm focus on the individual.

Lucan, however, lavishly employs all the traditional virtues in his grim settings of death and despair, but at the same time does so with such apparent disgust that the dignified spirit of Roman tradition dissipates. Thus, both Velleius Paterculus and Lucan – however differently – articulate their disbelief in the old system of the virtues and the need for a completely new way of contemplating the purpose and options of *the individual* in the Roman Empire.

Notes

* I would like to thank Ewen Bowie, Otto Steen Due, and Timothy J. Moore for valuable suggestions and advice.

1. On the problems of the word 'silver', see Jenkyns 1986, 267-68, Wight Duff 1909, 661 & 664-70, Wight Duff 1927, 1-22, and Johnson 1987, 131-32; on the decline in statesmanship after Augustus, see Tac. *Ann.* 1.54, 1.81 & 2.2, Suet. *Tib.* 59.1-2; for a more loyal account of Tiberius' difficulties, see Scullard 1959, 268-70 & 283; on the decline in literature, see e.g. Butler 1909, 1-22; for a more recent and much more convincing attempt at a diagnosis, see Fantham 1996, 126-52; for an interesting discussion of the way in which literature has portrayed Tiberius, see Downey 1975, 95-130. All classical texts and translations quoted in this article are taken from the Loeb Classical Library Series.
2. On the meaning and importance of *virtus* as a Roman virtue, see Curtius 1967, 370-71, Hellegouarc'h 1963, 244-45, and of course Eisenhut 1973. On continuity and change in the concept of *virtus* in the Republic and early Principate, see Büchner 1967, 378.
3. On further aspects of *fides* and *pietas*, see Meister 1967, 13-19.
4. For definitions and use of the concept *humanitas*, see Cic. e.g. *De or.* 1.27, 1.53 & 1.72, *Leg.* 3.1, *Off.* 3.41 & *Tusc.* 5.66.
5. With the exception, perhaps, of the conscientious description of Julius Caesar vs. Cato Uticensis in Sall. *Cat.* 54.3-6. For a brief introduction to the nature of *mos maiorum*, see Conte 1994, 799-800.
6. On Livy's use of traditional, Roman virtues in *Ab urbe condita libri*, see Moore 1989, and on Augustus' attempts to uphold Republican *concordia* by eliminating powerful individuals from politics, see Syme 1939, 310ff.
7. See e.g. Hor. *Carm.* 3.24.53-62 on 'the seeds of greed' exemplified by Julius Caesar throwing dice before crossing the Rubicon, and Luc. 1.84-89 on 'excess of ambition' bringing about the doom of Rome.
8. On *the individual* as a hero, see e.g. Augustus *Res gestae* 1.1: *Annos undeviginti natus exercitum privato consilio et privata impensa comparavi, per quem rem publicam*

(do)minatione factionis oppressam in libertatem vindica(vi. [...])] ('At the age of nineteen, on my own initiative and at my own expense, I raised an army by means of which I restored liberty to the republic, which had been oppressed by the tyranny of a faction'), and also Ramage 1987, 43-50; on the making of the myth of Romulus and Remus in Roman literature, see Wiseman 1995.

9. For a comparative analysis of the changes in Roman portraits from Republic to Principate, see Zanker 1990.
10. For a high quality display of Roman coins, see Kent 1978; for reflexions on *virtus* and *Victoria* on Augustan coins, see Benario 1975, 80-83.
11. Cf. Kent 1978, 280-81 & 21, plate 45, and Shotter 1992, 86.
12. On the *fides* of the soldiers, see Vell. Pat. 2.104.4, on the *pietas* of Tiberius towards Augustus, i.e. Rome: 2.105.3, 1.107.3 & 2.120.1-3, consoling Augustus on his deathbed: 2.123.1-2, obeying his last will: 2.124.1-4, and restoring the Roman Republic: 2.126.1-4, on the *clementia* of Julius Caesar towards his enemies: 2.52.4-6 & 2.56.3, on Augustus and his *clementia* towards enemies together with his moderation in connexion with victories: 2.86.2-3, as opposed to the cruelty of Anthony: 2.87.2, showing *clementia* towards the son of Antony: 2.100.4, and finally, Tiberius displaying *humanitas*: 2.114.1.
13. For *virtus* in the Roman army, see Livy e.g. 24.16.8-9, 40.32.5-8 & 42.49.1-6; for *gloria* in connexion with *virtus*: e.g. 22.12.3-4, 38.17.8-20, 38.48.15-16 & 42.47.5; on consulting the gods before a battle: e.g. 8.30.1-8.32.8 & 10.39.2-14. In what is left of Livy's *Ab urbe condita libri*, *virtus* is employed no less than 297 times, as opposed to *humanitas*, a term only used twice, both times to describe non-Romans, cf. Moore 1989, 8-10, 151-52 & 209-15.
14. Vell. Pat. 2.115.5.
15. On Roman soldiers being sacrificed for the sake of victory, see Livy e.g. on Manilius being killed by his own father in order to set an example for the army: 8.7.13-22, on the self-sacrifice of Decius Mus: 8.9.4-14 & on the young Decius Mus imitating his fathers heroism: 10.28.12-18.
16. On *virtus* and the necessary approval of the gods in Livy, see Moore 1989, 10-11; on the importance of observing the gods in religious rituals, see Livy 5.51.5. On Tiberius neglecting the gods, see alternatively Suet. *Tib.* 69.
17. On Tiberius sparing the lives of his soldiers, see Vell. Pat. 2.95.1-2, 2.97.4, 2.107.2-3 & 2.120.2; on Tiberius' calmness in providing for the soldiers during conscription: 2.130.2.
18. Ibid. 2.114.1-2.
19. Ibid. 2.114.3, where it is also described how Tiberius preferred to travel on horseback like his officers, as well as sitting upright in a chair at dinner instead of reclining on a couch.
20. On Julius Caesar as a bloodthirsty monster, see Lucan e.g. 1.476-80, 2.439ff., 3.358ff. & 9.15-16; on him fearing his own soldiers: 5.240ff.
21. Ibid. 5.289-90.
22. Ibid. 5.340-43.
23. On *virtus*, *pietas* and *fides* together with despair, see ibid. 4.490ff., on *virtus* and sui-

cide: 4.556-58, on balancing *virtus* and *fides* when confronting countrymen in battle: 7.311ff., on *virtus* together with the sense of shame and wickedness: 4.26ff., Lucan stating that *virtus* is a crime in civil war: 6.147-48, *virtus* and death: 7.382-83; on atrocious crime being called heroism: 1.667-8; on Lucan's redefinitions of Roman notions of value and virtue, see also Masters 1992, 44 & 64; for a fascinating outline of Lucan's Stoicism, see Due 1968, 201-32, and for a tour de force through Lucan's play with *virtus*, the hero, and the *exemplum*, see Leigh 1997, esp. 158-90.
24. Cf. Verg. *Aen.* 2.717-29.
25. Luc. 4.502-6.
26. On Julius Caesar as a pack leader, see ibid. 7.574ff., on his soldiers as beasts: 1.353ff., 4.235ff. & 6.207ff.
27. Ibid. 7.760-67.
28. On dead soldiers seen as lives wasted: ibid. 4.490-91: *Conferta iacent cum corpora campo, in medium mors omnis abit, perit obruta virtus* [...] ('When the dead lie thick upon the field, each death is merged in a common account, and valour, thus overlaid, is wasted').
29. On molested bodies, see ibid. e.g. 2.98ff. & 3.567ff., on mankind not being governed by gods: 7.444-59, on Julius Caesar laying out justice as a trophy of victory, thus freeing the winning side of guilt: 7.257-58: [...] *haec, fato quae teste probet, quis iustius arma sumpserit; haec acies victum factura nocentem est.* ([...] 'this day must decide, on the evidence of destiny, which of the two combatants had justice on his side: this battle will pronounce the guilt of him who loses it').
30. Ibid. 5.385-86. See also Johnson 1987, 98-100 for the argument that both *libertas* and history are lies to Lucan.
31. Ibid. 7.454-59.
32. Ibid. 5.262-67.
33. Ibid. 5.274-77 & 5.284-85.
34. Ibid. 5.310-11.
35. Ibid. 5.360-64.

CHAPTER 9

Plutarch's *Lives* and Their Roman Readers

Philip Stadter

Who was the initial *audience* for Plutarch's *Parallel Lives*, and how did Plutarch hope to influence them? I wish to offer some thoughts on this broad topic, looking first at the question of audience, and Plutarch's motivation for writing, then specifically at the life of Tiberius Gracchus, with the aim of describing more precisely how Plutarch hoped that his *Lives* would function in their contemporary setting, especially among Romans in the imperial administration. Clearly, many questions must be left to one side, but even such a narrow focus may prove useful.

The *Parallel Lives* are addressed to Plutarch's friend, the extremely distinguished general and twice consul Sosius Senecio. This fact would seem to imply an audience which consists of members of the Roman political elite,[1] and not simply the cultured Greeks who might normally be expected to read Greek literature of Plutarch's literary level. Yet several objections have been raised against this conclusion.

I believe, however, that these objections are quite mistaken, and that Plutarch's intended audience consisted in fact of Romans as well as Greeks. Moreover, as the Romans represented an especially important segment of that audience, in as much as they were more powerful, they were therefore in greater need of the kind of moral education he could offer. Before going further, therefore, it is necessary to look more closely at these objections, beginning with Plutarch's practice of explaining Roman institutions and Latin words.

Simon Swain has recently described the exceptional significance of linguistic purity to Greek writers of the second century.[2] An elegant use of classical Greek was a symbol of education, of attachment to the Greek tradition, and of their own elite status. For this reason educated Greek authors devoted immense care to their choice of words, their use of syntax, and the sound and arrangement of their phrases. In this context, a cultivated Greek writer would not choose to use foreign phrases without conscious apology. Stylistically, it would have been impossible for Plutarch to insert Latin words, no matter how familiar to his Greek readers, into his artfully contrived sentences.[3] The glosses which he offers, then, should be seen as an appropriate way for him to bring Latin terms into his text, and do not imply ignorance on the part of his audience.

Often, in fact, these glosses play a rhetorical function which contributes to the overall meaning of a passage. Let me offer two examples. In *Romulus* 13, Plutarch explains some fundamental terms of the Roman political system: *legio, populus, patricius, senatus, patronus, patres conscripti, clientes*. In defining these terms, the passage emphasizes the nature of the relation of senate to people, wealthy to poor. Plutarch focuses on the term *patricius*, derived from *pater*, which he suggests was used by Romulus to convey the fatherly care and thoughtfulness that the more powerful should show for the weaker, and the trust that the poorer should show their betters. The implications of the *patronus-cliens* relation are similar: Romulus called the powerful *patroni*, that is, 'advocates' (*prostatai*), and the masses *clientes*, that is, 'neighbors'. In explaining the Roman terms, Plutarch sets out his own ideal version of the Roman social system.

In a quite different context, a passage of *Antony* (4.7-9) explains that a *decies* is equivalent to 250,000 drachmas, the sum which a friend of Antony's asks to borrow. Here the explanation gives force to the anecdote of which it is a part. When Antony's steward, wishing to make him aware of the size of the sum, dumps the coins out in front of him, Antony exclaims in reproof, 'I thought a *decies* was more! This is a small amount: double it.' Plutarch uses the very brevity of the Latin word to make his point; like the steward, he places the large sum before us – 250,000 drachmas – which Antony reduces to a *decies*. The indication of these and many other examples is that Plutarch consciously employs Latin words and their explanations as a means of enhancing his content, as he also does with poetic quotations or other literary devices.[4] Can we really imagine that there were educated, cultivated Greeks, whatever their knowledge of Latin, who needed the words *populus* and *senatus* explained to them, when their slaves were so steeped in Latin that they called a breadbasket a *panarion*?[5]

A striking passage in *Quiet of Mind* raises a second problem, that of Plutarch's attitude towards Greeks pursuing Roman careers:

There are other provincials – from Chios, Galatia, or Bithynia – who are dissatisfied with having obtained a portion of status or power among their compatriots, and who weep because they do not wear senatorial shoes; and if they do, then because they have not been praetor at Rome, and if they have, then because they are not consuls, and if they are, then because they were proclaimed not first but later. The only possible description of this is self-mortification and self-inflicted punishment, as a result of scrabbling for reasons to be ungrateful to fortune. (470C)[6]

This passage has been interpreted as expressing scorn for Greeks who try to follow an imperial career.[7] However, this view has been rightly rejected by Swain, who notes that two of Plutarch's Greek friends were senators, and that the work itself is dedicated to the Roman Paccius, an orator and probably a senator.[8] Moreover, Plutarch's close friend Sosius Senecio, who may have been of Greek descent, was consul ordinarius in AD 99 and 107.[9] The passage is rather part of an argument about not always wanting more than what you have, a sure road to unhappiness. Just before speaking of the ambitious Greeks, Plutarch recalls the story of the Stoic philosopher Antipater of Tarsus, who, when close to death, 'added up the good things that had happened to him, and included even the easy voyage he had had from Cilicia to Athens' (469D). The same story is repeated in *Marius* (46.2), along with Plato's praise on his death bed of his own *daimôn* and fortune. In contrast, Marius was never content, to the extent that after seven consulships he was able to lament his adverse fortune (*Marius* 45.12).

Throughout *Quiet of Mind* Plutarch considers it natural that one wishes to hold office, and often high office: but what he encourages is freedom from the fear of losing it, and from a constant desire for more. Even the senatorial shoe is an unreliable token of security.[10] Plutarch, like Epictetus, addresses people who may have power at court, but are tormented.[11] He addresses people who feel miserable because they are not consuls or governors (470F), and who are not content with being friends of emperors and magistrates of cities (471E).[12] The point is that an 'increased enjoyment of wealth, fame, power, and status (*dunamis kai archê*) depends on a decreased dread of the opposite' (474C). Although many of his examples were traditional, derived from his reading, Plutarch obviously is also thinking of contemporaries who are active in public life, whom he reproaches not for being active or even ambitious, but for tormenting themselves by refusing to be content with what they have achieved. Plutarch does not mock those who would wish to be senators from Chios or Bithynia, but reproves those who, like Marius, are never satisfied.[13]

Rules for Politicians is often cited as evidence that Plutarch does not encourage political activity at the imperial level. However, this work is addressed specifically to a young man, Menemachus, who desires to enter political life 'in his homeland,' Sardis (798B, ἐν τῇ πατρίδι). The local context, politicians in Sardis contending for honour among themselves, defines the purpose of Plutarch's oft-quoted reminder to Menemachus:

You are in command, but you are under command; you rule a city subject to proconsuls, to Caesar's procurators ... look at the orator's platform from the standpoint of the proconsul's residence, don't attach much pride to your garland, or trust in it; you can see his senatorial boots above your head! (813E).[14]

Plutarch here attacks the irrational but common habit of inflaming a city by invoking past glories: Sardis is no longer the capital of Croesus, but a city under the dominion of Rome. The job of a leader in the city therefore is to promote harmony among the different groups of the city,[15] so that he can do the very best for his city.[16] In fact, Plutarch immediately reminds Menemachus of the grim results which removed his friend Pardalas when that man forgot his limits of action.[17] Rabble-rousing seems expedient, but can easily lead to disaster.

Significantly, Plutarch at the beginning of the treatise notes that Menemachus has no time for philosophical thinking: he wants to do great things, and is already immersed in politics (798B). This is already a bad sign for Plutarch, for whom a firm philosophical foundation is essential for the politician, but he tries to respond to Menemachus' request for handy rules as best he can. Two quotations from the *Iliad*, spoken by Nestor and Phoenix to Diomedes and Achilles respectively, establish Plutarch's role as elder advisor to an impulsive youth.[18] Plutarch's first and most important rule follows: political activity must have motives 'which are based on judgement and reason, not on the emotional excitement of vanity or combativeness, or mere lack of other occupation' (798C). The sharp way in which Plutarch later reminds Menemachus of the fate of Pardalas (813F) suggests that he feared that Menemachus himself would be all too ready to forget this rule, and much of the treatise is devoted towards pointing him towards a calmer, more rational path. Plutarch pointedly returns to the question of faction and the punishment of Pardalas at the end of the treatise. Without a philosophical foundation, it is too easy to be swept up in the passion of demagogery – and meet disaster.[19]

Menemachus' passion is for local politics: what of the larger world? Can a man from a small town make his mark outside his home town? Plutarch considers the question in the proem to *Demosthenes*, and finds it central not only to the lives of Demosthenes and Cicero, but to his own life.

Other arts, whose end it is to acquire riches or honour, are likely enough to wither and decay in poor and undistinguished towns, but virtue ... may take root and thrive in any place where it can lay hold of a noble nature and an industrious mind. I, for my part, shall ascribe any deficiency of mine in right judgement or action to myself, and not to the size of my native town.

The life of Demosthenes begins with Euripides' dictum on happiness, but Plutarch defines happiness not as prosperity or wealth, but a life of virtue. Moreover he shifts the focus from the abstract to his own life, his residence in Chaeronea, and the difficulty which staying in Chaeronea creates for historical research and intellectual exchange. Plutarch chooses to make Chaeronea his principal residence,[20] but his modesty should not conceal his pride in his own accomplishments. For Plutarch measures himself against Demosthenes and Cicero, who rose from small beginnings to great heights,[21] and Plutarch wishes to do the same. He too wishes to influence his world through the persuasive power of his writing. However, beneath Plutarch's humane and tranquil persona lies a fiercely ambitious spirit: ambitious not for money or power, but for the philosophic life, to win it for himself and for others. The enormous outpouring of works devoted to popular philosophy and ethics, and especially the massive project of the *Parallel Lives*, indicates a man *driven* by the need to achieve the philosophic life, and to share it with his friends and readers. The philosophic life is not limited by the size of the city, nor was Plutarch's audience for his philosophic gospel limited to his Greek acquaintances.

We must not measure Plutarch's ambition against that of modern academics, especially classical philologists and philosophers, who see themselves far removed from the political realm. His master Plato is a more suitable model. Plato, who turned to philosophy in disgust after witnessing the folly of democracy, the tyranny of his uncle Critias and the Thirty, and the irrationality and vindictiveness of Socrates' execution, nevertheless decided to take the extraordinary step of travelling to Syracuse and undertaking the training of Dionysius II as a philosopher-king. Despite his misgivings about the project, he resolved to go ahead, lest he forever reproach himself that he had fled from the opportunity of putting his ideals into practice.[22] As a philosopher, Plutarch strongly felt this need to descend from the abstractions of philosophical study back into the cave of politics. But again, modesty is deceptive. He speaks lightly of his own service as magistrate in the lowly Chaeronea,[23] but in the *Lives* he focuses on the greatest statesmen of the ancient world. Time and again he comments on the contribution philosophy made – or could have made – to their political career, and singles out the contributions of philosophers as advisers to statesmen. Anaxagoras trains Pericles to highmindedness (*Per.* 4-6), Aristotle tames the ungovernable Alexander (*Alex.* 5.7-8.5),[24] Brutus has learned Academic philosophy, and Cato was a Stoic. Plutarch praises Lycurgus for having accomplished in a real city something that philosophers had done only in books (*Lyc.* 31.1-3).

The *Solon-Publicola* pair represents a lesson in the usefulness and limitations of philosophy.[25] Solon himself is more philosopher than statesman. Unlike Lycurgus, when Athens suffered from faction he refused to take dictatorial power, but instead created a body of law for the city. He then went abroad to instruct the kings Philocyprus and Croesus (and through him Cyrus), and finally returned, first to advise the Athenians and then Peisistratus. His laws and advice always had limited effect, however, because he did not hold power himself.²⁶ But his Roman counterpart, Publicola, actually put into effect what Solon had only dreamed, both in his personal life and in what he did for the state, as Plutarch argues in his extraordinary syncrisis of the two.²⁷ The Greek philosopher serves as instructor to the Roman man of action, who converts Solon's noble thoughts into pragmatic reality in a way that the philosopher could not. Does Plutarch see himself as a philosopher, advising Roman leaders, and even the Roman emperor? He hints himself at an answer. In one of the notable scenes of *Solon* (27.2-4), the philosopher enters the court of Croesus, and sees the king himself,

whose outfit lacked nothing that men regard as remarkable or extraordinary or desirable in the way of precious stones, dyed clothing, and wrought gold jewellery – nothing that might help him present a thoroughly impressive and gorgeous spectacle. Contrary to Croesus' expectations, however, Solon stood there opposite him unmoved by the spectacle and without passing any comment on it; in fact, anyone with any sense could see that he actually despised the vulgarity and tawdriness of it all.²⁸

The scene recalls the splendor of the Roman imperial court, especially the audiences in the *domus Flaviana*, newly erected by Domitian.²⁹ Domitian's faulty taste is explicitly criticized at *Publ.* 15.3-6. There, Plutarch recalls seeing columns lying ready for the reconstruction of the temple of Jupiter Capitolinus,³⁰ which he had seen already cut in Athens. They had now been recut, and had lost their beauty and proportion. But an observer's marvel at the extravagance of the temple would be nothing, Plutarch asserts, if he saw one stoa, great hall, bath, or apartment for concubines of Domitian's *domus*, and he would say 'this is neither piety nor magnificence, but a disease of building, like Midas converting everything into gold or stone'.³¹ Plutarch has stood in the palace of Domitian, and like Solon, has seen only 'vulgarity and tawdriness'. Unlike Domitian, Publicola, in Plutarch's account, took an important step in winning the favor of the Romans by pulling down his ostentatious house after he observed the distress it caused (*Publ.* 10).³² Plutarch sees himself as being in a position to evaluate from a moral perspective a recently deceased emperor, comparing himself to Solon evaluating Croesus, and thus implicitly to Solon advising Publicola through his laws.³³ In a fundamental article, Swain has shown that Plutarch took a deep interest in the Hellenic culture of his Roman heroes, and its effect on their behavior, and bids his reader to 'take notice of the benefits which Hellenic culture has to offer and of the detriment which may be occasioned by its absence.'³⁴ But we must go one step further: Plutarch himself is the representative of Hellenic culture, the philosopher who wishes to teach his contemporaries. The *Parallel Lives* are his means of bringing philosophy to Rome. He, in his own time, will be Anaxagoras to Pericles, Aristotle to Alexander, Solon to Publicola.[35]

Granted that Plutarch intended to instruct contemporary politicians at the highest level, as well as those active in the Greek cities, how did he do this in the *Parallel Lives*? The twin pair *Agis and Cleomenes—Tiberius and Gaius Gracchus* furnishes an example. I will restrict myself here to the Roman pair, and in particular *Tiberius*. These *Lives* demonstrate that statesmen who are noble and well-intentioned can act for the worse under pressure of men and circumstances. The particular problem is how the well-meaning statesman attempts to remedy serious injustices suffered by the people. In the initial chapters (1-3), both Gracchi are described as men of excellent nature and education, inspired by their mother to seek glory in the state. Plutarch then turns to Tiberius. After outstanding service in Africa and in Spain, where his handling of the Numantia treaty negotiations won the favor of the people (7.3), Tiberius is elected tribune and decides to attack the problem of public lands. Plutarch gives five explanations for his decision (8): the advice of his advisors Blossius and Diophanes, the urging of his mother Cornelia, his rivalry with a contemporary orator, Spurius Postumius, his own experience in Etruria, where he saw the impoverishment of the land, and the clamor of the people. The first three reflect standard influences: advisors, desire for glory, and political rivalry. The fourth, the vision of Etruria, is not only the most honourable, but is supported by contemporary evidence: a *biblion* written by Gaius. But, Plutarch asserts, the *dêmos* provided the strongest incentive to ambition, plastering stoas, walls, and monuments with slogans spurring him to recover the public land for the poor.

In the beginning, Tiberius acted prudently, consulting with distinguished older men such as Crassus, Scaevola, and Appius Claudius, and proposing a mild and gentle law, which he defended with stirring rhetoric (9). Only when Octavius vetoed his proposal did Tiberius react in frustration by withdrawing the lenient law and proposing one more pleasing to the people (*hêdiô tois pollois*, 10.4). Even so, he was always restrained in his dealings with Octavius: Plutarch notes that even in times of emotion and ambition, a nature which is naturally good and trained in self-control keeps the mind well-balanced (10.6). Finally, however, the intransigence of the wealthy, manifested in threats of murder, the theft of the voting urns, and the senate's refusal of his direct appeal, leads Tiberius to force the issue. Here is the turning point, which Plutarch marks clearly: 'he turns to an illegal and unseemly action', the deposition of Octavius.[36] Although Tiberius tries in every possible way to get Octavius to yield, he must carry out his plan, and Octavius is removed. The *dêmos* goes wild, rushing to attack Octavius and behaving like a mob, and blinds one of his attendants (12.6). The land law is passed, but Tiberius has transgressed a limit, as the sequel shows. The situation becomes worse. Nasica insults Tiberius in the senate, and Tiberius goads the anger of the crowd by putting on mourning clothes (13.6). When King Attalus bequeathes the kingdom of Pergamum to the Romans, Tiberius at once seeks the favor of the crowd by introducing a populist bill to distribute the land to the citizens (14.1). Compromise has been forgotten: in every way he can he tries to hold the favor of the people. But the people are fickle, and the removal of Octavius has made them more hostile to him (15.1). He defends himself in a moving speech, which Plutarch quotes at length, but of which he pointedly does not approve. Finally, to protect himself from the opposition, Tiberius must seek a new term as tribune, and therefore propose new laws to win the masses. Plutarch notes that he now does not act for what is right, but to preserve his position with the people (16.1).[37] When later he is deterred by bad omens from going to the Capitol, his advisor Blossius urges him on: he must not disregard the citizens when they call (17.5). The argument seems reasonable, but is specious: Tiberius, rather than follow his better judgement, is forced to follow the people's demands.[38] He goes up to the Capitol, and is killed.

I have traced this process at length to make clear the stages which Plutarch assigns to Tiberius' political and moral progress. The reader can follow step by step how Tiberius replaces a good bill with bills and actions designed to please the people, and in the process forces civil war and his own death. Of course, Plutarch sees clearly that the opposition was more violent and desperate than Tiberius, but they were not the subject of his study. Rather he wishes to focus on how a good man, with the best intentions, can create a disastrous situation.

The tribunate of Gaius progresses much more rapidly, but the basic pattern is the same, and need not be repeated.[39] The dream in the first chapter foretells the tragedy of Gaius' life: he will die, pursuing Tiberius' course. His means to power is the oratory which he uses to rouse the people. However, the crowd turns to Livius Drusus when he outbids Gaius for their favor. The people are irrational, and a leader cannot trust them.

It is not difficult to see the relevance of the Gracchi's tragedy for Plutarch's contemporaries. The central theme of Plutarch's advice to Menemachus at Sardis was to work for harmony among the leaders of the city and not try to use the populace as a tool for personal gain or ambitions.[40] More significantly, the problem recurs in imperial Rome. Plutarch reads the same lesson in the fate of emperors or others who try to win over the army to achieve their own ends. *Galba* and *Otho* are the examples which survive. Plutarch had lived through their brief time upon the stage, coming and going like tragedy kings (*Galba* 1.8). In AD 69 he would have been in his mid twenties, and already active in political affairs in Greece.[41] The cause, Plutarch believed, was especially the greed and indiscipline of the troops, which had begun when Nymphidius paid the pretorian guard to betray Nero (*Galba* 1.6, 9). Thereafter the shifting allegiance of the armies, and their anger at not receiving promised donatives, controlled the fortunes of the contenders, until Vespasian was able to stabilize the situation. There was no fighting in Greece, but it must have been a time of great fear and tension. Chaeronea had often been a battlefield, and could have been again. Later, after the assassination of Domitian, the new emperor Nerva had seemed on the right track, consciously working to defuse the tense situation in the capital, restoring exiles and confiscated property. He gave special attention to the populace, giving a *congiarium* to the people, promoting a *lex agraria*, and building granaries to ensure the grain supply for the populace.[42] A donative was given to the troops. Nevertheless, in AD 97 he was forced by his praetorian prefect, Casperius Aelianus, at the head of mutinying soldiers, to execute the assassins of Domitian. The moment was ominous. Would irrational soldiers once more dictate policy in Rome?

For Plutarch, army and people were intimately tied.[43] The connection goes back to his Platonic understanding of the forces within the soul, which are divided between rational and irrational. The leaders of the city or the state, the elite, should be the rational element;[44] the people and the army represent the irrational.[45] It is the role of the politician to lead this irrational mass, and not be led by it. The Gracchi had begun well, but had yielded their leadership to the emotions of the crowd. Nerva had had to yield to the pressure of the praetorians. This was not an abstract problem for Plutarch: civil war could have followed.

Nerva, realizing the instability of his position, acted quickly to proclaim Trajan as his successor. When Nerva died naturally a few months later, Plutarch could not have felt sure that no further problems would arise. Did the new ruler and his associates have the character and inner resources to follow a sound and peaceful course in handling the pressures from the people and the troops? Would he be able to walk the thin line between winning their support and pandering to their irrational desires? There were no guarantees, and Plutarch's own experience of history gave little reason for confidence. By this time he had already written the *Lives of the Caesars*, from Augustus to Vitellius,[46] and he knew well enough the weaknesses of emperors.[47] The duty of a philosopher to educate was never of greater importance.

Trajan began his reign by taking firm control of the armies of the north, executing Casperius and the leaders of the pretorian revolt against Nerva,[48] and granting a *congiarium* to the people and a donative to the soldiers.[49] He seemed to have begun well. In this climate of hope and uncertainty Plutarch undertook his *Parallel Lives*. We do not know when under Trajan *Gracchi* was written, but there is no reason to think that it was occasioned by a particular crisis. The challenges to judgement and right behavior which *Gracchi* explores so powerfully were ever-present in imperial Rome as well as in individual Greek cities. Plutarch does not have answers for politicians, for he is well aware of the complexity of political action. Circumstances greatly affect the situation: he notes, for example, that if Scipio Aemilianus had been present when Tiberius was tribune, the course of history might have been different (*Gracch.* 7.7). Rather he allows his readers to discover fundamental guidelines in the life histories of great men, and invites them to consider the implications of their stories for their own action in the contemporary world.[50] It was not by chance that he chose to dedicate the *Parallel Lives*, his most ambitious work, to Sosius Senecio, an old friend who just happened to be one of Trajan's most trusted associates.

Notes

1. For Plutarch's Roman friends, see Jones 1971, 48-64, Puech 1992.
2. Swain 1996, 1-64.
3. See Swain 1996, 40-42.
4. On Plutarch's use of citations, cf. e.g. Di Gregorio 1976; Van der Stockt 1987; Carrara 1988.
5. See Swain 1996, 63, quoting Sext. Emp. *Adversus mathematicos* I 234.
6. Translated by Waterfield 1992, with some changes.
7. E.g. Russell 1972, 9.
8. Swain 1996, 169-171: the senators were C. Julius Eurycles Herculanus, the addressee of *De laude ipsius*, and C. Julius Antiochus Epiphanes Philopappus, addressee of *Quomodo adul. ab amico internosc.* and suffect consul in 109, on whom see also Puech 1992.
9. It has been suggested that Sosius was of Eastern origin: cf. Syme 1958, 599, n. 8; 1968, 101 n. 127; Jones 1970, 103; 1971, 53, 136. Provincial origin is doubted by Swain 1996, 144 and 426-27.
10. See the wonderfully ironic anecdote, *Pomp.* 24.11-13, in which pirates capture a man who complains that he is a Roman and an important person: the pirates pretend to be abashed, present him with senatorial shoes and toga, then invite him to walk the plank.
11. Cf. 466C and 467D. For Epictetus, cf. *Diss.* e.g. 1.10 and 3.7, and Millar 1965; Brunt 1977.
12. The whole passage is an interesting statement of the competitive instinct in Plutarch's world, which extended to all sorts of activities: 'they not only expect to be rich, erudite, strong, outgoing, pleasant, friends of kings (or emperors), and magistrates of cities, but they are discontented if their dogs, horses, quails, and cocks are not the best at what they do'.
13. Swain 1996, 170, seems wrong on this point. Mocking of this sort is not Plutarch's

style, nor does it fit the tone or argument of the treatise. For his positive attitude toward small cities, see *Dem.* 1-2, discussed below.
14. Translated in Russell 1993. The meaning of στρατήγιον and βῆμα here is disputed: see Jones 1971, 133 and Swain 1996, 166. The latter would render 'look from the magistrate's office to the proconsul's tribunal.' The two terms are usually used together by Plutarch as a synecdoche for political life (*Per.* 37.1, *Phoc.* 7.5, *An seni* 788C, 789C). Plutarch uses στρατήγιον for *praetorium* at *Brut.* 42.6 (Cassius' battlefield tent). For an extended analysis of this section of Plutarch's treatise, see now Swain 1996, 165-173, which my discussion is meant to modify and to a limited extent correct.
15. Cf. on Plutarch Wardman 1974, 57-63, and on Dio, Jones 1978, esp. 83-94.
16. This focus on what is good for the city seems to be the reason why Plutarch urges making a friend of a powerful Roman rather than pursuing an imperial equestrian career as procurator (814DE): the latter, though potentially profitable for the individual, is demeaning and forces one to abandon one's civic affairs, while the other, while it may be demeaning, helps the city. In this passage, the expression διοικήσεις τῶν ἐπαρχιῶν, which normally is translated 'governorships of provinces', may mean 'procuratorships of provinces': διοίκησις and related forms, besides the general meaning of administration, may have the sense of procurator: cf. Mason 1974, 38, s.v. and Plutarch *Ant.* 67, *Apophth. Reg.* 207B (referring to Eros, procurator of Egypt, and Areios, the friend of Augustus mentioned at 814D and procurator of Sicily). This would be significant, because it might restrict the offices to which he was referring to the equestrian career. To be a senatorial governor of a province would imply much greater standing: in fact the governor would be one of those 'higher authorities' with whom Plutarch recommends becoming friends.
17. Plutarch alludes to Pardalas' fate only through a tragic quotation, 'the punishing axe, sharp severer of the neck', which implies that he was executed (thus Jones 1971, 117), though he may have been exiled.
18. *Praec. ger. reip.* 798 A-B, quoting *Il.* 9.55-56 and 443.
19. The introduction to the treatise suggests that Menemachus' lamp of philosophy lacked oil. At the conclusion Plutarch returns to the lamp image: 'Fire rarely starts in temples or public buildings. Most often, a neglected lamp or some rubbish catching alight in a house starts a conflagration which ends in widespread public damage. Likewise, ... differences arising out of private difficulties and offences throw the whole city into turmoil.' This leads once more to the case of Pardalas, and his enmity with Tyrrhenus, 'which came near to ruining Sardis, plunging the city into war and rebellion for a trivial, private cause.' (825C-D). It looks very much like there had been extremely serious trouble in Sardis not too long before, and Plutarch is very worried that Menemachus may not have the strength to resist rekindling it. This same Menemachus may be the addressee of *De exil.*, a wealthy citizen of Sardis, now banished (600A, 601B, 604B): cf. Jones 1971, 117; Swain 1996, 184. The exile is disconsolate because he no longer holds offices; Plutarch notes that he no longer has factional strife, or expenses, or long waits at the governor's door (604B).

20. Of course, he would have had a residence in Delphi, where he was priest for so many years, and probably in Athens as well, where he was a citizen.
21. *Dem.* 3.4.
22. Plato, *Epistle* 7. Plutarch considered the epistle genuine and frequently quoted it in *Dion*.
23. *Praec. ger. reip.* 811BC.
24. See Stadter 1996, esp. 291-94.
25. For this paragraph I am endebted to Hadavas 1995, 241-45.
26. Note Plutarch's comparisons of Solon and Lycurgus at *Sol.* 16 and 22.
27. *Comp. Sol.-Publ.* 1-4.
28. Translated by Waterfield 1998.
29. On the *domus* Flaviana see Statius, *Silv.* 4.2, Martial 8.36, 39; Nash 1969, 1:316-38; Richardson 1992, 114-17.
30. Consecrated in AD 80. The expense of the gilding alone, Plutarch notes, was 12,000 talents, which can be compared to the 1,000 talents he associates with the Parthenon (*Per.* 12.2).
31. Dryden translation. The palace was completed in AD 92. C.P. Jones (1971, 23) notes that Plutarch may have visited it as an ambassador or on other business in AD 92, or later.
32. Nerva took a similar step after his accession, declaring the *domus Flaviana* a public building for general use: cf. Pliny *Paneg.* 47.4.
33. For comparisons between Plutarch's Pericles and Trajan, see Moles 1992, 293-94.
35. Plutarch clearly wished a role rather different from the house philosopher described by Rawson 1989 or Lucian *De merc. cond.*
36. *Gracch.* 11.4 τρέπεται πρὸς ἔργον οὐ νόμιμον οὐδ' ἐπιεικές.
37. For Plutarch's apparently simplistic dichotomy between the people and the senate in *Gracchi* and often in the *Roman Lives*, see Pelling 1995b, especially 331-37.
38. The same situation occurs with Caesar before his assassination, *Caes.* 64.
39. On the many powerful echoes between the two lives, see Ingenkamp 1992, especially 4298-4323. Plutarch gives a rather different picture of Gaius' motivation at *Praec. ger. reip.* 798F: when the memory of Tiberius' death was still fresh, he hung back from politics, but then, 'inflamed with anger because of insults and attacks, he rushed into public life.' These would be the attacks while Gaius was in Sardinia and after his return: cf. *Gracch.* 23-24.1.
40. Cf. most recently the analysis by Swain 1996, 161-83.
41. *Praec. ger. reip.* 816C. Quite possibly he had witnessed Nero's announcement of Greek freedom at Corinth in November 67: cf. *Flam.* 12.13 and Jones 1971, 15-17.
42. Cf. Bennett 1997, 37-41.
43. For Rome, see the important treatment of de Blois 1992. De Blois clarifies the thinking behind Plutarch's *dêmos-boulê* dichotomy noted by Pelling 1995b.
44. 'Should be', because all too often they also ceded their rational role, as frequently in *Gracchi*. This would seem to explain the frequency with which in these lives Plutarch speaks of 'the wealthy' or 'the powerful' rather than 'the senate'. The *equites*, which Pelling notes rarely figure in Plutarch's thinking (although he him-

self probably was one), would fall on one side or the other of the senate-people division, depending on the moment. The analysis is more theoretical than historical.

45. Cf. the image he uses of Pericles' work force: 'each skill, like a general his troops, had its own laboring and private mass (ὄχλος) under it' (*Per.* 12.6).
46. Perhaps under Domitian, and before 93: cf. Jones 1971, 72-73.
47. Cf. Plutarch's comment at *Rules for Politicians* 816A, after recalling the violence of Sulla at Praeneste, 'Let us pray that such times do not come upon us, but if they do, expect a better outcome than this'.
48. Dio Cass. 68.5.4.
49. For the evidence, cf. Bennett 1997, 59-62, citing especially Pliny *Paneg.* 25-26. By 101, Trajan had also set up a system of support for impoverished citizens called *alimenta*, perhaps building on a plan initiated by Nerva. This seems to respond to problems not unlike those seen by Tiberius Gracchus when travelling through Etruria (*Gracch.* 8.9). On the difficulties of Italian agriculture at this time, cf. Bennett 1997, 79-81; on *alimenta*, cf. 81-84, with the bibliography cited in his n. 60.
50. For Plutarch's aim of creating a more nuanced and vivid sense of the ongoing moral implications of political action, see Pelling 1995a and Stadter 2000.

CHAPTER 10

Plutarch and Roman(ized) Athens

Frances B. Titchener

Plutarch, a pragmatist, was most circumspect in his writings about Rome and Romans when it came to expressing his own opinion. He could be very negative about Roman individuals (Crassus immediately comes to mind), but his attitude towards Romans in general is harder to discern, despite the recent excellent work, particularly of Simon Swain, in this area.[1] His decision to live his life in Chaeronea may provide a key to his underlying feelings. Plutarch says he chose to stay there because it was such a small town that even one absent citizen would be noticed. Although this is a charming sentiment, it is a little disingenuous to be accepted at face value. Perhaps first and second century AD Athens was a little too Roman for Plutarch. Whether that means expensive, bureaucratic, crowded, impersonal, dangerous, or a combination of the above is the subject of this paper.

Let us first examine Plutarch's own words on this subject, from the first three chapters of his *Demosthenes*. Several points jump out. The biography (like the *Parallel Lives* as a whole, as well as the *Quaestiones Convivium* and *Quomodo quis suos in virtute sentiat profectus*) is specifically addressed to a Roman, Q. Sosius Senecio. Although it has been suggested that Sosius was of provincial origin,[2] possibly the Greek east, he rose through the *cursus honorum* and was close to Trajan, meaning only that these words were most certainly going to be heard by Roman ears. Then Plutarch sets a kind of program for the importance of where one lives. He begins with 'true happiness' (ἀληθινὴν εὐδαιμονίαν) which he says does NOT depend on birthplace, pace the author of Alcibiades' encomium for his Olympic chariot-victory. Then he goes on to 'virtue' (ἀρετή), which he says *unlike the arts* (my emphasis) can take root and flourish anywhere there is 'a generous nature and a spirit that shuns no labour'. He concludes the chapter with a rhetorical flourish, saying that we should not blame small-town life for our own failure to achieve happiness and virtue. The next chapter takes a strong turn away (μέντοι). When it comes to composing history based upon less accessible readings, the author must *first and foremost* (again, my emphasis) live in a city which has access to books and intellectual discussion. In this way he will avoid publishing a work which lacks many and even necessary things. In answer to the chapter's opening μέντοι, he now says

But I (ἡμεῖς δὲ), living in a small city, and preferring to live there in order that it might not be even smaller, while in Rome and during other Italian travels, there not being leisure to practice the Roman language because of political duties and the number of philosophy students, came late and advanced in age to Roman grammar.

He then digresses on how he learned Latin from knowing already what it said. He begins the third chapter saying this is why he will not examine the speeches of Demosthenes and Cicero, but rather examine their deeds and public careers to compare their natures and dispositions. Next is a fine quotation from Ion and a gentle denunciation of Caecilius as a kind of smokescreen, brought together by the excellent observation that if it were that easy to 'know thyself' the god wouldn't need to tell us to do so. He then begins his comparison of Demosthenes and Cicero.

What Plutarch has said is that since he does not read Latin well enough to take advantage of the writings and literary conversations in Rome, there is no need for him to do so and it seems very clear that he has no other interest in going. It seems equally clear that this it not a sentiment he wants to express baldly, hence the little joke about 'lest it become any smaller.' This brings to mind Juvenal's Umbricius. At the beginning of Satire III, Juvenal attributes motives to Umbricius that sound very much like Plutarch's statement at the beginning of Demosthenes:

Quamvis digressu veteris confusus amici laudo tamen, vacuis quod sedem figere Cumis destinet atque unum civem donare Sibyllae.

Although confounded by the departure of an old friend, I nevertheless commend that fact that he has decided to relocate his operation to empty Cumae and provide at least one citizen for the Sibyl.

Anderson[3] interprets the *unum* as follows: 'The movement from a negative concept of solum as loneliness to a positive definition as individual independence is thus gradually effected by the use of unus and the implications of Umbricius' words' (Anderson 1957, 62). Anderson is uncertain, earlier, about that unus, saying 'it is uncertain whether Juvenal conveys a positive concept or whether he implies rather deprecatingly 'at least one' (Anderson 1957, 62). In fact, I think this is exactly what it means, and perhaps some kind of 'one-horse town' joke was even popular about that time. Such a joke could reflect the changing, urbanized Roman world of ca. 100 AD. The cities were bursting with urban poor by then, as Juvenal's satires and, among other things, the rise of Christianity makes clear. Emperors like Hadrian were 'on tour' constantly, perhaps as part of the effort to keep country life alive as well as pacify the army. At that time, it was still true that the vast majority of the people needed to live in the country to make city life possible in the absence of refrigeration, the complicated nature of transport, etc. Even though Plutarch does not ever cite Juvenal, it is dangerous to assume he had never read or heard Juvenal's work read, and I suspect the same applies to Vergil, Ovid, Martial, Plautus, Terence, and all the other Roman poets Plutarch never cites. If so, then the 'one citizen' joke gives Plutarch a graceful way to explain his antipathy toward Roman and/or urban life. But the question still remains: why not live in Athens, where the writings and intellectual conversation would be accessible?

I myself live in a small town (under 50,000 inhabitants), and am periodically hampered in my scholarship by the lack of library resources and community with whom to discuss research, as well as the lack of big city stimulation in the form of restaurants and entertainment. Yet I like it very much, I think it suits me, and I'd be very unwilling to change. Hence, my own experience may shed some light on this subject. First, expense. Jones makes a convincing case for Plutarch's family being well-off, but not outrageously wealthy. Juvenal and Martial complain repeatedly about the expense of living in Rome, and it stands to reason that life in Athens or any big city of the time would be similarly expensive. Plutarch may not have wanted to incur the decrease in his standard-of-living or the increase in expenses that an urban lifestyle might entail.

What about fear of the unknown? Plutarch certainly had enjoyed plenty of opportunities to travel. Furthermore, despite the smallness of the town, Chaeronea was hardly isolated, situated as it was in such a way that it was easily accessible via the Corinthian gulf to Italy, Macedonia, and hence the Black Sea, as well as Egypt and the eastern Mediterranean, so friends and travellers from all those places would find it easy to visit him. Plutarch himself had made multiple trips to Rome, and at least one tour of northern Italy, during which he visited Bedriacum, Brixellum, Ravenna, where he saw Marius' statue, and perhaps other cities as well. He had visited Egypt in his youth, and perhaps Smyrna. He was in a position, then, to evaluate what it would be like to live somewhere else.

What about fear of the known? On top of the general unpleasantness of the type Juvenal describes so well, there could be real physical danger in coming to the emperor's attention. Plutarch's friend Arulenus Rusticus was executed by Domitian, and Rusticus' brother Junius was exiled over the Rustici's loyalty to Thrasea Paetus, one of Nero's victims. Domitian then expelled philosophers from Rome and Italy. Later on in the first year of Hadrian's succession, Plutarch's family friend C. Avidius Nigrinas (along with three other consulars) was executed on conspiracy charges. But even earlier, Jones makes the case for Plutarch's having learned practical political lessons early on in terms of the varying fortunes of Achaea. After Nero liberated that province, factionalism ran rampant until Vespasian revoked the Neronian liberty and restored order. As Jones sums up 'These were grim years in the internal affairs of Greece, and they may have given the young Plutarch his first practical lessons in politics. His later treatises on the subject show an abhorrence of faction and a liking for firm rule, guaranteed by the friendly presence of Roman power'.[4]

Perhaps Plutarch was unwilling to compete on the large scale implicit in becoming an inhabitant of a big city. He is apologetic in a number of places in the *Parallel Lives* (i.e. *Nicias* 1.1 vis-a-vis Thucydides) which could suggest that he anticipates criticism and perhaps feels inadequate, or it could be a biographical convention, along the lines of Cornelius Nepos' *Praefatio*. The opening of Demosthenes shows Plutarch's awareness of the sacrifice he made in depriving himself of the library resources he would have in a bigger place, despite his protestations about the quality of his Latin. Yet 'fear of competition' seems unlikely in view of Plutarch's extensive career in public service. Not only did he serve as priest of Delphi, he had undertaken diplomatic missions for Greece even as a young man, as is clear from the famous anecdote about his father's advising him to always use the first person plural for reports involving an ill colleague.[5] He was *archon* of Chaeronea and a citizen of Athens; he was also a citizen of Rome, possessed of equestrian status, and allowed the privilege of consular ornamenta. His writings express impatience and scorn for those who do not serve their countries, as in the *Comparison of Nicias and Crassus*, where Plutarch suggests that there is plenty of room for men afraid of action and service (like Nicias) to sit in the agora and weave a crown of *ataraxia*. Yet he had no patience with 'climbers' who deserted their Greek homes to chase after positions in the Roman government (*Prae. Ger.* 814D).

What about Plutarch's interest in providing moral instruction? We know he wanted to do so; shouldn't he have wanted the widest possible circulation? We know by now that Plutarch didn't like living in the big city and presumably had no interest in the sort of 'lecture circuit' we find others pursuing. He liked being a big fish in his little pond, and it was certainly safer. Plutarch knew well that Athens' heyday had passed (and Greece's, for that matter), and he was in a somewhat peculiar position in being aware of it. For most of us, it may not be so clear that we are on the downhill side. It can be argued that Plutarch believed that the Greek world still had much to offer the Roman world in terms of education, and was trying hard to do so. I think that while Plutarch is not a golden ager, he would just as soon not be confronted with the coarse successors to his country's leadership, and that he perhaps does not wish to expend the additional effort required to maintain his neutral attitude in the actual face of the oppressor. Is he 'trying to catch Trajan's ear' to borrow a phrase, or covering himself in case he does? And in any case, surely Trajan's or Hadrian's ear would be caught by anecdotes and phrases, not entire biographies. Plutarch was fairly safe in criticizing Roman militarism, luxury, and greed in biographies of those safely dead like Publicola and Lucullus with the friendly filters of the likes of Mestrius Florus and Sosius Senecio between himself and the emperor.

Yet if it is true that Plutarch wanted to maintain a low profile, we must account for his popularity and literary success. People were, after all, asking him to write things for them, and he had lectured in Rome. Surely there is no need to go beyond the statement that Plutarch was a good writer with an eye for historical detail in an age that was desperately seeking some way to make sense of the present by a moral assessment of the past. And he was certainly the man to make such an assessment. Plutarch is very clear about his purpose in writing the *Parallel Lives* – he is providing examples, good and bad, for men to emulate and avoid. Pelling has argued recently that Plutarch's moralizing is timeless, not geared to his own times.[6] He gives, as example, the fact that Trajan was probably planning a war against Parthia when Plutarch was preparing his *Antony* and *Crassus*. Pelling denies that Trajan was on Plutarch's mind at this point:

If any contemporary association had been caught, it would have been extraordinarily gauche, and Trajan surely never crossed Plutarch's mind. Plutarch has other reasons for emphasizing Parthia, where so many of Antony's frailties and virtues showed themselves so plainly; a few chapters later the Actium campaign reprises many of the same points, but this time events are even more catastrophic. Parthia can point many truths about an Antony, impetuous, valiant, irrepressible, lovable, and deeply flawed; but those are traits which might recur with other people at other times. They are points about a timeless human nature, not about ad 10-15 (Pelling 1995, 210).

In conclusion, Plutarch didn't like big cities, Rome in particular. He believed that living in a big city was not necessary for living a virtuous and happy life. He did not wish to compete in the international arena any more than was unavoidable through his local political work and his friendship with Roman officials like Sosius Senecio, perhaps because of a kind of apprehensive caution that should not be called by as strong a term as 'fear'. In light of his lack of confidence in his Latin, he could not make use of the library and intellectual resources that would make the expense and stress of life in Rome 'worthwhile'. Yet his natural diplomacy preferred to accentuate the positive aspect of life in Chaeronea rather than deplore the negative aspects of hyperurban life. Ironically, he thus rather inadvertently joins a long literary tradition of the very Roman poets whom his lack of linguistic confidence prevented him from citing. By the end of the millennium, the Empire was so huge and well-connected that there was little need to live in Rome to be a creative writer anymore. Catullus needed to live in Rome to be Catullus, but in the next generation it was becoming increasingly possible to live outside Rome and still be at the hub of literary action (pace Ovid's letters from exile!). Horace had his Sabine villa, Vergil his retreat, and even Martial talks about 'the farm'. Plutarch is then the furthest extension of that tradition, living in the 'boondocks' and writing frequently about Romans, in Greek. How different, in the end, is that from living on a Sabine farm and writing Greek-style poetry? Plutarch remained in Chaeronea because he disliked big city life and preferred small-town existence. This outlook was evidently sufficiently unusual to require the construction of a polite, and perhaps humorous *recusatio*.

Notes

1. Swain 1996, *passim*.
2. Jones 1971, 54-55.
3. Anderson 1957, 33-90 (55-68 on Satire III); other interpretations support this general interpretation of the satire (Motto and Clark 1965, 267-76; Witke 1962, 244-48).
4. Jones 1971, 22-23.
5. I recollect that when I was still a young man I was sent with another as envoy to the proconsul; the other man was somehow left behind; I alone met the proconsul and accomplished the business. Now when I came back and was to make the report of our mission, my father left his seat and told me in private not to say 'I went' but 'we went', not 'I said' but 'we said' and in all other ways to associate my colleague in a joint report (Loeb translation, *PraecGer* 816d-e).
6. Pelling 1995, 205-20.

CHAPTER 11

Plutarch's 'Roman' Women

Victor Castellani

The purpose of Plutarch of Chaeronea, philosopher, author, priest of Delphic Apollo, in writing his Roman *Lives* was moral and didactic rather than 'social scientific'. He did not intend to provide a social history, let alone a sociology of the Romans, but rather cautionary stories about character, motivation, and action among their great public men, from the legendary Romulus and Numa to 'Caesars' who lived during his own youth. His best efforts to understand the Romans, however, so as to give background and detail to the lives of his biographical subjects were not entirely successful. For example, the Boeotian Greek seems to have attempted to comprehend the Roman *matrona / materfamilias* as no different from the Greek women and the few thoroughly Hellenized Italian ones he knew, personally or from *Greek* literature.

All who work in this area owe a debt to France Le Corsu (1981) for giving us a better insight into how Plutarch dealt with the condition of women and to Philip A. Stadter's discussion of Plutarch's strategies in describing them (1965). Other more recent scholarship is also helpful (for example Boulogne 1994). However, the problem with all of these studies seems to be the same as Plutarch's was: a tendency to homogenize Greek and Roman women because of the 'cultural continuum' that undeniably embraced the entire Mediterranean region. A continuum, however, is not necessarily uniform, and there were major differences between the 'Roman' women Plutarch acknowledged and their real-life models in Italy and at Rome.

Some differences between Greeks and Romans in the matter of women concerned their legal position, others their personal moral – or practical – authority, and even their emotional life. In political rights, of course, Roman women were not at all better off than Greek ones; on the other hand, although there were a few powerful Greek women who exercised their influence through husbands or sons, such women were much more frequent in early and late Roman history. Regarding legal rights, Roman women had, at least in the later Republic and Empire, notably more actual control than Greek ones over their property and their persons, which, they frequently deployed, however, to advance dynastic ambitions, by marriages, divorces, and other liaisons in collaboration with their 'men' (fathers, brothers, sometimes sons – and even husbands!).

Within the family, moreover, women in Rome seem to have been much more active advisers, even instigators of policy, to their male kinsmen. This applied especially to mothers, who frequently invested not only emotion but vicarious ambition in their sons. Divorce and widowhood may have been common enough to make wives somewhat less eager to put as much into husbands, though there was an occasional Fulvia who really threw herself into her 'Mark Antony' politics.

There is no 'life' of any woman, of course, Greek or Roman, among Plutarch's biographies. Except perhaps in the unique case of Sappho, women were not the subject of that ancient genre. Many nevertheless appear in his parallel lives, on both sides, the Greek as well as the Roman. Memorable Greek women emerge in the stories of Cimon and Pericles, Alexander, and Agis and Cleomenes. These, however, are neither so numerous nor so prominent as the women in very many of the Roman *Lives*.

Although in Plutarch's accounts of Publicola, Fabius Maximus, Marcellus and Flamininus neither mother nor wife is ever mentioned, the biographies of most of the leading Romans from Romulus to Mark Antony would never have been the same without mothers, wives, sometimes also daughters, and other females who affected these men from childhood to death – and even beyond. Occasionally the great lady is not a Roman; Cleopatra, first Caesar's and later, more tragically, Antony's woman, is the chief example. For the most part, however, the women are Romans, and often noble ones in both senses: distinguished in character and in ancestry.

Some Roman *Lives* teem with women.

Those of Romulus and of Coriolanus will be considered in detail below. The *Life of Cato the Elder* passes along some of that curmudgeon's thinking about women in general. Concerning the power of wives, the Censor paraphrases Themistocles the Athenian: 'We rule the world, but our wives rule us' (*Cat. Mai.* ch. 8). Individual women appear in this *Life*, too: the mother of an unnamed dissolute young man (ch. 8) and Cato's own wives (chs. 17 with a joke!, 20, and 24) and daughter-in-law (ch. 20).

Plutarch's historical biographies from the Civil War period, those of Marius and Sulla, of Pompey and Caesar, of Cato the Younger and Cicero, of Mark Antony and Brutus, all present important political women. Plutarch deserves credit for this presentation. He always seems a bit alarmed by the influence of wives, however, and above all by that of mothers. He is surprised not by the moral effect of a mother upon her growing son (something enlightened Greeks since Homer had appreciated) but rather by her practical, political counsel. Daughters, too, are sometimes forces to be reckoned with, not only in their fathers' affections but also in their politics. Perhaps a Greek understood this last fact, for there is ample evidence of strong father-daughter relationships in Hellenic mythology and history. Greek daughters were not expected to *do* much, however. When a girl was given in a political marriage, her actions and sufferings, not to mention her thoughts, were unimportant.

Let us review Roman women, by category and by instances, beginning with mothers.

Significant, sometimes magnificent mothers, ones who probably in some way shaped their sons' character, are to be found in at least eleven lives.[1]

Leaving (1) Coriolanus' Volumnia for later, we shall begin with

(2 and 3) the mother of the Gracchi, the grand patrician *matrona* Cornelia, daughter of Scipio Africanus Major, whose excellence as a wife and widow to her plebeian-noble husband (raising his twelve children!) must be noted. Cornelia's part in bringing to adulthood two ambitious and energetic populist leaders is a highlight of Plutarch's twin biography of the brother-tribunes. Despite what Plutarch says about the humble, working-class status of

(4) Marius' mother Fulcinia, she was quite likely nobler in pedigree than the Marii, and, one suspects, may have instilled in her equestrian son those aspirations which led to a brilliant military career and, alas, a horrendous political one. In this case Plutarch minimizes her effect, perhaps because he prefers not to associate the man's later brutality with a 'humble' municipal woman. In the case of

(5) Sertorius, on the other hand, our Greek author emphasizes the part played by that man's widowed mother – named, if we can believe Plutarch, Rhea! (Does he misunderstand a joke?) Whatever her Roman name, she had young Quintus well educated in law and oratory, and he doted on her: τραφεὶς δὲ κοσμίως ὑπὸ μητρὶ χήρᾳ πατρὸς ὀρφανὸς ὑπερφύως δοκεῖ φιλομήτωρ γενέσθαι, 'raised fittingly by his widowed mother, since he was orphaned of his father, he seems to have been exceptionally devoted to her' (*Sert.* ch. 2). In sharp contrast,

(6) Caecilia, Lucullus' mother, noble though she was, daughter and sister of consuls, was also notorious for licentious behavior: ἠδόξησεν ὡς οὐ βεβιωκυῖα σωφρόνως, 'she had a bad reputation, as not having lived chastely' (*Luc.* ch. 1). Lucullus' own proverbial self-indulgence is thus in part ascribed to her influence, although Plutarch observes further that his father was an outright crook ἑαλώ κλοπῆς, 'he was convicted of embezzlement').

(7) Helvia, the mother of Cicero, was clearly higher in class than her husband; for Plutarch informs us that they say she καὶ γεγονέναι καλῶς καὶ βεβιωκέναι, 'was noble in birth and in conduct of life' (*Cic.* ch. 1). The Tullii Cicerones, like the Marii who were related to them, apparently liked to

'marry upward' and thereby to gain valuable cognate connections for their sons.

(8) Caesar, on the other hand, was the issue of an alliance at the end of the second century between two patrician families who needed allies, his own *gens Iulia* and the Aurelii. Women of both houses were major influences upon him, but especially his mother Aurelia, who, as in so many of these stories, survived her husband through their son's adolescence and young adulthood. She lived, in fact, to hear her son say, as he left for an electoral assembly: Ὦ μῆτερ, τήμερον ἢ ἀρχιερέα τὸν υἱὸν ἢ φυγάδα ὄψει, 'Mother, today you will see your son either Pontifex Maximus or an exile' (*Caes.* ch. 7). One should note that Plutarch melodramatically describes the elderly lady οὐκ ἀδακρυτί 'not without tears'; yet as one who had been through so many crises with her audacious son it could be doubted whether at this crisis she lost her composure. His being with her that morning probably indicates the value he attached not only to her person, but also to her advice and support. Caesar's younger contemporary and lifelong arch enemy

(9) Cato the Younger, had likewise a noble woman for mother, a Livia, daughter of a consular and sister to the Italians' patron just before the Social War, the tribune Livius Drusus. She had been previously married to Servilius Caepio, an Optimate leader, and therefore offered in her life story and in her affinities quite a range of choices, and much personal experience to her son, whose father appears to have died when he was very young. Thanks to his widowed mother, Porcius Cato was brought up in Uncle Drusus' home, and received an excellent education as well as some vital lessons in *Realpolitik*.

(10) Mark Antony was son of a Julia, who was related to the line of the Caesars and who, Plutarch says, imposed some restraint upon the prodigal Antonius *père* until his death; from that time on, that is from the time little Mark was ten years old or so, she raised him, probably without much help from his step-father Cornelius Lentulus – who would himself be executed by Cicero in 63, when Antonius *fils* was about twenty years old and still several years away from the first steps in a public career. Her Julian strain seems to have brought her son to the attention of Julius Caesar, with fateful results throughout the last decades of his life. Finally there is

(11) Marcus Brutus. Two prominent Servilias were half-sisters of Cato the Younger, and were, like him, raised by the aforementioned Livia. Brutus' mother was one of these, and was indeed one of the most remarkable women of her day.[2] Caesar is reported to have been an admirer, and an erstwhile lover of this Servilia, so that she was able to get Brutus nicely connected among the Populares despite her husband's and own ancestors' traditional conservatism.

Through all of this Plutarch pays little attention to family-factional affiliations and combinations, and virtually none at all to the role of the Livias and

Servilias of the Late Republic in family *consilia*, just as if they were mere Greek women, heeded as little as Aristophanes' Lysistrata and her co-conspirators had been until they took fantastic action.

At this point we should observe that this frequent biographical 'matrix' of Plutarch's, however often it recurs, does not suggest to him a social principle. He never comments, never generalizes on the phenomenon of powerful widowed Roman mothers. Such mothers are simply there, without explanation, not to provide a manly example of how to conduct affairs of state (as a good Greek father would do), but instead to give personal, emotional exhortation, and very often to offer familial ties that encouraged a young Roman to advance further in prestige and power than his late father had done. Plutarch, however, misses the point about how important these women were, not only to fill voids left by orphanhood, but as such sources of counsel and mediums of power in their own right as non-royal Greek mothers seldom, if ever, were.

Significant wives also deserve our attention, even though very young women usually married only when their *viri* were already formed in character and committed as rising politicians. Caesar's teenage marriage to Cinna's daughter was unusual. Another limiting fact must also be noted: first spouses were seldom the last ones for groom or bride because many marriages ended suddenly either with divorce, which was much more common among Romans of the political classes than among Greeks; the wife's death in childbirth; or by the man's death in battle or other violence.

Space does not permit me here to relate everything that could be said about the wives of all the Romans that Plutarch deals with in Roman *Lives*. Nevertheless, some of them play such a conspicuous role, as partners in their husbands' enterprises, that we must take notice.

Again with the exception of Romulus and Coriolanus, there were no fewer than thirteen Romans of the *Lives* with a wife (or two or three!) who had a major impact upon their achievement or fate. Two of these wives are so striking in Plutarch that Shakespeare, using the Elizabethan English translation by Sir Thomas North as his source, dramatized them in moving interaction with their famous husbands in his *Tragedy of Julius Caesar*:

(1) Caesar's last of three wives, loving and loyal Calpurnia, daughter of a consular ally of her husband; and

(2) Marcus Brutus' beloved Porcia, whose late father Cato had been Caesar's implacable foe.

The other eleven Romans with politically helpful wives were:

(3) Numa Pompilius, a Sabine, who married the only child of the Sabine co-king Titus Tatius, Tatia of course, and (whatever Plutarch insists about Numa's reluctance to rule) thereby clearly put himself in a politically advantageous position.

(4) Cato the Elder, who for his first wife married a woman of higher pedigree than his own, a patrician Licinia. Not a wealthy woman, Plutarch says, since Cato esteemed intrinsic nobility more than money, but well connected.

(5) The older Gracchus brother, Tiberius, who married an Appia Claudia from a remarkable demagogic patrician line much vilified in the conservative tradition.

(6) Marius, whose alliance by marriage to a Popularis patrician family, the Julii, has already been remarked.

(7) Sulla, who consolidated his position as a darling of the most deeply entrenched element among the Roman nobility by marrying a Caecilia Metella, his third wife, at age fifty. During the crisis of 85 this woman took brave measures to save her family, fleeing with her children from Rome to Greece, and urged her husband to return home from the Mithridatic War to combat the radical tyranny of Cinna and Carbo. She was obviously an emissary of her family and her class.[3]

(8) Lucullus, who, as great a philanderer as Sulla, likewise made some political capital by marrying as his third wife a Clodia of the Appii Claudii, and then, as his fourth, the second of those Servilias already mentioned as half-sisters of Cato and daughters of the *grande dame* Livia.

(9) Pompey's first marriage to an Antistia was, like the first marriage of many others, inconsequential and very temporary. His second wife Aemilia, however, brought him abruptly into partisan politics, for she was a stepdaughter of Sulla, who ordered her married to young Pompey although she was pregnant by her previous husband. Pompey freely chose his third wife Mucia, with excellent and venerable pedigree, but then just as freely abandoned her, not because of her notorious unfaithfulness (*Pomp.* ch. 42), but so he could marry Julia, the daughter of his triumviral colleague Caesar. His fifth and last wife, after the adored Julia's untimely death in childbirth, was a Republican Cornelia, very young and very talented. Plutarch has a great deal to say in Chapter 55 of the *Life of Pompey* about this charming daughter of the despicable Metellus Scipio, but nothing, really, about her fatal influence upon the 'great' generalissimo during the crisis that led to Pharsalus. Even though her prior confidence in Pompey's victory does come out, Plutarch dwells instead upon the pathos of her reunion with her unexpectedly defeated husband after the battle (chs. 75 and 76).

(10) Cicero, who abandoned his honest wife Terentia, her substantial dowry notwithstanding, because he could marry a pretty younger woman, really just a girl, who was even wealthier, to please him in his late middle age and to get him out of considerable debt. Yet Terentia, probably of noble class, had been a power. She played an important intermediary role in the Catilinarian crisis, bringing (she said) word from the Vestal Virgins that Cicero should be re-

solute in his planned course of action. She apparently did sharpen his resolve. Plutarch adds parenthetically καὶ γὰρ οὐδ' ἄλλως ἦν πραεῖά τις οὐδ' ἄτολμος τὴν φύσιν, ἀλλὰ φιλότιμος γυνὴ καὶ μᾶλλον ... τῶν πολιτικῶν μεταλαμβάνουσα παρ' ἐκείνου φροντίδων ἢ μεταδίδουσα τῶν οἰκιακῶν ἐκείνῳ, 'indeed she was never a meek person nor lacking boldness in nature, but was an ambitious woman, and readier to take a part in his political counsels than to give him a share in household matters' (*Cic.* ch. 20). Yet another exceptional, even a somewhat unnatural woman, the Greek writer seems to mean. But perhaps she was not so exceptional in Rome!

(11) Cato the Younger. This dour man was involved in one of the oddest of all political transactions with his wife, ex-wife, and again wife Marcia, whom he loaned, as it were, to an important ally, the orator Hortensius. Plutarch (*Cat. Min.* chs. 25 and 52), although with less pathos than the Roman poet Lucan (*De Bello Civili* 2.326-391), tries to make the nasty business noble or at least morally acceptable. She herself, daughter of the consular fence-sitter Marcius Philippus whose consent was necessary for this to happen, may well have been a willing participant in a dance of alliances so much the more sordid because of Cato's hypocritical comments on other political marriages (*Caes.* ch. 14) and his ostentatious refusal to undertake one himself. The *Life of Pompey* relates how Cato, despite the wishes of his sister and his wife, refused to marry a niece of his to the Triumvir Pompey (*Pomp.* ch. 44; cf. *Cato Min.* ch. 30).

(12) Mark Antony, whose wife Fulvia played an extraordinary role in diplomacy and even in military affairs to defend her husband's interests, his widely known unfaithfulness to her notwithstanding. She was true to him till the end, and true as well to her Fulvian family's political home on the popular Left: widow of Publius Clodius, widow of Scribonius Curio! Antony's last *Roman* wife, Caesar Octavian's sister Octavia, was a different story, equally sad: a sacrifice to her brother's political maneuvering. She is quite a major character in Chapters 31 through 57 in the *Life* of her unloving husband, according to which she seems to have been her brother's instrument, in separation as in marriage, as a well-publicized deserted wife and mother in the Caesarian propaganda of the 30s BC.

(13) Otho, who saved himself and procured a province, albeit a remote one (Lusitania), by surrendering his beautiful Poppaea to Nero, first indulged himself in adultery, then in remarriage.

Divorce, of course, was as important a device as marriage for the Romans. The women in most cases seem to have been powerless, particularly when an aging Sulla or a Cicero (or an Aemilius Paulus) became enamored of some sweet young thing. The frequency of divorce seems to have made some of the divorcees exceptionally self-reliant; and every intelligent woman of the upper class must have been ever ready to live a new life, as a widow, as a deserted wife, or as some new person's wife, rearing children of her own by more than one husband and/or stepchildren.

Daughters and sisters are self-evidently important persons, their fathers' or brothers' pawns in the game of alliances. Among the most striking of these are Caesar's daughter Julia, Caesar Octavian's sister Octavia, and, not politically exploited yet equally sad, Cicero's Tullia.[4]

Non-related women also played major roles. Besides plenty of mistresses, some, like Cleopatra, non-Roman, there were other powerful women like Fannia, the considerate enemy of Marius, and the outrageous Clodia, Cicero's nemesis. In their likes Plutarch the Greek seems to see monsters, unnatural, unwomanly figures, resembling Aeschylus' Clytemnestra or Euripides' Medea. We see Roman women.

Two legendary episodes – those of Romulus and the Sabine Women, among them the king's wife Hersilia; and of Coriolanus and the patrician women of Rome, including his mother and wife – will show concretely how Plutarch de-Romanized exemplary Roman women. These early stories, legend rather than solid history, permitted more creative license than later ones, and greater flexibility in treating his sources, of which the chief ones evidently were Livy and Dionysius of Halicarnassus.

First, the Sabines. These women reconciled the Roman men, who had seized them at the inaugural Consualia festival, with their Sabine fathers and brothers, who had gone to war to punish that violation of hospitality and to recover them. Dionysius, Plutarch's favorite source for the earlier antiquities of Rome, tells their story in an unusually restrained manner. One noteworthy feature of his account is that Romulus addresses women from two Sabine towns he has conquered, Caenina and Antemnae, promising to make their people one with his Romans in settlement and in polity (*Ant. Rom.* 2.35). This anticipates the event, of course, but also embodies a principle of Roman government, much admired by Dionysius, that defeated enemies be incorporated into the Roman state (2.16). Therefore, when the rest of the Sabines and the Romans are ready to square off for a decisive battle, and the women intervene, the plan of fusing the two nations is nothing new – and not the women's, but rather that of Romulus. Indeed they pathetically implore Tatius and the Sabines; yet (a) they have the express permission of the Roman proto-senate (συνέδριον) to do so, and (b) they promote an established policy of Romulus that he himself has explained to them. On the other hand, it is the women's own idea to make such an appeal to their birth-relatives. They decide to do so at a meeting by themselves, with no men present. Hersilia is their leader. Dionysius explains that she was perhaps the only married woman that Romulus' men seized among the maidens on the occasion that provoked the war in the first place, and thus perhaps a bit wiser and more mature. Dionysius does not associate her with Romulus, however.[5] In fact, the women do not interpose themselves dramatically on the battlefield, but rather visit the camp of the Sabine army. Dionysius uncharacteristically passes up the chance to compose a dramatic speech, writing merely that Ἑρσιλία μακρὰν καὶ συμπαθῆ διέξηλθε δέησιν, ἀξιοῦσα χαρίσασθαι τὴν εἰρήνην ταῖς δεομέναις ὑπὲρ τῶν ἀνδρῶν, δι' ἃς ἐξενηνέχθαι τὸν πόλεμον ἀπέφαινεν, 'Hersilia made a long and moving plea, urging that they should rightly grant the favor of peace to women who sought it on behalf of their husbands – women because of whom, she pointed out, the war had been joined' (2.45). The whole delegation of women and their children then threw themselves to the ground and lay there, until the men raised them back to their feet and promised to accept reasonable terms from the Romans – which, of course, they did receive and accept, making the two peoples officially one, as the children their women had borne were already doing in fact.

Livy the Roman tells the tale quite differently, in a form probably more familiar. The Romans have defeated the Sabine Antemnates and occupied their city. Hersilia is again involved. *Victoria ovantem Romulum, Hersilia coniunx, precibus raptarum fatigata, orat ut parentibus earum det veniam et in civitatem accipiat: ita rem coalescere concordia posse. Facile impetratum*, 'as Romulus celebrated the victory, his wife Hersilia, wearied by the pleas of the Sabine women, begged him to pardon their fathers and receive them into the citizen body: thus the affair could end in harmony and union. She easily won her request' (*Hist.* 1.11). But the war continued. The Sabines attacked Rome, and confronted the Romans on the low ground between the Capitoline and Palatine hills. The battle was hard fought. Jupiter Stator stayed a Roman retreat. The Romans had the upper hand, when the Sabine women ran out between the very battle-lines, pleading that the war end, *hinc patres hinc viros orantes ...ne parricidio macularent partus suos, nepotum illi, hi liberum progeniem*, 'begging their fathers on one side, husbands on the other ...not to pollute with parricide the children the women had borne, grandsons of the one party, legitimate sons of the other' (1.13). *Si adfinitatis inter vos, si conubii piget*, they said, *in nos vertite iras. Nos causa belli ...melius peribimus quam sine alteris vestrum viduae aut orbae vivemus*, 'If you disdain relationship by lawful marriage between your peoples, turn your wrath against us. We are the cause of the war ...Better we shall die, than live without one group or the other of you, as widows or as orphans'. It works, *Movet res cum multitudinem tum duces*: The appeal moves troops and commanders alike. The nations combine.

Contrast Plutarch's version, in the *Life of Romulus*. Romulus not only spared but incorporated into his nascent state first the Sabines of the town Caenina that he conquered early in the Sabine War, and thereafter those of Fidenae,

Crustumerium, and Antemnae. No mention of women. Then the Battle of Rome was joined. The defending Romans had first the worse, later somewhat the better of the fight against Tatius' Sabines Ἐνταῦθα δ' αὐτοὺς ὥσπερ ἐξ ὑπαρχῆς μάχεσθαι παρασκευαζομένους ἔπεσχε δεινὸν ἰδεῖν θέαμα καὶ λόγου κρεῖττων ὄψις, 'at this point as they were preparing to renew the combat, they were checked by a remarkable spectacle, a sight beyond description' (*Rom.* Ch. 19). The women rushed between the opposed armies ὥσπερ ἐκ θεοῦ κάτοχοι ... πᾶσαι δ' ἀνακαλούμεναι τοῖς φιλτάτοις ὀνόμασι ποτὲ μὲν τοὺς Σαβίνους, ποτὲ δὲ τοὺς Ῥωμαίους, 'as if possessed by a god ...all of them calling out with terms of greatest endearment on one side to the Sabines, on the other to the Romans'. The warriors stopped, stood, and listened. The women then proceeded into a fine speech, too long to quote in full, that begins with the pathetic rhetorical question, Τί γὰρ ὑμᾶς δεινὸν ἢ λυπηρὸν ἐργασάμεναι, τὰ μὲν ἤδη πεπόνθαμεν, τὰ δὲ πάσχομεν τῶν σχετλίων κακῶν; 'What awful or hurtful thing have we done to you, that we have endured dire sufferings already before, and are enduring them now?' They continued with reasonable arguments. These arguments, however, consisted mainly of appeals to love and to pity; and they were addressed almost entirely to the Sabines. Hersilia spoke, among others. (According to Plutarch, Hersilia was probably the wife of the Roman Hostius Hostilius, not of Romulus, although he is aware of the other tradition. See *Rom.* ch. 14.) Truce was made and the Sabines became citizens of Rome and Quirites.

What the biographer has done here is to remove the deliberateness and the politics from the women, something that even his fellow Greek Dionysius allowed them (although, as we saw, he insisted upon Senatorial authority for their intervention). Instead Plutarch makes them as pathetic as possible. His women do not present a balanced argument to husbands as well as to fathers; they plead not as citizens to the Romans to make one state, but rather, as daughters to the Sabines, their fathers, to make peace with their de facto sons-in-law. In contrast to the women in Livy, moreover, Hersilia and her compatriot women are not consciously advancing Romulus' programme of unification; and, of course, they do not bravely offer themselves as targets for misguided violence, as they do in the Roman historian's account. According to our Greek, they are inspired, 'as if by a god', not wise in themselves. (This is not to minimize the emotional intensity of Livy's Sabine women. They, however, *victo malis muliebri pavore, ausae se inter tela volantia inferre*, 'their womanish fear overcome by their evil plight, dared to bring themselves between the volleys of javelins'. They assessed the situation and acted in the only way they could. At most Plutarch allows them pathetic reasoning, but nothing of what could be called in Latin *virtus*, the excellence of a man and a citizen.)

Finally we have the legend of Coriolanus. The basic story is familiar. Accounts by both Dionysius of Halicarnassus and Livy are again before Plutarch as he composes his own version. Dionysius is quite enthusiastic about the entire history of Coriolanus, which he tells at considerable length (and with several lengthy speeches) in Books Six through Eight of his Ῥωμαϊκὴ ἀρχαιολογία. The outline of events is as follows, starting after Marcius Coriolanus carried the Volscian War onto the *ager Romanus* and almost to the walls of the City: First, the Romans had sent as ambassadors Marcius' best friends in the Senate, and then ten distinguished consulars to ask the enemy leader to relent in his campaign against his native land. Both embassies failed. At that point, according to Dionysius, the senators' wives, panicked ὡς ἐγγὺς ὄντος ἤδη τοῦ δεινοῦ, καταλιποῦσαι τῆς οἴκοι μονῆς τὸ εὐπρεπὲς ἔθεον ἐπὶ τὰ τεμένη τῶν θεῶν ὀλοφυρόμεναί τε καὶ προκυλιόμεναι τῶν ξοάνων, 'because a terrible outcome was imminent, abandoning the decorousness of staying home, they ran into the temples of the gods, lamenting and bowing to the ground before the statues' (8.39). Then Valeria, sister to the late great patrician leader Publicola, brought them back to their senses and gathered a group of noble matrons who, with her, approached Volumnia (here Coriolanus' wife) and Veturia (the name used in this account for Coriolanus' mother). The old lady was at first very reluctant to help, since she did not know how she could rightly ask her son to relax his indignation against a nation that had wronged him. But finally, after a second long speech by Valeria, Veturia agreed to join the women's mission. Before they set out, however, Valeria brought the idea before the Senate. A heated deliberation took place there. Should the Roman government allow all the noble women to go (potential hostages, if Coriolanus wished) or only those related to the man? All were allowed to go.

Veturia approached her son, who received her in respectful silence. He greeted his wife, too, but asked his mother to say whatever she came to say. She insisted upon doing so in public. First she wept a brief while. A speech followed from each. Coriolanus interrupted his mother urging mightily that she stand by him in his indignation against Rome. In her lengthy reply, six chapters long, we eventually learn (8.51) that she had been widowed when Marcius was quite young, had raised him alone, had never remarried – thus imposing a stepfather on him and causing her own loyalties to be divided – not even after he had reached adulthood and entered public life. She included some arguments for the Volscians' ears, about the advantages of peace and friendship with the Romans. She threatened to kill herself, bringing a curse upon her son who, if he did not yield to her, would be guilty of her death. Her very last words refer to her next, shocking gesture: Ταῦτ' εἰποῦσα ἔρριψεν ἑαυτὴν χαμαὶ καὶ περιπλέξασα ταῖς χερσὶν ἀμφοτέραις τοὺς πόδας τοῦ

Μαρκίου κατεφίλησε, 'after saying this, she threw herself to the ground and, with both her hands embracing Marcius' feet, she kissed them' (8.54). The other women burst into tears and groans, the Volscian men averted their gaze from such a dreadful scene. Coriolanus relented.

Livy's much more concise version of the same legendary episode differs in several salient features. The entire intervention of the women transpires in a single chapter, 40, of Livy's *Ab Urbe condita*, Book Two. The second state embassy in his account consisted of *priests* in their sacred garb. They fail: no help from the supernatural here. A group of *matronae* approach Veturia (which here, too, is the name of Coriolanus' mother). The Roman historian adds: *Id publicum consilium an muliebris timor fuerit, parum invenio; pervicere certe, ut et Veturia magno natu mulier et Volumnia duos parvos ex Marcio ferens filios secum in castra hostium irent, et, quoniam armis viri defendere urbem non possent, mulieres precibus lacrimisque defenderent*, 'Whether this was by state policy or the result of womanish fear, I have too little evidence to say; but they certainly prevailed, so that old Veturia and, bringing the two infant boys of Marcius with her, Volumnia went into the camp of the enemy and, seeing that the men could not defend the city with weapons, the women did so with pleas and tears' (2.40). In Livy, Coriolanus' first reaction to the female delegation is gruff; but he softens when he sees his mother with her daughter-in-law and grandsons. *Prope ut amens consternatus* – therefore, 'extremely upset!' – he moves to embrace her. *Sine, priusquam complexum accipio, sciam ... ad hostem an ad filium venerim, captiva materne in castris tuis sim*, 'Wait: I must know, before I accept your embrace, whether I have come to an enemy of the state or to a son, whether I am a prisoner of war or your mother in your camp'. She says rather little, but all to the point. He is a traitor to his country if he persists. She calmly hints that defeat of Rome would kill her, and maybe the rest of his family as well. *Nec, ut miserrima sum, diu futura sum; de his videris, quos, si pergis, aut inmatura mors aut longa servitus manet*, 'I, in my awful misery, will not live long; but consider these [that is, his wife and sons] who face either untimely death [the boys] or long enslavement [their young mother]'. His wife and children embrace him, but his mother does not, whom we imagine to stand firm, facing him. However, the rest of the women weep and bemoan the imminent fate of themselves and their fatherland. He relents.

Now to Plutarch. Plutarch names Coriolanus' women differently, following neither Dionysius nor Livy. Furthermore, he turns Livy's doubt about whether or not the women had public authorization to try a desperate final appeal to Marcius, which they did have according to Dionysius, into a negative certainty: their mission in the *Life of Coriolanus* is purely private. Let us look closer. The women gather for supplication in the temples, with Valeria, as according to Dionysius. However, in Plutarch this *grande dame* πάθος ἐξαπίνης παθοῦσα, καὶ κατ' ἐπίνοιαν οὐκ ἀθείαστον ἁψαμένη τοῦ συμφέροντος, αὐτή τε ἀνέστη καὶ τὰς ἄλλας ἀναστήσασα πάσας, 'suddenly felt a strong compulsion [such as Plutarch has just digressed to describe] and seizing upon the suitable action in accordance with a divine inspiration, herself rose and made the all the others do the same' (ch. 33). They went straight to Volumnia, Coriolanus' mother in this account, and appealed to her and to Vergilia, her daughter-in-law, οὔτε βουλῆς ψηφισαμένης οὔτ' ἄρχοντος κελεύσαντος, 'neither by resolution of the Senate nor at a consul's command.' Instead, a god took pity and instructed them. They could surpass the fame even of the Sabine women[6] if they should succeed in saving the state at the present crisis. Here, old Volumnia shows no reluctance. She immediately agrees to do what she can for the fatherland (never mind the injustice Rome has done her son), though she is uncertain whether it will be enough. When the women[7] enter the Volscian camp, pity seizes all who see them – except, initially, Coriolanus himself. He, however, subsequently γενόμενος δὲ τοῦ πάθους ἐλάττων καὶ συνταραχθεὶς πρὸς τὴν ὄψιν, 'overcome by emotion and thoroughly distressed at the sight' (34), leaves his seat of command and runs to meet his women. The expatriate commander greets and embraces all his family, beginning with his mother. Then she speaks. She reasons well with him, using several of the arguments that Veturia had deployed in Dionysius; but she also explicitly mentions her possible death. She suggests that her son will have to attack Rome over her dead body, whether she will kill herself or will stand defensively before the city. Then she threatens and uses the same 'last hope' (ἐσχάτη ἐλπίς) as Dionysius' Veturia, throwing herself at his feet, where his wife and children immediately join her. He gives in, as usual.

Much of this is modelled upon Dionysius, although wordiness and melodramatic pathos are notably reduced. Once again in Plutarch the women are distinctly unpolitical. Nor are they quite rational, inspired as they are to actions, and presumably also to words and accompanying gestures, by divine Providence, just as in Plutarch's story of their ancestresses the Sabines. The mother does not use her maternal dignity and authority, except to sacrifice it by abject grovelling at the end of her speech. She has none of the imperious grandeur of Livy's terse Veturia. This is especially striking because we have in Plutarch's Volumnia yet another widow-mother. (Livy knows, or says, nothing at all about this circumstance.) In the opening Chapters of the *Coriolanus* Plutarch provides a memorable story of how the fatherless boy was raised by his mother, and paradoxically attained an almost unique degree of ἀνδρεία, *virtus*, the martial virtue of a *man*. Ἦν δὲ τοῖς μὲν ἄλλοις ἡ δόξα τῆς ἀρετῆς τέλος, ἐκείνῳ δὲ τῆς δόξης ἡ τῆς μητρὸς εὐφροσύνη, we read in Chapter 4, 'while other men's goal was to be famous for excellence, his was the satisfaction of his mother in his fame'. And yet, when he grew up, and she grew old, her ultimate appeal to him could only be womanish and personal, not authoritative, not political, not *Roman* because, although he portrayed numerous Roman women – many of them, as we have seen, in detail, often in admiring detail – Plutarch the Greek never really comprehended their distinctiveness as noble parents and noble consorts to those noble men whose achievements, triumphs, and tragedies he related. His purpose, of course, was to draw moral examples from the lives of the great men whose lives he reviewed; an unintended corollary, on the other hand, was to belittle the great women who often guided – or misguided – those men.

Notes

1. We must therefore greatly regret the loss of Plutarch's biographies of some of the Julio-Claudians: Tiberius, Gaius Caligula, and Nero!
2. In independent-mindedness this Servilia ranked with the notorious Sempronia, known from Sallust's *Catiline* (ch. 25), whom Plutarch, perhaps to his considerable relief, never had to treat.
3. Later still Sulla wedded a much younger woman, Valeria, out of sheer lust, as Plutarch describes the event in *Sull.* chs. 35-36.
4. How much we have lost in Plutarch's *Life of Augustus*, where we would not only have found his interesting daughter to contemplate but also his granddaughters, his mother Atia and *her* mother, Grandmother Julia – that is, Caesar's sister Julia, who is not mentioned in the *Life of Caesar*; and, of course, Livia Augusta could not but have received a great deal of attention!
5. Whether he knew of a tradition that made her Romulus's wife is not clear: he mentions no Roman husband at all.
6. Plutarch himself therefore is conscious of the similarity between these two cases where women had to save the Roman state.
7. The women here may be *only* those of Coriolanus' family, unaccompanied by other *patriciae*.

CHAPTER 12

The Ox, the Crow, and the Orator:
Image, Allegory, and Motive in Dio Chrysostom's *Second Tarsian Oration* (*Oration* 34)

R. Anthony Kugler

In his thirty-fourth oration, one of two delivered in the city of Tarsus, Dio Chrysostom introduces two images, the fable of the ox and the crow in chapters five and six and the boxing metaphor of chapters twelve and thirteen, that together bear meaningfully upon the project of self-characterization that he undertakes there. By setting Dio's performance into its sociohistorical context, I demonstrate, in particular, the extent to which these images extend the range of Dio's persona, transforming him from a mere announcer of the divine will to an enforcer of it. As a final point, I argue that Dio equates divine will – in this case, at least – with Roman Imperial will.

Among the most distinctive characteristics of Tarsus at the end of the first century AD are these: it apparently enjoyed the status of a 'free' city,[1] exempt from Imperial levies, and it was decidedly plutocratic, its citizens assembly open only to those able to pay a poll tax of 500 dr.[2] It is to these fortunates that Dio addresses himself.[3] In his opening statement to them, Dio introduces an issue that will animate much of what follows: namely, the tendency to prefer as speakers those who have performed liturgies and have done so admirably. By definition, then, these are men possessed of both citizenship and considerable means. Dio questions the wisdom of such limitations, noting that in other fields discrimination is based not on wealth or civil status but on talent. He then dwells on the implications of this situation for someone like himself, whose physical appearance resembles that of the prestige- and property-scorning Cynics but who nevertheless has something of substance to say. This emphasis on appearance is perhaps the clearest manifestation of Dio's desire to create a distinctive persona in Tarsus, a carefully constructed identity quite unlike the prosperous burgermeister visible in the Bithynian speeches. In this context, the seemingly offhand reference to his studiously unkempt countenance serves in part as a thematic template for the rest of the oration; as the boxing metaphor, in particular, will vividly demonstrate, appearances, and the preconceptions they generate in the minds of onlookers, matter. Tarsus is not the only town where Dio chooses to play the wandering, other-worldly Cynic, but it is there that he achieves the most seamless integration of theme and persona. In pointing to his physical appearance, the speaker points to his project. It is apt material, then, for an introduction.

At this point Dio elaborates upon two assumptions triggered, he contends, by his appearance: namely, that those who dress as he does are crazy and that, as a philosopher, he bears some deep affinity with certain philosophers who recently felt the just wrath of an offended Tarsian populace. Both preconceptions are summarily dismissed. In the latter case, Dio destroys the assumption's central thesis by denying one of its premises; the individuals who earned the opprobrium of the Tarsians were not philosophers, for true philosophers, of whom the speaker himself is an implicit but obvious model, avoid the sort of malicious mischief characteristic of the others.

The first preconception, namely that the speaker is crazy and thus unreliable, is handled differently. Here Dio takes advantage of the wide semantic range of μαίνομαι (*mainomai*), deliberately blurring the distinction between ordinary madness and the kind of divinely inspired, prophetic madness that reveals the truth to those willing and able to perceive it. In sum, Dio's argument is this: if he appears crazy, if he wears wretched clothes and speaks without the 'normal' motivations of money or friendship, that is merely a sign of his 'other-worldliness', his privileged access to the divine fount of truth. As such he resembles birds of omen, though his messages lack the obscurity and ambiguity of augury.

Here Dio is able to make an apparently effortless and spontaneous transition to the fable of the ox and the crow:

καίτοι τὰ μὲν τῶν οἰωνῶν εἰκάζειν δεῖ, τῶν δὲ ὑπ᾽ ἐμοῦ λεγομένων ἔστιν ἀκούσασι συνιέναι καὶ σκέψασθαι, ἐὰν ἄρα σαφῶς ᾖ τι χρήσιμον. βούλομαι δέ, ἐπεὶ τῶν τοιούτων ἐμνήσθην, ἐν Φρυγίᾳ τι συμβὰν εἰπεῖν, ἵν᾽ εὐθὺς ἐνθένδε μου καταγελᾶν ἔχητε. ἀνὴρ Φρὺξ ἐπὶ κτήνους ἐβάδιζεν. ὡς δ᾽ ἐθεάσατό τινα κορώνην, οἰωνισάμενος, οἱ γὰρ Φρύγες τὰ τοιαῦτα δεινοί, λίθῳ βάλλει καί πως τυγχάνει αὐτῆς. πάνυ οὖν ἥσθη, καὶ νομίσας εἰς ἐκείνην τετράφθαι τὸ χαλεπὸν ἀναιρεῖται καὶ ἀναβὰς ἤλαυνεν. ἡ δὲ μικρὸν διαλιποῦσα ἀνέσφηλε· τὸ δὲ κτῆνος πτοηθὲν ἀποβάλλει τὸν ἄνδρα, καὶ ὃς πεσὼν κατάγνυσι τὸ σκέλος. ἐκεῖνος μὲν οὖν οὕτως ἀπήλλαξεν, ἀχάριστος γενόμενος περὶ τὸ σύμβολον. ἐγὼ δὲ πολύ μοι δοκῶ τῆς κορώνης ἀσφαλέστερον βεβουλεῦσθαι καὶ πρὸς εὐγνωμονεστέρους ἄνδρας ἥκειν τοῦ Φρυγός. ἐὰν γὰρ ὑμῖν δοκῶ φλυαρεῖν, οὐ δήπου λίθοις βαλεῖτέ με, ἀλλὰ θορυβήσετε.

Yet it is necessary to make inferences about the doings of birds, but on the other hand it is possible for those who have listened to the things said by me to understand and to consider if in fact [what I've said] is something useful. But, since I've made mention of such things, I want to tell something that happened in Phrygia, so that straightaway here you may have a chance to laugh at me. A Phrygian man was making his way on a ox, but when he saw a crow, having interpreted the bird sign, for the Phrygians are clever at such things, he cast at it with a stone and somehow hit it. Accordingly he was very pleased, and thinking that he had turned his bad luck toward the bird, he picked it up, mounted his ox, and rode off. But after a short time the crow recovered and the ox, terrified, threw off the man, who fell and broke his leg. Thus did he fare, ungrateful as he was for the sign. But I seem to myself to have planned much more safely than the crow and to have come to men more thoughtful than the Phrygian. For if I seem to you to speak nonsense, surely you will not cast at me with stones, but raise a commotion. (34.5-6).

Pace Crosby and Cohoon,[4] Dio is no Aesop, nor is his strange tale of the ox and the crow a mere fable, a pious and moralistic vignette of the sort familiar to every schoolchild. On the contrary, one suspects that Dio's story is perhaps not the most appropriate material for the young and impressionable. What is disturbing in Dio's tale is not the cast of the stone itself but the implications of its allegorical interpretation, a project explicitly endorsed by the speaker. In comparing himself to the crow and his audience to the Phrygian (ἐγὼ δὲ πολύ μοι δοκῶ τῆς κορώνης ἀσφαλέστερον βεβουλεῦσθαι καὶ πρὸς εὐγνωμονεστέρους ἄνδρας ἥκειν τοῦ Φρυγός.), Dio belies his own halfhearted attempt to portray the tale as nothing more than an amusing trifle, a brief diversion before the serious business at hand. Indeed, the story serves to underscore the seriousness of Dio's message by symbolizing the disastrous consequences of ignoring him. In a sense, then, it could be described as a meta-fable, a fable on the importance of listening to fables, metaphors, and other tools of the rhetorician's art. This self-referential quality and its implications for Dio's relationship with his Tarsian audience can best be seen, perhaps, through a detailed exegesis of the fable's primary motifs. As it is the identification of a particular motif as Dionic that promises the clearest evidence of the speaker's Tarsian agenda, we begin with the search for topical and thematic comparanda.

We note, first, that Dio's assertion of divine inspiration is not limited to this oration. In making the same claim before the people of Alexandria, however, Dio strikes a balance between allusiveness (note the echo of the Platonic Socrates in *daemonion*) and clarity that is lacking in Tarsus:

ἐγὼ μὲν γὰρ οὐκ ἀπ' ἐμαυτοῦ μοι δοκῶ προελέσθαι τοῦτο, ἀλλ' ὑπὸ δαιμονίου τινὸς γνώμης. ὧν γὰρ οἱ θεοὶ προνοοῦσιν, ἐκείνοις παρασκευάζουσι καὶ συμβούλους ἀγαθοὺς αὐτομάτους καὶ λόγους ἐπιτηδείους καὶ ξυμφέροντας εἰρῆσθαι.

For I do not think that I have chosen this by myself, but by the will of some *daemonion*. For those for whom the gods have concern – for those men the gods provide good and spontaneous advisors and useful arguments and beneficial ones. (32.12).

Before proceeding, we need to inquire into Dio's motives for such stylistic *variatio*. Why a parable in Tarsus but not in Alexandria? Indeed, given Dio's own characterization of the typical Alexandrian audience as immature and overly fond of jokes,[5] the story of the ox and the crow would seem more appropriate there than among the politically minded elite of Tarsus.

Dio's own representation of his motives here is of little use by itself. He introduces the parable, he tells us, for two reasons: (1) his mention of augury in chapters four (ἀετοὺς μὲν καὶ ἱέρακας προσμαίνειν ἀνθρώποις...) and five (...τὰ μὲν τῶν οἰωνῶν εἰκάζειν...) called it to mind; and (2) it offers the audience an immediate opportunity to laugh *at him* (emphasis mine):

Βούλομαι δέ, ἐπεὶ τῶν τοιούτων ἐμνήσθην, ἐν Φρυγίᾳ τι συμβὰν εἰπεῖν, ἵν᾽ εὐθὺς ἐνθένδε μου καταγελᾶν ἔχητε. (34.5).

But, since I made mention of such things, I want to tell something that happened in Phrygia, in order that you may right away here have the opportunity to laugh at me.

The first of these is acceptable, though not for the reason implied; the story might indeed spring suddenly to the forefront of consciousness, not because the incident it relates occurred recently, but because its central conceit, that sophists resemble birds of omen in their foresight and perspicacity, seems to have been a longstanding and familiar one. Philostratus, for one, seems thoroughly at ease with the general idea (i.e. sophist=oracle) of Dio's simile, extending it with considerable wit to the realms of style and stage manner.[6] A sophist *is* like an oracle; each uses deliberately obscure and enigmatic language, and each strives to sound as if in possession of true knowledge.

Here we have a clue to the meaning of Dio's second motive. As elsewhere, Dio presents himself in Tarsus as a plainspoken and straightforward speaker. Indeed, his Phrygian tale is immediately preceded by a reminder of the alleged simplicity of his orations:

καίτοι τὰ μὲν τῶν οἰωνῶν εἰκάζειν δεῖ, τῶν δὲ ὑπ᾽ ἐμοῦ λεγομένων ἔστιν ἀκούσασι συνιέναι καὶ σκέψασθαι, ἐὰν ἄρα σαφῶς ᾖ τι χρήσιμον.

Yet it is necessary to make inferences about the doings of birds, but on the other hand it is possible for those who have listened to the things said by me to understand and to consider if in fact [what I've said] is something useful. (34.5)

That this assertion by Dio of his oratorical straightforwardness is set against the enigmatic difficulties of augury appears paradoxical in light of the parable which follows, according to which Dio is comparable to a bird of omen. Admittedly, Dio does distinguish himself from the crow, but only in terms of planning – he has done so more carefully than the bird – not simplicity of expression. Which assertion, then, are we meant to take seriously? Is Dio as enigmatic as a bird of omen or not? The answer depends upon the individual audience member. To those uninitiated in Dio's verbal wizardry, he may indeed appear to be a simple, straightforward speaker, full of amusing anecdotes and charming flattery. To the rhetorically sophisticated listener, however, the idea that all is as it seems with Dio, that the story of the ox and the crow is the trifle it appears – is nothing short of laughable. In this context, the otherwise unintelligible use of the phrase μου καταγελᾶν 'to laugh *at* me', makes sense. Dio is playing the fool here, an idiot savant who fails to apprehend the import of his own words. The true fools, of course, are those in the audience who really are unaware of the joke.

It is difficult to estimate the relative numbers of sophisticates and neophytes in the audience. To judge from Dio's allegorizing, however, the latter seem to form a large majority; we recall here that the bumbling Phrygian who misapprehends the meaning of the crow's omen is explicitly compared to the audience at hand in Tarsus. As in the case of Dio and the crow, it is true that the comparison is made in the course of distinguishing the two; the Phrygian and the audience are not in fact so similar, because the latter is more considerate (… εὐγνωμονεστέρους ἄνδρας ἥκειν τοῦ Φρυγός). Nevertheless the essential similarity of their roles – both, after all, are the recipients of a message – is broad enough to suggest a close affinity in other respects as well. In other words, the fact that Dio sees no reason to qualify the comparison in terms of rhetorical sophistication ('Of course, you Tarsians are much more astute than that bumbling Phrygian …') strengthens one's suspicions that it is precisely that characteristic, rather than some vague notion of the need to be considerate of others, that motivates the comparison in the first place. Despite the speaker's claims to the contrary, the fable has very little to say on the issue of altruism; whether or not the Phrygian should have struck the crow with a stone is not a question of concern for the bird's well-being but of accepting the inevitability of the omen it represents. To cast a stone at such a creature is to fail to recognize the inescapable truth of its divinely-sanctioned message.

The implications of this paradigm for Dio's Tarsian listeners are ominous. The correspondences between Dio and the crow, on the one hand, and the Phrygian and the audience, on the other, imply a similarity of message as well. Our suspicions in this regard are borne out, in particular, by Dio's remarkable claim of divine inspiration:

μὴ γὰρ οἴεσθε ἀετοὺς μὲν καὶ ἱέρακας προσημαίνειν ἀνθρώποις τὸ δέον, καὶ τὴν παρὰ τῶν τοιούτων συμβουλὴν πιστὴν εἶναι διὰ τὸ αὐτόματον καὶ τὸ θεῖον, ἄνδρα δὲ ἀφιγμένον οὕτως καὶ μηδαμόθεν ὑμῖν προσήκοντα μὴ κατὰ τὸ δαιμόνιον ἥκειν ἐροῦντα καὶ συμβουλεύσοντα.

For you must not think that eagles and falcons foretell to mankind what is required of them and that the counsel derived from such creatures is trustworthy because of its spontaneity and its divine inspiration, while refusing to believe that a man who has come, as I have come, having no connection with you from any point of view, has come by divine guidance to address and counsel you.[7]

Like the crow, Dio is on a mission from God. His admonitions to the Tarsians do not spring from earthly motives – neighborly concern, perhaps, or a desire for some tangible expressions of gratitude. On the contrary, they are of a piece with the grand designs of heaven. Thus Dio deprives himself of a measure of free will; like the crow, he is merely a vehicle for the dissemination of divine mandates. He has arrived in Tarsus, it seems, despite himself.

Dio's reluctance to play the role of prophet is not surprising, for the message he bears is full of critical admonitions. Such chastisement is rarely received by its targets with unalloyed gratitude, as Jeremiah, among others, learned,[8] especially when its immediate source is an outsider, someone lacking membership in the social, economic, and political groupings that unite the targets and give them common cause. The danger Dio faces in Tarsus is real; that some audience members may not grasp the full import of his words says nothing about their ability to recognize that something untoward is going on, and to resent it. Like Jeremiah, Dio responds to that danger by invoking the authority of a higher power.

What, exactly, could an angry audience do to Dio? Consider again his conclusion to the fable: 'For if I seem to you to speak nonsense, surely you will not cast at me with stones, but merely cause a disturbance.' I submit that the violence alluded to here is thematically as well as structurally relevant. To mention stoning is to conjure up the whole range of antisocial behaviors to which a foreign speaker, pronouncing upon local topics of controversy without apparent invitation, potentially subjects himself. Seen in this light, stone-throwing and commotion-raising differ in seriousness, not in character. Both are direct challenges to the speaker's personal authority. Dio himself, in his remarks to the people of Alexandria, seems to regard the prospect of *thorubos* with palpable fear:

τάχ᾽ <ἂν> οὖν καὶ ὑμεῖς ἐμὲ θορύβῳ καταπίοιτε καὶ τῇ ταραχῇ, βουλόμενον ὑμᾶς ὠφελεῖν.

Perhaps you might swallow me up in your clamor and uproar, though I want to help you. (32.24).

To all appearances, the Tarsians seated before Dio are rather more tolerant, for the speaker's citation of their polite behavior in chapter six – i.e. immediately following the fable – cannot have been utterly implausible:

Φέρε οὖν, ἐπεὶ σιωπᾶτε καὶ ὑπομένετε, πρῶτον μὲν ἐκεῖνο, εἰ μὴ σαφῶς ἴστε, ἐπιδείξω, ὅτι δεῖσθε γνώμης ἐν τῷ παρόντι, καὶ τοιαῦτα ὑμῶν τὰ πράγματά ἐστιν ὥστε βουλῆς ἄξια εἶναι καὶ πολλῆς προνοίας·

Well now, since you are quiet and are bearing with me, I will first point out this one matter, namely that you are in need of counsel in the current circumstances, and your affairs are such as to be worthy of advice and a good deal of forethought. (34.6).

Thus Dio uses the topos of audience behavior to make the transition from his Phrygian fable to the situation at hand in Tarsus. Immediately apparent here is the extent to which the speaker deliberately predicates the tone and direction of the remainder of his oration upon the audience's reaction to his fable. Specifically, their subdued behavior, that is, their failure to respond audibly or physically, drives Dio to begin to unveil the meaning and relevance of the fable by explicating the current political climate (ἐν τῷ παρόντι) in Tarsus. He alone of those present is capable of doing so accurately, for only an outsider can hope to escape the perils of ignorance, fear, or self-interest:

ἔπειθ', [ἐπιδείξω] ὅτι μηδεὶς ὑμῖν δύναται ῥᾳδίως τούτων τὸ δέον παραινέσαι, οἱ μὲν ἀγνοίᾳ τοῦ συμφέροντος, οἱ δέ τινες καὶ δειλίᾳ τῇ πρὸς ὑμᾶς ἢ τῇ πρὸς ἑτέρους καὶ τὸ αὑτῶν ἴσως μᾶλλον ἔνιοι σκοποῦντες.

Then [I will show] that no one of these men [at hand] is able easily to advise you as to what is necessary, some through ignorance of what is beneficial, some even through fear of you or of others, and some, perhaps, because they are watching out rather for their own [personal] interests. (34.6).

It is an extraordinary position, one which calls into doubt the efficacy of one of the most basic communal institutions, the public assembly of citizens. The alternative Dio offers, namely that the city should heed his personal advice as that of a well-informed and benevolent outsider, is a blow to local autonomy and an integral part of the Imperial myth, according to which cities will inevitably collapse into strife and chaos without the guiding hand of a wise and kindly overseer. Thus is the message of Dio's fable – ignore me at your peril – reemphasized.

Much of the remainder of the speech can be characterized as the speaker's attempt to apply this lesson, expanded now to include other observers besides Dio, to a variety of Tarsian problems, both internal and external. Prominent among the latter is the city's dispute with its neighbor Mallus:

τὰ δὲ νῦν οἵ γε Μαλλῶται διαφέρονται πρὸς ὑμᾶς, αὐτοὶ μὲν ἅπαντα ἀδικοῦντες καὶ θρασυνόμενοι, τῷ δὲ ἀσθενεῖς εἶναι καὶ πολὺ ἥττους [ἀεὶ] μᾶλλον τὴν τῶν ἀδικουμένων τάξιν ἀεὶ λαμβάνοντες. οὐ γὰρ ἃ ποιοῦσιν ἔνιοι σκοποῦσιν, ἀλλὰ τίνες ὄντες, οὐδὲ τοὺς ἀδικοῦντας ἢ βιαζομένους ἐθέλουσιν ἐξετάζειν πολλάκις, ἀλλ' οὓς εἰκὸς βιάζεσθαι τῷ δύνασθαι πλέον. εἰ γοῦν ὑφ' ὑμῶν ἐπράχθη τι τοιοῦτον οἷον ὑπ' ἐκείνων νῦν γέγονε, πορθεῖν ἂν ἐδοκεῖτε τὰς πόλεις καὶ ἀποστάσεως ἄρχειν καὶ πολέμου, καὶ στρατοπέδου δεῖν ἐφ' ὑμᾶς.

But as to the situation now the people of Mallus, at least, are at loggerheads with you, and though they themselves are in the wrong and acting insolently in every respect, because of their being weak and greatly inferior they always take rather the position of the injured party. For some men look not at what people do, but at who they are, nor are [these observers] often willing to scrutinize those who do wrong or act violently, but those from whom it is reasonable to expect violence by virtue of their greater power. If, at any rate, some such thing had been done by you as has now occurred at their [i.e. the Malleans'] hands, you would seem to be sacking cities and starting a revolution and a war, and it would seem necessary to lead an army against you. (34.10-11).

Clearly the emphasis here is not on the dispute itself, but on the damage it may cause Tarsus in the realm of public relations. Certain observers (ἔνιοι), in particular, are apt to misinterpret the situation, wrongly conflating strength with the intent to cause injury. Dio's formulation is thus dual-purpose; it allows his audience to maintain beliefs in both the physical superiority of their city and its victimization at the hands of wicked neighbors, while simultaneously suggesting that observers may treat this self-portrait with scepticism. That these observers can raise armies, moreover, hints at an identification with the Romans.

The same motifs – the paradox of the victimized winner and the powerful observer – animate the second image under discussion, namely the metaphor of the boxing match:

τὸ γὰρ συμβαῖνον ὅμοιόν ἐστι τῷ περὶ τοὺς ἀθλητάς, ὅταν ἐλάττων πρὸς πολὺ μείζω μάχηται. τῷ μὲν γὰρ οὐδὲν ἔξεστι παρὰ τὸν νόμον, ἀλλὰ κἂν ἄκων ἁμάρτῃ τι, μαστιγοῦται· τὸν δ' οὐδεὶς ὁρᾷ πάνθ' ἃ δύναται ποιοῦντα. τοιγαροῦν κἀκεῖ σωφρονοῦντος ἀνδρός ἐστι καὶ ταῖς ἀληθείαις κρείττονος τῇ δυνάμει περιεῖναι,

τὰς δὲ πλεονεξίας ταύτας ἐᾶν, <καὶ> ὑμεῖς <ἂν> ἔχητε νοῦν, τοῖς δικαίοις περι-
έσεσθε καὶ τῷ μεγέθει τῆς πόλεως τῶν φθονούντων, πρὸς ὀργὴν δὲ οὐδὲν οὐδὲ
ἀγανακτοῦντες δράσετε.

For your situation is similar to the one with athletes, whenever a weaker man fights with a much stronger one. For nothing against the rules is possible for the latter, but should he do something wrong, even unintentionally, he is whipped. But as to the other man, no one sees *him* doing everything he can. There as well, therefore, it is the part of a sensible man and one who is truly stronger to win with his ability and to leave aside these advantages, and should you have sense, you will through justice and the size of your city be victorious over those who are jealous of you, and you will do nothing in anger or annoyance. (34.12-13).

Dio's basic point here is clear enough: namely, that Tarsus, a city superior in every way to Mallus, should not stoop to the kind of unscrupulous behavior and inflammatory slander characteristic of the smaller city. What is remarkable, however, is Dio's concern with the source of such scruples. Tarsus should avoid Mallean tactics not because they are inherently demeaning, but because the city's size and strength make them inappropriate for it *in the view of others*. Once again, then, we find Dio constructing a world in which onlookers hold sway over participants. And once again Dio's reaction to his own creation is telling; specifically, the fact that the onlookers are sometimes wrong, that they overlook the misdeeds of the weaker party, does not lead Dio to question the fairness of the situation as a whole. Or, to use the terms of the metaphor, the fact that the referee is sometimes blind does not seem to arouse in Dio any feeling that perhaps the referee ought to be replaced, or done away with altogether, on the grounds that a fight without rules is to be preferred to one in which the rules are applied sporadically and unfairly. On the contrary, Dio recommends a policy of silence and endurance to those persecuted by a referee's preference for the underdog. That he does so, moreover, on utilitarian grounds (this is the way to secure victory) rather than vaguer existential ones (this is the way to lead a victorious life) is striking, for it suggests that the metaphor is no mere embellishment, but a lesson in political pragmatism adapted to suit the current situation. As such its individual terms may themselves resonate within that context. The stronger and weaker fighters clearly represent Tarsus and Mallus, respectively, but who is the referee? Who is it who wields the whip?

It is my contention that, if the observers with armies resemble the Romans, the referee describes them to a T. Though his existence must be inferred as the agent of the passive μαστιγοῦται, his traits are clear enough:

(1) He enforces rules or laws.
(2) He punishes offenders.
(3) His judgment in disputes is compromised at times by a bias in favor of the weaker party.

The parallels between these traits and those of Roman authority in the provinces can be best illustrated, perhaps, through a brief consideration of Imperial *Realpolitik*, some of the best evidence for which is contained in the nearly contemporary correspondence between Trajan and his special legate in Bithynia-Pontus, Pliny the Younger:

10.77
C. Plinius Traiano Imperatori

Providentissime, domine, fecisti, quod praecepisti Calpurnio Macro, clarissimo viro, ut legionarium centurionem Byzantium mitteret. Dispice, an etiam Iuliopolitanis simili ratione consulendum putes, quorum civitas, cum sit perexigua, onera maxima sustinet tantoque graviores iniurias, quanto est infirmior, patitur.

10.78
Traianus Plinio

Ea condicio est civitatis Byzantiorum, confluente undique in eam commeantium turba, ut secundum consuetudinem praecedentium temporum honoribus eius praesidio centurionis legionarii consulendum habuerimus.

Si Iuliopolitanis succurrendum eodem modo putaverimus, onerabimus nos exemplo. Plures enim, et quanto infirmiores erunt, idem petent. Fiduciam diligentiae tuae habeo, ut credam te omni ratione id acturum ne sint obnoxii iniuriis.

Si qui autem se contra disciplinam meam gesserint, statim coerceantur...

10.77
Pliny to Emperor Trajan

You acted with a great deal of foresight, my lord, in instructing the most illustrious Calpurnius Macer to send a legionary centurion [and his men] to Byzantium. Consider whether you think that a decision by similar reasoning [i.e. a similar decision] ought to be made for the people of Iuliopolis, whose city, though it is very small, bears very great burdens and is open to injuries that are so much the more serious as it is too weak [to bear them].

10.78
Trajan to Pliny

The condition of the city of the Byzantines, with a mob of visitors flowing into it from all directions, is such that, in accordance with the custom of preceding ages, I thought it best that measures be taken on behalf on the city's officials for [the establishment of] a legionary centurion's guard.

I considered that, if we aided the people of Iuliopolis in the same manner, we would weigh ourselves down with a precedent. For many cities will seek the same benefits, and all the more so the weaker they are. I have such faith in your diligence as to believe that you will by every tactic bring it about that they are not exposed to injuries.

If, however, anyone has acted contrary to my standards of public order, let him be immediately restrained...

Concisely illustrated here are precisely those traits that characterize Dio's referee. Roman authority, as it is concentrated in the person of Pliny, is intimately concerned with law enforcement and the punishment of those who offend Imperial standards of conduct. Given the kinds of behavior, visible elsewhere in the correspondence, that violate those standards – meeting with one's fellow craftsmen, for example,[9] it becomes apparent that provincial authorities, even those specially appointed by the Emperor himself, often had to involve themselves in matters more mundane and perhaps more distasteful than elaborate engineering schemes[10] or high finance.[11] If a general theme can in fact be found in Trajan's directives to Pliny, it is that public order and 'provincial peace'[12] must be maintained. Such concerns are likely to have transcended provincial boundaries and administrative changes; if we cannot find the Emperor himself involved in the dispute between Tarsus and Mallus, we can be reasonably certain that the Roman authorities on the scene in Cilicia were keenly aware of it as a threat to *quies provinciae*.

To sum up, then, the referee who plays such an important, if implicit, role in Dio's metaphor of the boxing match possesses characteristics that are highly consonant with those of Roman provincial authorities, at least insofar as these are typified by the correspondence between Pliny and Trajan. To the concern with criminal punishment and the maintenance of public order, we may perhaps add a third parallel, namely a bias in favor of the smaller and weaker of two parties. Dio claims that referees give carte blanche to these underdogs, while Pliny argues that the small city of Iuliopolis deserves the same degree of Imperial protection as Byzantium. While it is hard to identify Pliny's motives here precisely, it is possible that the favor he bestows upon Iuliopolis is part of a larger program in which the status quo of *quies provinciae* is maintained by unilaterally equalizing the powers of the strong and the weak. If so, the dynamic would be similar to the referee's attempt to make the boxing match 'fair'. In any event, the correspondences between the referee and Roman authority are too deep to be coincidental. Dio's referee stands for Roman authority, and does so powerfully and evocatively.

It is here, in the uneasy intersection between ruler and ruled, that Dio locates himself. It is a position that offers considerable opportunity for personal aggrandizement, insofar as he is able to play both sides of the fence. To his primary audience, the Tarsians before him, Dio presents himself as a solicitous samaritan whose only concern is to steer them away from the problems that have dogged them in the past. To his secondary audience, the Romans who surely soon learned of his remarks in sum if not verbatim, he is a stern disciplinarian, using his fame and prestige to bring an annoyingly vocal and freespirited city to heel. The skill with which he integrates these two presentations into a seamless and coherent whole is a substantial one, highly valued, in particular, by forces of colonialism.

There can be little doubt as to where Dio locates his own interests along this continuum: namely alongside those of the occupying Romans. Only thus is the tone of his remarks, at once threatening and paternalistic, explicable. An outsider's claim to know what is best for a given group of people is a hallmark of the colonialist mindset;[13] what may sound like brotherly concern is often more akin to an impatient parent's treatment of a recalcitrant child, at once an affirmation of intellectual superiority (Do this because I say so, and I know better) and of the justice of hierarchical structures in general (I am above you, and you are above him. Your job, therefore, is to obey me and indulge him). Yet this is the tone Dio adopts again and again in his analyses of Tarsian affairs both foreign and domestic. Here, for example, is his verdict on the city's border dispute with Mallus:

εἰ μὲν οὖν παρὰ τὰς θῖνας ἔμελλε Μαλλὸς μείζων ἔσεσθαι τῆς Ταρσοῦ καὶ παρὰ τὴν ἐπὶ τῆς ψάμμου νόμην, τάχα ἔδει σπουδάζειν ὑμᾶς ἐπὶ τοσοῦτον.

If, then, Mallus were destined to become greater than Tarsus on account of the dunes and the beach pasture, it might perhaps be necessary for you to be as determined as you are. (34.46).

Dio's vicious denigration of the disputed property as 'sand-dunes and swamp-land'[14] is designed to imply that ownership of it is not worth contesting, that yielding to the demands of the Malleans would cost the Tarsians little. Even if true, however, such arguments ignore any symbolic importance the property may have; even materially trivial scraps of land often assume enormous significance in the context of a given group's collective aspirations. What would the Romans stand to gain from a Tarsus so willing to compromise? *Quies provinciae*, of course, but of a very particular sort. It is the peace and quiet born of resignation, if not outright complacency. A city unilaterally willing to cede its claim to a stretch of beach is not apt to raise troubling questions about the nature of other, conceptually more difficult territorial claims. Boundary disputes arise naturally between ambitious neighbors; one field is more fertile than the one adjacent, one hilltop better situated than the next, and feelings of envy arise easily. But what of Imperial claims? In what sense could the Romans claim to have a right to the land and bounty of cities hundreds of miles away? As Fanon has noted in the context of twentieth-century imperialism, such questions, once asked, tend to remain in the collective consciousness, ultimately serving to focus the resentment of the colonized and to destabilize the status quo.[15] Insofar as Dio's brand of *quies* hinders the asking of such questions, then, it can be said to aid in the the never-ending work of maintaining the Empire. As he reminds the Tarsians, 'the jobs of leading and ruling belong to others' (τὸ γὰρ προεστάναί τε καὶ κρατεῖν ἄλλων ἐστίν. 34.48).

In short, then, what Dio advocates in Tarsus is not self-improvement vis-à-vis the Romans; the subjugation inherent in that relationship is non-negotiable. What the Tarsians need to do is to advance themselves at the expense of other subject cities, to distinguish themselves in Roman eyes. The need to do so, moreover, is pressing, for the Tarsians have lost the Imperial favor that once served to set them apart from the colonized masses:

καὶ μὴν ὅ γε ἔφην τὸ πρότερον αὐξῆσαι τὴν πόλιν, τοῦτο οὐχ ὁρῶ νῦν ὑμῖν ὑπάρχον, τὸ ἐξαίρετον εὐεργεσίαν καὶ χάριν καταθέσθαι τῷ κρατοῦντι, δῆλον ὅτι τῷ μὴ δεηθῆναι μηδενὸς αὐτὸν τοιούτου· πλὴν ὅτι γε [εἰ] μηδὲν τῶν ἄλλων ἔχετε πλεῖον πρὸς αὐτόν·

Indeed, as to that which I said earlier increased the city, I do not see it at hand for you now, namely the deposit of special favor and goodwill with the Ruler, and it is clear that this is because he is in no need of any such thing. But it is the case that you have no advantage with him over the others. (34.25).

In Dio's formulation, it is not the Romans against whom the Tarsians should struggle, but the other cities of Asia Minor. The Empire is a fait accompli; what matters is the securing of Imperial favor, the supply of which is evidently limited. Thus is the dialectic of colonizer versus colonized transformed into a zero-sum struggle among the colonized.

It might be possible to conceive of Dio's role in Tarsus as that of a genuine peacemaker, were the tone of his remarks not so disturbing. We remember here the threat that permeates the two central images of the oration, namely the fable of the ox and the crow and the metaphor of the boxing match. In each case, Dio's demand that his audience be a good audience – i.e. that its members sit still, *be quiet*, and obey – is backed up with a threat of violence; the Phrygian who attempts to silence the oratorical crow with a stone meets with violent misfortune, while the superior boxer who disregards the rules receives a whipping. Though the latter is somewhat imprecise about the kind of behavior that would provoke such violent retaliation – anything that offends the sensibilities of the referee, it seems, would suffice – its underlying premise is the same as the fable's: authority, whether embodied in an orator, a referee, or the Imperial administration, must be obeyed.

This last consideration leads us back to the question of what Dio perceives his role in Tarsus to be, or, more precisely, whether he invokes the claims of authority as any orator might or as an individual specially qualified to do so by some personal connection to that authority. Our analysis suggests the latter; as Dio himself points out, any old orator simply will not do:

ἔπειθ', [ἐπιδείξω] ὅτι μηδεὶς ὑμῖν δύναται ῥᾳδίως τούτων τὸ δέον παραινέσαι, οἱ μὲν ἀγνοίᾳ τοῦ συμφέροντος, οἱ δέ τινες καὶ δειλίᾳ τῇ πρὸς ὑμᾶς ἢ τῇ πρὸς ἑτέρους καὶ τὸ αὑτῶν ἴσως μᾶλλον ἔνιοι σκοποῦντες·

Then [I will show] that no one of these men [at hand] is able easily to advise you as to what is necessary, some through ignorance of what is beneficial, some even through fear of you or of others, and some, perhaps, because they are watching out rather for their own [personal] interests. (34.6).

Thus Dio manages to dismiss the great advantage of the locals – namely their longstanding familiarity with their own situation – in favor of the outsider's bird's-eye view. It has been argued above, moreover, that Dio does much to imply that this view – his view – represents the official Imperial one, that his analysis is fortified with inside information. Central to this project are the threats articulated through the fable and the boxing metaphor, as these reinforce Dio's self-presentation as a traveling representative of temporal power. The relationship between the motifs of inside information and threatened violence is a synergistic one; the idea that Dio knows what the Romans are planning lends credence to the thought that he knows under what circumstances they would consider violence, and vice-versa. Again it is not necessary to prove the existence of an official role for Dio in Tarsus. Indeed, if there were one, he likely would have emphasized it; modesty, particularly with regard to information that might strengthen his position or improve his standing before the audience, is not much in evidence anywhere in Dio.

Thus we return to the eternal question of Dio's motivations. Why travel to a distant city for a speaking engagement if it were not part of one's official duties? Though personal motives of money or vanity surely had some influence, they are notoriously prone to concealment or misrepresentation. Nevertheless they demand further study. I begin here by suggesting that Dio speaks in part to exploit the ambiguities inherent in his position as a Greek member of an elite bound economically and politically to Rome. Far from paralyzing him with conflicted loyalties, this position offers a kind of flexibility highly useful to those interested in pragmatic solutions to the conflicts that divide 'native' populations and their foreign dominators. Fanon notes the tendency for 'native' elites to act as mediators, to remind each disputant of their obligations toward the other parties; he cites the attempts by Algerian intellectuals to dissuade the French from some of their worst and most violent abuses of power and, *simultaneously,* to remind the Algerian revolutionaries of French contributions to infrastructure, public health, etc.[16] Such attempts are inherently pragmatic, insofar as they impel the disputants to reassess their particular situations realistically. I submit that Dio may be taking the same kind of pragmatic approach in Tarsus. In urging his audience to yield – to fellow citizens and neighbors alike – Dio is urging them, with arguments, fables, and threats, to accept the reality of their powerlessness. To fight every battle to the end is to kick against the pricks, to refuse to accept the fact of Roman domination. It is to act not as subjects but as emperors.

Notes

1. Cass. Dio 47.31.
2. 34.23: τί οὖν σὺ κελεύεις ἡμᾶς; τοὺς ἅπαντας ἀναγράψαι πολίτας [ναί φημι] καὶ τῶν αὐτῶν ἀξίους, ἅμα μηδὲ ὀνειδίζειν μηδὲ ἀπορρίπτειν, ἀλλὰ μέρος αὐτῶν, ὥσπερ εἰσί, νομίζειν. οὐ μὲν γάρ, ἄν τις καταβάλῃ πεντακοσίας δραχμάς, δύναται φιλεῖν ὑμᾶς καὶ τῆς πόλεως εὐθὺς ἄξιος γεγονέναι· I have relied upon the text of von Arnim 1962 exclusively, though I have tried to exclude all arguments hinging upon questionable or disputed readings. Translations are my own unless otherwise noted.
3. Note the use of the second person in the passage cited in n.2.
4. Crosby and Cohoon 1940, 3.341n.
5. Jokes: τὸ θέατρον...κρουμάτων δὲ ἀεὶ μεστόν ἐστι καὶ θορύβου καὶ βωμολοχίας καὶ σκωμμάτων οὐδὲν ἐοικότων χρυσῷ. (32.4). General immaturity: ἐπειδὴ παίζοντες ἀεὶ διατελεῖτε καὶ οὐ προσέχοντες καὶ παιδιᾶς μὲν καὶ ἡδονῆς καὶ γέλωτος, ὡς εἰπεῖν, οὐδέποτε ἀπορεῖτε· (32.1).
6. Philostr. *VS* 480-81.
7. 34.4. This felicitous translation is found in Crosby and Cohoon 1940, 3.341.
8. e.g., Jeremiah 11.18 (RSV):
   > The LORD made it known to me
   >   and I knew;
   > then thou didst show me their
   >   evil deeds.
   > But I was like a gentle lamb
   >   led to the slaughter.

9. See *Ep.* 10.33-4, on the subject of Pliny's proposal for a *collegium fabrorum* to fight fires in Nicomedia. Trajan vetoes the *collegium* as a potential threat to political stability.
10. Cf., e.g., *Ep.* 10.41-2 on Pliny's proposal for a canal in the territory of Nicomedia.
11. Cf., e.g., *Ep.* 10.54-5 on possible uses of a budgetary surplus.
12. *Quies provinciae*: The phrase appears in *Ep.* 10.117.
13. As stated the formulation owes much to the analyses of Fanon 1967-68, *passim*.
14. Crosby and Cohoon's tonally apt translation of αἱ μὲν οὖν θῖνες καὶ τὸ πρὸς τῇ λίμνῃ χωρίον... (34.45). Crosby and Cohoon 1940, 3.379.
15. Fanon 1967, *passim*.
16. Fanon 1968, 46 (infrastructure) and 59 (pacifism).

CHAPTER 13

Hadrian and Greek Poetry

Ewen Bowie

The section of Denys Page's *Further Greek Epigrams* containing epigrams by imperial Romans has twelve composed by emperors. On his attribution, these comprise two by Germanicus, one possibly by Tiberius, one by Trajan, seven by Hadrian and one by Julian.[1] Even once we have subtracted the poem inscribed on a statue base in Ephesus by the sophist Hadrianus of Tyre, that Page mistakenly attributed to the emperor,[2] Hadrian's surviving output places him clearly in a unique class. If he was not the 'Greekest' Roman of them all, he was certainly in this matter, as in many other things, the most Hellenic Roman emperor of them all. Of course an interest in Greek poetry and writing Greek poems are only two criteria on which the Hellenism of a person originating from the Latin-speaking West might be judged. They do, however, merit inclusion in any attempt to explore this broad and complex subject.

In this paper, then, I shall first look at Hadrian's tastes in established Greek poetry: those canonical texts which he liked and those which he didn't. Then I shall examine briefly the poetry that he himself composed. Finally I shall consider some examples of Greek poetry composed by some of his friends or close associates. I shall regularly stray from Greek into Latin texts, because, symptomatically of this period, Hadrian and his friends of western origin showed equal facility in both, though it is unlikely that many πεπαιδευμένοι brought up in the Greek language and culture were even competent in Latin in this period.

I

First, then, what was Hadrian's own taste in poetry? The answer of the ancient tradition is clear: he wished to dethrone established classics. So, after noting Hadrian's preference in Latin literature for Cato over Cicero, for Ennius over Virgil and for Coelius Antipater over Sallust, the *Historia Augusta* says:

amavit praeterea genus vetustum dicendi... Ciceroni Catonem, Vergilio Ennium, Salustio Coelium praetulit, eademque iactantia de Homero et Platone iudicavit

Moreover he liked an archaic style ... He preferred Cato to Cicero, Ennius to Vergil, Coelius [Antipater] to Sallust, and he uttered the same pretentious verdicts on Homer and Plato.³

I take it that this means that Hadrian preferred other writers in the same genre, and that would also seem to be suggested by Cassius Dio's related remark talking of his envy:

καὶ οὕτω γε τῇ φύσει τοιοῦτος ἦν ὥστε μὴ μόνον τοῖς ζῶσιν ἀλλὰ καὶ τοῖς τελευτήσασι φθονεῖν. τὸν γοῦν Ὅμηρον καταλύων Ἀντίμαχον ἀντ' αὐτοῦ ἐσῆγεν, οὗ μηδὲ τὸ ὄνομα πολλοὶ πρότερον ἠπίσταντο.

And he was so strongly of this natural bent that he envied not only the living but even the dead: for example he tried to unseat Homer and introduce Antimachus in his place, a poet whose very name was hitherto unknown to many.⁴

In fact, as will be noted later, Hadrian rewarded at least one Homerising poet, Pancrates, and I am inclined to dismiss Dio's assertions as silly gossip, as I have tried to demonstrate are the earlier parts of his chapter about Apollodorus of Damascus.⁵ That Hadrian tried to persuade members of his entourage that the *Thebais* of Antimachus was a better poem than Homer's *Iliad*, or tried to replace Homer by Antimachus in libraries or school curricula, is barely credible, although Antimachus had been given qualified approval by Domitian's professor of rhetoric, Quintilian, and was later read in second-century Oxyrhyncus.⁶ But no doubt there was some truth in this claim. Part of the explanation may lie in the poetry of Hadrian that allegedly emulated Antimachus (this is discussed below), and part in the fact that, as we can infer from a comparison mounted by Plutarch in his *Timoleon* between the poet Antimachus and the painter Dionysius on the one hand, and Homer and the painter Nicomachus on the other, in the early second century AD comparison of Homer with Antimachus was an established literary critical game.⁷

II

Another contribution to our understanding of Hadrian's liking for Antimachus is to be found in the Greek poetry he himself wrote. First, there is no evidence that he wrote any long poems. That is hardly surprising, since he had many other calls on his time, but some equally busy emperors did write poems of some length. According to Suetonius, Augustus was responsible not only for epigrams – composed like all good epigrams in the bath – but also a one-book work *Sicilia* and a tragedy *Ajax*. We also know that Domitian wrote a *Bellum Capitolinum*.[8] It may be significant therefore that the positive evidence for Hadrian's poetic activity is different. According to Dio, as well as prose compositions 'in verse he left poems of all sorts'.[9] Dio does not say whether these were in Greek or in Latin, but since he has just been talking about Hadrian's devotion to letters in either language and since poems by Hadrian in both languages are preserved, I infer that he means in both languages.

The surviving poems are not only short but deploy considerable variety of metre. The Latin poems are in hexameters, Anacreontics, and a metre which alternates iambic dimeters and Aristophaneans; the Greek are in elegiacs and hendecasyllables.

The production of different sorts of poem in a variety of metres puts Hadrian in a tradition that can be traced back through Hellenistic poetry as far as Archilochus. It is a tradition one branch of which was represented in Hadrian's youth by the Latin *Silvae* by Statius, published between AD 93 and 96 (i.e., so when Hadrian was between seventeen and twenty). In AD 104 (when Hadrian was already twenty-eight) the younger Pliny praised the elderly Arrius Antoninus for epigrams that rivalled those of Callimachus, and *mimiambi* that rivalled those of Herodas, and embarked upon some translations into Latin of Arrius' Greek epigrams. He then sent a friend a *libellus* of Latin hendecasyllables that he himself had composed while travelling, bathing or dining.[10] A year or two earlier he had talked of the *lyrica doctissima* written by Vestricius Spurinna for relaxation in both Latin and Greek, and later, in AD 107, he was putting together a book of poetry in various genres and metres.[11] In the Greek world a Pergamene who had been honoured with Athenian citizenship, Q. Pompeius Capito, was commemorated, perhaps before the end of the first century, as extemporising 'in every rhythm and metre'.[12] The composition of short poems in various metres and in either language was a trend already vigorous in Hadrian's twenties, and not one that he had set.

That Hadrian had a special interest in some 'post-classical' poetry and poets may also be argued on the basis of his decision to restore the tomb of Parthenius of Nicaea and furnish it with a new sepulchral epigram. The text of that epigram is extremely uncertain, but unfortunately the stone on which it was inscribed, which was situated near Rome, perhaps at Tivoli, has long been lost. It seems, however, to allude to Parthenius' poetry of mourning for his dead lady Arete.[13] That theme might itself recall the *Lyde*, which Antimachus allegedly composed to console himself after the death of his wife of that name.¹⁴ Parthenius himself seems generally to have been neglected after Vergil and Propertius, whose echoes may be a tribute as much to Parthenius' patron Gallus as to Parthenius. He is not mentioned by Ovid or by Quintilian, and that Tiberius liked Parthenius, Euphorion and Rhianus and wrote poems in imitation of theirs, as well as ensuring that their poems and statues were in public libraries, is recorded by Suetonius as an aspect of Tiberius' unusual taste – perhaps with a glance at imperial taste in his own time, the 120s.¹⁵ One element in Parthenius' literary output seems to have been unrestrained criticism of Homer, as we know from an epigram by Erucius whose target is certainly a Parthenius and is conjecturally this one.¹⁶ Hadrian's interest in Parthenius may be not unrelated to Parthenius' attack on Homer, and it is doubtless partly in response to imperial taste that another epigram, by the Asian poet Pollianus, praises poetry in the elegiac tradition of Callimachus and Parthenius and vilifies imitators of Homer who plagiarise Homeric phraseology.¹⁷ Later in the second century Parthenius is mentioned in the company of Callimachus and Euphorion by Lucian and his 'Elegies' are referred to by Artemidorus.¹⁸

Such an attack on 'theft' is not, of course, an attack on Homer himself. Nor do I think there is a serious attack on Homer in Hadrian's own epigram which purports to be for the tomb of Archilochus:

> Ἀρχιλόχου τόδε σῆμα, τὸν ἐς λυσσῶντας ἰάμβους
> ἤγαγε Μαιονίδῃ Μοῦσα χαριζομένη.

> This is the monument of Archilochus, whom the Muse diverted into raging iambics, doing a favour to Homer.¹⁹

A nice point is made in complimenting Archilochus: as an epic poet he would have been a serious rival to Homer. But Homer is not thereby dethroned. We might, however, see the composition of such an epigram as one of the starting points for Dio's exaggeration.

A final candidate for an epigram that purports to relate to a tomb is the single line:

> Τῷ ναοῖς βρίθοντι πόση σπάνις ἔπλετο τύμβου.

> For one so heavy with temples what scarcity was shown by his tomb!

Appian cites the line in his account of Pompey's death. After recounting his murder, he says that somebody buried him and that someone else composed an epigram for the tomb – then goes on to narrate how in his day Hadrian cleared the tomb of encroaching sand-dunes and re-erected its statues of Pompey. Xiphilinus' epitome of Cassius Dio, however, claims that during Hadrian's visit to Egypt (i.e., in autumn of AD 130) he performed a sacrifice to Pompey, uttered this line and restored Pompey's monument.[20] Hadrian's enthusiasm for restoring dilapidated constructions, of which we may already have seen an example in the case of Parthenius' tomb, is well attested by other cases throughout the empire.[21] It is surprising that Appian, who originated precisely from Alexandria, was wrong when in citing the line he said 'and someone else inscribed an epigram "For one so ..."'. But it is conceivable that Appian was working from memory of a personal visit, and was not aware that the epigram was Hadrian's simply because it was not signed, whereas Dio was drawing on a narrative which (like that of the Augustan History) had access to a collection or selection of Hadrian's poetry.

Just what the epigram's composer meant is also unclear. The Budé notes point out the difficulty in the usual translation 'weighed down by temples': we have no other evidence of Pompey receiving divine honours in the form of a temple. Unless Hadrian is confused on the pre-history of the imperial cult, he is more likely to mean 'who was so generous with temples', a quality in which of course Hadrian could well see himself as similar to the great Pompey.[22]

A declamatory epigram that is not overtly sepulchral, although its source claims that it was, is a hexameter three-liner ascribed to Hadrian in a Bodleian manuscript and first published by Bühler twenty years ago. It expresses envy of Achilles for the publicity given him by Homer. I accept Bühler's strong arguments against Hadrianic authorship.[23]

What, then, of Hadrian's alleged attempt to exalt Antimachus? As well as Hadrian's disinclination to emulate Homer, one particular work may have given rise to this claim. According to the Augustan History, Hadrian wrote 'most obscure books [called] *Catachannae* in imitation of Antimachus'.[24] The manuscripts are corrupt, but as Bernhardy saw in 1847, their readings (*catacannas, catacaimos, catacaymos*) should render the same word that we find in a letter of Fronto, where it is the name of a tree seen about AD 140 by Fronto in the garden of a *villa suburbana* owned by Hadrian's friend Q. Pompeius Falco, his colleague in the consulate of 108 and proconsul of Asia during his visit there in AD 123-24. It was an unusual tree 'bearing on a single stock shoots of almost every tree'.[25] There must be some connection between Hadrian's books of poetry and Fronto's pet name (*suum nomen*) for this tree. Was this tree already flourishing when Hadrian composed his poetry, so that he gave the name as a title to a heterogeneous, probably polymetric collection? That cannot be excluded. But another possibility is more attractive. The word should be Greek, and the nearest attested (as is noted in the *Oxford Latin Dictionary*) is καταχῆναι, which happens to be the title of a Comedy, [26] while in the singular καταχήνη means mockery. I suggest that καταχῆναι meant 'mockeries', on the analogy of titles like ἴαμβοι and σίλλοι, and that Hadrian's book was a collection comprising satirical poems in various metres: on this hypothesis Pompeius Falco then named his tree in allusion – perhaps overtly mocking allusion, if the name was given after Hadrian's death in AD 138 – to the emperor's heterogeneous collection. By AD 163, the date of the word's next surviving appearance in another letter of Fronto, the name of the tree is well enough known to be used as an analogy for a style of rhetoric with strikingly diverse constituents.[27]

Nothing in all this, however, helps us to understand the assertion that the collection imitated Antimachus. The poet of Colophon is remembered chiefly as the composer of a hexameter *Thebais* and an elegiac *Lyde*. These can never have circulated in a single *volumen*. It is possible that there were papyrus books of Antimachus that had copies both of the elegiac *Lyde* and of some short poems from other genres or in other metres (as we now know that Simonides' elegiac narrative of the battle of Plataea could be read on the same roll as some shorter sympotic elegies)[28] but that is unlikely to have been the basis of a perception of Antimachus as the author of a diverse and polymetric book. We do know of another Antimachus, a melic and apparently comic poet who was attacked by Aristophanes for ill-treatment of his comic chorus,[29] but it is unlikely that his name, far less his poetry, was familiar to anyone in the early second century other than scholars working on Aristophanes. The Antimachean element in Hadrian's collection remains obscure.

It remains possible that the *catachannae* were not in fact satirical but simply diverse. If so they might have included the mock epitaph on Archilochus already discussed. They might also have contained the many erotic poems that Apuleius recalls having read from Hadrian's pen and that were known to the Augustan History, but of which no other trace remains.[30] Whether they were diverse or only satirical it is possible that they included one of the epigrams attributed to him in the Palatine Anthology, 9.137, allegedly a reply to a starving γραμματικός. The γραμματικός had quipped:

ΓΡΑΜΜΑΤΙΚΟΣ   ἥμισύ μου τέθνηκε, τὸ δ' ἥμισυ λιμὸς ἐλέγχει
             σῶσόν μου, βασιλεῦ, μουσικὸν ἡμίτονον·

    Half of me is dead, and half succumbs to the logic of starvation:
    save, o king, a semitone of this man of the Muses.

Hadrian's reply was likewise a couplet:

ἈΔΡΙΑΝΟΣ   Ἀμφοτέρους ἀδικεῖς, καὶ Πλουτέα καὶ Φαέθοντα,
            τὸν μὲν ἔτ᾽ εἰσορόων, τὸν δ᾽ ἀπολειπόμενος.

> You wrong both Pluto and the sun
> in still seeing the one and breaking your appointment with the other.[31]

However the close relation between the two couplets raises problems about their authorship. It is possible that in a sympotic context a γραμματικός had indeed uttered a couplet that made a bid for financial support, but it is also conceivable that a real exchange that took place in 'prose' was later encapsulated in pithy verse. In that case the composition of the first couplet could well be by the author of the second; and this draws attention to the more unsettling possibility that neither couplet is in fact by Hadrian, but that a third party composed both couplets as a pair.

A further candidate for inclusion in the *catachannae* is the well known riposte to Florus, presumably the historian. According to the Augustan History, Florus had sent Hadrian a poem:

> *ego nolo Caesar esse*
> *ambulare per Britannos*
> *<latitare per Pelasgos>*[32]
> *Scythicas pati pruinas*

> I don't want to be a Caesar
> want to walk among the Britons
> <want to lurk among the Hellenes>
> or endure the frosts of Russia

In reply Hadrian sent the following lines picking up each of those in Florus' stanza:

> *ego nolo Florus esse*
> *ambulare per tabernas*
> *latitare per popinas*
> *culices pati rutundos*

> I don't want to be a Florus
> want to stroll among the taverns
> want to lurk among the bistros
> or endure the plump mosquitoes.[33]

It is not likely that Florus was trying to be rude or seriously critical – Favorinus had had the last word on attempting to compete with the emperor in wit or erudition when he said: 'You give me bad advice, friends, in not allowing me to believe the man who has thirty legions to be more learned than everyone else'.[34] Florus does in fact offer a clearer reflection of the imperial ideology of *patientia* than any other poem of the reign, and of course gives Hadrian an opportunity to dissociate himself from the life of self-indulgence in which Juvenal represents the governing class as totally immersed. Hadrian also achieved pungent wit, perhaps including bilingual puns: Florus can be heard or read as φλαῦρος 'bad, worthless, trivial', and *culices* might suggest the Greek κύλικες, also suitably described as *rutundos* (though of course a Greek accusative would be κύλικας).[35]

If this exchange did appear in the *catachannae* alongside Greek poems, then this was a bilingual collection. That would not be an unprecedented innovation. We have no knowledge of such a practice in the late Republican or Augustan period. Latin poets had indeed included translations of Greek poems in collections: already Lutatius Catulus, then Catullus with poems 51 and 66 translating (and developing) Sappho and Callimachus respectively. But it does not seem that Catullus' *lepidum novum libellum* included texts of the Greek poems translated. However we have noted that Vestricius Spurinna was credited by Pliny with *lyrica doctissima utraque lingua* (n.11 above), and later in the second century AD the letters of Fronto included Greek letters and the Attic Nights of Aulus Gellius had extensive quotations of Greek. The survival of a number of poems in each language whose preservation might have been assisted by such a collection also supports the hypothesis that it existed.

So much for the *catachannae*. Hadrian's remaining extant poems belong in what both the Palatine Anthology and the Suda call (τὰ) ἀναθήματα.[36] The context in which we learn that title is a ten-line epigram accompanying a dedication by Trajan to Zeus Kasius, on Mount Kasius in Syria, during the preliminaries to the Parthian war, presumably during the winter of AD 113/14.[37] Although the corrector has added an ascription to Trajan (Τραιανοῦ Καίσαρος) the original ascription of the anthology and that of the Suda to Hadrian should be accepted. Trajan's literary skills were limited, and it is probable that the epigram came to the Anthology and the Suda *via* the *Parthica* of Arrian.[38] Since both Arrian and Hadrian were involved in Trajan's Parthian expedition and Arrian seems to have become close to Hadrian, Arrian's authority, if it is behind the tradition, is certainly to be preferred.

Ζηνὶ τόδ' Αἰνεάδης Κασίῳ Τραιανὸς ἄγαλμα,
      κοίρανος ἀνθρώπων κοιράνῳ ἀθανάτων,
ἄνθετο, δοιὰ δέπα πολυδαίδαλα καὶ βοὸς οὔρου

>   ἀσκητὸν χρυσῷ παμφανόωντι κέρας,
> ἔξαιτα προτέρης ἀπὸ ληίδος, ἦμος ἀτειρὴς
>   πέρσεν ὑπερθύμους ᾧ ὑπὸ δουρὶ Γέτας.
> ἀλλὰ σύ οἱ καὶ τήνδε, κελαινεφές, ἐγγυάλιξον
>   κρῆναι εὐκλειῶς δῆριν Ἀχαιμενίην,
> ὄφρα τοι εἰσορόωντι διάνδιχα θυμὸν ἰαίνῃ
>   δοιά, τὰ μὲν Γετέων σκῦλα, τὰ δ' Ἀρσακίδεων.

> Trajan, Aeneas' son, dedicated this image to Kasian Zeus,
>   the lord of men to the lord of the immortals,
> a pair of much-decorated cups and from an aurochs
>   a horn adorned with all-shining gold,
> set aside from previous booty, when tireless
>   he destroyed the proud Getae with his spear:
> but do you promise to him, dark-clouded one, this
>   strife too to accomplish gloriously against the Achaemenids,
> so that as you gaze on them your heart may be doubly warmed
>   by a pair, the Getae's spoils, and the Arsacids'.

The epigram is neat in its concise inclusion of the chief relevant facts and in the way it holds back to the last line the identification of the finely-wrought mixing bowls and gilded ox-horn[39] as Getic spoils, so that they can balance the hoped for Arsacid spoils also mentioned in that line. It is not a great poem, but its tropes may help us with another shortly.

One dedicatory poem that rises decisively above the ordinary is the elegant hendecasyllabic epigram preserved on stone from Thespiae:

> ὦ παῖ τοξότα Κύπριδος λιγείης
> Θεσπιαῖς Ἑλικωνίαισι ναίων
> Ναρκίσσου παρὰ κῆπον ἀνθέοντα,
> ἱλήκοις, τὸ δέ τοι δίδωσι δέξο
> ἀκροθίνιον Ἀδριανὸς ἄρκτου,
> ἣν αὐτὸς κάνεν ἱππόθεν τυχήσας.
> σὺ δ' αὐτῷ χάριν ἀντὶ τοῦ σαόφρων
> πνείοις οὐρανίας ἀπ' Ἀφροδίτης.

> O archer child of clear-voiced Aphrodite,
> dwelling in Heliconian Thespiae
> by the blooming garden of Narcissus,
> be gracious, and accept what Hadrian offers,
> the spoils of his hunt, a bear
> which he slew himself with a cast from horseback.

> And may you in exchange for this chastely
> breathe favour upon him from Heavenly Aphrodite.[40]

The bear is unlikely to be one hunted down in the relatively tame country around Thespiae. Rather it is almost certainly, as Louis Robert argued in 1978,[41] the one that he slew during a famous hunt in Mysia – a hunt which allowed one of the cities he established there to be named Hadrianoutherae: both the killing of the bear and the city's foundation passed into the Augustan History.[42] One of the cities in this group, Stratoniceia, could still be termed 'recently created' in AD 127,[43] so that both the hunt and foundation of Hadrianoutherae should fall during Hadrian's long visit to Asia Minor in AD 123-24.[44] One of a series of coins of Hadrianoutherae commemorating the hunt shows Hadrian on horseback casting his javelin, precisely the manoeuvre of the poem.[45] In September 124 Hadrian travelled by sea from Asia to Achaea, and there, based in Athens, spent the last months of 124 and the first half of 125.[46] From Athens he could easily have visited Thespiae, perhaps at a time when one of its two great four-yearly festivals, the Mouseia or Erotidia, was being celebrated.[47]

The belief that the bear is the one slain in Mysia entails the supposition that the head was preserved in the imperial baggage-train until a suitable dedicatee was found. This is not perhaps as absurd as it may sound. It seems to be just what we have seen Trajan doing with an aurochs-horn that was booty from his Dacian campaigns. That must have been kept for some seven years (from AD 106 to 113/14), whereas the bear's head might have had to be kept for no more than a few months in the calendar year 124.[48] But the choice of dedication to Eros ought perhaps to have prompted more thought. What connection is there between a successfully hunted bear and love? The metaphor of hunting is common in love-poetry,[49] and in Roman art Erotes are represented hunting – as they are on the frieze of the 'Piazza d'Oro' in Hadrian's villa at Tivoli, part of the villa that seems likely to have been built around AD 125.[50] But neither of these facts seems sufficient to explain this dedication at Thespiae. I would guess – but of course it must be only a guess – that Hadrian had met Antinous during his passage through Bithynia in AD 123-24, and that Antinous was already a companion in Hadrian's favourite sport of hunting, as we know that he later was from the lion hunt in Egypt mentioned by Athenaeus, written up in hexameters by Pancrates[51] and commemorated on one of the Hadrianic tondos from the Arch of Constantine.[52]

I turn now to two more epitaphs. First, one in Latin which also ties in with Hadrian's interest in hunting. Cassius Dio, in a discussion of Hadrian's enthusiasm for hunting, says that when his favourite horse Borysthenes died, he built him a tomb, erected a memorial and equipped it with an epitaph.[53] A stone was found in Provence which offers just such an epigram, and oddly it was also found in a single manuscript, but both are now lost.[54] Neither source assigned it an author, but its first editor, Pierre Pithou, was probably correct in suggesting that it was by Hadrian.[55] It may be a forgery, but in favour of its authenticity is the unusual metre, which alternates iambic dimeters catalectic and Aristophaneans.[56]

> *Borysthenes Alanus*
> *Caesareus veredus*
> *per aequor et paludes*
> *et tumulos Etruscos*
> *volare qui solebat*
> *Pannonicos in apros*
> *nec ullus insequentem*
> *dente aper albicanti*
> *ausus fuit nocere*
> *– ut solet evenire –*[57]
> *vel <si> extimam saliva[m]*
> *sparsit ab ore caudam*
> *sed integer iuventa*
> *inviolatus artus*
> *die sua peremptus*
> *hoc situs est in agro.*

> Borysthenes, from Alan lands,
> the stallion of Caesar,
> who used to fly
> across the plains and marshes
> and the hills of Etruria
> after Pannonian boars,
> nor ever as he pursued
> did a boar dare injure him
> with white-flashing tusk
> – as it often happens –
> even if he sprayed its tail's tip
> with saliva from his mouth
> but in the full flower of youth
> and with his limbs unmauled,
> carried off in his due time
> he is laid to rest in this land.

The date should be AD 121 or 122, when Hadrian was passing through Gaul en route to and from Britain. The reference to Borysthenes' death is mysterious. How did he die? If we think ahead to AD 130, when one reconstruction of events would involve Hadrian drowning Antinous, perhaps as some sort of sacrifice,[58] while he was still *integer iuventa inviolatus artus*, we may wonder whether this was, as it were, a prequel to that turning point in Hadrian's life.

The last sepulchral epigram I want to discuss is a poem whose authorship is uncertain. It is an epitaph from Rome:

> ὁ κλεινὸς ἶνις βασιλέως Ἀμάζασπος
> ὁ Μιθριδάτου βασιλέως κασίγνητος,
> ᾧ γαῖα πατρὶς Κασπίας παρὰ κλήθρας,
> Ἴβηρ Ἴβηρος ἐνθαδὶ τετάρχυται
> πόλιν παρ᾽ ἱρήν, ἣν ἔδειμε Νικάτωρ
> ἐλαιόθηλον ἀμφὶ Μυγδόνος νᾶμα.
> θάνεν δ᾽ ὀπαδὸς Αὐσόνων ἁγητῆρι
> μολὼν ἄνακτι Παρθικὴν ἐφ᾽ ὑσμίνην,
> πρίν περ παλάξαι χεῖρα δηίῳ λύθρῳ,
> ἴφθιμον αἰεὶ χεῖρα δουρὶ καὶ τόξῳ
> καὶ φασγάνου κνώδοντι, πεζὸς ἱππεύς τε·
> ὁ δ᾽ αὐτὸς ἶσος παρθένοισιν αἰδοίαις.

> The glorious scion of a king, Amazaspus,
> the brother of king Mithridates,
> whose native land was by the Caspian gates
> An Iberian, son of Iberian, here is buried
> by the sacred city, which Nicator built
> burgeoning with olives by Mygdon's stream.
> And he died a squire to the Ausonians' leader
> going for his lord (?) to the Parthian conflict
> before even he stained his hand with enemy gore
> a hand ever mighty with spear and bow
> and the blade of his sword, on foot and horse.
> But he himself was like unto modest maidens.

This poem commemorates the brother of an Eastern client king, Mithridates of Iberia: this brother, Amazaspus, accompanied a Roman emperor on a Parthian expedition and died at Nisibis, i.e. Antiocheia Mygdonia, 'before even he had stained his hand with enemy gore'. The emperor must be Trajan, the context is his Parthian campaign of AD 114-17, when Nisibis was conquered, lost to an insurrection, and then reconquered.[59] Perhaps Amazaspus was killed in the insurrection, or perhaps he was simply carried off by one of those virulent Eastern Turkish tummy bugs. Oddly the stone talks as if it is set up in Nisibis (ἐνθαδὶ) but it was copied by Fulvio Ursini in Rome: Mommsen conjectured that Amazaspus was ultimately cremated, not inhumed, and that his bones were taken to Rome where the epigram, originally intended for a tomb at Nisibis, was reused. Moretti conjectured that the bones were taken to Rome under Pius, but as far as I can discover Nisibis was then no longer in Roman control. The puzzle remains. Odd too is the metre, choliambics (or scazons), usually used for invective or scabrous narrative, and a strange choice for an epitaph, even if, as we have seen, scazons were being written ten years earlier in Rome, as they were by Arrius Antoninus, maternal grandfather of the emperor Pius, in imitation of Herodas.[60] On grounds of the metre and of the ornate language I would infer that the epigram on Amazaspus comes from the pen of a litterateur who happened to be in Trajan's company during the Parthian expedition, and (to judge from the last line comparing him to 'modest maidens') one who was not unaware of the Eastern prince's personal charm. Further conjecture is of course irresponsible, but we should recall that Hadrian was himself on the expedition; that during it he composed, as we have seen, at least one 'official' epigram (the poem for the dedication to Zeus Kasius); and that he had a penchant for wily metres, not to mention handsome orientals. That the poem was by Hadrian, and had been included by him in a collection which circulated on a roll or in a codex, would offer an explanation of how a text was available to be inscribed in Rome. The pathos brought out in the modest prince's death before he had even contributed to the campaign might also suit the attitude to the campaign of the emperor who rapidly gave up almost all that Trajan had conquered; and if the stone was erected in a public place in Rome during Hadrian's principate, then it might be seen as a reminder of the cost to Rome and her friends of the policy of expansion.

I have left to last in this section the Latin poem attributed to Hadrian that has excited most interest, his 'farewell to life':

> *animula vagula blandula*
> *hospes comesque corporis*
> *quo nunc abibis? in loca*
> *pallidula rigida nubila*
> *nec ut soles dabis iocos.*

> Little soul, little wanderer, little charmer
> body's guest and companion,
> to what places will you set out for now?
> To darkling, cold and gloomy ones –
> and you won't make your usual jokes.

The Augustan History ascribes the poem to Hadrian on his death-bed, and a number of leading scholars have defended its authenticity vigorously, in recent years notably Cameron and Birley.[61] It is secured for Hadrian neither by the apparent echo of Ennius, a poet favoured not only by Hadrian but also by the likes of Gellius and Fronto, nor by Cameron's observation that it is too good to have been composed by the author of the Augustan History. If we accept that author's claim that it was uttered by Hadrian on his death-bed (*moriens*) then the likelihood of its authenticity becomes minimal – those authentic poems of Hadrian that survived did so because he included them in a collection that he himself circulated, whereas *ex hypothesi* the 'farewell' poem must depend on a supposed third-party witness. Add to that the tendency of many cultures to fabricate impressive – and characteristic – 'last words' and one must conclude that scepticism is legitimate. The poem may well have been composed in or not long after AD 138, but more probably by another than by Hadrian.

So much for Hadrian's own poetry. Some of what survives is rewarding, and if his καταχῆναι had survived complete they would tell us much more of his literary tastes and qualities.

III

I conclude this paper with a brief consideration of two poems by friends and associates of Hadrian that display some connections with his own.

First, an epigram which was probably composed by one of those Greek πεπαιδευμένοι who enjoyed an equestrian career under Hadrian, L. Iulius Vestinus. In Book fifteen of the Palatine Anthology and alongside the bucolic poets in a Vatican manuscript of the fourteenth century is preserved a poem which both purports to be 'spoken' by an altar and when written out forms an altar's shape.

ὅλος οὔ με λιβρὸς ἱρῶν
λιβάδεσσιν οἷα κάλχη
ὑποφοινίῃσι τέγγει
μαύλιες δ' ὕπερθε πέτρης Ναξίης θοούμεναι
παμάτων φείδοντο Πανός. οὐ στροβίλῳ λιγνύι
ἰξὸς εὐώδης μελαίνει τρεχνέων με Νυσίων.
ἐς γὰρ βωμὸν ὁρῇς με μήτε γλούρου
πλίνθοις μήτ' Ἀλύβης παγέντα βώλοις,
οὐδ' ὃν Κυνθογενὴς ἔτευξε φύτλη
λαβόντε μεκάδων κέρα,
λισσαῖσιν ἀμφὶ δείρασιν

ὅσσαι νέμονται Κυνθίαις,
ἰσόρροπος πέλοιτό μοι.
σὺν οὐρανοῦ γὰρ ἐκγόνοις
εἰνάς μ' ἔτευξε γηγενής,
τάων ἀείζῳον τέχνην
ἔνευσε πάλμυς ἀφθίτων.
σὺ δ', ὦ πιὼν κρήνηθεν, ἣν
ἶνις κόλαψε Γοργόνος
θύοις τ' ἐπισπένδοις τ' ἐμοὶ
Ὑμηττιάδων πολὺ λαροτέρην
σπονδὴν ἄδην. ἴθι δὴ θαρσέων
ἐς ἐμὴν τεῦξιν. καθαρὸς γὰρ ἐγὼ
ἰὸν ἰέντων τεράων, οἷα κέκευθ' ἐκεῖνος,
ἀμφὶ Νέαις Θρηικίαις ὃν σχεδόθεν Μυρίνης
σοί, Τριπάτωρ, πορφυρέου φὼρ ἀνέθηκε κριοῦ.

Not me does the black ink of rites
like the murex with droplets
tinged with crimson moisten,
and knives being sharpened above a stone from Naxos
spared the possessions of Pan: not with twists of smoke
does fine-fragrant gum blacken me from Nysian saplings.
For you behold an altar neither with golden
bricks constructed nor with clods from Alybe,
nor that which the Cynthian-born stock made
taking horns of bleaters
that graze around about the
Cynthian ridges precipitous
would be my counterpart.
For with Ouranos' daughters
the earth-born nine made me
to whose craft eternal life
was granted by immortals' emir.
But you, drinker from a spring
which Gorgon's scion sculpted,
may you sacrifice and pour
much sweeter than the girls of Hymettus
a libation in plenty. Come now with courage
to encounter me: for I am pure
of monsters that shoot forth poison, such as harboured that
which near to Thracian Neai, not far from Myrine,
to you, three-fathered one, the red ram's thief dedicated.

The Palatine codex does not ascribe an author, but the *index vetus* of the Anthology and the Vatican manuscript give it to Βησαντίνου, 'Besantinus'.[62] Haeberlin's conjecture that this is a corruption of 'Vestinus' is generally accepted, but it is important to remember that it is only a conjecture. Certainly several factors point to Hadrian's principate: the poem's metrical diversity, necessary to the attempt to present on a page the shape of an altar in imitation of the *Altar* of Dosiadas, probably of the second century BC; its recondite language and mythological allusions; and the acrostich, a trick also used in the contemporary hexameter *Periegesis* by Dionysius of Alexandria.[63] But the most powerful argument comes from the content of the acrostich. The first letters of each line read

Ὀλύμπιε πολλοῖς ἔτεσι θυσείας

Olympian, may you sacrifice for many years

We can conclude that the addressee was someone who both performed sacrifices and yet had the title Olympian. Hadrian is perhaps the only individual who matches this description. In his titulature Ὀλύμπιος appears from AD 128/9, but it may be possible to narrow down still further the probable date of the poem's composition to between AD 128 and Hadrian's death in 138. Although the initial adoption of the title 'Olympian' in AD 128-29, apparently while Hadrian was at Athens, remains one possible occasion,[64] a more attractive one is the final dedication of the completed temple of Olympian Zeus at Athens, late in AD 131 or early in AD 132.

A third possibility is the visit of Hadrian to Egypt between August AD 130 and spring of AD 131. This should be considered a candidate because L. Iulius Vestinus may have been in a procuratorial post in Egypt about that time: some discussion of him and of his family is now necessary.

Vestinus is known chiefly from two sources. The Suda reports his epitome of Pamphilus' γλῶσσαι and selections of words from Demosthenes, Thucydides and Isocrates,[65] and some other book titles are attested elsewhere. An inscription from Rome gives us his career:[66] he was ἀρχιερεύς of Alexandria and all Egypt and superintendent of the Museum, *procurator* in charge of the Latin and Greek libraries at Rome, *a studiis*, and finally *ab epistulis* – these last two posts are specifically described as in Hadrian's service. The chronology of Vestinus' appointments cannot be precisely established, and Pflaum's suggestion that his Egyptian posts (which he plausibly argues were held concurrently, as they were already under Claudius by Claudius Balbillus)[67] fell about AD 130 and his post *ab epistulis* towards AD 138 may put them all too late.[68] But if Pflaum's chronology is right, L. Iulius Vestinus may actually have been in charge of the Museum when Hadrian visited Egypt in AD 130, and as *archiereus* would have been the highest official of the imperial cult in Egypt. It might seem appropriate that abstruse Alexandrian learning and grateful piety should be combined in a poem purportedly composed for inscription on an altar upon which the emperor was exhorted to sacrifice. Its virtuosity might even have been one factor in persuading Hadrian to promote Vestinus from his Egyptian post to those in Rome, and thence finally to that of *ab epistulis* – a move made before him by Dionysius of Alexandria, father of the Periegete who also fancied acrostichs.[69]

But the appointment of the head of the Museum was itself imperial,[70] so Vestinus must have come to an emperor's attention before it was made. Indeed he is almost certainly from a family from Vienne in Narbonensien Gaul already well entrenched in the Roman élite, with an ancestor, perhaps his grandfather, L. Iulius Vestinus prefect of Egypt under Nero (59-62 AD) and a M. Vestinus Atticus, perhaps the prefect's son, rising to the consulate in AD 65, only to lose Nero's favour and be forced to suicide in that very year.[71] Moreover the poem itself has no hint of an Alexandrian geographical context but does have pointers to Attica, Boeotia and the Aegean: in the Callimachean tradition these features are of course quite compatible with composition in Alexandria, but the mode of address to the unnamed reader whom the acrostich identifies as Hadrian tips the balance (17-22): its reference to drinking from Hippocrene on Helicon, created by the hoof of Pegasus, together with the reference to the honey-bees of Hymettus, best suits publication in a mainland Greek context, and points to one of Hadrian's visits to Athens and neighbouring parts of Greece, whether in AD 128/9 or in AD 131/2. That he had earlier visited Thespiae by Helicon we have already seen from his poem to Eros. This visit was most probably in 124, but it need not have been forgotten four or even eight years later: and indeed Hadrian may well have returned to Thespiae again, perhaps even to attend the μουσεῖα Ἀδριάνεια which were celebrated in his honour in the month Demetrius, appparently the equivalent to the Attic Pyanepsion, i.e. October / November.

In choosing between AD 128/9 and AD 131/2 one factor points us to AD 131/2. With the consecration of the Olympieion in AD 131/2 and the simultaneous founding of the Panhellenion is associated an extraordinary crop of almost one hundred small altars (a high proportion of them carved from Hymettus marble) set up in Athens to Hadrian as σωτὴρ καὶ κτίστης and (invariably) Ὀλύμπιος.[72] Such altars are indeed found elsewhere before 131/2 (though not before AD 128/9 with the title Ὀλύμπιος) but the address Ὀλύμπιε would most aptly reflect the ceremonies in Athens in AD 131/2, at which another leading πεπαιδευμένος, the sophist and grandee who had based himself in Smyrna, M. Antonius Polemo, was chosen by Hadrian to deliver an epideictic oration to mark the inauguration of the finally completed temple of Zeus Olympios.[73] The formula 'for many years' also suggested to Buffière that a birthday might be an appropriate occasion for the poem:[74] if that guess is correct, then an exact date emerges, 24th January AD 132, Hadrian's fifty-sixth birthday.

This date and indeed the Athenian context can only be attractive possibilities. But wherever and whenever the poem was composed, it presumably presented an image of Hadrian that his equestrian official Vestinus had some reason to think was welcome to the emperor: as sacrificer, Hadrian stands in the tradition of Greek piety, as the implied reader of the poem he is assumed to belong to the connoisseurs of recondite hellenistic poetry. Several of the rare words in Vestinus' *Altar* had also been used by Dosiadas in his;[75] πάλμυς had been used by Lycophron, probably taking it from Hipponax; ἶνις was a tragic word also exploited by Lycophron and, of course, the epigram on Amazaspus.[76]

Another dedicatory epigram that can be plausibly claimed to be by one of Hadrian's friends in the governing class was discovered three decades ago at Cordoba. Signed by 'Arrianus, proconsul', it relates to a dedication to Artemis:

> Κρέσσονά σοι χρυσοῖο καὶ ἀργύρου ἄμβροτα δῶρα,
>   Ἄρτεμι, καὶ θήρης πολλὸν ἀρειότερα
> Μουσάων. ἐ[χ]θρῶν δὲ καρήατα δῶρα κομίζειν
>   εἰς θεὸν οὐχ ὁσίη δαίστορας ἀλλοτρίων.
> Ἀρριανὸς   ἀνθύπατος

> I offer to you, Artemis, immortal gifts of the Muses,
> better than gold and silver, and far finer than the catch;
> it is not right for those who feast on others' property to bring as gifts
> to a goddess the heads of their enemies.[77]
> Arrian   Proconsul

Given the interest in hunting displayed by the philosopher and historian Arrian in his Xenophontic *Cynegeticus* it is likely that this poem is by him, though attribution as well as interpretation have been much disputed since its first publication in 1971. The insistence on the superiority of literary creations to other artefacts and to ἀκροθίνια of animals, as well as being a *locus communis* of dedicatory epigram,[78] blends Arrian's belief in the primacy of λόγοι (expressed pugnaciously in his *Anabasis* 1.12) with a Stoic view he may have learned from Epictetus, i.e., that man is not master of anything outside him. It may be, as Bosworth suggests, that the reference to 'gold and silver' is to be connected with the Celtic practice which Arrian in his *Cynegeticus* tells us he adopted, of setting aside money for each animal killed, money which he then used to finance an annual sacrifice to Artemis,[79] though the reference to precious metals and to hunted animals could simply be to characteristic objects of dedication. It is much harder to know what is being said in the second couplet. However best sense is given by reading (as above) (e.g.) ἐ[χ]θρῶν δὲ καρήατα in the third line: ἐ[χ]θρῶν is not required by, but is compatible with, the traces, and the stone's dative καρήατι has not been accommodated in any plausible reconstruction of the couplet, requiring as it does the male dedicant to be carrying gifts (of water?) on his head in a mode that ancient practice and iconography seem to restrict to females. 'Heads', however, are regularly the objects of dedication, whether those of sacrificial or of hunted animals. It is less clear that ἐ[χ]θρῶν 'of their enemies' is right, although Bosworth has made an attractive case for referring this term to predatory or destructive animals, above all the rabbit which wreaked havoc in Spain and southern France. This interpretation involves taking δαίστορας ἀλλοτρίων in apposition to καρήατα, whereas it might rather be expected to be in apposition to ἐ[χ]θρῶν, and hence in the genitive. Moreover the assertion that such dedications are οὐχ ὁσίη chimes better with a depreciatory description of the dedicator than the dedication: perhaps Arrian is saying that regular consumption of animals who really belong to Artemis makes dedication of no more than their heads an act of impiety, but if so he was reversing the standard perceptions of greco-roman sacrifice.

Whatever the nuances, the issues of sacrifice are debated. That the debater is indeed the philosopher and historian has been doubted, most recently on the grounds that the lettering on the stone is third century AD,[80] but like many scholars I accept the identity. Arrian's tenure of the proconsulate of Baetica was not previously known, but can be fitted into the years before his consulate, probably ca. AD 124/5. The poem is thus almost certainly earlier than that of Vestinus, which plays with the same notion of the superiority of the Muses' creations to real objects (in Vestinus' poem altars of animal horns, lines 8-12). Although Arrian's poem was inscribed in Spain we must allow for the probability that Arrian circulated a text which Vestinus could have seen – it is unlikely in the literature-oriented Greek world of the 120s that Arrian would have restricted the readership of an epigrammatic composition to the inhabitants of an overwhelmingly Latin-speaking city in a western province.

More striking is a possible link with Hadrian's epigram composed for Trajan's dedication to Zeus Kasius. That had been a dedication of silver cups and a gilded animal horn plundered from Rome's enemies, the Dacians: could it be to this that the mysterious 'enemies' in Arrian's poem alludes? In the case of the Kasius epigram a literary text almost certainly circulated in Hadrian's reign, but it is probable that Arrian was himself in the Roman expeditionary force when the epigram was composed in AD 113/4. It is possible that Arrian alludes to that epigram, composed by Hadrian on Trajan's behalf, and that the phrase ἐ[χ]θρῶν δὲ καρήατα means not 'enemies' [own] heads' but 'heads belonging to enemies': Arrian would be suggesting that spoils both of the hunt and of war are of questionable appropriateness as dedications.

Arrian and Vestinus are but two of a number of cases where Hadrian's interests – admittedly, in the former case, more his interest in hunting – can be seen to have an impact on poetry composed by others.[81] In the context of a book entitled 'Greek Romans and Roman Greeks' they are as significant for their careers as for their literary output. Vestinus was a westerner of Narbonensian ancestry who divided his procuratorial career between the East and the largest Greek city of the empire, Rome, and his literary works of which we know were all in Greek. Arrian was from a family well-established in the élite of Nicomedia, though possibly of Italian descent. His Latin linguistic skills must have been considerable to administer Baetica as *proconsul*, perhaps even to execute his duties as suffect consul in Rome (probably in AD 129), and he sent Hadrian reports from the Black Sea in Latin as well as in Greek.[82] Yet his substantial philosophical and historical writing was all in Greek. Though things must still have seemed different to many members of the Greek city élites, here were men for whom, as for Hadrian, the question 'Are you Roman or Greek?' would have been one to which it was impossible to give a simple answer.

Notes

1. Page 1981, 555-73. Of those ascribed by Page to others which are also given to Hadrian in the tradition, *Anth. Pal.* 9.17, where the Corrector having written Γερμανικοῦ Καίσαρος then added Ἀδριανοῦ in the margin, is argued forcefully by Page to be by Germanicus. *Anth. Pal.* 9.387, of which a Latin translation is ascribed to Germanicus in the *Anthologia Latina* (*PLM* 4.102), has the ascription Ἀδριανοῦ Καίσαρος, then qualified by the Corrector οἱ δὲ Γερμανικοῦ Ἡσύχιος δὲ εἰς Τιβέριον τὸν Καίσαρα ἀναφέρει αὐτό. Page ascribes it to Tiberius, and its translation to Germanicus: the tone of exultation in which Roman control of Thessaly is described should be added to the arguments against Hadrianic authorship. Other recent, but less full, discussions of these and other poems are to be found in Fein 1994, Birley 1997.
2. *IEphesos* 1539 = *Epigr.Gr.* 888a, Page 1981, 566-8. For discussion and further references see Bowie 1989, 247.
3. SHA *Hadr.* 16.6. Presumably the alternative to Plato was Xenophon, especially popular in the imperial period and emulated by Hadrian's friend Arrian, on whom see below.

4. Cass. Dio 69.4.6.
5. Bowie 1997, 1-15. Note however the reservations of Jones 1997, 527-30.
6. Quint. 10.1.53. For the remains of Antimachus see the editions of B. Wyss (1936) and Matthews 1996. Given that genre is the basis of Dio's comparison the claim must relate to the *Thebais* (as Wyss t. 31, followed by F. Williams in OCD³) and not to the *Lyde*, whose merits were the subject of hot poetic debate in the third century BC (see Cameron 1995, esp. 303-338) or the *Artemis* (about which we know nothing, but its title is not that of an epic) as suggested by Birley 1997, 171.
7. Plut. *Tim.* 36.3.
8. Suet. *Aug.* 85, Mart. 5.5.7.
9. καί τινα καὶ πεζὰ καὶ ἐν ἔπεσι ποιήματα παντοδαπὰ καταλέλοιπε, Cass. Dio 69.3.1.
10. Arrius, Plin. *Ep.* 4.3; 4.18; 5.15; Pliny's hendecasyllables, 4.14 cf. 7.4.
11. For the *lyrica* of Vestricius Spurinna *utraque lingua*, see *Ep.* 3.1.7; Pliny's own *liber. et opusculis varius et metris*, *Ep.* 8.21.4. For a review of Latin polymetric poetry in the second century see Steinmetz 1989.
12. *IG* 2-3².3800, see Hardie 1983, 22, 83-4; note also C. Iulius Longianus of Aphrodisias, honoured at Halicarnassus for ποιημάτων παντοδαπῶν ἐπιδείξεις ποικίλας ('diverse performances of all manner of poems'), *MAMA* 8.418.
13. *IG* 14.1089 = *Epigr.Gr.* 2050. For a further attempt to establish a text see Page 1981, 568-71. For discussion of Hadrian and Parthenius see also Fein 1994, 48-9, with bibliography, Lightfoot 1999, 82-4 (and **T** 4).
14. Ps.Plut. *consol. ad Apollonium* 9.106b.
15. Suet. *Tib.* 70.
16. *Anth. Pal.* 7.377 = Gow-Page 1968, Erucius xiii, lines 2274-81, with a full discussion of the identity of the Parthenius attacked.
17. Τοὺς κυκλίους τούτους, τοὺς αὐτὰρ ἔπειτα λέγοντας
    μισῶ, λωποδύτας ἀλλοτρίων ἐπέων.
    καὶ διὰ τοῦτ' ἐλέγοις προσέχω πλέον. οὐδὲν ἔχω γὰρ
    Παρθενίου κλέπτειν ἢ πάλι Καλλιμάχου.
    θηρὶ μὲν οὐατόεντι γενοίμην, εἴ ποτε γράψω,
    εἴκελος, ἐκ ποταμῶν χλωρὰ χελιδόνια.
    Οἱ δ' οὕτως τὸν Ὅμηρον ἀναιδῶς λωποδυτοῦσιν,
    ὥστε γράφειν ἤδη μῆνιν ἄειδε, θεά
    Pollianus, *Anth. Pal.* 11.130.
18. Lucian, *Hist. conscr.* 56; his 'Elegies' are referred to by Artemidorus, *Oneirocr.* 4.63 as a source of recondite stories (along with Lycophron and Heraclides Ponticus), cf. further Lightfoot 1999, 82-4.
19. *Anth. Pal.* 7.674 = Page 1981, Hadrian ii, 563-4. Although Page is right to insist that this poem may not be a reply to *Anth. Pal.* 7.352 on Archilochus (perhaps by Meleager, see Gow-Page, 1965, Meleager cxxxii, lines 4742-9) which ends Πιερίδες, τί κόρῃσιν ἐφ' ὑβριστῆρας ἰάμβους / ἐτράπετ', οὐχ ὁσίῳ φωτὶ χαριζόμεναι, it undoubtedly shows knowledge of it.
20. Τὸ δὲ λοιπὸν σῶμά τις ἔθαψεν ἐπὶ τῆς ἠιόνος καὶ τάφον ἤγειρεν εὐτελῆ, καὶ ἐπίγραμμα ἄλλος ἔγραψε, Appian *BC* 2.86; εἰς Αἴγυπτον παριὼν καὶ ἐνήγισε τῷ

Πομπηίῳ, πρὸς ὃν καὶ τουτὶ τὸ ἔπος ἀπορρῖψαι λέγεται... Cass. Dio (=Xiphilinus) 69.11.1. Cf. SHA *Hadr.* 14.4 *peragrata Arabia Pelusium venit et Pompeii tumulum magnificentius extruxit*. The line also appears in the *Anth. Pal.* 9.402 ascribed to Hadrian. For discussion see the Budé notes in *Anthologie Grecque* vol. 8, containing 9.359-827, for the complex authorship of which see its introduction vii-x; Pekáry 1970, 195-8; Page 1981, Hadrian iv, 564-5; Fein 1994, 55-6; Birley 1997, 235-7.

21. Note his addition of a στήλη to the tomb of Epaminondas at Mantinea and the composition of an epigram for it (Paus. 8.11.8), his attention to Alcibiades' tomb at Melissa, where he commissioned a statue of Alcibiades in Parian marble and instituted an annual sacrifice of an ox (Athen. 574f) and his refurbishment of Ajax's tomb in the Troad (Philostr. *Her.* 288).

22. The Budé cites Od. 6.159 ἐέδνοισι βρίσας as a parallel for this sense: it perhaps counts in favour of the traditional translation that this sense only appears with the aorist, and the present tense seems always to have the sense 'be heavy with'. However the Budé's alternative proposal, that Hadrian alludes to a verse initially composed about Alexander, is unsupported speculation. See now Boatwright 2000, 140-2.

23. Bühler 1978, 55-60. The epigram runs:

ὄλβιε Πηλέος υἱέ, τεῆς τάχα χειρὸς ἀέθλους
ἄλλος ἀνὴρ ῥέξειε, τυχεῖν δ' οὐκ ἔστι καμόντα
τοσσαυτῆς σάλπιγγος ἀεὶ ζώοντος Ὁμήρου

The superscription in codex Bodl. Grabianus 30 f.33 (in which it was found) runs Ἀδριανοῦ στίχ(οι) καίσαρος εἰς τὸν Ἀχιλλέως τάφον which Bühler compared with that on *Anth. Pal.* 9.387 in its citation by the Venetus scholiast at the end of book 24 of the *Iliad* (schol. Ven. Hom. p. 532 de Villoison): Ἀδριανοῦ καίσαρος εἰς τὸν Ἕκτορος τάφον'. Bühler argued for a post-Nonnan composition on the grounds of the similarity between line 3 and the ending of Nonnus *Dion.* 25.269 σάλπιγγος Ὁμήρου.

24. *catachannas libros obscurissimos Antimachum imitando scripsit*, SHA *Hadr.* 16.2. The manuscripts have *catacannas / catacaimos / catacaymos*, emended to *catachannas* by Bernhardy.

25. *anno abhinc tertio me commemini cum patre meo a vindemia redeuntem in agrum Pompei Falconis devertere; ibi me videre arborem multorum ramorum, quam ille suum nomen catachannam nominabat. sed illa arbor mira et nova visa est mihi in uno trunco omnium ferme germina <arborum ferens>* ... Fronto 2.6 = 1.141 Haines = 29.7 van den Hout, a letter written in AD 143. The link with the tree in Fronto was already seen by F. Orioli, cited by A. Mai in his second edition of Fronto (Rome 1823) 106, cf. Cantarelli 1898, 157. For discussion of the *catachannae*, see also Schanz-Hosius 3.³ 8; Bardon 1968, 414-5; Fein 1994, 42-3; Birley 1997, 171.

26. *IG* 14.1097.8. The inscription (which at the time of the publication of *IG* 14 was in the Villa Albani) records victors at Athenian festivals in certain archon years in the second half of the fifth century; where identifiable the category of competition is comedy.

27. *Ad Marcum Antoninum de orationibus* 2 (2.102 Haines): *confusam eam ego eloquentiam, catachannae ritu partim pineis nucibus Catonis partim Senecae mollibus et febriculosis prunulis insitam, subvertendam censeo radicitus, immo vero, Plautino ut utar verbo, exradicitus.*
28. *P.Oxy.* 59 (1992), no. 3965 edited by P.J. Parsons.
29. Ar. *Ach.* 1150-2.
30. *ipsius etiam divi Hadriani multa id genus* [i.e. what Apuleius has just called *lasciva*] *legere me memini*, Apul. *Apol.* 11, in the context of Hadrian's epitaph for Voconius Romanus, cf. SHA *Hadr.* 14.9 *nam et de suis dilectis multa versibus composuit.* The phrase that follows in the MSS, *amatoria carmina scripsit*, is usually deleted as being a gloss.
31. *Anth. Pal.* 9.137 = Page 1981, Hadrian iii, 564-5.
32. Birley 1997, 143, discussing the poems, suggests that the people in the missing line should relate to Hadrian's tour of the Rhine and upper Danube in AD 121, hence *latitare per Sugambros* (as Steinmetz 1989 274 n.10) or *Batavos* (he also suggests, unmetrically, *Germanos*). But *latitare* demands rather some people among whom Hadrian seemed to withdraw from other activities, hence my preference for *Pelasgos*.
33. SHA *Hadr.* 16.3-4: see for discussion (including the question of the identity of this Florus) and bibliography Hermann 1950; Steinmetz 1989, 274-5; Fein 1994, 53; Birley 1997, 143.
34. SHA *Hadr.* 15.13: for the broader context of Favorinus' confrontations with Hadrian see Bowie 1997.
35. Both *calices* and *culices* are found in the manuscript tradition, see Fein 1994, 53 n.74.
36. *Anth. Pal.* 6.332 gives the heading Ἀδριανοῦ ἐν τοῖς ἀναθήμασι and the Suda s.v. Κάσιον ὄρος refers a quotation from the epigram to ἐπιγράμματα ἐν ἀναθήμασιν Ἀδριανοῦ πεποιημένα. For good arguments for accepting this title see Page 1981, Hadrian i, 561-3.
37. *Anth. Pal.* 6.332 = Page 1981, Hadrian i, 561-3.
38. The Suda entry (quoting only the first two lines) was attributed to Arrian's *Parthica* by Roos 1912, 33, and included by him in his Teubner (2nd edn 1968) as fr. 36, though not admitted as a secure fragment by Jacoby in his commentary in *FGrH* IId p. 575.
39. The horns of sacrificial animals were regularly gilded, cf. Plato *Alc.*II 149c, but the horn here offered along with two cups should be a drinking horn, the use of which Greek perceptions associated with Thracians and Getae: so Theopompus (*FGrH* 115 F 38) ap. Athen. 476d-e attributes their use to Paeonians, Diod. Sic. 21.12.5 to Getae (in a third century BC context). For the gilding of such horns see Krausse 1996, 146ff. (I am grateful to Susanne Ebbinghaus for these references).
40. *IG* 7.1828 = *Epigr. Gr.* 811 = Page 1981, Hadrian v, 565-6. For a very full and illuminating discussion see Gamberale 1993.
41. Robert 1978, 440ff = Robert 1987, 136ff.
42. SHA *Hadr.* 20.13. Cass. Dio 69.10.2 also mentions the foundation.

43. ἄ[ρ]τι γεινομένῃ πόλει, in Hadrian's letter to Stratoniceia from Rome dated 1 March AD 127, *IGR* 4.1156a = *SIG*³ 837, discussed by Robert 1948, 80-4.
44. Hadrian's movements in Bithynia and in *provincia Asia* during the years 123 and 124 cannot be determined with precision, but we now know that he was in Ephesus on 29 August AD 124, the date of the letter sent to Oenoanda published by Wörrle 1988 (*SEG* 38 (1988) 1462), and other indications are compatible with the hypothesis that he was touring cities in the north-west part of the province in the first half of AD 124, cf. Halfmann 1986, 199-201.
45. Imhoof-Blumer 1911, 10-11 pl. 1, von Fritze 1913, nos. 558, 564-7, 569-70 with plates ix 17, 22, 23, 25 and, with the legend Ἀδριανοῦ θήρα, no. 564 with pl. ix 22.
46. See Halfmann 1986, 201-3.
47. Cf. Wörrle 1988, 231-3. For the bulk of the inscriptions see Jamot 1895, 311-365; for more recent discoveries Plassart 1926, J. & L. Robert *Bull.épigr*. 1978, no. 215, Moretti 1981. It is clear that there was a revival in the second century AD, probably due to Hadrian, and the Museia are now called μεγάλα Τραιάνεια Ἀδριάνεια Σεβαστεῖα Μουσεῖα, Jamot 1895, no.16. For a collection of the evidence, see Schachter 1986, and for a discussion of the festivals in the hellenistic period, Knoepfler 1992.
48. Fein 1994, 55 (with n. 186) exaggerates the interval in describing it as 'rund ein Jahr', and metamorphoses the bear into a lion. For the question whether the bear's head (Robert 1978) or skin (as most others have supposed) was dedicated see Gamberale 1993, 1099, noting the regular offering of the skin in hunters' 'dedications' in the *Anthology* but the bear's head on the Hadrianic tondo on the arch of Constantine (cf. below n.52).
49. E.g. Thgn. 949-50 = 1078c-d, Rhianus *Anth. Pal.* 12.146 = Gow-Page 1965, lines 3226-9 (Rhianus v). Cf. Aymard 1951, 129ff.
50. See Conti 1970, 18ff. with pll. ix-xiii, and on date 10.
51. Athen. 677d-f, Heitsch 1961, no. xv, 51-3. See also Bowie 1990, 81-3.
52. For discussion and illustrations of the tondi see L'Orange & van Gerkan 1939; Aymard 1951, 527-37 with plates 35 and 37-9; Maull 1955. For Hadrian's interest in hunting, see also Anderson 1985, 105ff.
53. καὶ τάφον κατεσκεύασε καὶ στήλην ἔστησε καὶ ἐπιγράμματα ἐπέγραψε, Cass. Dio 69.10.2.
54. *CIL* 12.1122 = *CLE* 2.1522 cf. Schizzerotto 1968, 276-83, Stadter 1980, 209 n.5, Fein 1994, 50 with n.165, Birley 1997, 144-5.
55. Pithou 1590, 145 and addendum 465.
56. A number of modern scholars have accepted Hadrianic authorship (Bücheler in *CLE*, Bardon 1968, 419-20, Fein 1994, 50) but it is doubted by Cameron 1980, 172 n.8. For a full discussion of the poem, see Vinchesi 1988.
57. Both sense and metre suggest that this line should follow *ausus fuit nocere* and not, as in the renaissance copies, *sparsit ab ore caudam*.
58. For a full discussion of a problem to which we are unlikely ever to have a definitive answer, see Lambert 1984, 128-42.

59. *IG* 14.2139 = *Epigr. Gr.* 728 = *GVI* 722 = *IGUR* 1151.
60. The other epitaphs in *GVI* in scazons are 187, a one-liner from Rome of the first to second century AD; 246, of the second or third century AD from Traiana Augusta, whose metre may have something to do with its subject having been a writer of mimes; 538, of the same period from Amorgos, home of the archaic iambographer Semonides; and 1935, a very long and affected poem from second-century Alexandria whose choice of metre is unlikely to be casual.
61. SHA *Hadr.* 25.9, defended by Cameron 1980 and Birley 1994 (with extensive bibliography, to which should be added Bejarano 1975). The text and translation I print are those of Birley, who (like Bejarano) accepts the conjecture of Sajdak 1914-5, 147ff., of *nubila* for MS *nudula*. Sajdak saw in *nubila* an echo of Ennius' description of the underworld. The lines which, following Ribbeck, he took to be by Ennius, *Acherunsia templa alta Orci pallida leti nubila tenebris loca*, quoted by Cic. *Tusc.* 1.48 without ascription, are denied to Ennius by Jocelyn 1967, 256 (on fr. 35, from the *Andromacha*): perhaps correctly, but they are certainly from early Latin poetry, and their quotation by Cicero raises the probability that they would be known to Hadrian.
62. *Anth. Pal.* 15.25. The Palatine Anthology is preserved in the late 10th century manuscript Palatinus 23 + Paris. suppl. gr. 384; the Vatican MS is Y in Gallavotti's edition of Theocritus (Rome 1946, 3rd edn 1993). For a brief account of the collection of *technopaignia* see Gow 1952, 552. For an edition and full discussion see Haeberlin 1887.
63. Dionys. *Per.* 109-133 and 513-32, see Bowie 1990, 77.
64. For the evidence see Weber 1907, 209ff.
65. Suda s.v Οὐηστῖνος, Ἰούλιος 835.
66. *IG* 14.1085 = *OGIS* 679 = *IGR* 1.136 = *IGUR* 62, cf. *PIR*² I 623 (Stein – Petersen); Pflaum 1960-61, no. 105; Bowie 1982, 40f., Fein 1994, 267-9: ἀρχιερεῖ Ἀλεξανδρείας | καὶ Αἰγύπτου πάσης Λευκίωι | Ἰουλίωι Οὐηστίνωι καὶ ἐπισ | τάτηι τοῦ Μουσείου καὶ ἐπὶ τῶ | ν ἐν Ῥώμηι βιβλιοθηκῶν Ῥωμαικῶν τε | καὶ Ἑλληνικῶν καὶ ἐπὶ | τῆς παιδείας Ἀδριανοῦ τοῦ αὐτοκράτορος καὶ ἐπισ | τολεῖ τοῦ αὐτοῦ αὐτοκράτορος.|
67. See Pflaum 1960-61, no.105.
68. Birley 1997, 142 with n.2, puts Vestinus' move to the post of *ab epistulis* early in the 120s, immediately after Suetonius: as he says, there is no evidence either way.
69. See Bowie 1982, 77-8; Fein 1994, 269-70.
70. Strabo 17.1.8, 794C. On the highpriest's functions cf. Rigsby 1985, 279-89.
71. *PIR*² I 622 and 624.
72. Benjamin 1963, 57-86. On the Panhellenion see Spawforth and Walker 1985 and 1986; Jones 1996.
73. A L. Vestinus was one of the magnates who contributed sums of money to the reconstruction of buildings in Smyrna in AD 123/4, a project for which Polemo extracted assistance in kind – marble columns from the imperial quarries – from Hadrian, as attested by *IGR* 4.1431.11 = *ISmyrna* 595.11 Given the procurator Vestinus' presence in Athens, Rome and Egypt (where he may have observed the

despatch of the 6 porphyry columns of *ISmyrna* 595.43) it is surely likely that he is also the benefactor recorded in Smyrna.

74. Buffière 1970, 138 n.1.
75. φώρ (Vest.26 ... Dos.16) (ἔ)τευξε (Vest.9 ... Dos.3) ἶνις (Vest.19 ... Dos.17) ἰός (Vest.24 ... Dos.13); others echo similar words (Τριπάτωρ Vest. 26 ... ἀπάτωρ Dos.7; ἀείζωον Vest. 16 δίζωος Dos.17).
76. πάλμυς, Hipponax 3W, 38.1W etc., Lycoph. *Alex.* 691, ἶνις ibid. 570.
77. *SEG* 26 (1976-7) 1215, first published by Tovar 1971. For bibliography to ca. 1990 see Bosworth 1993.
78. Bosworth 1993, n.72 compares *Anth. Pal.* 6.321 and 325 by the Julio-Claudian poet Leonides of Alexandria (= Page 1981, Leonides i and iv).
79. *Cyn.* 34-35.1, Bosworth 1993, 239.
80. Beltrán Fortes 1993, 238ff. If the lettering is indeed third-century (which Birley 1997, 337 n.16 doubts), one might postulate the recutting of an inscription originally set up by a figure who was by then famous.
81. I have explored others in Bowie 1990.
82. Arrian, *Peripl. M. Eux.* 6.2, 10.1.

CHAPTER 14

The Self-portrait of an Antonine Orator:
Aristides, *or.* 2.429ff.

Jaap-Jan Flinterman

Among the extant works of Aelius Aristides, there are three texts in which the Antonine orator makes a stand against the attack by Plato's Socrates, in the *Gorgias*, on oratory and on the four leading statesmen of fifth-century Athens: Miltiades, Themistocles, Cimon and Pericles. In the edition by Lenz and Behr, these are the second, third and fourth orations: *To Plato: In Defence of Oratory*, *To Plato: In Defence of the Four*, and *To Capito* respectively.[1] The titles of the second and third orations speak for themselves; the fourth oration is in fact a letter addressed to a Plato fan who had taken offence at the way in which Aristides, in *To Plato: In Defence of Oratory*, had dealt with the philosopher's Sicilian adventures. *To Capito* is, therefore, later than *In Defence of Oratory* and earlier than *In Defence of the Four*. Charles Behr has made an attempt to assign more precise dates to these so-called Platonic orations,[2] but his arguments are less than compelling. In fact, his hypothesis that *In Defence of Oratory* was occasioned by a confrontation with the alleged Platonic school of Gaius in Pergamum has been shown to be built on quicksand.[3] On the other hand, it is evident that already *In Defence of Oratory* attests an intimate knowledge of the procedures in the Pergamene sanctuary of Asclepius.[4] Aristides spent two years of forced inactivity in this sanctuary; he himself labels this period the *Cathedra*.[5] His arrival in Pergamum, in AD 145, is therefore a certain terminus post quem for the composition of the orations, and as has been correctly pointed out by David Sohlberg, that is all that we can say with a reasonable amount of certainty.[6]

This paper on Aristides' Platonic orations has a slightly apologetic tone: I shall try to explain why, as an ancient historian, I think that these orations are worth studying. As some ancient historians – including rather eminent members of the profession – consider the Second Sophistic in general a suspect hobby rather than a legitimate object of historical interest,[7] this is not a wholly superfluous exercise. I shall argue that these colleagues of mine are wrong. At the same time, by using Aristides' Platonic orations as the main evidence in arguing my case, I hope to demonstrate that they are indeed an important source for the history of the mentality and ideology of the social elite in the Greek-speaking provinces of the Roman Empire, and that they, therefore, deserve to be studied by historians just as much as by literary scholars.

Before I start with the implementation of this programme, however, a couple of preliminary points should be brought up. Firstly, what do I mean by the term 'Second Sophistic'? I think that 'Second Sophistic' is a workable historical concept as long as it is used as the designation of a phenomenon that encompasses a social as well as a cultural aspect. The cultural aspect is, of course, a specific oratorical practice, characterized by a combination of rhetorical instruction and extempore declamation on historical or fictional themes in avowedly Attic Greek. As for the social aspect, from the second half of the first century AD onwards this oratorical practice became an immensely popular and prestigious pastime among the elites in the Greek-speaking provinces of the Roman empire, and it is for this phenomenon that I reserve the term 'Second Sophistic'.[8] It should be clear that this usage does not imply that I regard the Second Sophistic as just a cultural phenomenon:[9] in fact, the social position of the imperial sophists is explicitly taken into account. At the same time, it should be said that my approach deliberately focuses on the declamatory practice of the representatives of the Second Sophistic, a practice that was, after all, the most distinguishing characteristic of their activities.[10]

The second preliminary point I want to bring up concerns the relationship of Aristides to the Second Sophistic. Aristides himself would have taken serious offence at being labelled a 'sophist'. Charles Behr has convincingly demonstrated, most recently in his contribution in *Aufstieg und Niedergang der römischen Welt*, that for Aristides the word 'sophist' is a term of abuse.[11] By calling himself ῥήτωρ, 'orator', he wanted to distinguish himself emphatically from the sophists of his day, whom he accused of greed and cheap sensationalism. Should we therefore avoid the term when speaking of him?[12] I do not think so. Would we, if confronted with a person who composes and performs rock music, and who labels himself a composer, refrain from calling him a rock musician?[13] For similar reasons, we should have no qualms about calling Aristides – who wrote deliberative declamations for and against sending reinforcements to Sicily in 413 BC,[14] to mention only one example – a sophist; and I feel encouraged to do so by Behr himself, who accuses Aristides of 'perverse disregard of contemporary usage'.[15]

So much for my preliminary points. I want to start my defence of the historical importance of Aristides' Platonic orations by presenting a summary of Aristides' conception of oratory as set out in the second oration.[16] *In Defence of Oratory* is the most voluminous apology for oratory against Plato's attacks that was produced in Antiquity: the author was able to draw on the complete arsenal of arguments in favour of oratory that had been developed since the fourth century BC. Although Sohlberg has made a plausible case for at least some Stoic influence,[17] it is clear that the conception of oratory that Aristides unfolds is strongly reminiscent of the Isocratean ideal.[18] For Aristides, oratory is a comprehensive intellectual and moral project. It encompasses philosophy.[19] Its discovery and practice are inextricably linked up with the possession of the cardinal virtues.[20] Moreover, oratory is a bulwark against the rule of force and, as such, an essential condition for the existence of human society.[21] Legislation and jurisdiction are nothing but parts of oratory.[22] According to Aristides, 'to be an orator is to discover what is necessary and to order and present it in a proper manner with adornment and force'.[23] Therefore, the only person who can lay claim to the title 'best orator' is the best man, the ἀνὴρ ἄριστος, and with characteristic modesty Aristides presents himself as the embodiment of the lofty ideal implied in this thesis (*or.* 2.429-33).[24] It is to this self-portrait of the Antonine orator that I would like to draw your attention.

(429) What then is oratory by itself and the orator? I should not hesitate to say that he is the best speaker who is the best sort of man. (430) If someone should be of such a nature that he does not easily appear before the people with his oratory and engage in political disputes, since he sees that the government is now differently constituted, although as far as reputation, honour and important distinctions are concerned, he is not among the last, but if he should speak in solitude, and show honour to oratory's nature and the beauty in it, and should enlist god as the leader and patron of his life and speech, not even this man would find it hard to answer Plato, but he would be well supplied with the fairest and most just arguments. (431) My dear sir, I have honoured this faculty from the start and have valued it above all profit and affairs, not so that I might be a flatterer of the people nor so that I might conjecture at the desires of the masses, nor for money – but whoever looks to this and belongs to those who pay him, I call a hireling not an orator, and I say that I have left room for many others to dispute about felicity, if they are proud of this. But guided by speech itself and believing that good oratory is a fitting possession for men, I work according to my ability. (432) Why then do you accuse me of flattery, I who am so far from being a flatterer that I do not even consider how others will be flatterers toward me? Nor does it matter to me if I shall not be admired among the masses. But just as the lover of wine does not feel it a loss, if no one at all will know that he drinks, and the lover of boys and the lover of women do not pursue their passions for others to witness but are glad if they have what delights them, so I in my association with oratory and in my use of this in place of those other practices, have a joy and pleasure perhaps more fitting for

a free man. Therefore I do not count it an injury, even if none of my neighbors knows of me. (433) You call him a doctor who possesses the art of medicine, even if he does not publicly practice his art, and him a politician who possesses the art of politics, even if he remains in private life. [*Plt.* 259a-b] What then prevents the true orator in solitude from being such a man? [Translation: Behr 1986, 146]

In commenting on this text, we should observe in the first place that it is replete with allusions. Aristides models his self-portrait on the Socrates of Plato's dialogues, especially the *Gorgias* and the *Apology*. Just as Socrates was the only real politician in fifth-century Athens (*Grg.* 521d), in spite of his aloofness from political life (*Ap.* 31c-d), so is Aristides, even though he does not appear before assemblies and does not discuss policies, a real orator – perhaps the only one. After all, Aristides argues, one does not have to practise medicine or politics to be a doctor or a politician, provided that one possesses the relevant art. The reference to the *Statesman* (259a-b) serves to underline the Platonic inspiration of Aristides' self-portrait.[25]

In modelling himself on Socrates, Aristides is again following the example of Isocrates, who had done exactly the same in his lengthy self-defence, *On the Exchange*.[26] Isocrates even went so far as to pretend that he was standing trial for corrupting Athenian youth.[27] Now Aristides' claim that he himself 'does not easily appear before the people with his oratory' (*or.* 2.430) may very well echo Isocrates' repeated protestations that, due to his shyness and to the weakness of his voice, he is unable to deal with the mob.[28] Isocrates does not abstain from politics, though. What he abstains from is participation in the decision-making process of the democratically run Athenian state. At the same time he emphasizes his willingness to give advice to his fellow-citizens, to the Greeks in general and especially to the most distinguished among them, the ἐνδοξότατοι.[29] In her recent study of Isocrates, Yun Lee Too has aptly characterized this posture as 'the politics of the small voice'.[30] Aristides' position, on the other hand, at least in the passage under discussion, could well be described as 'the politics of muteness' – strange though the word 'mute' may sound when applied to an author as verbose as Aristides.

Aristides' self-portrait as the ideal orator is the crowning of an exhaustive encomium on oratory in which, time and again, its social function is emphasized (*or.* 2.362-437). The function of oratory is to think right as well as to convince oneself and others of what should be done (*or.* 2.392). Oratory brings up proposals, acts in embassies, and is thus constantly engaged in modelling the circumstances of human life (*or.* 2.401). Aristides characterizes it as a βασιλικόν, a royal thing (*or.* 2.392). It is somewhat surprising that the embodiment of this art of authoritative communication turns out to practise it in splendid isolation (*or.* 2.430: αὐτὸς δὲ ἐφ' ἑαυτοῦ). The fact that Aristides in actual practice did give advice to Greek cities on a couple of occasions only serves to sharpen the contrast.[31] The striking inconsistency between Aristides' eulogy of oratory and his self-portrait cries out for an explanation.[32]

Charles Behr has looked for an explanation of Aristides' professed silence in the so-called *Cathedra*, the orator's period of forced inactivity from 145 to 147 AD, spent in the Pergamene sanctuary of Asclepius. Without going into the details of chronological controversy, I would like to point out that there is a strong element of circularity in Behr's argument. First the American scholar interprets the passage under discussion as an attempt by Aristides to cope with the situation in which he found himself during the *Cathedra*, and then this seemingly self-evident interpretation as 'Aristides' defense of his retirement' is adduced as evidence for a date in the years 145-147. As far as I can see, however, it is Behr's dating of *In Defence of Oratory* more than anything else which enables him to state without further qualms that here 'Aristides speaks of his own inactivity during the incubation at Pergamum'. Since Behr's other arguments for a dating of *In Defence of Oratory* to the *Cathedra* are fragile, to say the least, I do not find this reasoning very satisfactory.[33] Besides, it tends to hide from view the much more interesting explanation for the muteness of the ideal orator given by Aristides himself: ὁρῶν ἑτέρως ἔχοντα τὰ πράγματα, 'seeing that political conditions have changed' (*or.* 2.430). As was noticed already in Late Antiquity, witness a scholium on the passage under discussion, these five words amount to the contention that deliberative oratory has lost its function under the Roman empire.[34]

This is a remarkable claim, and one could maintain that it is exaggerated.[35] After all, city politics may still have offered at least some room for deliberative oratory around the middle of the second century AD. Aristides' own speeches to the cities of Asia and to the Rhodians, though not deliberative in the strict sense of the word, are concerned with problems of civic life.[36] Nevertheless, in his *Defence of Oratory* Aristides expresses a different point of view, and that is what matters for the moment. Even if one considers Aristides' appeal to a change of political conditions a lame excuse for a silence caused by health problems,[37] the statement itself should be taken seriously. Besides, there were other voices in the camp of oratory which openly declared that eloquence as taught in the schools and practised by the declaimers had become a rather pointless exercise outside the educational and cultural field. In an article published in 1982, Ewen Bowie has drawn attention to a couple of anecdotes in Philostratus' *Lives of the Sophists* which show that sophistic eloquence might very well be counter-productive in the context of an embassy speech to an emperor.[38] In this connection, Philostratus' comment on a story about the Lycian sophist Heraclides is instructive too.[39] During a declamation in the presence of Septimius Severus, the Lycian lost the thread of his argument and broke down. In explaining Heraclides' misfortune, the author of the *Lives of the Sophists* recognizes that there is a wide gap between the insolence of forensic orators, on the one hand, and the mentality of sophists, who spend their days among schoolboys and are easily disconcerted by adverse conditions, on the other (*VS* 614). Simon Swain has correctly pointed out the tongue-in-cheek character of the passage under discussion,[40] and this becomes even more manifest when one realizes that Philostratus reproduces a traditional argument against oratory: the inability of the rhetorician to speak in court.[41] I want to suggest that Philostratus' self-mockery and Aristides' emotional outburst are different ways of dealing with a similar awareness of the loss of function of oratory. Whereas the Antonine orator professes to prefer a life of solitary dedication to his art under the guidance of his divine saviour, the Severan sophist unabashedly espouses the cause of belles-lettres.[42]

At this point, the attentive reader may experience an urge to retort that I have succeeded in proving precisely the opposite of what I had promised. After all, when even the sophists themselves had lost faith in the socio-political function of their profession, the futility of the whole practice of sophistic oratory should be obvious. Grateful though I am for the incentive to consistency implied in this objection, I must draw the attention of this reader to the fact that he or she has apparently missed a point of considerable interest, namely, the perception of the loss of function of oratory by prominent practitioners of the art of persuasion themselves, and the development of a belles-lettres mentality. Moreover, I want to argue that sophistic oratory was important as a medium for the affirmation of *elite* identity *precisely because it was devoid of any practical use*. I have borrowed the theoretical tools for this part of my argument from *The Theory of the Leisure Class*, a sociological classic by the American author Thorstein Veblen, published almost a century ago. Thanks to the late Moses Finley, most ancient historians are familiar with Veblen's concept 'conspicuous consumption'.[43] In Veblen's work, however, conspicuous consumption has a conceptual twin brother, namely 'conspicuous leisure'.[44] This concept amounts to the simple observation that, among the members of a leisured class, the more useless an activity is the more prestige it imparts to those who excel in it. Veblen himself considered classical studies an excellent contemporary illustration of his theory.[45] I want to suggest that Veblen's concept of 'conspicuous leisure' has considerable explanatory value for the fact that sophists could at the same time affirm the value and the uselessness of their art: precisely because sophistic oratory was devoid of practical use, it could function – in Veblen's words – 'as serviceable evidence of an unproductive expenditure of time'.[46] An analysis along these lines fits in very well with the interpretation by Simon Swain, in the first chapter of *Hellenism and Empire*, of Atticism as a 'badge of elite identity'.[47]

A more fashionable sociological approach recently applied to the Second Sophistic is Pierre Bourdieu's theory of practice.[48] Bourdieu-ian concepts such as habitus and symbolic capital have been used by Maud Gleason in a stimulating monograph on Favorinus and Polemo,[49] while in an impressive study on the Second Sophistic published in 1997, *Bildung und Macht*, Thomas Schmitz stresses the usefulness of two closely interrelated ideas in Bourdieu's oeuvre. The first of these is the notion that proficiency in activities expected to impart symbolic capital to the practitioner should be presented as the consequence of inbred refinement rather than of acquired expertise.[50] In the phrasing of Maud Gleason: the competitive performances of the sophists made the gap between the educated and the uneducated appear to be 'in no way arbitrary, but the result of a nearly biological superiority'.[51] The second is the notion that the effectiveness of activities in the literary or artistic field in securing a 'profit of distinction' is dependent on an appearance of disinterestedness.[52] Incidentally, there seems to be a considerable overlap between this idea and Veblen's concept 'conspicuous leisure'.[53]

Are theoretical tools such as these of any use in studying Aristides' Platonic orations? The proof of the pudding is in the eating, so let us have a look at two passages from *In Defence of Oratory*: the myth about the origin of oratory and the passage we have been discussing so far.[54] As we have seen before,[55] Aristides regards oratory as an essential condition for the existence of human society; this claim is underpinned by an aetiological myth (*or*. 2.394-99) which is modelled on the myth told by Protagoras in Plato's dialogue of the same name (320c-23a). There is, however, an important difference between the two. Whereas in Protagoras' myth Hermes is ordered by Zeus to make the survival of mankind possible by distributing conscience and justice among *all* people (322c-d), in Aristides' version the gift of oratory is given to 'the best, the noblest and those with the strongest natures' only, in order that they might save themselves and others.[56] By making a salient variation on the myth of Plato's Protagoras, Aristides makes explicit the link between oratorical excellence and social prominence. The fact that he presents the gift of oratory as a concomitant of natural rather than of social superiority should come as no surprise after the observation by Maud Gleason quoted above.[57] In Aristides' myth, eloquent supermen turn out to be the saviours of their less gifted fellow humans. In Aristides' self-portrait, on the other hand, the Antonine orator admits that such pretensions indeed belong to the realm of myth. Oratory still has a function, though: for a gentleman, it is a worthier pastime than hitting the bottle and chasing boys or women.[58] The fact that oratory has become an end in itself enhances rather than diminishes its value as a strategy of social distinction.[59]

Unlike other representatives of the Second Sophistic, Aristides defends his art with deadly seriousness. As a consequence, *In Defence of Oratory* does not exactly make exciting reading. It is precisely because of this serious-mindedness, however, that the inconsistency we have traced so far becomes so apparent to the reader. Whereas Philostratus takes the loss of oratory's political function for granted, Aristides struggles with it, thereby throwing it into relief. For both, oratory remains a socially significant phenomenon as a strategy of social distinction. In Aristides, this is a far cry from the power that, in the larger part of his *Defence* and elsewhere, the Antonine orator still claims for his art. *We* can argue that the loss of oratory's political function was conducive to the emergence of sophistic oratory as a symbol of elite identity. For Aristides' attempt to defend his art, on the other hand, the recognition of these developments creates an insoluble problem.

Aristides himself holds a change in political circumstances responsible for a situation in which the function of oratory has been reduced to a leisure activity for gentlemen. Despite the cautious phrasing, there can be no doubt that he is referring to the effects of Roman rule on city politics. Therefore, it is hardly coincidental that an inconsistency similar to the one that we have traced so far can be detected in Aristides' defence of the heroes of the Greek past against Plato's 'slanderous attack'.

It goes without saying that the classical past of Hellas in general, and of Athens in particular, was of inestimable value to Aristides. It was the intellectual and emotional link with this past that constantly nourished his self-confidence as a Greek living under Roman rule. Accordingly, saving the reputation of the champions of Greek liberty and of Athenian greatness against Plato was not a futile exercise for him.[60] The point is well brought out in *In Defence of the Four* 645ff. Plato has, in the metaphorical sense of the word, branded the most honoured of the Greeks, who fought for their common freedom (*or.* 3.651). In doing so, he has robbed Athens of the reputation which it owes to the memory of these men (*or.* 3.654-58). Aristides uses the metaphor of a reserve fund for this memory: it is due to this reserve fund that the Athenians, even in times of misfortune, could hope for a respectful and decent treatment (*or.* 3.654). This claim is illustrated with an example taken from fifth-century history: the Spartan refusal to destroy Athens after its defeat in the Peloponnesian war (*or.* 3.656). It is quite obvious, however, that Aristides thinks that the memory of the Four still has a contribution to make in ensuring the Athenians the goodwill of all men, τὴν συνεχῆ παρὰ πάντων εὐμένειαν (*or.* 3.658). It is a distinct possibility that he refers to Roman attitudes; in his oration *To Rome*, the ruling power's consideration in dealing with the Greek cities in general, and with the 'leaders of old' in particular, is singled out for praise (*or.* 26.96).

Aristides, it should be said, succeeds remarkably well in combining loyalty to Rome with pride in the Greek past.[61] And yet, in the defence of Themistocles, as if carried away by his own eloquence, he urges yearly prayers for the birth of a man such as Themistocles, and at the same time recognizes the political inappropriateness of such prayers (*or.* 3.347). The passage in question serves to illustrate the 'unsatisfactory contradictions and anomalies' – I borrow the phrase from Simon Swain[62] – involved in constructing Greek elite identity under Roman domination on the basis of past greatness, just as Aristides' self-portrait as an orator reveals the tensions involved in expressing it through an outmoded medium. Even though, as I have argued, in the latter case the liability could be turned into an asset, the constant harking back to the Hellenic past was a potential source of frictions and inconsistencies within elite ideology in the Greek world of the Roman empire.

Notes

* The research for this paper was done during a stay at Oxford in the spring of 1997 as a visiting scholar of Corpus Christi College, made possible by the College's φιλοξενία and by grants from the Netherlands Organization for Scientific Research (NWO) and from the Faculty of Arts of Utrecht University. Previous versions were given as part of a talk in the Seminar Room of Corpus Christi College and as a paper at the 1998 European Social Science History Conference. I am grateful to those present on these occasions and at the Congress at Lund for their comments and criticisms. Special thanks are due to Ewen Bowie and Simon Swain. Over the last few years they have been immensely supportive, and their willingness to discuss subjects of shared interest occasioned exchanges as pleasurable as they were inspiring. I am also indebted to Jona Lendering, who pointed out to me the relevance of modern social theory for a correct understanding of the Second Sophistic's historical importance. None of them should be held responsible for any factual errors that remain or for the opinions expressed in this paper, which is deliberately one-sided in its emphasis. While adding the paraphernalia of scholarly discourse, I have retained the format of an oral presentation. Not for the first time, Peter Mason corrected my English.

1. Text: *P. Aelii Aristidis Opera Quae Exstant Omnia*. Volumen I Orationes I-XVI complectens. Leiden: E.J. Brill 1976-80. Translation: Behr 1986. The discussion of *orr.* 2-4 by Boulanger 1923, 210-39 still makes instructive reading; Pernot 1993 is the best and most up to date treatment. Sohlberg 1972 is an investigation into the ancestry and origins of Aristides' conception of oratory; Karadimas 1996 offers a reconstruction of the conflict between philosophy and oratory in the second century on the basis of the evidence of Sextus Empiricus' attack on oratory and of

Aristides' *or.* 2. Vickers 1989, 170-78 summarizes *or.* 2; for perceptive comments cf. Wardy 1996, 104-7.
2. *Or.* 2 (AD 145-47): Behr 1968, 54-56 with n. 52; cf. Behr 1986, 449 n. 1. *Or.* 4 (towards the end of the same period): Behr 1968, 59f. with n. 60; cf. Behr 1986, 479 n. 1: 'around August AD 147'. *Or.* 3 (AD 161-65): Behr 1968, 94f. with n. 2; cf. Behr 1986, 460 n. 1.
3. For this hypothesis see Behr 1968, 54 with n. 50, where – as is pointed out by Göransson 1995, 35 n. 2 and 39 n. 7 – Galen's *De affectuum curatione* 5.41 Kühn is misinterpreted; cf. Behr 1986, 449 n. 1. See also Moreschini 1994, 1241f., referring to Dillon 1977, 266f.: 'The place of Gaius' teaching activity remains uncertain'.
4. See *or.* 2.66-71 and 2.75. Besides, it seems reasonably certain that the addressee of *or.* 4 was a citizen of Pergamum, see *or.* 4.5 and 4.22, with Behr 1986, 480 n. 31. The tentative identification of this Capito by Behr 1968, 59f. n. 60 is, on the other hand, quite speculative; see also Behr 1986, 479 n. 1.
5. *Or.* 48.70 Keil, *or.* 49.44 Keil, and the subscription to *or.* 30 Keil; cf. Behr 1968, 26 with n. 20; Swain 1996, 257 with n. 15.
6. Sohlberg 1972, 178 n. 6. Behr 1994, 1165f. n. 117 is overconfident in dismissing Sohlberg's questioning of his previous dating of the Platonic orations. In appealing to 'the improbability of Aristides writing II, IV and III with little time intervening' he ignores the fact – noticed already in Late Antiquity, witness H_1 158.9-12 Lenz with Lenz 1959, 24 – that *or.* 3 is a δευτερολογία. The arguments adduced by Behr 1968, 55 n. 52 for a dating of *or.* 2 to the *Cathedra* (e.g. the 'abnormally high – even for Aristides – insistence on medical and disease metaphors, and unfavorable comparisons of medicine with divine healing') fail to take into account (a) the function of such metaphors and comparisons in Aristides' argument, viz. that an activity does not have to be an art in order to be highly respectable (esp. *or.* 2.35, 61-72) and that using conjecture does not disqualify an activity as an art (esp. *or.* 2.149-56); and (b) the fact that Aristides is answering the contention by Plato's Socrates that oratory is to justice as cookery to medicine (*Grg.* 465c, quoted in *or.* 2.22). For Behr's interpretation of *or.* 2.430 as 'Aristides' defense of his retirement' see below, n. 34. The arguments for a dating of *or.* 3 to the period 161-65 (Behr 1968, 94f. n. 2) are inconclusive too, cf. Pernot 1993, 316 n. 4.
7. See especially Brunt 1994.
8. Cf. Goudriaan 1989, 55f. and 59f.; Flinterman 1995, 32-34 and 1996, 135-140; and now Schmitz 1997, 11-18. For a slightly different perspective see Swain 1996, 1-7 and 87-100, who uses the term 'second sophistic' as a 'convenient shorthand' for the period 50-250 AD (p. 2), defines it as 'the manifestations of [an] intensified feeling of Greekness' among the civic elites in the Greek-speaking provinces during this period (p. 88), and stresses (rightly in my opinion) the political-ideological importance of such manifestations (p. 6 and 88).
9. Cf. Swain 1996, 88: '... "cultural" is far too innocent and passive a word'.
10. In concentrating on an oratorical practice seemingly devoid of any social relevance I side with Schmitz 1997, 9-11, 18-26 and passim. Russell 1983 remains the best introduction to the sophistic scene; see also Anderson 1993, esp. 47-68.

11. Behr 1994, 1168-1177.
12. As is maintained by Wilamowitz 1925, 349 and Swain 1996, 255.
13. I have taken and adapted the musical analogy from Reardon 1971, 111-14.
14. *Orr.* 5-6 Lenz/Behr; see also Pernot 1981.
15. Behr 1968, 106. See also Reardon 1971, 127: 'Il affecte de mépriser les sophistes, mais il ne fait lui-même que transposer leur façon de faire.'
16. Cf. the summaries in Sohlberg 1972, 178-83 and 191-200; Pernot 1993, 317-23.
17. Sohlberg 1972, 261-77; cf. Pernot 1993, 322.
18. See Hubbell 1913, 54-64, esp. 64: '... [Aristides'] point of view is essentially Isocratean ...'; Boulanger 1923, 233: 'La plupart semblent provenir d'Isocrate ...'; Karadimas 1996, 240: '... he bases his ideas on Isocratean views and positions ...'; Swain 1996, 255: 'His conception of oratory was drawn from Isocrates.'
19. Aristides holds that oratory is nothing else than φρόνησις λόγων δύναμιν προσειληφυῖα (*or.* 2.302) and thus either a kind of philosophy or a more perfect accomplishment than philosophy (*or.* 2.305), and also that dialectic is a part of oratory (*or.* 2.450; cf. *or.* 3.509). There is an undeniable amount of common ground between Aristides' position in this regard and the claims made by Isocrates for his educational programme (see esp. *Antid.* 277; cf. *Antid.* 256f. = *Nicocles* 8f.), alternately referred to as ἡ τῶν λόγων παιδεία (*Antid.* 168) and φιλοσοφία (esp. *Antid.* 270ff.). Cf. Eucken 1983, 16: 'Sie [i.e. die Philosophie] ist als weitergefasster Begriff (...) dem (...) Ausdruck παιδεία τῶν λόγων gleichgestellt.' In *or.* 3.677f. Aristides explicitly and approvingly refers to Isocrates' labelling of 'himself and the orators, and those concerned with political matters' as philosophers, and claims that philosophy traditionally was φιλοκαλία τις (...) καὶ διατριβὴ περὶ λόγους, καὶ οὐχ ὁ νῦν τρόπος οὗτος, ἀλλὰ παιδεία κοινῶς. Cf. Sohlberg 1972, 180 and 276; Pernot 1993, 320f.; Karadimas 1996, 216-18 and 222f.
20. *Or.* 2.235f. and 2.382; cf. Sohlberg 1972, 198-200; Karadimas 1996, 102-4. Sohlberg 1972, 273f. thinks that Aristides knew the Stoic tenet that the virtues are reciprocally implied, and traces back to Diogenes of Babylon the combination of this doctrine with the idea that oratory is a virtue; see also Boulanger 1923, 235 n. 3. Karadimas 1996, 230-32 refers for related ideas to Isoc. *Panath.* 30-32, *Antid.* 274-82 and *C. soph.* 21.
21. *Or.* 2.205-11 and 2.394-99; cf. Karadimas 1996, 76. For an Isocratean parallel see *Antid.* 253-57 = *Nicocles* 5-9, with Hubbell 1913, 55-57; Karadimas 1996, 220f. and 232f.
22. *Or.* 2.212-33 and 2.401; cf. Karadimas 1996, 77f. and 81f. For an Isocratean parallel see *Antid.* 255 = *Nicocles* 7, with Hubbell 1913, 55-57; Karadimas 1996, 232f.
23. *Or.* 2.382: ἔστι μὲν γὰρ δήπου ῥητορεύειν τὸ τὰ δέοντα ἐξευρεῖν καὶ τάξαι καὶ τὰ πρέποντα ἀποδοῦναι μετὰ κόσμου καὶ δυνάμεως. Aristides gives a moral interpretation to rhetorical terms; the resulting ambiguity is intentional. Cf. Karadimas 1996, 52f. with n. 14 and 102-4.
24. That in *or.* 2.429ff. Aristides is speaking about himself was already noticed by the scholiast, III, 430, 9-11 Dindorf: τοῦτο εἰ καὶ ξενοπροσώπως δοκεῖ λεγέσθαι, ἀλλ' ἔμφασιν ἔχει περὶ ἑαυτοῦ λέγειν. The fact that the ideal orator 'enlists god as the

leader and patron of his life and speech' (*or.* 2.430) points in the same direction; the scholiast (III, 430, 19-24 Dindorf) rightly observes that the god in question must be Asclepius. Note also that *or.* 33.18ff. Keil, where Aristides is speaking without further ado in the first person, shows remarkable similarities to *or.* 2.429ff.
25. Note that Wilamowitz 1925, 350 seems to deny Aristides' knowledge of the *Statesman*.
26. Cf. Too 1995, 108: 'The *Antidosis* (...) constitutes Isocrates' attempt at being Socrates.'
27. *Antid.* 30; cf. Too 1995, 192f.
28. See e.g. *Philippus* 81; cf. Too 1995, 74f.
29. *Philippus* 82.
30. Too 1995, 74-112.
31. See esp. *orr.* 23 and 24 Keil; cf. below, at n. 37.
32. Karadimas 1996, 143 tries to eliminate the inconsistency by contending that the passage under discussion refers to epideictic oratory. I fail to see how this interpretation finds support in the text. It seems to be a corollary of Karadimas' conviction that Aristides' defence of his art reflects the practical usefulness of oratory in the second century AD rather than its importance as a socio-cultural and ideological phenomenon; see Karadimas 1996, 42-44 and 243f. and cf. 40f. for his criticism of the opinion expressed by Behr 1968, 55 with n. 53: 'What is so unreal about this whole argument is that Plato wrote of the instrument of political power, and Aristides of an art which was nearly reduced to a form of entertainment.' For a balanced view of the reflection of the contemporary role of oratory in Aristides' Platonic orations see Pernot 1993, 331-36.
33. Behr 1968, 51 and 55 n. 52; Behr 1986, 459 n. 314. For discussion of Behr's other arguments see above, n. 7.
34. III 430, 9-18 Dindorf, esp. 14-18: διὰ τοῦτο ὁ τοιοῦτος ῥήτωρ οὐκ ἀμφισβητεῖ ἑτέρῳ περὶ πολιτείας, ἀλλ᾽ ἡσυχίαν ἄγει, ὁρῶν οὐχ ὑπὸ δημοκρατίαν ὄντα τὰ πράγματα, ἀλλ᾽ ὑπ᾽ ἀρχὴν, ἐν ᾗ κινδυνεύειν ἀνάγκη τὸν τὰ δοκοῦντα ἑαυτῷ λέγοντα. Cf. Sohlberg 1972, 193f. with n. 24; Behr 1986, 459 n. 315. Aristides' words offer a modest parallel to the anonymous philosopher's contribution to the short dialogue which forms the epilogue to *De sublimitate* (44) and to Maternus' speech in Tacitus' *Dialogus* (36-41).
35. Thus Pernot 1993, 336 n. 89.
36. On *orr.* 23 Keil (*To the cities, on concord*) and 24 Keil (*To the Rhodians, on concord*) see Reardon 1971, 127-34; and Swain 1996, 288-95 and 96, contrasting with the passage under discussion *or.* 23.4. Here Aristides claims that his continuous practice of declamation has prepared him to speak on serious subjects οὐ γὰρ ὅπως μηδέποτ᾽ εἴπωμεν τῶν χρησίμων μηδέν, διὰ τοῦτο ἀεὶ μελετῶμεν, ἀλλ᾽ ὅστις τὰ δέοντα λέγειν ἔχει τε καὶ θαρρεῖ, οὗτός ἐστιν ὁ καὶ τὴν μελέτην δεικνὺς ὡς οὐχὶ μάτην οὐδ᾽ εἰκῆ πεποίηται. But the fact that this needed saying is significant in itself.
37. The view of the scholiast, III, 430, 9-18, esp. 13-15 Dindorf: ἵνα δὲ μή τις αὐτῷ εἴπῃ ὡς οὐκ εὐφυῶς εἶχε πρὸς τοῦτο, ὅπερ ἦν ἀληθές, ὥσπερ ἀπολογούμενος λέγει· διὰ τοῦτο ὁ τοιοῦτος ῥήτωρ κτλ. Cf. Pernot 1993, 336 n. 89: 'Comme le notent les

scholies, c'est une mauvaise excuse qu'il se donne (...). Son abstention politique n'était pas due à une possibilité extérieure, mais à des raisons personelles, notamment à sa maladie'.

38. *VS* 570f. and 622f., with Bowie 1982, 33.
39. On the incident cf. Anderson 1986, 47.
40. Swain 1996, 97.
41. See e.g. Sext. Emp. *Math.* 2.18; cf. Karadimas 1996, 62 and 194-98.
42. On the emergence of a belles-lettres mentality see Reardon 1971, 9f., 69-71, 95f., and 198; on Philostratus' outlook see Flinterman 1995, 29-51; cf. Reardon 1971, 185-98, esp. 190: 'Il crée une oeuvre variée, dont l'élément commun est qu'elle est surtout le produit d'un artiste en littérature, et non d'un homme convaincu de quoi que ce soit.'
43. Veblen 1899, 68-101; Finley 1973, index s.v. 'consumption, conspicuous'.
44. Veblen 1899, 35-53.
45. Veblen 1899, 394-98.
46. Veblen 1899, 45.
47. Swain 1996, 64 and esp. 29: 'Language was taken up as the badge of the elite because it particularly showed the possession of wealth and leisure by taking the classics as its point of reference.' See also Schmitz 1997, 83-91.
48. Helpful introductions to Bourdieu's oeuvre are Harker/Mahar/Wilkes 1990 – especially the chapters by Mahar/Harker/Wilkes 1990, Harker 1990 and Codd 1990 – and Thompson 1991.
49. See Gleason 1995, xii and xxi.
50. See e.g. Bourdieu 1990, 139: 'When distinctive dispositions are accepted and acquired as self-evident from early childhood, they have all the appearances of naturally distinguished nature, a difference which contains its own legitimation.' Schmitz 1997, 146, 149f. with n. 37, 152 with n. 43, 155 with n. 50, and 156-59.
51. Gleason 1995, xxi.
52. See e.g. Bourdieu 1977, 177, 194, and 197, esp. 194: 'But in reality such denials of interest (...) satisfy interest in a (disinterested) manner designed to show that they are not satisfying interest.' Cf. Thompson 1991, 16. Schmitz 1997, 28, 31, 155 with n. 50 and 157f.
53. I owe this observation to Jona Lendering. See esp. Veblen 1899, 44f., with Hobson 1936, 92f.
54. On these passages see also Wardy 1996, 106f.; and on the myth about the origin of oratory now Wissmann 1999.
55. Above, n. 21.
56. *Or.* 2.397: ... ἐπιλεξάμενον τοὺς ἀρίστους, καὶ γενναιοτάτους καὶ τὰς φύσεις ἐρρωμενεστάτους, τούτοις ἐγχειρίσαι τὸ δῶρον, ἵνα ὁμοῦ σφᾶς τε αὐτοὺς καὶ τοὺς ἄλλους σῴζειν ἔχοιεν.
57. Above, n. 51.
58. *Or.* 2.432. Cf. Philostr. *VS* 605: Damianus of Ephesus spent his money on fees for his tutors, Aristides and Hadrian of Tyrus, rather than on male or female beauties. For the justification of charging fees as a way to teach young men to get their pri-

orities straight see *VS* 494, with Flinterman 1995, 37 and 1996, 144f.; Schmitz 1997, 60. Note that Diogenes Laertius (2.72) attributes this justification to Aristippus.
59. On oratory as 'ein Ziel an sich' for Aristides see Schmitz 1997, 157, referring to *or.* 33.19f. Keil, a personal outpouring which shows considerable similarities to *or.* 2.429ff.; and cf. Nicosia 1979, 67-69, referring to *or.* 2.429ff.
60. Cf. Pernot 1993, 330f.
61. Cf. Swain 1996, 260.
62. Swain 1996, 109.

CHAPTER 15

Polyaenus:
A Greek Writer as a Job-seeker in the Roman World

Anthon Xenophontov

Polyaenus as a writer cannot be placed among the famous persons of the time of the Second Sophistic. However, his surviving principal work *Strategica* undoubtedly reflects some cultural trends of this period.[1]

The *Strategica* as a text is interesting for us, not only because it is a valuable collection of ancient military trickeries or because it has preserved many fragments from lost historians, but also because *Strategica* is an exciting example of a very provocative self-presentation of its author, Polyaenus. From my point of view this example has a certain relation to the problem of self-promotion of some Greek intellectuals in the Roman Empire.

We can ask the question: Who was Polyaenus? Was he an ambitious careerist who tried to climb the official ladder, contemplating every advantageous opportunity? Or was he just an unlucky person patiently awaiting his moment of triumph?

There could be many different answers to this question but I shall try to present just one possible interpretation of this problem. My suggestion is based not only on the study of sources about Polyaenus's life but also on a careful examination of his own work. I am sure that by analysing the text we can gain a better understanding of the fundamental ideas and intentions of its author than by merely studying the scanty sources available about his life. Indeed, these sources on the life and career of Polyaenus are not numerous. They are limited to some scattered notes in some later Greek texts.

From the Byzantine lexicon of *Suda* we know that Polyaenus was a Macedonian by origin and rhetor by occupation (s.v. Polyainos).[2] It is evident that his family was well-off but not necessarily rich. Although he could get quite a good education and he knew Latin and Roman law, he did not belong to a family with influential links. Therefore, Polyaenus was obliged to seek jobs as a teacher of rhetoric or as an attorney in imperial courts.[3] Although not necessarily by his own choice, Polyaenus later appeared in Macedonia and in Rome as an attorney.[4]

Furthermore, Polyaenus, in comparison with other successful contemporaries and rivals of sophists, was not perhaps so gifted a writer that he was able to receive literary patronage from noble Romans.[5] Therefore, he constantly travelled in search of new possibilities.

In spite of his probable ambitions he fell short of his goals but lived until an advanced age when, at last, fortune seemed to smile on him. This was at the beginning of the Parthian War in the autumn of AD 161.[6]

Suddenly, he decided to compose a kind of anthology of stratagems which he now could directly dedicate to the contemporary co-emperors – Marcus Aurelius and Lucius Verus.[7]

Then, during quite a short period of time he published eight books. His haste was evident. This is revealed in the lack of correspondence between the prefaces and the content of his books, in a certain disorder in the arranging of stratagems, and in the repetition of slightly different versions of the same story. Because of all these errors Polyaenus more than once is criticized by modern scholars who blame him for carelessness and absence of diligent searching for the historical truth. [8]

But why did he rush so much? Maybe he was afraid that the war would stop before he could complete his writing. Or, perhaps, he did not expect to live long enough to receive his possible reward. We can only guess.

We can hardly assume that Polyaenus did not care about the clarity of his writing. By means of analysis of the author's remarks, as well as from his main narration, it becomes clear that *Strategica* does not represent a chaotic collection of different types of military trickeries. It is designed according to a certain plan which originally had to cover a central theme, people, or chronological period. At the same time, *Strategica* is not simply a sort of conventional military treatise. It has some implicit level of narration which could be revealed to thoughtful and experienced readers in sophistic matters.

Although *Strategica* does not represent itself as a consistent narration and seems to be a multitude of separate narrative elements where every aspect is dedicated to quite different persons or peoples, we can nevertheless see how the author of *Strategica* develops his concept of stratagem throughout the text. Actually this concept is introduced already at the beginning of the First Book where Polyaenus explains that he has chosen from history the acts that have shown generalship when confronted with public and private enemies (I.13). Then, during the publication of his next books he gradually constructs the pattern of the ideal *strategos*. For Polyaenus the race of origin does not matter so much – Greek, Roman or even barbarian. This model of ideal *strategos* should conform to the qualities of a clever and tricky general – like Odysseus who appears as a first example of its kind in Polyaenus's work (I.8-12).[9] Among similar persons Polyaenus depicts examples of other great *strategoi* of the Hellenic and Roman past – Agesilaus (II.1.1-33) and Iphicrates (III.9.1-63), Alexander (IV.3.1-32) and Dionysius (V.2.1-23), Hannibal (VI.38.1-10) and Caesar (VIII.23.1-33). Thus Polyaenus invites his crowned readers to follow his model.

It is also a very indicative fact that Polyaenus took all of his examples from the distant past, completely ignoring the data of the Roman imperial history. This omission is too glaring to be unintentional. One can offer some possible explanations: first (and more traditional) is to consider this marginalization of Romans as conventional among many Greek writers.[10] The second explanation (and in my view more consistent with the views of Polyaenus) concerns the merits of *strategos*, the foremost characteristics of which are cleverness and trickery. That is why he himself tried to adhere to this rule. He understood that it is imprudent to remind his imperial readers about the recent Roman disaster at Armenian Elegeia (AD 161).[11] It is better merely to hint at it in a certain camouflaged form. Polyaenus resorted to using analogies and by way of inclusion in the only Parthian stratagem he presented an anecdote which recalls the Roman defeat at Carrhae (VII. 41).

Thus he, first of all, tried to warn his Roman sovereigns against underestimating their eastern adversaries. Because, he says, the barbarian race finds more delight in trickery and guile than even in arms (VII. Pref.). Polyaenus is sure that he knows the way to overcome Parthians. He maintains that being a Macedonian he has inherited the ability to conquer the Persians in war (I. 1). Therefore, in this way, he tries to send a special message to his Roman sovereign: 'if you follow my advice, which is not only of a military nature, you will tower above all your predecessors and rank with the most famous heroes of ancient times such as Odysseus, Alexander and Caesar'.

Thus Polyaenus could be described as a job-seeker in the Roman world, trying to draw the attention of his imperial reader and in this way promoting his own social status.

We don't know for certain whether Polyaenus ever succeeded in his aspirations. His writings reached us in an uncompleted form. However Polyaenus stated (hinted at) in the Preface to Book Five that the emperors actually read his book – a statement too bold to publish unless some truth lay behind it. It is also possible that he died even before the end of the Parthian War (AD 166) because his book on Parthian affairs was never written.[12]

In conclusion, we can suppose that the example of Polyaenus was not exceptional in this period of history, although we have no evidence that other prominent Greek writers like Arrian or Plutarch were granted their offices in return for their writings.[13] We are sure, however, in spite of Polyaenus's remarks, that he is worthy of the emperor's favor, this writer did not belong to 'those Graeculi who shamelessly exploited, to their own profit, the tastes of certain Romans'.[14]

Notes

1. Wheeler 1984, 253-74; Wheeler 1988, 12-13.
2. However, the recent edition of *Strategica*, mentioned below, is of the opinion that Polyaenus was born into a family of Macedonian descent living in Bithynia (possibly at Nicaea). See: Wheeler & Krentz 1994, 9-10. See also: Lammert 1952, 1432-36 and Melber 1887, 5-7.
3. About connections between the legal profession and sophists see: Bowersock 1969, 50, 56-7.
4. The fragment of Polyaenus's speech *On Behalf of the Macedonian Assembly* can confirm this fact. Also, Polyaenus notes in *Strategica* that he was busy with pleading in the Roman courts (Praef. libri II).
5. Polyaenus tried to write in a pure Attic dialect using dual and optative forms but not always successfully. His style leaves much to be desired. In general see: Bowie 1970, 23 and Wheeler & Krentz 1994, 14.
6. Strobel 1994, 1317-24.
7. It was ordinary practice for many authors to dedicate their writings to the Emperor. See: Janson 1964, 100-6 and Russell 1973, 9-11. In some cases a work's dedication was really targeted at promoting the social status of its author. See, for example, Apollonius Citiensis, *Kommentar zu Hippokrates*. [I would like to mention the helpful comment by Professor Jerker Blomqvist].
8. See, for example, Stadter 1965, 18-19.
9. About Odysseus as a favourite hero of the Second Sophistic, see Anderson 1993, 75-78.
10. See discussion of this problem: Bowie 1970, n. 5, 1-41 and Anderson 1993, 101-19.
11. See: Strobel 1994, 1319.
12. Polyaenus tells about his intention to write this book in Prefatio to Book VI. However, Suda knows just another work of Polyaenus – *Tactica* in three books, considered by some critics as *Strategica*. See discussion of this question: Lammert 1952 n. 2, 1433.
13. Plutarch, see: Russell 1973, n. 7, 8-9 and Pelling 1988, 2-3; Arrian, see: Bowie 1970, 25-27 and Syme 1982, 181-211.
14. Bowersock 1969, n. 3, 115-16: 'The more vicious imputations in Lucianus in the *Nigrinus* or treatise on hired philosophers are directed either against weakness generally or against men of the East, like himself. Lucianus criticized those Graeculi who shamelessly exploited, to their own profit, the tastes of certain Romans'.

CHAPTER 16

The Meaning of Greek Historiography of the Roman Imperial Age

Paolo Desideri

1. Giacomo Leopardi on the Later Greek Historians

In one of the most penetrating thoughts of his *Zibaldone*, the Italian writer Giacomo Leopardi observed, on the 30th of May 1823, that only the Greek historians had continued to narrate the history of Rome, long after the Latin ones had stopped.[1] According to him, Tacitus – whose *Historiae* ended with Domitian's death – was the last of the great Roman historians. In fact, if Appian, Dio, Herodian, and later Procopius, Agathias, Zosimus and so on, had not continued the task of registering the new events, we would know hardly anything now about the history of the second century AD and of the subsequent centuries. One could add that, as many of these historians also narrated the events of past ages again, if they had not written their histories – and if their works had not been preserved – we would be very poorly informed of the history, both Greek and Roman, of previous periods as well. With great emphasis Leopardi proceeded in exalting the nation – Greece, of course – which, having long before invented historiography, and narrated its own magnificent deeds, after so many centuries, when its political fortunes had fallen into complete decay, could still 'be the instrument of the memory of the centuries; so that its writers alone could be able to tell the stories of mankind, and of the nation itself (Rome) which had destroyed its independence'.

This comment on the longue-durée of Greek historiography can easily be connected to the general high appreciation with which Leopardi considered the cultural achievements of the Greek world, as compared to those of the Roman and of other ancient and medieval peoples.

Greek civilization went on for an exceptionally long time – he said – so that it was able to see the birth and the death of the other peoples...; Greece – he insisted – never lost its civilization, and after tremendous vicissitudes..., after communicating its own culture to many a people, in which this same culture flourished and decayed, emerged once again – in what can be called the beginning of the modern age – as the one and only civilized nation in the world, and gave again the other nations the light and the impulse towards a new and modern civilization.

We need not dwell here on the philosophy of history of the great nineteenth century thinker and poet; it will be enough to gather up some of his suggestions referring to the field of our present concern: suggestions which, as in many other cases, are of great interest. First of all, we can find here the idea of the autonomous value of the Greek literature of the Roman Imperial period, and, as regards historiography at least, of the Byzantine period as well. Second – and more important for us today, while looking for the intellectual profiles of the Greek historians of the Flavian and Antonine periods – we see that Leopardi stressed their importance as historians of contemporary events: which may appear surprising.

2. Contemporary and Non-Contemporary History

As is well known, the more-or-less well-preserved Greek historians of the second century AD make up what can be considered the most impressive group of ancient historians of one and the same period throughout classical antiquity. Beginning with Plutarch – whose exclusion from the group, based on his being a biographer rather than a historian, I would regard as absolutely unjustified – passing through Appian, Arrian and Dio Cassius, and ending with Herodian, we have a corpus of historical writing which, taken in its entirety, represents a sort of general rethinking of all the Greek and Roman historical – mostly political and cultural – experience from Theseus up to Severus Alexander. Some periods, historical themes or personalities – like Alexander the Great, or the Roman civil wars – were in fact reconsidered more than once. More important, anyway, is that contemporary history had indeed a relevant place: all of the authors just mentioned dedicated – as we will soon see – some part at least of their works to narrating events which had occurred during their own lifetime. Putting aside, for now, the problem of why and how this corpus has largely been preserved, it is in fact appropriate for our purpose to point out the elements which show the interest of the authors for their own times.

Plutarch, the oldest of the group, may appear disappointing from this point of view. It is evident that his *Vitae Parallelae*, even if we take into consideration the few *Lives* which are lost, are completely orientated towards the past. In fact their heroes, both Greek and Roman, belong to ages which are very far from the author's own lifetime – Philopoemen, 'the last of the Greeks', lived in the second century BC, whereas the last of the Romans is Cicero, whose death dates from 43 BC. Besides that, at least once Plutarch makes an explicit statement that his biographies allow him to become estranged from the present: in the Prooemium of Aemilius Paulus' *Life* he says:

the study of history and the familiarity with it which my writing produces enables me, since I always cherish in my soul the records of the noblest and most estimable characters, to repel and put far from me whatever base, malicious, or ignoble suggestion the relations I need to establish with my contemporaries may intrude upon me, calmly and dispassionately turning my thoughts away from them to the fairest of my examples (Perrin's Loeb translation, with slight modifications)

Incidentally, I would like to stress his using the term *historia* to define his biographical activity. Admittedly, statements like that would legitimate the conclusion that, as far as Plutarch is concerned at least, historiography can be considered as a sign of being dissatisfied by the events of one's own age. This can also be witnessed elsewhere in other non-historiographic works of Plutarch – such as the ironic and painful description of the Roman tribunals in some Asian town which can be found in the brief fragment of an essay *Animine an corporis affectiones sint peiores*, for instance (*Mor.* 501e-502a), not to mention well-known passages of the *Praecepta gerendae rei publicae*.[2] This disenchantment with events in one's own time was not something unique to the Greek people of this period: the Roman great families themselves were discontented all the same, admittedly because of different reasons. On the other hand Plutarch himself lets one of his characters declare, without raising objections: 'I am well content with the settled conditions prevailing at present, and I find them very welcome...; there is, in fact, profound peace and tranquillity: war has ceased, there are no wanderings of peoples, no civil strifes, no despotisms, nor other maladies and ills in Greece requiring many unusual remedial forces' (*De Pythiae oraculis*, 408bc). Anyway, most important, from our point of view, is the fact that Plutarch also wrote on contemporary, or nearly contemporary, subjects, such as biographies of the Roman emperors from Augustus to Vitellius – of which only the *Lives* of Galba and Otho are preserved. In this way the system, as it were, of a universal history in biographical form was completed. We cannot therefore affirm that present times were deliberately excluded from his historiographical interests.

Passing to Appian, of Alexandria in Egypt, who lived until the reign of Antoninus, his historical work, the *Historia Romana*, was mainly divided into geographical sections, corresponding to the various regions and provinces of the Empire, the fundamental historiographical idea being to show how the

Romans had succeeded, through decades or centuries of wars, in taking possession of the single portions (and peoples) of their immense dominion. So one could say that Appian's history was at the service of geography; in other words, that the author's main interest was to describe and explain his own world, using the history of each region as a means of identification of its fundamental characteristics. In fact, if we take into consideration the five books of *Bella Civilia*, or even the strongly personalized Ἀννιβαϊκή and Μιθριδάτειος, some doubts must be raised about the real nature of his historiographic plan, or at least about his ability to carry it out. As for our present concern, anyway, what is extremely important is that the *Historia Romana* included, or was intended to include, a section of a completely different kind. 'The last book' – Appian says at the end of his Preface (15) – 'will show the present military force of the Romans, the revenues they collect from each province, what they spend for the naval service, and other things of that kind'. The project of a book like this – which we can no longer read – would reinforce the idea of a spatial, rather than diachronic, dimension of the whole work, and therefore of its fundamentally contemporary outlook. But even if this book had never been written, as some scholars think,[3] we know from the abstract of Photius' *Bibliotheca* (cod. 57) that Appian's work also included a book in which the Imperial conquests from Augustus to Trajan were narrated, whose title was Ἑκατονταετία, as well as a *Dacian* and an *Arabic* book. This is enough to conclude that in Appian's *Historia Romana*, too, contemporary history played a significant role.

As for Arrian of the Bithynian Nicomedia (of nearly the same age as Appian), whose most important historical work was certainly the *Anabasis* which we can still read, we know from Photius' *Bibliotheca* (cod. 58 + 92) that he had also written eight books of Βιθυνικά, two biographies (*Dio* and *Timoleon*), ten books of Τὰ μετ' Ἀλέξανδρον, (a history of the short period from 323 to 321 BC), and finally seventeen books of Παρθικά, which, according to Photius, ended with Trajan's war. The dimensions of this last work – of which unfortunately only some few fragments remain in modern times (see Jacoby's collection, 156 FF30-48) – make us think of an ethnographic, not strictly historical, approach; but at least the Photian indication of its terminal point obviously also implies an exhaustive treatment of the political and military history of the region, as far as its relations with the Roman world were concerned.[4]

With Dio Cassius, who was also of Nicomedian origin, we are of course in a much later generation, that is at the passage from the Antonine to the Severan period; which enabled the historian himself to say at the end of his seventy-second book (72.36), commenting on Marcus Aurelius' death, that 'our history now descends from a kingdom of gold to one of iron and rust, as affairs did for the Romans of that day'. There is no need to dwell here on the structure of Dio's *Historia Romana*, which in its final form looks like an annalistic work, beginning presumably with the Aeneas legend and the founding of Rome, and proceeding up to the author's lifetime. For my purpose it is only useful to underline that Dio – as he informs us in a celebrated passage (73.23) – originally wrote and published 'a little book about the dreams and portents which gave Severus reason to hope for the Imperial power'; that after receiving the emperor's approval for this booklet he devoted himself to writing a history of the contemporary events of his age; and that, after a second Imperial approval, he 'conceived a desire to compile a record of everything else that concerned the Romans'. Other details of this passage need not detain us for the moment; it is sufficient to conclude that evidently Dio's point of departure was contemporary history, and that only later on he was led to start on the long journey through past history, even the remotest periods.

Even fewer words need be spent, from our point of view, on Herodian's *Ab excessu divi Marci libri octo*, whose eight books covered, according to the author himself (1.1.5), nearly sixty years, that is from Marcus' death (180) to Gordian's accession (238); in fact, he also explicitly added that he had 'written a history of the events following the death of Marcus which I saw and heard in my lifetime' (1.2.5). The dignity of the present – especially, it must be pointed out, as a proper subject for historiographical treatment – is strongly stressed, as compared, for instance, even with the recent past of the first two centuries of the Roman Empire.

3. Being Roman Does Not Exclude Greek Identity

The great majority of the Greek historiographical works written in the period from Plutarch to Herodian have been lost. To realize the entirety of the loss one can refer to the wonderful, still unsurpassed, picture drawn twenty-eight years ago by Ewen L. Bowie[5] – whose general tenets, though, I don't always agree with. For example, the 'group' of historians whose works have at least been partially preserved – i.e., those about whom we have been speaking so far – is a group only in a very debatable sense of the word. In fact, it would surely be hazardous even to think of the possibility of tracing the criteria, if any, which could have determined the partial preservation through so many centuries of Byzantine cultural history, both of the single authors and works, and of the whole of them. It is tempting, of course, to imagine that the idea of preserving the essentials of the political and military history of the Empire may have played some role. The concept itself of the group is however a modern one: I have been able to trace it back to the second half of the sixteenth century, when it can first be found in the *Methodus ad facilem historiarum cogni-*

tionem (1st edition 1566) by Jean Bodin; a book which represents, inter alia, the first modern attempt at a systematic evaluation of the ancient (and modern) historians. In fact, the great French jurist, historian, philosopher, and political thinker stressed the special historical meaning of the group of Greek historians of Rome – in which admittedly he placed Polybius and Dionysius of Halicarnassus too (see esp. 132a, 10 ff., P. Mesnard, ed.). In his opinion they had themselves, and could offer to others, the possibility of looking at the Roman historical experience as a developing political system – a look which the Roman historians, who lived, so to speak, inside this same system, could not manage to acquire: a very stimulating approach indeed, but one which is not very helpful to our present concern.[6]

The problem is, on the one hand, if we want to obtain from these historians an idea of the Greek mentality of the age, we ought to consider them not as the sole historians of this same age, but as just a part of the contemporary historiographical production, putting them, as it were, in perspective. On the other hand, one is not allowed to forget these authors in the general panorama, even if one starts from the idea that it is necessary, as far as possible, to give the proper place to the authors whose works have been lost. Once the problem has been put in the terms which – in my opinion at least – are correct, one can better appreciate the fact that, as we have just seen, contemporary history played a role which cannot be considered irrelevant in all the historians of whose works we have some direct information. It is in some way surprising to observe that, on the other hand, the interest for their own age seems almost absent on the part of the historians of whose works we have only titles or scanty fragments. But it would be too easy to ignore the first group of historiographers, on the basis that they ought primarily to be considered as members or high officers of the Roman government – and as such, more interested in the fortunes of the Roman Empire than in asserting their own identity as Greeks. In fact, most of these historians, beginning with Plutarch, cannot be credited with immoderate sympathy towards Rome; and, on the other hand, they devoted not the least of their work to the history of Greece and of what we call the Hellenistic world; they were not less Greek than the others.

What one can suspect is that, at least from a certain moment on, they could not really see any fundamental difference between being Greek and being part of the Roman Empire. It would be superficial to try to synthesize in only a few words the cultural elements of the historical process which culminated in the birth and subsequent development of the Empire which we call Byzantine; but we can be reasonably certain that Byzantium was, from Constantine on, the *Nea Rhome*, and that the inhabitants of the new Empire called themselves *Rhomaioi*. It is useful to recall in this perspective the well-known passage of Aelius Aristides' Εἰς Ῥώμην, where the Smyrnean sophist, speaking – probably in AD 143 (at any rate during Antoninus Pius' reign) – in front of the Imperial court and the Senate, said that 'you (Romans) don't now divide the races into Greeks and barbarians...; you have divided people into Romans and non-Romans' (63; Behr's translation). Even if one cannot believe that an idea like this was universally accepted and shared throughout the Greek world at this time, it evidently could be stated without creating a scandal on an official occasion, in the presence too – one may suppose – of other Greek people. What the cultivated and well-to-do Greeks after an age of humiliation had been convinced of was that the Imperium Romanum could become a Greek and not only a Roman concern; the acquisition of Roman citizenship being the easiest way open to 'the best' to take full part in the material advantages of the Imperial peace: 'you have caused the word 'Roman' to belong not to a city, but to a sort of common race, and this not one out of all the races, but the one which alone equals all the others' (Behr's translation, with slight variations).

Anyway, becoming Roman did not imply, on the part of Greeks, renouncing their own identity and civilisation, first of all their language and cultural physiognomy. On the contrary, it had been a very long time since the Romans themselves had begun to remould their cultural identity in Greek terms, actually to become Greek, as Greece – to say it as Cicero did – had invented humanitas, and the other peoples, including the Romans, had to learn it from Greece itself (*Ad Quintum Fratrem* 1.1.27-28). In the same way, they did not have to renounce their history, which was to become – with the Roman conquest – part of the main history of humanity. Plutarch, with his idea of parallel biographies – a Greek idea, even if based on Roman premises – and above all with the historical system he was able to build on it, provided the intellectual framework of a conception which was to become dominant afterwards: Greeks and Romans were nearly one and the same people, or at least they had the same moral and political values, the same religious beliefs, the same cultural interests; in a sense, they had lived the same history too, even if in different times. Of course, Plutarch simply gave, as it were, a final form to the cultural trend which had begun to reveal itself in the first decades of the third century BC, and had steadily developed in the second and first centuries: a trend in which both Romans and Greeks – admittedly in different ways – had been involved, one of whose most significant moments had been Dionysius of Halicarnassus' theory of the Hellenic origin of the Romans. Thanks to the Plutarchean formula, the process which nowadays we usually refer to as the Greek acculturation of Rome received its final historical configuration, the different Greek and Roman experiences being amalgamated; whereas the histories of all the other peoples were excluded, or reduced to more or less meaningless episodes of the sole, really important course of events.[7]

The Romans consented to leave to the Greeks their own history, or even adopted it as a component of, or a parallel to, their own history. They even used it, just like the Greeks did, as a part of their rhetorical training. But it was, of course, for the Greeks that the reconsideration of their history was vital; together with religious customs and beliefs, public festivals, civic institutions, it ensured the preservation of their local and national identity and pride. A famous passage in Plutarch's *Praecepta gerendae rei publicae* shows that history-telling could even be a risk for civic order, and that it was therefore necessary to select the historical exemplification in public speeches with great care: 'Marathon – he said – the Eurymedon, Plataea, and all the other examples which make the common folk vainly to swell with pride and kick up their heels, should be left to the schools of sophists' (814c). Plutarch recommended other examples, more appropriate to the present situation, while at the same time censuring those magistrates in the towns, who 'foolishly urge the people to imitate the deeds, ideals and actions of their ancestors, however unsuitable they may be to the present times and conditions' (814a). Plutarch himself narrated, of course, the celebrated events of the epic struggle between Greeks and Persians; but he did so in his *Vitae*, that is not in a political, but in a cultural context. In fact, he was well aware that ancient histories needed to be told – in the appropriate way – to public audiences over and over again, to avoid the risk of their fading away from the people's minds.

Greek identity was to become more and more a cultural and moral, rather than a political, identity, since the political aspect had been resorbed by the universal breadth of the Roman Imperial state, in which the Greeks were called to play a privileged role anyhow. With regard to the collective psychology of their citizens, the same thing was happening now, more or less, which had happened some two hundred years earlier to the Italian communities, following the social war. These communities had all been incorporated into Roman citizenship with the resulting consequences which Cicero from Arpinium had so well described at the beginning of the second book of his *De legibus*. 'Surely I think' – he said – 'that Cato and all natives of Italian towns have two fatherlands, one by nature and the other by citizenship. Cato, for example, though born in Tusculum, received citizenship in Rome'... 'That fatherland' – he continued – 'must stand first in our affection in which the name of republic signifies the common citizenship of all of us... But the fatherland which was our parent is not much less dear than the one which adopted us...'. Due to many reasons, which of course it is not possible to enumerate here, the Greek case was much more complicated than the Italian one, and the results of the process of incorporation were very different in the two cases. One could even say that it was the Greeks that incorporated the Romans rather than the reverse. In fact, the Greeks, unlike the Italians, were able to preserve their cultural identity, and in later times even to build on it a new, so-called Roman, political identity.

However, our purpose here is to underline the fact that the effort of the Greeks towards preserving their cultural identity was not felt as contradictory to the acceptance of Roman political rule in their territories. Of this effort both the recalling of the ancient glories of the classical age, and the narrating of the histories of the new, Roman, times were equally significant elements, even if, of course, not all historians were interested in the same way in the two themes, and even if one admits that the majority of them preferred to devote themselves to recounting the great past. The important fact – I conclude – as Leopardi rightly stressed nearly two centuries ago, is that those historians who practised the noble Thucydidean and Polybian art of contemporary history were not Latin any longer, but Greek.

Notes

1. P. 2731 f. I translate from G. Pacella's edition (G. Leopardi, *Zibaldone di pensieri*, Milano 1991, vol. II, pp. 1453 f.).
2. I refer to my 1986 and 1996 articles.
3. Meister 1994, 126; see Gabba 1993, 103-115, for a very clear survey of Appian's historiographic features.
4. Ambaglio 1994, 5-32; Stadter 1980, especially 167 ff.
5. 1970 = 1974; see now also Bowie 1996.
6. On the meaning of the Greek historians in the *Methodus* see now Couzinet 1996, 143 ff. (ch. VI *Les historiens grecques de l'histoire romaine*).
7. See now Desideri 1998.

CHAPTER 17

Hellenism and Romanization:
A comparison between the Greek novels and the tale of Psyche in Apuleius' *Metamorphoses*

Sophie Lalanne

The English title of this conference 'Greek Romans or Roman Greeks?' suggests in the most appropriate way the complexity of the problem submitted to our reflection. It gives in a few words a clear idea of a subject that the French expression '*Des Romains grecs ou des Grecs romains*' cannot precisely define. Today it is generally acknowledged that the notion of imperial Hellenism is rather delicate to handle considering the fact that it covers very different individual situations. However, progress has been made in the study of the matter due to several recent works which illuminate a double phenomenon of Romanization and resistance in the Greek elite.[1] But which Romanization are we talking about? It is obvious for anyone that the Roman culture has gone through an important evolution from the end of the Republic to the beginning of the Roman Empire, and that the Greeks in the 3rd century AD are not Romanized in the same way as the Greeks in the first century BC.

Taking this way of thinking a little further I shall examine a particular literary genre which illustrates this evolution, it is to say the Greek novel and more precisely the model it proposes for youth education. In fact five complete novels have been handed down to us in the form of manuscripts and through a certain number of fragments preserved on *papyri* which will not be considered here. To our actual knowledge it is almost certain that the five complete novels have been composed in a rather restricted scope, historically limited to the 2nd and 3rd centuries AD and geographically to the Eastern provinces of the Empire, more particularly to Asia Minor. I shall not take up the tricky question of dating the novels here and shall just consider that they have been written in the following chronological order: *Callirhoë* by Chariton, the *Ephesian Tale* by Xenophon of Ephesus, *Daphnis and Chloe* by Longus, *Leucippe and Clitophon* by Achilles Tatius and the *Aethiopica* by Heliodorus. These five novels deal with only one subject, situated in the Greek world of the classical period or in the imperial times: they tell the story of unfortunate love between a boy and a girl, both members of the highest aristocracy of their city and gifted with remarkable qualities granted by their descent (*eugeneia*). In order to prove themselves worthy of marriage or marital love, but also of their rank within the city, the two heroes make a long journey and have to give proof of their moral qualities through innumerable vicissitudes. The account of these ordeals forms the plot of the novel. In my opinion, this *paideia* is conceived on the pattern of a rite of passage reserved for an elite; it indicates a certain conception of the aristocracy in general and of the Hellenic identity in particular.

Therefore I will pay specific attention to love and adventure novels, of which many other examples probably existed in the Hellenistic and Roman period though they have been lost to us, and which inspired the Latin writer Apuleius to write the tale of Psyche. This story is included in the *Metamorphoses*, a novel contemporary with the Greek novels quoted above for it was written between 160 and 180 AD. One finds here a good deal of the themes one can find in the Greek novels, such as choosing a girl as the principal character, wandering, hard trials, faithful love, piety, etc. Thus, this group of six texts will be used as a sort of telescope permitting us a somewhat closer observation of the object of our study, these Greek speaking notables, learned persons and men of letters who lived, under Roman rule, in the first centuries AD. After having clarified the specific features of the Greek novel by studying how a Latin author like Apuleius has treated his model, we shall consider some aspects of the progressive Romanization of the Greek novel.

To begin with, I shall make conspicuous the common elements of the five Greek novels and of the tale of Psyche. We already know that Apuleius in writing his novel was inspired by one or more Greek models like the *Metamorphoses* by a certain Lucius of Patrae (as mentioned by Photius) or *Lucius or the Ass* ascribed to Lucian; as to the tale of Psyche, it has probably been borrowed from a Greek author or written in the Greek manner, as suggested by Apuleius himself when he announces a 'Milesian story'.[2] What immediately strikes us is that the status of protagonist has been given to a woman, as is usual in the Greek novels, and the remarkable value of marital – meaning heterosexual – love.[3] Notice that the girl to whom this story is told holds herself the attributes and the tragic fate of the Greek novels' heroines; this is made conspicuous in her lamentations:[4] thus, the character of Psyche appears in the framework of a timeless, novelistic Greek world, somehow frozen within the stream of history.

From the Greek heroines Psyche has the age, the beauty, the name, the qualities (simplicity and tenderness), the social status, the fame. Like Anthia of Ephesus, Chloe of Mytilene and Leucippe of Byzantium she is no doubt a native of a city in Asia Minor, for her father consults the oracle in Miletus.[5] As Callirhoë and Anthia fear – though in reality Chaireas and Habrocomes are aimed at – her beauty inflames jealousy in the heart of the divine Venus-Aphrodite, who is assisted then by her son Cupid.[6] Like Callirhoë, Chloe, Leucippe, Charicleia, she is abducted and taken far away, and if the sea was not missing, her monstruous marriage [7] would take place in the setting of a Greek epic, tragedy or novel. One thinks anyhow of the tragic fate of Iphigeneia who *in extremis* was drawn away from the bloody sacrifice to which her own father had condemned her by divine order. After the mistake that has caused her fall Psyche thinks repeatedly of suicide.[8] Her adventurous way of behaving can only recall that of Greek heroines:[9] she even meets Pan and Echo as if they had been reconciled at the end of Longus' novel and had left to Psyche's sister the sinister doom of the nymph.[10] The heroine is not even spared violence, notwithstanding her pregnancy, and just like Anthia, Leucippe and Charicleia she is handled roughly and tortured.[11] Then Venus submits her to a series of trials which end with an episode of apparent death[12] and finally marriage,[13] two elements that readers of the Greek novel know so well.

Notably, Apuleius makes no mention of two specific themes: the sea journey and the education of the heroine. However, in my opinion we are talking here about the most characteristic features of Hellenism in the field of fiction. In fact, the sea journey puts the two heroes in a marginalised position which is needed for the proper development of a rite of passage; this radical change of status is most often suggested in the texts by the word 'stranger' (*xenos*) and sometimes by 'foreign slave' (*doulos kai xenos*), and it is precisely this invert phenomenon, turning the heir of a great aristocratic family into a slave, which makes possible the learning of social and religious values, if not political values. As to the ordeals, these have not the same status in the work of Apuleius as in the Greek novels where they are set in sequences and form some sort of ritual. In fact, Apuleius has perceived how important the theme of travelling is but he has reduced it to a wandering; he has retained from the Greek novels the model of initiation, but Psyche's behaviour hardly changes through the course of events. So, on one hand Apuleius has understood that these two themes were essential to the genre of the novel, since he has kept them in another form, on the other hand he has assessed that he didn't really feel concerned by them. Indeed, he considers more important the jealousy of the two sisters, the hard trials Psyche goes through,[14] and the debates within the Pantheon, all themes which are of no interest to the Greek novelists.

Nevertheless, it is almost certain that the Greek novel has been influenced, if not by the Latin novel, at least by the Latin civilization. Evolution is clearly perceptible between Chariton, Xenophon of Ephesus and Achilles Tatius. The spectacular and the macabre tone of the narration are the two elements I will study now as good examples of this transformation of the genre. Both features relate to the hard trials the heroes go through and give a specific colour to rites of passage.

The taste for spectacular scenes appears as early as in the novel of the *Ephesian Tale*. Where Chariton showed delicacy, Xenophon of Ephesus dwells on it even more. It would not be honest to ascribe this systematic exaggeration to the doubtful nature of Xenophon of Ephesus' novel which might be an *epitome*; on the contrary, a summary would very well induce a greater simplicity. Let us take two examples: the description of heroines and the narration of fights.

When Chariton wants to give an idea of Callirhoë's beauty, he is satisfied with this sort of characterization:

She was a wonderful girl, the pride of all Sicily; her beauty was more than human, it was divine, and it was not the beauty of a Nereid or mountain nymph at that, but of the maiden Aphrodite herself.[15]

Xenophon of Ephesus enlarges on the subject:

Anthia's beauty was an object of wonder, far surpassing the other girls'. She was fourteen; her beauty was burgeoning, still more enhanced by the adornment of her dress. Her hair was golden – a little of it plaited, but most hanging loose and blowing in the wind. Her eyes were quick; she had the bright glance of a young girl, and yet the austere look of a virgin. She wore a purple tunic down to the knee, fastened with a girdle and falling loose over her arms, with a fawnskin over it, a quiver attached, and arrows for weapons; she carried javelins and was followed by dogs.[16]

The spectacular dimension is considerably increased here for Anthia leads the line of girls in a majestic epiphany which Chariton only suggested. In the novel of Heliodorus the description assumes even more obviously an artistic character which lies on spectacular:

On a rock sat a girl, a creature of such indescribable beauty that one might have taken her for a goddess. Despite her great distress at her plight, she had an air of courage and nobility. On her head she wore a crown of laurel; from her shoulders hung a quiver; her left arm leant on the bow, the hand hanging relaxed at the wrist. She rested the elbow of her other arm on her right thigh, cradling her cheek in her fingers. Her head was bowed, and she gazed steadily at a young man lying at her feet.[17]

If one reads also the description of Theagenes, wounded and lying down, one can contemplate in imagination the mere spectacle of a group of Pergamene statues from the Hellenistic period. Let us consider for instance the detailed account of clothing and attitudes, the arrangement of corporal volumes, the expression of *pathos*.

The narration of fights, which quite obviously is something more and more appreciated by the novelists, provides us with a second example. Once more, Chariton mentions the heroic victories of Chaireas who has become an admiral in the navy of the Egyptian pharaoh, but he does not dwell on the events in spite of the fact that he could have imagined an encounter with his rival Dionysos, victorious on earth. Longus dedicates time to the war between Methymnians and Mytilenians but elaborates more on diplomatic exchanges than on regular battles. Heliodorus in return offers us the magnificent spectacle of the siege of Syene, the amazing scene of the duel which Thyamis fights with his brother Petosiris, the incredible pursuit of a furious bull in Meroe, and Theagenes' final wrestling against the champion of the Ethiopians. In these two categories, the description of heroines and the narration of fights, the spectacular dimension of the scenes is constantly progressing from Chariton to Heliodorus. One cannot help comparing this more and more outspoken taste for the spectacular with the well-attested phenomenon of the introduction in the Greek city-states of circus games, which were very characteristic of Roman civilization. Indeed, the Greeks easily and rapidly got accustomed to this new way of entertainment.[18]

The macabre is the second tonality which gains more and more foothold over time. The abduction of the heroine by the pirates will illustrate this point. First, Chariton describes with many details the apparent killing of Callirhoë and her descent to the grave. The only episode which could interest us here would be the moment when the pirates refuse to go into the grave where they believe they will see a ghost; Theron, the chief of the pirates, is the only one who enters, and after having considered to kill the young girl he decides to sell her at a good price. As for Anthia, the brigands of Hippothoos hang her upon a tree intending to riddle her with their javelins and to offer her as a sacrifice to Ares; then she is locked up in a cavern and almost raped by the brigand Anchialos, whom she has to kill. Finally Leucippe is eviscerated by the brigands before the eyes of her lover and later on exposed on the deck of a ship, both hands tied, then beheaded and thrown into the sea. These descriptions illustrate the way Latin theatre – I think of tragedies by Seneca such as

Medea or *Thyestes*[19] – poetry[20] and painting[21] have been able to influence the setting of certain episodes, more particularly the cruelties inflicted on the heroines.

So here we have two characteristics of the Greek novels, the spectacular and the macabre, which are not present at the beginning of the beginning, but become more and more evident over time from Chariton to Heliodorus, and which I think are the mark of a Latin influence and of the tastes of a more and more Romanized public.[22] In Heliodorus' novel these characteristics join forces with a jubilant dexterity, and one may assert that an important change has occured.[23] But which Romanization are we talking about? While the question 'Greek Romans or Roman Greeks?' makes sense concerning Longus or Achilles Tatius, it is less relevant when reading the *Aethiopica* which was probably written in the first half of the 3rd century AD. Is this novel really coloured by the Roman culture or has this culture itself been influenced from outside? For instance, it seems that the notion of nobility (*eugeneia*) is opened more in Achilles Tatius and Heliodorus than in Chariton and Xenophon of Ephesus due to the fact that in their period nobility lay more within the reach of Hellenized non-Greek people. Thus, Heliodorus develops an oriental notion of nobility as reserved for a sacerdotal cast, whether of Delphi, Memphis or Meroe.[24] One might draw a parallel with the progressive opening up of Roman citizenship, even if it also has to be related to the probable Syrian origins of Heliodorus. It could be suggested that the novelists were more and more imbued with the Roman culture, which in the same time took on and developed new forms. Thus, Hellenism seems to have reached the borders of the Empire, in short the limits of universal in those times, at the risk of being dissolved within it.

Let us stress, as a conclusion, the need of studying cultural influences in their historical dimension, it is to say the necessity of taking into account exact places and periods, as well as the limits of our actual knowledge concerning the diversity of cultures in imperial times. In this context, it can be of some interest to underline the remarkable continuity of the initiation scheme within the genre of the novel, but also to keep in mind the evolution of the imperial customs and mentalities themselves. One would take a great interest in a methodic comparison between the Greek and the Latin novels, which might allow us to define some of the characteristics of Hellenism. It is indeed very difficult to have a clear idea of what Hellenism meant to a Greek living in the first centuries AD. One may be surprised to find out some invaluable information where one has not expected. For instance, it is astonishing how a good understanding of the Greek archaic period can be much more useful than the knowledge of Greek civilization in the 5th and 4th centuries. In fact, in the first centuries of the Greek city-state the problems and solutions that the city ran into afterwards appeared. In order to hoist the bright colours of Hellenism, the contemporaries of the Empire had to leap over the era of the Athenian democracy and to go back to the foundations that Greeks had established in the 8th century: a Greek is a human being who speaks the Greek language, who takes part in Greek culture and religion and who lives in a city-state. It is these features that have been taken up in the 2nd century AD and appear through the questions raised by the Greek novels. The remarkable permanence of the reading of Homeric poems evidenced by *papyri* could be interpreted in this way. In the Homeric epic one finds indeed several notions, like the aristocratic *arete* or the community of Hellenes, which quite obviously serve as a frame of reference for the Greek novelists.

Notes

* Translation from French into English: Nanny Renkema and Mary Waters Lund.

1. Recently, Swain 1996.
2. Apul. *Met.* 4.32. Cf in particular Sandy 1997, chapter 6.
3. Konstan 1994.
4. Apul. *Met.* 4.24.
5. Apul. *Met.* 4.32.
6. Apul. *Met.* 4.29-30.
7. Apul. *Met.* 4.33-35.
8. Apul. *Met.* 5.25; 6.12 & 17. See Mc Alister 1996 on the frequency of this theme.
9. Apul. *Met.* 5.26 and 28; 6.1.
10. Apul. *Met.* 5.25 and 27.
11. Apul. *Met.* 6.9.
12. Apul. *Met.* 6.21.
13. Apul. *Met.* 6.23-24.
14. Fehling 1977, 43-46.
15. Charit. *Call.* 1.1.2, translated by B. Reardon in Reardon 1989.
16. Xen. Ephes. *Eph.* 1.2.5-8, translated by G. Anderson in Reardon 1989.
17. Heliod. *Aeth.* 1.2.1-2, translated by J. Morgan in Reardon 1989.
18. On the mythological colouring given to executions during the first and second centuries AD, cf Coleman1990, 44-73; on the way how, according to Livy, the Romans introduced Greek athletic games in their cities making a 'spectacle (*spectaculum*) of athletic contests' reserved for professionals, cf Roman 1994, 177-78.
19. On the subject of *Thyestes*, it is interesting to notice that this was never treated by the Greeks and that Homer ignores it. Seneca on the other hand seems to have at least three Roman predecessors.
20. Richlin 1992, 158-79.

21. The *ecphraseis* contained in the novels often suggest a pictorial source of inspiration, in particular when they describe scenes of violence. See for example the prologue of *Daphnis and Chloe* in which Longus describes 'an attack by pirates, an enemy invasion', or *Leucippe and Clitophon* in which we witness the abduction of Europa or the rape of Philomela (5.3.4-8). Cf Brown 1992.
22. At first, humour seemed to me to be among the signs of an increasing Romanization of the Greek novel, but after discussion, it seems more plausible that the novelists simply drew their inspiration from the classical Greek tradition. Cf on this subject, Goldhill 1995, 16-20 and Hoffmann-Trédé 1998.
23. See, for instance, the necromantic Egyptian scene. Heliod. *Aeth.* 6.14-15.
24. Baslez 1990, 115-28.

CHAPTER 18

Language, Culture and Identity in Ancient Palestine[1]

Joseph Geiger

Meleager of Gadara, a city situated not far from the Eastern shore of the Sea of Galilee, was the foremost poet of his generation and the gatherer of the Garland that was to become the first component of the Greek Anthology. In one of the sepulchral epigrams he composed for himself he addresses the stranger at the grave: 'If you are a Syrian, say Salam; if a Phoenician, Naidios – or whatever stands behind the textual corruption, – if a Greek, Chaire'.[2] Clearly, for Meleager, identity was based on language – Syrian (that is, Aramaic), Phoenician and Greek. It is notable that there is no pretence of an absolute ignorance of barbarian languages or of being unable to distinguish between different barbarian ethnicities. Moreover, whatever the conventions of the poetic genre, it is also remarkable that it includes the assumption of both the Syrian and the Phoenician reading and understanding the Greek on the tombstone. If so, this bilingualism does not detract from their definition as Syrians or Phoenicians. Another point to be noticed is that a generation or so before Pompey's decisive interference on behalf of his freedman Demetrius in the affairs of Gadara[3] no Romans are mentioned – unless these are included among the Greeks as Greek speakers.

Nevertheless, the linguistic criterion is not the only one Meleager applies to identify non-Greeks: in his only allusion to Jews[4] he complains that white-cheeked Demo prefers a Sabbath-keeper to the poet. Thus, a cultural, or religious, distinguishing mark could be as decisive as language: one imagines that the putative Jewish lover of Demo was Aramaic-speaking – though perhaps bilingualism with Greek as a second language would have come in useful, as the story shows. By the way, both epigrams attest to some degree, at least, of 'interracial mixing' in Gadara.

I have said nothing yet of Meleager's self-presentation. In another of his sepulchral epigrams he describes his birthplace as Ἀτθίς ἐν Ἀσσυρίοις

...Γάδαρα (*Atthis en Assyriois ... Gadara*) and asks then rhetorically: 'What wonder, if I am Syrian? We all inhabit one fatherland, one world', μίαν ... πατρίδα κόσμον ναίομεν.[5] This comes immediately after a reference to his fellow citizen Menippus, so that the Cynic attitude may well be a tribute to the cosmopolitanism of the famous philosopher of the city. Clearly, 'Syrian' here cannot be more than merely a geographical term for the son of a city that prides itself on its pure Attic tongue.[6]

In parentheses, since it belongs to a somewhat later period than the one I venture to consider here, we should regard not very differently, perhaps, the statement of Heliodorus, the author of the *Aethiopica* as to his being a Phoenician from Emesus.[7] Nor do I believe myself to be far off the mark in surmising that Ammianus Marcellinus' self-presentation as a one-time soldier and a Greek[8] was, in fact, tongue-in-cheek.

Back to the Early Empire, other cases may be more ambiguous. Most striking is the encounter of Jesus with the gentile woman in the neighbourhood of Tyre, whose daughter he first refuses to heal, since he came to the lost sheep of the house of Israel. Matthew 15.22 describes the woman as Χαναναία (*Chananaia*), Mark 7.26 clarifies: the woman was Ἑλληνίς, Συροφοινίκισσα τῷ γένει (*Hellênis, Syrophoinikissa tôi genei*). Assuming no conflict between the two Gospels exists, one concludes that the woman was Greek speaking, a non-Jew (that is, a Canaanite) and from the Syro-Phoenician region[9] – surely at home in the neighbourhood of Tyre. One notes, among other things, the contrast with Meleager, who clearly distinguishes between Syrians and Phoenicians: but there the contrast is linguistic, here the woman is a Greek speaker, albeit apparently not of Greek-speaking stock, though there is no knowing whether her forbears spoke Phoenician, Aramaic or both. One wonders how the authors of the Gospels could have known so much about the woman, since the exact description of a Hellenized native in such terms as in Mark is rare if not unique – the only fact that is of any relevance for the story is that she is a gentile. Or is it that in contrast to the Greek Meleager the Jewish authors of the Gospels did not care to distinguish between the various ethnicities or linguistic allegiances of gentiles inhabiting the Land of Israel and its immediate vicinity? This would well agree, e.g., with the standard rendering of 'Philistines' in the Septuagint and other Jewish-Hellenistic writings as ἀλλόφυλοι (*allophyloi*).

However, a curious light is shed on the combination 'Syrian-Phoenician' by the fact that Diogenes Laertius (6.99) describes Menippus, the earliest of the famous Greek intellectuals from Gadara, to whom I have referred above, as Φοῖνιξ (*Phoinix*). Also the latest known of these, the sophist Apsines of Gadara,[10] is called a Φοῖνιξ (*Phoinix*) by Philostratus (*VS sub fin.*). It appears that some people on some occasions would clearly differentiate between Syrians and Phoenicians, some would hold that there existed Syro-

Phoenicians, while again some would describe a compatriot of a self-described Syrian as a Phoenician.[11]

Then there is another case, of mistaken identity. Paul's revealing his Roman citizenship (*Acts* 22.25-28) is among the most often repeated stories of Roman Imperial history, but it is still worth the while to recall the circumstances of his first arrest in Jerusalem. When Paul addresses the tribune the latter is astonished: 'Do you know Greek? Are you not the Egyptian...' alluding to the false prophet who assembled his followers on Mount Olives and intended to conquer Jerusalem (cf. Jos. *BJ* 2.261-63, *AJ* 20.169-72), and Paul replies 'I am a Jewish man of Tarsus, citizen of no mean city of Cilicia' (*Acts* 21.37-39).[12] What are we to make of this story? Indeed, it would be self-evident that the false prophet addressed his followers in their own vernacular, Aramaic, but did the Roman officer assume, in his ignorance, that the language of an Egyptian Jew was not Greek? Did the Police 'Wanted' description designate him as Aramaic speaking? And then there is his declaration of being a Jew. The circumstances of the arrest of Paul could leave no doubt in the mind of the tribune that he was in fact a Jew. Asking him whether he was the Egyptian must be equivalent to 'the Egyptian Jew'; is Paul's specifying his being a Jew stating the obvious, or is it a tactful correction of the officer's ignorance – Diaspora Jews can be Greek speaking citizens of Greek cities? It seems to me also significant that in this case *Acts* and Josephus agree in consistently referring to the false prophet as 'the Egyptian'[13] – this must have been his common designation by all and sundry.

With Paul we have reached an intriguing case of self-presentation – in fact of three kinds of such acts: as we have seen, he declares himself a Jew, a citizen of the Greek city of Tarsus when mistaken for 'the Egyptian', and a Roman citizen when threatened with corporeal punishment. In fact, it is worthwhile putting on record that the contradictory statements of Paul (including *Acts* 22.3) have been noticed already by Porphyrius.[14] It is instructive to contrast these cases with his self-presentation in his epistles, written in Greek and sent to Diaspora communities. Here he ignores both his Greek city and his Roman citizenship and instead he emphasises not only his being a Hebrew, a circumcised Israelite, but he also twice mentions the fact that he belongs to the tribe of Benjamin, a fact devoid of any practical consequences in this period.[15] It is exactly this multi-faceted identity of Paul, also known by his Jewish biblical name Saul, – a Roman citizen, a Jew, a Greek-speaking citizen of a Greek city, a Hebrew and an Israelite of the tribe of Benjamin – which provides us with some valuable insights into the often complicated cases of civic, ethnic, cultural and religious identity in the Ancient Near East.

Another man of Jewish descent, a nephew of Philo of Alexandria, Ti. Julius Alexander[16] was procurator of the province of Judaea, later to ascend to the prefecture of Egypt and to the office of *praefectus praetorio*,[17] the very summits of an equestrian career. Tacitus, surely not ignorant of his descent, describes him as *inlustris eques Romanus* (*Ann.* 15.28) without ever alluding to his parentage. Certainly this looks as an example of the Romans classifying people politically, according to their citizenship – but then, why does he elsewhere mention Tiberius Julius Alexander's Egyptian background in connexion with his prefecture of Egypt (*Hist.* 1.11.1) but not his Jewish birth in connexion with his Judaean tenure?[18] Juvenal's 'Aegyptius atque Arabarches' (1.130) – if it indeed refers to the same person, as the scholarly consensus seems to make him[19] – chose among the three ethnic groups detested and ridiculed by the satirist, Greeks, Jews and Egyptians, presumably the most offensive alternative, not necessarily the most accurate one. At any rate, we are not to conclude that these different ethnic designations were necessarily mutually exclusive. Not surprisingly, it is the Jew Josephus alone who expands on Alexander's Jewish background and apostasy (*AJ* 20.100). Unfortunately, it is idle to speculate how the procurator would present himself to the Jewish inhabitants of his province – or, for that matter, to the Egyptians when ruling their land.

Rather unexpectedly, we can only guess at the self-presentation of such a well-known personality as King Herod, so that it seems worth the while to collect the available evidence. His father, Antipater, was an Idumaean, and it was in all probability only Herod's grandfather, also called Antipater, who belonged to the generation converted to Judaism under John Hyrcanus I.[20] His mother, Cyprus, was a Nabataean, judging by her name perhaps from a Hellenized family (Jos. *BJ* 1.181). Against the background of this last-mentioned fact it is interesting to note that during the civil war that led up to the establishment of his rule, Herod was mockingly called by his rival, the last Hasmonaean ruler Antigonus 'an Idumaean, that is, a half-Jew' – Ἰδυμαίῳ τουτέστιν ἡμιιουδαίῳ (Jos. *AJ* 14.403).[21] It may be noted in passing that we are dealing with the period before the great revolution in Jewish self-definition, from the Biblical patrilinear one, existing today only inside Judaism in its subdivisions of priests and Levites, to the later, and still valid, matrilinear system established by the rabbis.[22] Presumably in the view of Antigonus, Herod's gentile mother had nothing to do with his doubtful Judaism. Unfortunately we know very little about Nabataean self-definition,[23] but it would be interesting to know how Herod was regarded by a people, who could have with some justification claimed him as one of their own, but with whom they were in conflict during long stretches of his reign. It is not only the attitude of the Nabataeans to Herod's Judaism that eludes us, we also would dearly like to know whether it was acceptable to the inhabitants of the Greek cities of his realm, in constant contest with their Jewish fellow-citizens and jealously insistent on their Hellenic identity. We also don't know how people outside the

Roman Empire, the Parthians and Armenians in the first place, would regard such rulers as Herod. Be this as it may, there exists only one piece of contemporary documentary evidence expressly describing Herod as a Jew. The inscriptions on a load of amphorae of Italian wine discovered at Masada were sent to – or belonged to – Herod the Jewish king, rex Herodes Judaicus: it has been argued that this is the equivalent to 'king of the Jews'.[24] At any rate, there is no knowing who was responsible for the inscriptions or whether they accurately reflect Herod's wishes. In the very detailed narratives of Josephus, by far our most comprehensive source, Herod is only twice given an ethnic epithet: he is called 'king of the Jews' in a childhood prophecy (Jos. *AJ* 15.373), and again we are told (Jos. *BJ* 1.282) that Antony was determined to make him 'king of the Jews', which may well reflect the language of the ensuing decision of the senate (ibid. 284).[25]

Indeed, our acquaintance with Herod's ways and manner opens up possibilities of further enquiries. Though it is customary to view Herod as a Hellenized ruler – that is, as a person who regards himself if not a Greek, at least as somebody belonging to some extent to the Greek cultural sphere – there is also a Roman aspect to him. Elsewhere I have argued at some length that it was not only Herod's citizenship and obviously his political dependence on Rome and loyalty to her ruler, but also certain aspects of his policies, and above all his life-style, that rendered him a 'Roman' client-king in a deeper sense than we usually grant this designation.[26] Of course I do not wish to suggest, that the early acquisition of such Roman fashions as the building of amphitheatres, or the importation of artisans from Rome and a taste for luxury items from Italy rendered a man a Roman. Yet, on the other hand it can be demonstrated – and I have tried to do so – that Herod's Romanization was a no less important factor in the life of his country and his court than Hellenistic influences. A ruler living in villas affecting the latest fashions in Roman art and architecture, surrounded by body-guards trained and equipped after the Roman model, making use of such Roman institutions as the bath-house and conspicuously consuming imported Italian goods, may have appeared, perhaps to some of his subjects, and with greater probability to some of those regarding him from outside his realm and beyond the borders of the Empire, as a man not only representing and working in the interest of Rome, but also perhaps to some extent a Roman. On the other hand, it certainly agrees with what we know of the self-presentation of Greek and Eastern aristocrats and intellectuals, that his Roman citizenship is taken for granted and left – but for a brief reference regarding his father in Josephus' narrative (*AJ* 14.137) – virtually unmentioned. No doubt it was only people from the lower classes like Paul, who had to insist on this distinction. Nevertheless, it is an extraordinary mark of the limits of the Romanness of Herod the Roman citizen that he is described as 'Philorhomaios', an epithet that appears to be in direct contradiction to being a Roman citizen. Admittedly, it is found only in a decree of the People of Athens,[27] though I find it quite conceivable that the Athenians did not apply the term without reference to the King's usage or his wishes. The significance of this is perhaps deeper than would appear at first sight: the widespread notion that Greek identity was cultural and Roman identity political, appears to be contradicted by this epithet. A Roman citizen described as 'Philorhomaios' of necessity renders this appellation parallel to 'Philhellen', signifying a person friendly to Things Greek.

Another aspect of the Romanization of Herod's family was the education of the royal princes in Rome.[28] The education of Alexander and Aristobulus – as well as of a third son of Herod – by the Hasmonaean Mariamme in Rome, where they stayed it seems with Asinius Pollio, with one of the tutors conceivably a Roman[29] must have had profound effects not only on them, but also on the entire royal household. We are told[30] that Charops of Epirus had been sent to Rome with the express purpose of learning to speak and to write Latin: it seems inconceivable that Herod's sons, probably brought up bilingual, would not avail themselves of an opportunity – perhaps in this period already self-evident and thus not mentioned – to be in a position of gaining deeper insights into the workings of Roman government by acquiring the language of the rulers of the empire. Five more of Herod's sons were at one time or another in Rome to be educated and/or introduced to Augustus, presumably on similar terms as their half-brothers[31]. One can only guess at the influence of these sojourns on the definition of the position between Hellenism and Romanization of these Judaised Idumaeans of partly Nabataean descent.

We know somewhat more about another member of the Herodian dynasty. The Jewishness of Agrippa I, son of Aristobulus and grandson of Herod the Great and of his wife Mariamme the Hasmonaean[32] is, according to Talmudic legend, confirmed by the Jews[33] and asserted by himself, according to Philo. The latter, however, also calls him a Syrian, during Agrippa's sojourn in Alexandria.[34] It is the context that matters, and Agrippa's adherence to Jewish law and custom may have been decisive in the way he was seen by both Jews and foreigners. Indeed, if the famous jocular saying attributed to Augustus is genuine (Macr. *Sat.* 2.4.11), according to which he would prefer to be Herod's pig rather than his son, it marks Herod by one of the best-known characteristics of Judaism, irrespective of whether he in fact observed the Jewish dietary laws or not.[35]

Like his father and uncles, Agrippa was educated in Rome, a factor that must have left a deep impression on his personality and behaviour. Granted that his conversations with his highly – and most highly – placed Roman friends, including Caligula and Claudius, were conducted in Greek, one imagines that he must have picked up at least the necessary everyday Latin for life in the city. Given what we know of his background, character and ambition, as well as his bilingual, or probably trilingual upbringing – the Talmudic legend referred to above describes him as accomplishing his duty as King and reading from the book of Deuteronomy to the People, so he may well have been conversant with Hebrew, not only Aramaic – one would assume that in fact he did not deprive himself of this means to gain a useful insight into the workings of Roman government. Certainly Claudius' permission given to him and to his brother Herod of Chalcis to address the Senate in Greek (Dio 60.8.2) does not necessarily prove their ignorance of Latin, though it probably implies their less than complete mastery of the language.

Up to now I have dealt with designations and self-presentation as they appear in a variety of literary sources, from poetry and historiography to the more humble prose of the Gospels and *Acts*. It is illuminating to compare these with the daily transactions of the common people. In the documents from the Judaean desert, dating from the end of the first century and the first third of the second century and written in Greek and Aramaic (including its Nabataean variant), there appear many scores of people as litigants, parties to contracts and witnesses: only one of them carries an ethnic designation, and it is the task of the commentator to assign the rest, according to their names and family connexions, as well as to the script, to the various ethnic communities. Even the exception, in this case, is hardly a real one, since it appears in an official document issued by a political body. It became the business of the Council of the Metropolis Petra to appoint guardians for Babatha's orphan son. Accordingly the Council decided to appoint for 'Jesus, a Jew, son of Jesus, of the village Maoza' two guardians (*P.Yadin* 12.6-7), though in the sequel it did not even here appear worth mentioning that, judging by their names, one of the guardians was a Nabataean, the other a Jew. Even Babatha herself, the woman whose archive numbers more than thirty documents, and who was to die, in all probability, during the oppression of the Bar-Kokhba rebellion, is never explicitly described as a Jewess[36]. Of course, in small communities there could be little doubt about the allegiance of families or individuals, but it is still intriguing, that none of the persons involved felt the need for emphasising his ethnic or religious identity. It is this ambience that rendered it possible for a Jewish man to undertake a commitment to feed and cloth his bride and their future children 'in accordance with Greek custom'.[37]

Ethnicity and civic status could of course be explicitly contrasted. According to Josephus (*BJ* 2.308), the procurator Florus had scourged and crucified men of equestrian rank, who 'if Jews by birth, had this Roman dignity', ὧν εἰ καὶ τὸ γένος Ἰουδαῖον, ἀλλὰ γοῦν τὸ ἀξίωμα Ῥωμαϊκὸν ἦν. This might indeed seem like a clear antithesis between ethnic descent and citizenship, or rather status, or, at the very least, Josephus' awareness of the fact that identity had more than one aspect to it.[38]

So far I have been discussing a number of cases of doubtful or otherwise not self-evident identity and self-presentation, including its absence, of individuals from Late Republican and Early Imperial Palestine. But it is, of course, not only individual, but more often group identities that present themselves to the investigator and that appear to bear historical significance. Here I shall content myself with alluding to some problems notorious in the political history of the country and the province. Thus I shall bypass such issues as the identity of the Antiochenes in Jerusalem on the Jewish side, and of the Sidonians of Marissa and of Jamnia on the gentile side, and shall totally ignore the questions pertaining to the Samaritans and their becoming a separate entity from the rest of Jewry.

It is well known that the self-presentation as well as identification by others of cities as Greek was a matter of some consequence.[39] In Palestine a number of cities are described as Greek by Josephus. On the occasion of the division of Herod's kingdom between his heirs, Archelaus' share included the Greek cities of Gaza, Gadara and Hippos; these are juxtaposed with Strato's Tower, Sebaste, Joppe and Jerusalem (*BJ* 2.97; *AJ* 17.320), implicitly all non-Greek. Obviously Josephus, writing after the Jewish War, among whose causes he numbered the Jewish-Greek controversy over the character of Caesarea, made a point of not describing the city – to which he insists on giving its former name, Strato's Tower, in all probability commemorating a Sidonian dynast[40] – as Greek. Nevertheless, when speaking about the gentile inhabitants of the city he calls them indiscriminately Syrians and Greeks.

It would be pointless here to recount the struggles between the Jewish and gentile inhabitants of Caesarea, and, indeed, of some other towns, though one piece of testimony from a distant source for the city's Greek character is well worth mentioning. Apollonius of Tyana praises (*Ep.* 11) the councillors of Caesarea for their 'Greek manners' and for showing them by setting up 'public inscriptions' ἤθεσιν Ἑλληνικοῖς ... διὰ γραμμάτων κοινῶν.[41]

One other city in Palestine makes a point of its Greek self-presentation. An inscription in honour of Marcus Aurelius Antoninus – Mark Aurel, Caracalla or Elegabalus – is set up by the city of Nysa-Scythopolis, 'of the Greek cities of Coele-Syria', τῶν κατὰ Κοίλην Συρίαν Ἑλληνίδων πόλεων;[42] incidentally the inscription shows that this is the correct reading of one of the titles of the city on its coins. The 'other', against whom the Greekness is maintained, seems to be a matter of contention. Certainly in the case of Scythopolis I would maintain that it is a Greek city to differentiate itself from the surrounding Aramaic-speaking countryside as well as from the Jewish population of the province to which in all probability it was annexed.[43]

Jewish historians, as a rule, look at gentile ethnicities from their particular vantage point. Thus one wonders what exactly the author[44] of 2 *Macc.* (6.8) had in mind when he described Ptolemy as sending a *psephisma* 'to the neighbouring Greek cities', εἰς τὰς ἀστυγείτονας Ἑλληνίδας πόλεις. Could 'Hellenic' stand here for no more than 'non-Jewish', 'gentile'? This would in fact well agree with the usage of the author, who juxtaposes – and he is the first to do so in our extant literature – Judaism and Hellenism (4.13, 14.38, cf. 13.2).[45] The term is purely cultural, and indeed testifies to the fact that ethnic descent is not necessarily the key to a person's identity. It seems that to the mind of the author – for sure a Hellenized Jew – the contrast between Jews and Hellenes predominates: not only are the neighbouring cities 'Greek cities' (6.8), also Jason intended to settle 'Hellenes' in Jerusalem (11.2), and it is a Greek force that fights the Jews (13.2).[46] Not surprisingly, given the Jewish nationalistic attitude of the author, it hardly matters what sort of foreign nationality His Chosen People are up against. It is quite interesting to contrast this with the author of 1 *Macc.*, a book in the historiographic tradition of the Hebrew Bible and preserved for us in a Greek translation: here the opponents of the Jews are as a rule described as ἀλλόφυλοι (*allophyloi*), the 'kingdom of the Hellenes' is referred to only once, in the words of the Jewish embassy in Rome (8.18).

But the authors of both books of Maccabees precede the full impact of Rome in the region, so I shall return to Josephus. His view of the world is perhaps best conceived in the Preface to the *Jewish War*. First, there are the Jews and Romans opposed in war (1), then we are told about the earlier, vernacular version of the work, sent to the barbarians inland – οἱ ἄνω βάρβαροι – (3); later (6) we are informed that these included Parthians, Babylonians, the furthest Arabs as well as the Jews beyond the Euphrates and the (Jewish?) inhabitants of Adiabene. The translation was made in order to make it accessible to the Greeks and to those Romans who have not participated in the war (6; cf. 16). Josephus of course takes it for granted that Greek is read not only by Greeks but also by Romans – indeed, were we to go by the evidence of the passage of Josephus alone, we would never know that the Romans employed any language other than Greek. Nevertheless, he seems to make a very clear distinction in his mind between Romans and Greeks; while it is the first only who are mentioned as participating in the war, it is the Greek historians against whom he polemizes in a great outburst (13-16). Not that the identity of these Greek historians is at all clear: further on in the preface (17) Josephus refers to the Greeks who translated into their native tongue previous histories of Jews. Were these 'Greeks', as some seem to opine, Hellenized Jewish authors? [47] If so, a Jew could be described according to his country as 'Egyptian' or 'Syrian' when his Jewishness was obvious, and as 'Greek' when it was the linguistic or literary criterion that counted.

Furthermore, his identifying the Romans, and the Romans alone, as the opponents of the Jews in the war is not quite as self-evident as it might appear at first sight. Thus, for instance, at the siege of Gamala we are told by Josephus (*BJ* 4.37-38) that the centurion Gallus with ten soldiers, and we are expressly told that both he and they all were Syrians, overheard the plans of the Jews – they obviously understood the Aramaic spoken by them. Whether the soldiers belonged, as is most probable, to one of the three legions, the Fifth, the Tenth and the Fifteenth investing Gamala (*BJ* 4.13) or to some auxiliary troops, the centurion Gallus, at least, must have been a Roman citizen. Clearly, Josephus emphasises the point pertinent to his story, in this case the linguistic aptitude rather than the belonging to the Roman army or body politic.

Before concluding, one issue that I cannot pursue here is that of changing identities. Briefly it may be noted that there are two distinct aspects to such changes, the collective and the individual facet. On the collective plane, it is firstly to be seen how the Hellenized Idumaeans of Marissa or the inhabitants of the coastal city of Jamnia became Sidonians, or how some of the Jews in Jerusalem wished to be known as Antiochenes; secondly, a matter I have touched upon briefly above, how the Idumaeans, and the Ituraeans in their turn, were converted to Judaism. On the individual plane, there looms large the controversial issue of mission and conversion,[48] of some importance for the history of the Jews and of course crucial for the history of Christianity and of the Roman Empire.

If there is a general lesson to be learnt from this very incomplete, and rather impressionistic survey of some of the evidence, it is scarcely a surprising one: Greek Romans and Roman Greeks were not the only problematic identities. Except for the division 'we'/'the others' – where of course the definition of 'we' depended very much on the point of view and the personality of the speaker as well as on the occasion – there were no hard and fast rules for identifying and designating 'the other'. Identifying him was accomplished according to the circumstances and the needs of the occasion. Nor should these phenomena be viewed divorced from the historical processes and their time and space. Multiple and complex identities may have been almost the rule, rather than the exception, in a part of the world where Hellenization, the Roman conquest, the return from the Babylonian exile and the crystallisation of Jewish and of Samaritan identity, the turning of Aramaic into a lingua franca not confined to political or ethnic boundaries, and the geographic instability of the Nabataeans and the Idumaeans,[49] among other factors, call up the image of the kaleidoscope rather than that of the mosaic.[50]

Notes

* It is a pleasure to be able to thank again the organizers of the conference and all participants in the discussion. I should like also to thank Paolo Desideri and his colleagues for another opportunity to read a version of this paper at a conference at the Certosa di Pontignano in November 1998; Hannah Cotton very kindly read and commented on the manuscript.

1. S. Schwartz, 1995, a highly stimulating paper, deals, despite its title, only with the Jewish component in Palestine. On the contrary the present investigation seeks to consider the geographical unit with its multiple languages, cultures and national and religious backgrounds. Goodman, 1989, deals with one aspect of Jewish identity and is not restricted to Palestine. Millar, 1997, has important and pertinent observations.
2. *Anth.Pal.* 7.419.7-8, Gow and Page, 1965, no. 4, p. 217. For Meleager's standing as the first anthologist see Cameron, 1993, 5ff.
3. Plut. *Pomp.* 40 with Heftner, 1995, 278-81.
4. *Anth.Pal.* 5.160 = Gow and Page, 1965, no. 26, p. 223 – the sole surviving reference at all to Jews by any Greek author from Palestine, see Stern, 1974, no. 43, pp. 139-40.
5. *Anth.Pal.* 7.417, Gow and Page, 1965, no. 2, p. 216.
6. Meleager's self-definition could be compared with the famous self-definition of Favorinus as a Greek-speaking Gaul, Philostr. *VS* 489 and cf. ps.Dio Chrys. 37.27.
7. Heliod. 10.41.3.
8. Amm. Marc. 31.16.9: *ut miles quondam et Graecus*.
9. For the expression cf. Juv. 8.159, 160, where the Syrophoenix' abode is the Idymaea porta, perhaps the Porta Capena, associated by the satirist (3.12-14) with Jews, and Lucian, *Deor.conc.* 4; contrast this with the Συραττικός (*Syrattikos*), reminiscent of Meleager, coined for Ulpian of Tyre at Ath. 3.126f; 9.368c; cf. also 3.126a; 4.174e ff; 8.346c; 361f; 13.571a; 15.697c. The identity or otherwise of Ulpian with the jurist will not be pursued here
10. See Brzoska, *RE* 2.277.
11. NB that Ptolemy (Stern, 1974, no. 146 = Jacoby, *FGrH* 199 F 1 = Ammonius, *de diff. voc.* no. 243), an historian of Herod writing about the conversion of the Idumaeans, states that at first they were 'Phoenicians and Syrians'. This is of special interest, if Ptolemy is to be identified with the grammarian of Ascalon, a moot question: see, in addition to Stern and Jacoby, also Otto, *RE Suppl.* ii, 4.
12. For the rank of Tarsus see, e.g., both Tarsian Orations of Dio Chrysostom (nos. 33, 34) and esp. 34.7.
13. In Jos. *AJ* 20.16.9 he is introduced as 'someone from Egypt', thus explaining the appellation as geographic rather than ethnic.
14. See *adv. Christ.* frg. 28 Harnack = Macarius Magnes 3.31.
15. 2 Cor. 11.22; Phil. 3.5; Rom. 11.1. NB that in all three passages Paul calls himself an Israelite, in the first two also a Hebrew, in none of them a *Ioudaios*. I do not see any

evidence for Paul's wish to express in his reference to his tribe a geographical connexion with a certain part of the Land of Israel, as argued by Mendels, 1998, 28. Cf. e.g. *bBerakhot* 16b: 'we don't know whether we come from Reuben or from Simeon', though at some places, e.g. *bTaanit* 12a, descent from Benjamin is claimed. Nor do I see the evidence for the connexion of Paul's family with Galilean Gischala compelling in any way, contra Deissmann, 1957, 90 n. 5.

16. Schürer, Vermes and Millar, 1973, 456-57.
17. As against the doubts of Burr, 1955, 67ff see Turner, 1954, 61-64, Brunt, 1975b, 143.
18. Cf. Goodman, 1996, 87.
19. None of the commentators offers an alternative to Ti. Julius Alexander; nevertheless it seems to me quite incredible that an equestrian, of however exalted position and brilliant career, should have a statue in the Forum of Augustus or of Trajan (Juv. 1.128-29 *forum ... atque triumphales*). He is rightly not included in the list of recipients of triumphal ornamenta and statues in Gordon, 1952, 305ff.
20. For the conversion of the Idumaeans see Schürer, Vermes and Millar, 1973, 207, and, for a very different interpretation, Cohen, 1990, 204-23.
21. In fact the expression strikes one as somewhat odd. Such *composita* may be factual statements, as e.g. Oenom. apud Eus. *PE* 5.21.4, where Cyrus is described as Ἡμίμηδος ἢ Ἡμιπέρσης (*Hemimêdos ê Hêmipersês* and cf. Suet. *Gramm.* 1 on the *semigraeci* Livius [Andronicus] and Ennius), or else used in a bad sense, contemptuously; in such cases one either half descends to a lower level, e.g. ἡμιβάρβαρος (*hêmibarbaros*, of Greeks), Str. 13.1.58 (C 611), or else a barbarian is described as only a ἡμιέλλην (*hêmihellên*) 'half-Hellenized' (Lucian, *Salt.* 64). In our case it seems that a *compositum* of the ἡμιέλλην (*hêmihellên*) type is being used in a ἡμιβάρβαρος (*hêmibarbaros*) sense.
22. Cohen, 1985, 19-53. See the entire issue of *Judaism* 1985 on the problematics of the matrilinear principle.
23. See Millar, 1987, 143-64; id., 1993, 387ff.
24. Cotton and Geiger, 1989, 147-48 and Geiger, 1997, 75, 80.
25. In *BJ* 1.360 we are told that Cleopatra's desire for possessions (πλεονεξία, *pleonexia*) extended to the Jews and Arabs and their kings Herod and Malchus – by implication also here Herod is king of the Jews. For a late parallel, though in a 'correct' word-order, see Macrob. *Sat.* 2.4.11: *Herodes rex Iudaeorum*.
26. Geiger, 1997.
27. *OGIS* 414 = *CIA* III 550.
28. On the education of client-kings and princes in Rome, see Braund, 1984, 9-21.
29. Jos. *AJ* 15.342-43; the educators of Mariamme's sons were Andromachus and Gemellus (ibid. 16.242-43). The second name points with great probability, though not certainty, to a Roman, cf. Schalit, 1969, 414 n. 936. It seems that they were educated in the house of Asinius Pollio: Feldman, 1953; id., 1985; contra Braund, 1983.
30. Polyb. 27.15.4-5.
31. Antipater, the eldest son, came for purely political purposes, and not for educational ones, see Jos. *AJ* 17.52-53; *BJ* 1.573. Archelaus and Philip educated at Rome: *AJ* 17.80; *BJ* 1.602-3; Antipas and Herod: *AJ* 17.20-21; cf. Hoehner, 1972, 12-14.

32. His mother Berenice was the daughter of Herod's sister Salome and the Idumaean Costobar.
33. Schürer, Vermes and Millar, 1973, 447; D.R. Schwartz, 1990, App. 11.
34. Philo, *In Flacc.* 39: the crowd addressed Agrippa as 'Marin', for they knew that he was a Syrian by birth (γένει Σύρον, *genei Syron*) and ruler over a large part of Syria. A few sections earlier (29) we were told that because of their hostility to Jews they resented the fact that a Jew had been made king.
35. Our sources insist on Agrippa's strict keeping of the Jewish laws when king, even though clearly the manner of his youth in Rome was different. Nevertheless, some Jews may have viewed him as less than perfectly belonging to the nation, see D.R. Schwartz, 1990, 130ff. For Arabs in antiquity abstaining from pork see e.g. Sozom. *Hist. eccl.* 6.38. This must have been the rule with Nabataeans.
36. Cf. Cotton, 1993, 94 and n.5.
37. *P. Yadin* 18.16: ἑλληνικῷ νόμῳ (*hellenikôi nomôi*), and see Geiger, 1992 with previous bibliography.
38. Unfortunately Josephus' use of the term γένος (*genos*) does not allow precise conclusions. The entire incident is intriguing: not only is it unattested elsewhere, but also we have no knowledge whatsoever in this period of any Jews, in Palestine or elsewhere, of equestrian rank.
39. This is too large and complicated a matter to be tackled here. One may note the description and enumeration of some cities as Greek in the *Periplus* attributed to Scylax of Caryanda (see Flensted-Jensen and Hansen, 1996, 136-67) and such surprising items as the description of Ctesiphon as a Greek city in Jos. *AJ* 18.377.
40. Schürer, Vermes and Millar, 1979, 115.
41. Penella, 1989, does not commit himself on the question of authenticity.
42. Foerster and Tsafrir, 1986-7, 53-58.
43. For an excellent analysis see Stein, 1990, 274-91, esp. 281: '…in order to assert their Greek superiority over their new provincial associates in both Judaea and Arabia, the former Decapolis cities would have started emphasizing their belonging to an area long Hellenized'.
44. The matter does not become the less complicated by the fact that the terminology may issue from Jason of Cyrene, from his epitomator or conceivably from a compilator/redactor.
45. NB that he also employs the term ἀλλοφυλισμός (*allophylismos*, 4.13; 6.24). It is indeed instructive – and in support of the common view – to contrast this with the *hapax legomenon* Ῥωμαιότης (*Rhômaiotês*) in the first Cyrene Edict (Ehrenberg and Jones, 1955, no. 311 l. 39), 'Roman citizenship'.
46. The ἀλλόφυλοι (*allophyloi* 10.2; 5) is just a variant for these.
47. Thackeray, e.g., in his LCL edition, thinks of Demetrius, Philo the Elder, Eupolemus etc; there certainly exist no obvious gentile candidates one imagines as translators of Jewish treatises.
48. One may assume that the latest major contribution on the subject, Goodman, 1994, will not for long remain so.

49. If you were a Jew like Josephus, you never had to mention that so were the Idumaeans – their inclusion in the ethnic 'we' was well-established.
50. On the face of it, it might seem that my conclusions differ radically from those of Cohen, 1990, 204-23. Cohen argues, among other points, for a multiple, and complex, definition of *Ioudaios*; in my opinion such a situation is perfectly congruent with a certain degree of flexibility and of doubt as to ethnic and cultural definition and (self)-presentation.

Abbreviations

Adesp.	*Tragicorum Graecorum Fragmenta Adespota*, R. Kannicht & B. Snell (eds.), Göttingen: Vandenhoeck and Ruprecht 1981
AE	*L'année épigraphique*, Paris: Presses universitaires de France 1888-
ANRW	*Aufstieg und Niedergang der römischen Welt*, Berlin 1972-
CIA	*Corpus Inscriptionum Atticarum*, Berlin 1825- (= *IG* I-III)
CIL	*Corpus Inscriptionum Latinarum*, Berlin 1863-
CLE	*Carmina Latina Epigraphica*, F. Bücheler (ed.), 2 vols with supplement by E. Lommatzsch, 1895-1926
EE	*Ephemeris epigraphica*, Berolini: Institutum archaeologicum Germanicum 1872-
FGrH	*Fragmente der Griechischen Historiker*, F. Jacoby (ed.), Berlin 1923-
GVI	*Griechishe Vers-Inschriften* 1, *Grab-Epigramme*, W. Peek (ed.), Berlin 1955-
ICUR	*Inscriptiones Christianae urbis Romae septimo saeculo antiquiores*, Nova series. A. Ferrua & G.B. Rossi (eds.), In civitate Vaticana
IEphesos	*Die Inschriften von Ephesos*, H. Wankel, R. Merkelbach et al. (eds.), Bonn 1979-81 (=*IGSK* 11-17)
IG	*Inscriptiones Graecae*, Kirchhoff et al. (eds.), Berlin 1873-
IGR	*Inscriptiones Graecae ad res Romanas pertinentes*, R. Cagnat et al. (eds.), Paris 1906-27
IGUR	*Inscriptiones Graecae urbis Romae*, 1-4, L. Moretti (Studi pubblicati dall'Istituto italiano per la storia antica 17, 22, 28, 47), Roma: Istituto italiano per la storia antica 1968-90
ISmyrna	*Die Inschriften von Smyrna*, G. Petzl (ed.) 1982- (=*IGSK* 23-24)
LIMC	*Lexicon Iconographicum Mythologiae Classicae*, 1981-
MAMA	*Monumenta Asiae Minoris Antiqua*, Calder et al. (eds.), Manchester-London 1928-
NSc	*Notizie degli scavi di antichità*, Roma: Accademia dei Lincei 1876-
OGIS	*Orientis Graecae Inscriptiones Selectae*, W. Dittenberger (ed.),

	Leipzig 1903-5
*PIR*²	*Prosopographia Imperii Romani*, E. Groag & A. Stein (eds.), 2nd edition, Berlin 1933-
PLF	*Poetarum Lesbiorum Fragmenta,* E. Lobel & D. Page (eds.), Oxford: Clarendon Press 1955
PLM	*Poetae Latini Minores*, Vollmer & Morel (eds.), 1909-35
TrGF	*Tragicorum Graecorum Fragmenta* 4 vols., B. Snell, R. Kannicht & S. Radt (eds.), Göttingen: Vandenhoeck and Ruprecht 1971-85
SEG	*Supplementum Epigraphicum Graecum*, J.J.E. Hondius et al. (eds.), Leiden/Amsterdam: J.C. Gieben 1923-
SHA	*Scriptores Historiae Augustae*, with an English trans., D. Magie (ed.), Loeb Classical Library 1922-32
Schanz-Hosius	*Geschichte der römischen Litteratur bis zum Gesetzgebungswerk des Kaisers Justinian*, M. Schanz (ed.)/ Hosius & Krüger (eds. vol. 3³), München 1922
SIG	*Sylloge Inscriptionum Graecarum*, W. Dittenberger (ed.), 3rd edition, Leipzig 1915-24
TGF	*Tragicorum Graecorum Fragmenta,* A. Nauck (ed.), Lipsiae: in Aedibus B.G. Teubneri 1889²
IEG	*Iambi et Elegi Graeci*, M.L. West (ed.), Oxford: Clarendon Press 1971

Text editions used

Anacreon. *Anacreon*. Gentili, B. 1958. Romae: in Aedibus Athenaei.
Apollonius Citiensis. *Kommentar zu Hippokrates. Über das Einrenken der Gelenke.* Kollesch, J.& Kudlien, F. 1965. Berlin: Berlin Akad.- Verl.
Apollonius Rhodius. *Apollonii Rhodii Argonautica.* Fränkel, H. 1961. Oxford: Clarendon Press.
Aristides. *P. Aelii Aristidis Opera Quae Exstant Omnia.* Lenz, F.W. and Behr, C.A. (eds.) 1976-80. Leiden: Brill.
Aristotle. *Aristotelis Ars Rhetorica.* Ross, W.D. 1959. Oxford: Clarendon Press.
Catullus. *Catulli Veronensis Liber.* Ellis, R. 1878. Oxford: Clarendon Press.
Dionysius of Halicarnassus. *Roman Antiquities.* Cary, E. (ed. and trans.). Vols. I (Books I and II), II (Books III and IV), and III (Books V and VI.1-48) 1937-40. Cambridge, Mass.: Harvard University Press.
Euripides. *Euripides. Hippolytos.* Barrett, W.S. 1964. Oxford: Clarendon Press.
Euripides. *Euripides. Alcestis.* Conacher, D.J. 1988. Warmister, Wiltshire: Aris and Phillips Ltd.
Hesiod. *Hesiod. Theogony.* West, M.L. 1966. Oxford: Clarendon Press.
Hesiod. *Hesiod. Works and Days.* West, M.L. 1978. Oxford: Clarendon Press.
Homer. *Homère. Iliade.* Mazon, P. 1961. Paris: Société d'Édition 'Les belles lettres'.
Livy. *Livy.* Foster, B.O. (ed. and trans.). Vol. I (Books I and II) 1919. Cambridge, Mass.: Harvard University Press.
Moschus. *Die Europa des Moschos.* Bühler, W. 1960. Wiesbaden: F. Steiner Verlag.
Nepos. *Corn. Nepos.* Marshall, P.K. (ed.) 1991. Leipzig: Teubner.
Philostratus. *Vitae Sophistarum.* Cave Wright, W. (ed.) 1921. Cambridge, Mass.: Harvard University Press.
Plato. *Platonis Opera.* Burnet, J. 1905. Oxford: Clarendon Press.
Plutarch. *Plutarchus, Vitae Parallelae.* Ziegler, K. (ed.) 1968. Leipzig: Teubner.
Polyaenus. 'On Behalf of the Macedonian Assembly', *Die Fragmente der griechischen Historiker,* T. 3. Jacoby, F. (ed.) 1962. Leiden: Brill.
Polyaenus. *Strategematon libri octo.* Melber, J. 1887. Lipsiae: Teubneri.
Polyaenus. *Stratagems of War.* Krentz, P. & Wheeler, E.L. (eds.) 1994. Chicago: Ares Publishers.
Seneca. *Sénèque. Tragédies.* Herrmann, L. 1985. Paris: Société d'Édition 'Les belles lettres'.
Seneca. *Sénèque. Lettres à Lucilius.* Préchac, F. 1956. Paris: Société d'Édition 'Les belles lettres'.
Sophocles. *Sophoclis Fabulae.* Pearson, A.C. 1955[7]. Oxford: Clarendon Press.
Theocritus. *Theocritus.* Gow, A.S.F. 1952. Cambridge: Cambridge University Press.
Virgil. *Virgile. Énéide.* Perret, J. 1977. Paris: Société d'Édition 'Les belles lettres'.

Bibliography

Adams, A. 1989. 'The Arch of Hadrian in Athens', in: Walker & Cameron (eds.), 10-16.
Agnello, S.L. 1950. 'Christiana-Byzantina Siciliae II', *Nuovo Didaskaleion* 4, 55-66.
Agnello, S.L. 1956. 'Lavori di sistemazione nelle catacombe siracusane di Vigna Cassia', *Archivio storico siracusano* 2, 45-64.
Agnello, S.L. 1958. 'Problemi di datazione delle catacombe di Siracusa', in: *Scritti in onore di Guido Libertini*, Firenze: L.S. Olschki, 65-82.
Agnello, S.L. 1960. 'Iscrizioni cemeteriali inedite di Siracusa', *Rivista di archeologia cristiana* 36, 19-42.
Agnello, S.L. 1963. 'Ancora sull'iscrizione messinese di Ulpio Niceforo', *Cronache di archeologia e di storia dell'arte* 2, 79-83.
Alcock, S.E. 1993. *Graecia Capta: The Landscapes of Roman Greece*. Cambridge: Cambridge University Press.
Alcock, S.E. 1997. 'The problem of romanization, the power of Athens', in: Hoff & Rotroff (eds.), 1-7.
Allison, P. 1992. *The Distribution of Pompeian House Contents and its Significance*. Doctoral thesis, Ann Arbor, University Microfilms International.
Allison, P. 1997. 'Artefact distribution and spatial function in Pompeian houses', in: B. Rawson & P. Weaver (eds.), 321-54.
Ambaglio, D. 1994. 'Introduzione' to Arriano.
Anderson, G. 1986. *Philostratus. Biography and belles lettres in the Third Century AD*. London: Croom Helm.
Anderson, G. 1993. *The Second Sophistic. A Cultural Phenomenon in the Roman Empire*. London/New York: Routledge.
Anderson, J.K. 1985. *Hunting in the Ancient World*. Berkeley: University of California Press.
Aymard, J. 1951. *Essai sur les chasses romaines*. Paris: de Boccard.
Arafat, K.W. 1996. *Pausanias' Greece. Ancient Artists and Roman Rulers*. Cambridge: Cambridge University Press.
Arnim, H. von. 1898. *Leben and Werke des Dio von Prusa*. Berlin: Weidmann.
Arnim, H. von. 1899. 'Zum Leben Dios von Prusa', *Hermes* 34, 363-79.
Arnim, H. von. (ed.) 1962. *Dionis Prusaensis quem vocant Chrysostomum quae extant omnia*. 2 vols. Berlin: Weidmann.
Arriano 1994. *Anabasi di Alessandro*. Milano: Rizzoli.
Ault, B.A. 1994. *Classical Houses and Households: An Architectural and Artifactual Case Study from Halieis, Greece*. Doctoral thesis, Ann Arbor, University Microfilms International.

Babbitt, F.C. 1931. *Plutarch's Moralia III* (Loeb Classical Library). Cambridge, Massachusetts: Harvard University Press.

Baldassari, P. 1995. 'Augusto *Soter*: ipotesi sul *Monopteros* dell' Acropoli Ateniese', *Ostraka* 4, 69-84.

Bardon, H. 1968. *Les empereurs et les lettres latines d'Auguste à Hadrien*. 2nd edition. Paris: les belles lettres.

Barker, G. & Lloyd, J. (eds.) 1991. *Roman Landscapes: Archaeological Survey in the Mediterranean Region* (Archaeological Monographs of the British School at Rome 2). London.

Bartsch, S. 1994. *Actors in the Audience: Theatricality and Doublespeak from Nero to Hadrian*. Cambridge, MA: Harvard University Press.

Baslez, M.-F. 1990 'L'idée de noblesse dans les romans grecs', *Dialogues d'histoire ancienne* 16, 115-28.

Behr, C.A. 1968. *Aelius Aristides and the Sacred Tales*. Amsterdam: A.M. Hakkert.

Behr, C.A. 1986. *P. Aelius Aristides. The complete works. Volume I: Orations I-XVI*. Translated by Charles A. Behr. Leiden: E.J. Brill.

Behr, C.A. 1994. 'Studies on the biography of Aelius Aristides', in: *ANRW* II.34.2, 1140-1233.

Bejarano, V. 1975. 'El emperador Adriano ante la tradición romana', *Pyrenae* 11, 81-98.

Beltrán Fortes, J. 1993. 'Arriano de Nicomedia y la Bética, de nuevo', *Habis* 23, 171-96.

Benario, H.W. 1975. 'Augustus Princeps', in: *ANRW* II. 2, 75-85.

Benjamin, A.S., 1963. 'The altars of Hadrian in Athens and Hadrian's Panhellenic program', *Hesperia* 32, 57-86.

Benjamin, A. & Raubitschek, A.E. 1959. 'Arae Augusti', *Hesperia* 28, 65-85.

Bennett, J. 1997. *Trajan, Optimus Princeps. A Life and Times*. Bloomington and Indianapolis: Indiana University Press.

Bennett, S. 1990. *Theatre Audiences: A Theory of Production and Reception*. London: Routledge.

Bers, V. 1985 'Dikastic *Thorubos*', *History of Political Thought* 6, 1-15.

Bianco, M.G. et al, 1984-88. *Disiecti membra poetae: studi di poesia latina in frammenti* 3. Foggia: Atlantica.

Binder, W. 1967. *Der Roma-Augustus Monopteros auf der Akropolis in Athen und sein typologischer Ort*. Karlsruhe: Abhandlung.

Bingen, J. (ed.) 1996. *Pausanias historien. Entret. sur l' Ant. Class.* XLI. Vandoeuvres-Genève, 15-19 Août 1994), Genève: Fondation Hardt.

Bintliff, J.L. & Snodgrass, A.M. 1985. 'The Cambridge/Bradford Boeotian expedition: the first four years', *Journal of Field Archaeology* 12, 123-63.

Birley, A.R. 1994. 'Hadrian's farewell to life', *Laverna* 5, 176-205.

Birley, A.R. 1997. *Hadrian. The Restless Emperor*. London: Routledge.

Blomqvist, K. 1989. *Myth and Moral Message in Dio Chrysostom: A Study in Dio's Moral Thought, with a Particular Focus on his Attitudes towards Women*. diss. Lund.

Boardman, J., Griffin, J. & Murray, O. (eds.) 1986. *The Roman World: The Oxford History of the Classical World*. Oxford: Oxford University Press.

Boatwright, M.T. 2000. *Hadrian and the Cities of the Roman Empire*. Princeton, New Jersey: Princeton University Press.

Borsari, S. 1963. *Il monachesimo bizantino nella Sicilia e nell'Italia meridionale prenormanne*. Napoli: Istituto italiano per gli studi storici in Napoli.

Booth, W. 1974. *A Rhetoric of Irony*. Chicago: University of Chicago Press.

Bosworth, A.B. 1993. 'Arrian and Rome: the minor works', in: *ANRW* II.34.1, 226-75.

Boulanger, A. 1923. *Aelius Aristide et la sophistique dans la province d'Asie au IIe siècle de notre Ère*. Paris: Éditions E. de Boccard.

Boulogne, J. 1994. *Plutarque, un aristocrate grec sous l'occupation romaine*. Villeneuve d'Ascq: Presses universitaires de Lille.

Bourdieu, P. 1977. *Outline of a theory of practice*. Translated by Richard Nice. Cambridge: Cambridge University Press [Original edition: *Esquisse d'une théorie de la pratique, précédé de trois études d'ethnologie kabyle*. Genève: Droz, 1972].

Bourdieu, P. 1990. *The Logic of Practice*. Translated by Richard Nice. Cambridge: Polity Press [Original edition: *Le sens pratique*. Paris: Éditions de Minuit, 1980].

Bousquet, J. 1961. 'Inscriptions de Delphes', *Bulletin de correspondance hellénique* 75, 88-90.

Bowden, H. & Gill, D.W.J. 1997. 'Roman Methana', in: Mee & Forbes (eds.), 77-83.

Bowersock, G. 1961. 'Eurycles of Sparta', *Journal of Roman Studies* 51, 112-18.

Bowersock, G. 1964. 'Augustus on Aegina', *Classical Quarterly* 14, 120-21.

Bowersock, G. 1965. *Augustus and the Greek World*. Oxford: Oxford University Press.

Bowersock, G. 1969. *Greek Sophists in the Roman Empire*. Oxford: Clarendon Press.

Bowersock, G. (ed.) 1974. *Approaches to the Second Sophistic*. University Park, PA: American Philological Association.

Bowersock, G. 1982. 'The Imperial Cult: Perceptions and Persistence', in: Meyer & Sanders (eds.) 1982, 171-82.

Bowersock, G. 1984. 'Augustus and the East: The Problem of the Succession', in: Millar & Segal (eds.), 169-88.

Bowersock, G.W. 1987. 'The mechanics of subversion in the Roman provinces', in: Giovannini (ed.), 291-317.

Bowersock, G. 1990. 'The pontificate of Augustus', in: Raaflaub & Toher (eds.), 380-94.

Bowie, E.L. 1970. 'Greeks and their past in the Second Sophistic', *Past & Present* 46, 3-41 (now in Finley 1974, 166-209)

Bowie, E.L. 1974. 'Greeks and their Past in the Second Sophistic', in: Finley (ed.) 1974, 166-209.

Bowie, E.L. 1982. 'The importance of sophists', *Yale Classical Studies* 27, 29-59.

Bowie, E.L. 1989. 'Greek sophists and Greek poetry in the second sophistic', in: *ANRW* II.33.1, 209-58.

Bowie, E.L. 1990. 'Greek poetry in the Antonine Age', in: Russell (ed.) 1990, 53-90.

Bowie, E.L. 1996. 'Past and Present in Pausanias', in: AA.VV., 207-39.

Bowie, E.L. 1997. 'Hadrian, Favorinus and Plutarch', in: Mossman (ed.), 1-15.

Boyle, A.J. 1987. *Seneca's Phaedra: Introduction, Text, Translation and Notes*. Liverpool: Francis Cairns.

Braund, D. 1983. 'Four notes on the Herods', *Classical Quarterly* 33, 239-42.

Braund, D. 1984. *Rome and the Friendly King. The Character of Client Kingship*. London and Canberra: Croom Helm.

Brown, S. 1992. 'Death as decoration: scenes from the Arena on Roman domestic mosaics', in: A. Richlin (ed.), *Pornography and Representation in Greece and Rome*. Oxford: Oxford University Press, 180-211.

Bruneau, P. et. al. 1970. *Exploration archeologique de Delos 27: L'ilot de la maison des comédiens*. Paris, Ecole français d'Athènes.

Bruneau, P. 1978. 'Deliaca II', *Bulletin de Correspondence Héllenique* 102, 109-71.

Brunt, P.A. 1975a. 'Aspects of the Social Thought of Dio Chrysostom and the Stoics', *Proceedings of the Cambridge Philological Society* 19, 9-34.

Brunt, P.A. 1975b. 'The administrators of Roman Egypt', *Journal of Roman Studies* 65, 124-47.

Brunt, P.A. 1977. 'From Epictetus to Arrian', *Athenaeum* 50, 19-48.

Brunt, P.A. 1994. 'The bubble of the second sophistic', *Bulletin of the Institute for Classical Studies of the University of London* 39, 25-52.

Brunt, P.A. & Moore, J.M. 1967. *Res Gestae Divi Augusti. The Achievements of the Divine Augustus*. Oxford: Oxford University Press.

Büchner, K. 1974. 'Altrömische und horazische Virtus', in: Oppermann (ed.) 1967, 376-401.

Bühler, W. 1978. 'Ein unbekanntes, Kaiser Hadrian zugeschriebenes Epigram', *Zeitschrift fürPapyrologie und Epigrafik* 31, 55-60.

Buffière, F. 1970. *Anthologie Palatine 12 (livres xiii-xv)*. Paris: les belles lettres.

Burckhardt, J. 1864. 'Ueber den Wert des Dio Chrysostomus für die Kenntniß seiner Zeit', *Neues schweizerisches Museum* 4, 97-122.

Burnet, J. 1907. *Platonis Opera V.* Oxford: Clarendon Press.

Burr, V. 1955. *Tiberius Julius Alexander*. (Antiquitas 1). Bonn.

Butler, H.E. 1909. *Post-Augustan Poetry, from Seneca to Juvenal*. Oxford: Clarendon Press.

Calandra, E. 1996. *Oltre la Grecia – Alle origini del filellenismo di Adriano*. Napoli: Edizioni Scientifiche Italiane.

Calbi, A. et al. (eds.) 1993. *L'epigrafia del villaggio* (Epigrafia e antichità 12). Faenza: Lega.

Cambiano, G., Canfora, L. & Lanza, D. (eds.) 1994. *Lo spazio letterario della Grecia antica*. Vol. I: *La produzione e la circolazione del testo*. Part 3: *I Greci e Roma*. Roma: Salerno.

Cameron, A. 1980. 'Poetae novelli', *Harvard Studies in Classical Philology* 84, 127-75.

Cameron, A. 1993. *The Greek Anthology from Meleager to Planudes*. Oxford: Clarendon Press.

Cameron, A. 1995. *Callimachus and his critics*. Princeton: Princeton University Press.

Camp, J.M. 1992. *The Athenian Agora. Excavations in the Heart of Classical Athens*. London: Thames and Hudson.

Canetti, E. 1978. *Crowds and Power*. trans. Carol Stewart. New York: Seabury Press.

Cantarelli, L. 1898. 'Gli scritti latini di Adriano imperatore', *Studi e documenti di storia e diritto* 19, 113-70.

Carandini, A. 1969. *Vibia Sabina. Funzione politica, iconografia e il problema del classicismo Adrianeo*. Firenze: Leo S. Olschki Editore.

Carey, C. 1994. 'Rhetorical Means of Persuasion', in: Worthington (ed.) 1994, 26-45.

Carrara, P. 1988. 'Plutarco ed Euripide: alcune considerazioni sulle citazioni euripidee in Plutarco (De aud. poet.)', *Illinois Classical Studies* 13, 447-55.

Cary, E. 1914-1927. *Dio's Roman History in Nine Volumes*, (Loeb Classical Library). Cambridge, Mass.: Harvard University Press.

Castrén, P. (ed.) 1994. *Post-Herulian Athens. Aspects of Life and Culture in Athens AD 267-529*, (Papers and Monographs of the Finnish Institute at Athens 1). Helsinki: Foundation of the Finnish Institute at Athens.

Cavanagh, W. et al. (eds.) 1996. *Continuity and Change in the Greek Rural Landscape: The Laconia Survey II. Archaeological data*, (Annual of the British School at Athens suppl. 27). London.

Chamonard, J. 1906. 'Fouilles de Délos 1904: fouilles dans le quartier du théatre', *Bulletin de Correspondence Héllenique* 30, 485-606.

Chamonard, J. 1922. *Exploration Archeologique de Délos 8: le quartier du théatre 1-2*. Paris, Ecole français d'Athènes.

Chamonard, J. 1924. *Exploration Archeologique de Délos 8: le quartier du théatre 3: construction et technique*. Paris, Ecole français d'Athènes.

Cherry, J.F., Davis, J.L. & Mantzourani, E. 1991. *Landscape Archaeology as Long-Term History: Northern Keos in the Cycladic Islands from the Earliest Settlement until Modern Times*, (Monumenta Archaeologica 16). Los Angeles: UCLA Institute of Archaeology.

Clinton, K. 1989. 'Hadrian's contribution to the renaissance of Eleusis', in: Walker & Cameron (eds.), 56-68.

Clinton, K. 1997. 'Eleusis and the Romans: Late Republic to Marcus Aurelius', in: Hoff & Rotroff (eds.), 161-81.

Codd, J. 1990. 'Making distinctions: the eye of the beholder', in: Harker, Mahar & Wilkes (eds.), 132-59.

Coffey, M. and Mayer, R. 1990. *Seneca. Phaedra*. Cambridge: Cambridge University Press.

Cohen, S.J.D.1985. 'The origins of the matrilinear principle in Rabbinic Law', *American Jewish Studies Review* 10, 19-53.

Cohen, S.J.D. 1990. 'Religion, ethnicity, and "hellenism" in the emergence of Jewish identity in Maccabean Palestine', in: P. Bilde et al. (eds.), *Religion and Religious Practice in the Seleucid Kingdom*, (Studies in Hellenistic Civilization 1). Aarhus: Aarhus University Press, 204-23.

Cohoon, J.W. & Crosby, H. Lamar (eds. and trans.) 1932-51. *Dio Chrysostom*. 5 vols. Cambridge, MA: Harvard University Press.

Coleman, K.M. 1990. 'Fatal charades: Roman executions staged as mythological enactments', *Journal of Roman Studies* 80, 44-73.

Collart, P. 1937. *Philippes ville de Macedoine*. Paris: Boccard.

Conte, G.B. 1994. *Latin Literature, A History*. Baltimore and London: The Johns Hopkins University Press.

Conti, G. 1970. *Decorazione architettonica della 'Piazza d'Oro' a Villa Adriana*. Roma: 'L'Erma' di Bretschneider.

Cotton, H. 1993. 'The guardianship of Jesus, son of Babatha: Roman and local law in the Province of Arabia', *Journal of Roman Studies* 83, 94-108.

Cotton, H.M. and Geiger J. 1989. *Masada II. The Yigael Yadin Excavations 1963-1965. Final Reports. The Latin and Greek Documents.* Jerusalem: Israel Exploration Society.

Couzinet, D. 1996. *Histoire et méthode à la Renaissance. Une lecture de la Methodus ad facilem historiarum cognitionem de Jean Bodin.* Paris: Vrin.

Curtius, L. 1974. 'Virtus und Constantia', in: Oppermann (ed.) 1967, 370-75.

Dakaris, S.I. 1989. *Κασσώπη. Νεώτερες ἀνασκαφές* (1977-83). Ioannina: Ioannina University.

Davis, J.L. et al. 1997. 'The Pylos regional archaeological project. Part 1: overview and the archaeological survey', *Hesperia* 66, 390-494.

de Blois, L. 1992. 'The perception of politics in Plutarch's Roman *Lives*', in: *ANRW* II.33.6, 4568-4615.

Deissmann, A. 1957. *Paul. A Study in Social and Religious History.* New York: Harper & Brothers.

Dessau, H. 1899. 'Zum Leben Dios von Prusa', *Hermes* 34, 81-87.

Desideri, P. 1986. 'La vita politica cittadina nell'Impero: lettura dei *Praecepta gerendae rei publicae* e dell' *An seni res publica gerenda sit*', *Athenaeum* N.S. 64, 371-81.

Desideri, P. 1996. 'Barigazzi lettore di Plutarco', *Prometheus* 22, 3-10.

Desideri, P. 1998. L' impero bilingue e il parallelismo Greci/Romani, in: Settis (ed.), 909-39.

Despoine, A. 1988. 'Παρατηρήσεις στὰ ἀνάγλυφα τοῦ βήματος τοῦ Φαίδρου', in: Πρακτικά τοῦ XII Διεθνοῦς συνεδρίου κλασικῆς ἀρχαιολογίας, Ἀθήνα, 4-10 Σεπτεμβρίου 1983, τ. Γ. Athens, 70-73.

Di Gregorio, L. 1976. 'Plutarco e la tragedia greca', *Prometheus* 2, 151-74.

Dickmann, J. 1997. 'The peristyle and the transformation of domestic space in hellenistic Pompeii', in: Laurence and Wallace-Hadrill (eds.), 121-36.

Dillon, J. 1977. *The Middle Platonists. A study of Platonism 80 BC to AD 220.* London: Duckworth.

Dinsmoor, W.B. 1940. 'The Temple of Ares at Athens', *Hesperia* 9, 1-52.

Dontas, G. 1968. 'Μέγα Ἀδριάνειον κτήριον καὶ ἄλλα οἰκοδομικὰ λείψανα ἐπὶ τῆς ὁδοῦ Ἀδριανοῦ', *Athens Annals of Archaeology* 1, 221-24.

Dontas, G. 1969a. 'Νεώτερα περὶ τοῦ μεγάλου ρωμαικοῦ κτηρίου τῆς ὁδοῦ Ἀδριανοῦ', *Athens Annals of Archaeology* 2, 1-3.

Dontas, G. 1969b. ' Ἀρχαιολογικὸν Δελτίον 24', *Χρονικά*, 19-23.

Downey, G. 1975. 'Tiberiana', in: *ANRW* II. 2, 95-130.

Due, O.S. 1968. 'Lucain et la philosophie', in: Durry (ed.), 201-32.

Durry, M. (ed.) 1968. *Lucain. Entretiens, Tome XV.* Fondation Hardt pour l=Étude de l=Antiquité Classique. Vandoeuvres-Genève: Olivier Reverdin.

Ehrenberg, V. & Jones, A.H.M. 1955. *Documents Illustrating the Reigns of Augustus and Tiberius*[2]. Oxford: Clarendon Press.

Eisenhut, W. 1973. *Virtus Romana. Ihre Stellung im römischen Wertsystem.* München: Wilhelm Fink Verlag.

Etienne, R. 1960. *Le Quartier Nord-est de Volubilis.* Paris: Boccard.

Eucken, C. 1983. *Isokrates. Seine Position in der Auseinandersetzung mit den zeitgenössischen Philosophen.* Berlin/New York: De Gruyter.

Fanon, F. 1967. *A Dying Colonialism.* trans. Haakon Chavalier. New York: Grove Press.

Fanon, F. 1968. *The Wretched of the Earth.* trans. Constance Farrington. New York: Grove Press.

Fanon, F. 1974. *Les damnés de la terre.* Paris: F. Maspero.

Fantham, E. 1996. *Roman Literary Culture. From Cicero to Apuleius.* Baltimore and London: Johns Hopkins University Press.

Fayer, C. 1976. *Il culto della dea Roma. Origine e diffusione nell'impero.* Pescara: Trimestre.

Fehling, D. 1977. *Amor und Psyche.* Wiesbaden: Akademie der Wissenschaften und der Literatur.

Fein, S. 1994. *Die Beziehungen der Kaiser Trajan und Hadrian zu den Litterati. Beiträge zur Altertumskunde* 26. Stuttgart and Leipzig: B.G. Teubner.

Feldman, L.H. 1953. 'Asinius Pollio and his Jewish Interests', *Transactions of the American Philological Association* 84, 73-80.

Feldman, L.H. 1985. 'Asinius Pollio and Herod's Sons', *Classical Quarterly* 35, 240-42.

Ferrua, A. 1940. 'Due pseudoepigrafi cristiane di Siracusa', *Rivista di archeologia cristiana* 17, 276-78.

Ferrua, A. 1941. 'Epigrafia sicula pagana e cristiana', *Rivista di archeologia cristiana* 18, 151-243.

Ferrua, A. 1942. 'Dal greco al volgare', *Civiltà cattolica* 93.1, 207-16.

Ferrua, A. 1946-47. 'Florilegio d'iscrizioni paleocristiane di Sicilia', *Rendiconti della Pontificia accademia romana di archeologia* 22, 227-39.

Ferrua, A. 1974. Review of M.T. Manni Piraino, 'Iscrizioni greche lapidarie del museo di Palermo' (Palermo 1973), *Rivista di archeologia cristiana* 50, 431-33.

Ferrua, A. 1989. *Note e giunte alle iscrizioni cristiane antiche della Sicilia,* (Sussidi allo studio delle antichità cristiane 9). Città del Vaticano: Pontificio Istituto di archeologia cristiana.

Février, P.A.1964. 'Remarques sur les inscriptions funéraires datées de Maurétanie Césarienne Orientale (IIe–Ve siècle)', *Mélanges de l'Ecole française de Rome. Antiquité* 76, 105-72.

Fingarette, A. 1970. 'The Marmaria Puzzles', *American Journal of Archaeology* 74, 401-4.

Finley, M.I. 1973. *The ancient economy.* London: Chatto & Windus.

Finley, M.I. (ed.) 1974. *Studies in Ancient Society.* London-Boston: Routledge and K. Paul.

Fischer-Hansen, T. (ed.) 1995. *Ancient Sicily* (Acta Hyperborea 6). Copenhagen: Museum Tusculanum Press.

Fishwick, D. 1984. 'Coins as evidence: some phantom temples', *Classical Views* 28, 263-70.

Fishwick, D. 1993. *The Imperial Cult in the Latin West.* Leiden: E.J. Brill.

Flensted-Jensen P. & Hansen, M.H. 1996. 'Pseudo-Skylax' Use of the Term 'Polis', in: Hansen, M.H. & Raaflaub, K. (eds.), *More Studies in the Ancient Greek Polis,* (Historia Einzelschriften 108). Stuttgart.

Flinterman, J.J. 1995. *Power,* Paideia & *Pythagoreanism. Greek Identity, Conceptions of the Relationship Between Philosophers and Monarchs and Political Ideas in Philostratus'* Life of Apollonius. Amsterdam: J.C. Gieben.

Flinterman, J.J. 1996. 'De tweede sofistiek: een portie gebakken lucht?', *Lampas* 29, 135-54.

Flower, M.A. & Toher, M. (eds.) 1991. *Georgica. Greek Studies in Honour of George Cawkwel,* (Bulletin of the Institute of Classical Studies, Supplement 58). London.

Foerster, G. & Tsafrir Y. 1986-87. 'Nysa-Scythopolis. A new inscription and the titles of the City on its Coins', *Israel Numismatic Journal* 9, 53-58.

Fontana, M.J. et al. (eds.) 1980. Φιλίας χάριν. *Miscellanea di studi classici in onore di Eugenio Manni* 1-7. Roma: 'L'Erma' di Bretschneider.

Forbes, C. 1986 'Comparison, Self-praise, and Irony: Paul's Boasting and the Conventions of Hellenistic Rhetoric', *New Testament Studies* 32, 1-30.

Forni, G. 1980. 'Sicilia Romana tributim discripta', in: Fontana et al. (eds.), 949-61.

Forsell, R. 1996. 'The Roman period', in: Wells (ed.), 285-343.

Foucault, M. 1972. *The Archaeology of Knowledge.* trans. A.M. Sheridan Smith. New York: Pantheon Books.

Foxhall, L. 1990. 'The dependent tenant: land-leasing and labour in Italy and Greece', *Journal of Roman Studies* 80, 97-114.

Foxhall, L. 1997. 'Ancient farmsteads, other agricultural sites and equipment', in: Mee & Forbes (eds.), 257-68.

Frisk, H. 1960. *Griechisches etymologisches Wörterbuch* 1. Heidelberg: Winter Universitätsverlag.

Fritze, H. von. 1913. *Die antiken Münzen Mysiens.* Berlin: Akademie der Wissenschaften & Georg Reimer.

Führer, J. 1897. *Forschungen zur Sicilia sotterranea.* München: Königliche bayerische Akademie der Wissenschaften. (Distributed both in *Abhandlungen der königlichen bayerischen Akademie der Wissenschaften,* class 1, vol. 20.3, 673-862, and as a separate volume with independent page numbering).

Gabba, E. 1993. 'Roma nell' opera storiografica di Appiano', in: Reggi (ed.), 103-15.

Gabrici, E. 1925. 'Sicilia XIV – Girgenti', *Notizie degli Scavi* 50, 420-61.

Gamberale, L. 1993. 'L'epigramma dell' imperatore Adriano all' Eros di Tespie' in *Pretagostini,* 1089-1110.

Geagan, D.J. 1967. *The Athenian Constitution after Sulla,* (Hesperia, Supplement 12). Athens.

Geagan, D.J. 1979. 'Roman Athens: some aspects of life and culture I. 86 BC – AD 267', in: *ANRW* II.7.1, 371-437.

Geagan, D.J. 1992. 'A family of Marathon and social mobility in Athens of the first century BC', *Phoenix* 46, 29-44.

Geagan, D.J. 1997. 'The Athenian elite: romanization, resistance, and the exercise of power', in: Hoff & Rotroff (eds.), 19-32.

Geiger, J. 1992. 'A note on P.Yadin 18', *Zeitschrift für Papyrologie und Epigraphie* 93, 67-68.

Geiger, J. 1997. 'Herodes *Philorhomaios*', *Ancient Society* 28, 75-88.
Gentili, G.V.1961. 'Nuovi elementi di epigrafia siracusana', *Archivio storico siracusano* 7, 5-25.
George, M. 1997. *The Roman Domestic Architecture of Northern Italy*, (BAR International Series 670). Oxford: Oxbow Books.
Giomini, R. 1955. *L. Annaei Senecae Phaedra*. Roma: Signorelli.
Giovannini, A. (ed.) 1987. *Opposition et résistances à l'empire d'Auguste à Trajan*. Vandoevres-Genève: Fondation Hardt.
Gleason, M.W. 1995. *Making Men. Sophists and Self-presentation in Ancient Rome*. Princeton, New Jersey: Princeton University Press.
Goffman, Erving. 1967. *Interaction Ritual: Essays on Face-to-Face Behavior*. New York: Anchor Books.
Goldhill, S. 1995. *Foucault's Virginity*. Cambridge: Cambridge University Press.
Goodman, M. 1989. 'Nerva, the *Fiscus Iudaeicus* and Jewish identity', *Journal of Roman Studies* 79, 40-44.
Goodman, M. 1994. *Mission and Conversion*. Oxford: Clarendon Press.
Goodman, M. 1996. 'The Roman identity of Roman jews', in: I.M. Gafni et al. (eds.), *The Jews in the Hellenistic-Roman World. Studies in Memory of Menahem Stern*. Jerusalem: The Zalman Shazar Center for Jewish History, 85*-99*.
Göransson, T. 1995. *Albinus, Alcinous, Arius Didymus*, (Acta Universitatis Gothoburgensis). Göteborg.
Gordon, A.E. 1952. 'Quintus Veranius, Consul AD 49', *University of California Publications in Classical Archeology* 2: 5.
Goudriaan, K. 1989. *Over classicisme. Dionysius van Halicarnassus en zijn program van welsprekendheid, cultuur en politiek*. Amsterdam: Dissertation Vrije Universiteit.
Gould, J.P. 1980. 'Law, custom and myth: aspects of the social position of women in Classical Athens', *Journal of Hellenic Studies* 100, 38-59.
Gow, A.S.F. 1952. *Theocritus*. Cambridge: Cambridge University Press.
Gow, A.S.F. & Page, D.L. 1968. *The Garland of Philip*. Cambridge: Cambridge University Press.
Graindor, P. 1927. *Athènes sous Auguste*. Cairo: Université Egyptienne, Faculté des lettres.
Gray, N. 1948. 'The paleography of Latin inscriptions in the eighth, ninth and tenth centuries in Italy', *Papers of the British School in Rome* 16, 38-171.
Griesheimer, M. 1996. 'Nouvelles inscriptions funéraires de la catacombe Saint-Jean', *Rivista di archeologia cristiana* 72, 115-32.
Griffin, M. 1971. Review of Bowersock 1969 in *Journal of Roman Studies* 61, 279-81.
Grimal, P. 1965. *L. Annaei Senecae Phaedra*. Paris: Presses Universitaires de France.
Grobel-Miller, S. 1973. 'The Philippeion and Macedonian architecture', *Athenische Mitteilungen* 88, 189-218.
Habicht, C. 1990. 'Athens and the Attalids in the second century BC', *Hesperia* 59, 561-77.
Habicht, C. 1994. 'Athens and the Ptolemies', in: C. Habicht, *Athen in Hellenistischer Zeit*. München: Beck, 140-163.

Hadavas, C.T. 1995. *The Structure, Form, and Meaning of Plutarch's Life of Solon*, Diss. University of North Carolina at Chapel Hill, Chapel Hill, NC.

Haeberlin, C. 1887. *Carmina figurata graeca*, 2nd edition. Hannover: Hahn.

Halfmann, H. 1986. *Itinera principum*. Stuttgart: F. Steiner Verlag Wiesbaden.

Hänlein-Schäfer, H. 1985. *Veneratio Augusti. Eine Studie zu den Tempeln des ersten römischen Kaisers.* Roma: 'L'Erma' di Bretschneider.

Hahn, J. 1989. *Der Philosoph und die Gesellschaft: Selbstverständnis, öffentliches Auftreten und populäre Erwartungen in der hohen Kaiserzeit.* Stuttgart: Steiner.

Hardie, A. 1983. *Statius and his Silvae.* Liverpool: Francis Cairns.

Harker, R. 1990. 'Bourdieu: education and reproduction', in: Harker, Mahar & Wilkes (eds.), 86-108.

Harker, R., Mahar, C. & Wilkes, C. (eds) 1990. *An Introduction to the Work of Pierre Bourdieu. The Practice of Theory.* Basingstoke, Hampshire/London: Macmillan.

Harris, B.F. 1991. 'Dio of Prusa: A Survey of Recent Work', *ANRW* II.3.5, 3853-81.

Heftner, H. 1995. *Plutarch und der Aufstieg des Pompeius. Ein historischer Kommentar zu Plutarchs Pompeiusvita* Teil I: Kap. 1-45. (Europäische Hochschulschriften 639). Frankfurt am Main.

Heitsch, E. 1961. *Die griechischen Dichterfragmente der römischen Kaiserzeit* 1. Göttingen: Vandenhoek & Ruprecht.

Hellegouarc'h, J. 1963. *Le vocabulaire latin des relations politiques sous la république.* Paris: Société d'Édition 'Les Belles Lettres'.

Hermann, L. 1950. 'La réplique d'Hadrien à Florus', *Latomus* 9, 385-7.

Herzog, William R. II. 1994. *Parables as Subversive Speech: Jesus as Pedagogue of the Oppressed.* Louisville: Westminster/John Knox Press.

Hiller von Gaertringen, F. et al. 1899. *Thera I: Die Insel Thera in Altertum und Gegenwart.* Berlin, Georg Reimer.

Hiller von Gaertringen, F. et al. 1904. *Thera III: Stadtgeschichte von Thera.* Berlin: Georg Reimer.

Hobson, J.A. 1936. *Veblen.* London: Chapman and Hall.

Hoehner, H.W. 1972. *Herod Antipas.* Cambridge: Cambridge University Press.

Hoepfner, W. & Schwandner, E-L. 1994. *Haus und Stadt im Klassichen Griechenland* (2nd edition). Munich: Deutscher Kunstverlag.

Hoff, M. 1989a. 'Civil disobedience and unrest in Augustan Athens', *Hesperia* 58, 267-76.

Hoff, M., 1989b. 'The early history of the Roman agora at Athens', in: Walker & Cameron (eds.), 1-8.

Hoff, M. 1994. 'The so-called Agoranomion and the imperial cult in Julio-Claudian Athens', *Archaeologischer Anzeiger*, 93-117.

Hoff, M. 1996. 'The politics and architecture of the Athenian imperial cult', in: Small (ed.), 185-200.

Hoff, M. 1997. 'Laceratae Athenae: Sulla's siege of Athens in 87/6 BC and its aftermath', in: Hoff & Rotroff (eds.), 33-51.

Hoff, M. & Rotroff, S.I. (eds.) 1997. *The Romanization of Athens*, Proceedings of an

International Conference held at Lincoln, Nebraska (April 1996), (Oxbow Monograph 94). Oxford: Oxbow Books.

Hoffmann, P. & Trédé, M. 1998. *Le rire des anciens*. Paris: Presses de l'Ecole Normale Supérieure.

Höghammar, K. 1984. 'Dating the bath at Asine in Argolis', *Opuscula atheniensia* 15, 79-106.

Höghammar, K. 1993. *Sculpture and Society. A Study of the Connection between the Freestanding Sculpture and Society on Kos in the Hellenistic and Augustan Periods*, (Uppsala Studies in Ancient Mediterranean and Near Eastern Civilizations 23). Uppsala: Boreas.

Höghammar, K. 1997. 'Women in public space: Cos c. 200 BC to c. AD 15/20', in: Jenkins & Waywell (eds.), 127-33.

Holland McAllister, M. 1959. 'The temple of Ares at Athens. A review of the evidence', *Hesperia* 28, 1-64.

Hollegaard Olsen, C. et al. 1995. 'The Roman domus of the early Empire: a case-study: Sicily', in: Fischer-Hansen, 209-61.

Hollis, A.S. 1977. *Ovid Ars Amatoria* Book I. *Edited with Introduction and Commentary*. Oxford: Clarendon Press.

Hölscher, T. 1985. 'Die Geschlagenen und Ausgelieferten in der Kunst des Hellenismus', *Antike Kunst* 28, 124-28.

Hornblower, S. (ed.) 1994. *Greek Historiography*. Oxford: Clarendon Press.

Hubbell, H.M. 1913. *The Influence of Isocrates on Cicero, Dionysius, and Aristides*. New Haven: Yale University Press.

Hurst, A. & Schachter, A. (eds.) 1996. *La montagne des Muses*. Genève: librairie Droz.

Imhoof-Blumer, F. 1911. *Nomisma* 6. Berlin: Mayer & Müller.

Innes, D., H. Hine, & C. Pelling. (eds.) 1995. *Ethics and Rhetoric: Classical Essays for Donald Russell on his Seventy-Fifth Birthday*. Oxford: Oxford University Press.

Ingenkamp, H.G. 1992. 'Plutarchs "Leben der Gracchen". Eine Analyse', in: *ANRW* II.33.6: 4298-4346.

Jacoby, F. (ed.) 1923-. *Die Fragmente der griechischen Historiker*. Berlin: Weidmannsche Buchhandlung.

Jameson, M.H., Runnels, C.N. & van Andel, T.H. 1994. *A Greek Contryside: the Southern Argolid from Prehistory to the Present Day*. Stanford: Stanford University Press.

Jamot, P. 1895. 'Fouilles de Thespies. Les jeux en l'honneur des Muses', *Bulletin de Correspondence Hellénique* 19, 311-65.

Janson, T. 1964. *Latin Prose Prefaces. Studies in Literary Conventions*. Stockholm: Almqvist & Wiksell.

Jebb, R.1928. *Sophocles. The Plays and Fragments*, Part III, *The Antigone*. Cambridge: Cambridge University Press.

Jenkins, I. & Waywell, G.B. (eds.) 1997. *Sculptors and Sculpture of Caria and the Dodecanese*. London: British Museum Press.

Jenkyns, R. 1986. 'Silver Latin poetry and the Latin novel', in: Boardman, Griffin & Murray (eds.), 267-87.

Jocelyn, H. 1967. *The Tragedies of Ennius*. Cambridge: Cambridge University Press.

Johnson, W.R. 1987. *Momentary Monsters – Lucan and his Heroes*. Ithaca, New York: Cornell University Press.

Jones, A.H.M. 1937. *Cities of the Eastern Roman Provinces*. Oxford: Oxford University Press.

Jones, A.H.M. 1940. *The Greek City from Alexander to Justinian*. Oxford: Oxford University Press.

Jones, C.P. 1970. 'Sura and Senecio', *Journal of Roman Studies* 60, 98-104.

Jones, C.P. 1971. *Plutarch and Rome*. Oxford: Clarendon Press.

Jones, C.P. 1974. 'The reliability of Philostratus', in: Bowersock 1974, 11-16.

Jones, C.P. 1978. *The Roman World of Dio Chrysostom*. Cambridge Mass.: Harvard University Press.

Jones, C.P. 1984. 'Tarsos in the *Amores* ascribed to Lucian', *Greek, Roman, and Byzantine Studies* 25, 177-81.

Jones, C.P. 1996. 'The Panhellenion', *Chiron* 26, 29-56.

Jones, C.P. 1997. Review of Mossman 1997, *Echoes du Monde Classique/Classical Views* n.s. 14, 5.

Jones, R.P. & Gardner, E.A. 1906. 'Notes on a recently excavated house at Girgenti', *Journal of Hellenic Studies* 26, 207-12.

Jones, W.H.S. 1918-1935. *Pausanias' Description of Greece* I-IV, (Loeb Classical Library). Cambridge, Massachusetts: Harvard University Press.

Kaimio, J. 1979. *The Romans and the Greek Language*, (Commentationes humanarum litterarum 64). Helsinki: Societas scientiarum Fennica.

Kajanto, I. 1963a. *Onomastic Studies in the Early Christian Inscriptions of Rome and Carthage* (Acta Instituti Romani Finlandiae 2.1). Helsinki: Institutum Romanum Finlandiae.

Kajanto, I. 1963b. *A Study of the Greek Epitaphs of Rome*, (Acta Instituti Romani Finlandiae 2.3). Helsinki: Institutum Romanum Finlandiae.

Karadimas, D. 1996. *Sextus Empiricus against Aelius Aristides. The Conflict between Philosophy and Rhetoric in the Second Century AD*. Lund: Lund University Press.

Karamitrou-Mentesidi, G. 1982. 'Νόμος Κοζάνης: Ποντοκώμη', *Ἀρχαιολογικὸν Δελτίον* 37, Χρονικά Β2, 298.

Karivieri, A. 1994. 'The so-called Library of Hadrian and the Tetraconch Church in Athens', in: Castrén (ed.), 89-113.

Kennedy, G. 1963. *The Art of Persuasion in Greece*. Princeton: Princeton University Press.

Kennedy, G. 1972. *The Art of Rhetoric in the Roman World*. Princeton: Princeton University Press.

Kennedy, G. 1974. 'The Sophists as Declaimers', in: Bowersock 1974, 17-22.

Kent, J.P.C. 1978. *Roman Coins*. London: Thames and Hudson.

Kienast, D. 1971. 'Ein vernachlässigtes Zeugnis für die Reichspolitik Traians: Die zweite tarsische Rede des Dion von Prusa', *Historia* 20, 62-80.

Kiilerich, B. 1995. *Græsk skulptur fra dædalisk til hellenistisk*. Copenhagen: Gyldendal.

Knoepfler, D. 1996. 'La réorganisation du concours des Mouseia à l'époque hellénistique: ésquisse d'une solution nouvelle', in: Hurst & Schachter (eds.), 141-67.

Konstan, D. 1994. *Sexual Symmetry. Love in the Ancient Novel and Related Genres.* Princeton: Princeton University Press.
Kourouniotis, K. 1936. ''Ανασκαφαί ἐν Ἐλευσῖνι', *Πρακτικά* 1936, 34-40.
Krausse, D. 1996. *Hochdorf.* Stuttgart: Konrad Theiss.
Kreeb, M. 1985. 'Zur Basis der Kleopatra auf Delos', *Horos* 3, 41-61.
Kreeb, M. 1988. *Untersuchungen zur Figürlichen Ausstattung Delischer Privathäuser.* Chicago, Ares Publishers.
Kritzas, C.B. 1972. 'Ligourio', *Archaiologikon Deltion* 27 B1, 215-18.
Krystalli, K. & Papachristodoulou, I. 1967. 'Kiveri', *Archaiologikon Deltion* 22 B1, 179.
Kunst, K. 1924. *Phaedra, herausgegeben und erläuter.* Wien: Diss. Wien.
Kyle, D.G. 1987. *Athletics in Ancient Athens,* (Mnemosyne, Suppl. 95). Leiden: Brill.
Laín Entralgo, P. 1971. *Estudios sobre la obra de Américo Castro.* Madrid: Taurus.
Lambert, R. 1984. *Beloved and God. The Story of Hadrian and Antinous.* London: Weidenfeld & Nicholson.
Lammert, F. 1952. 'Polyainos' (8), *Real-Encyclopädie der klassischen Altertumswissenschaft* 21.2, 1432-36. Stuttgart.
Laurence, R. 1994. *Roman Pompeii: Space and Society.* London: Routledge.
Laurence, R. & Wallace-Hadrill, A. (eds.) 1997. 'Domestic space in the Roman world: Pompeii and beyond', *Journal of Roman Archaeology Supplementary Series* 22.
Lazaridis, D. 1973. *Φίλιπποι: Ῥωμαικὴ ἀποικία.* Athens: Centre for Ekistiks.
Lazenby, J.F. & Hope Simpson, R. 1972. 'Greco-Roman times: literary tradition and topographical commentary', in: McDonald & Rapp, Jr. (eds.), 81-99.
Le Corsu, F. 1981. *Plutarque et les femmes dans les Vies parallèles.* Paris: Les Belles lettres.
Leigh, M. 1997. *Lucan, Spectacle and Engagement.* Oxford: Clarendon Press.
Leiwo, M. 1994. *Neapolitana,* (Commentationes humanarum litterarum 102). Helsinki: Societas scientiarum Fennica.
Lenz, F. 1959. *The Aristeides Prolegomena.* Leiden: E.J. Brill.
Lightfoot, J.L. 1999. *Parthenius of Nicaea.* Oxford: Clarendon Press.
L'Orange, H.P. & van Gerkan, A. 1939. *Die spätantike Bildschmuck des Konstantinsbogen.* Berlin: Walter de Gruyter.
Lobel, E. & Page, D. 1955. *Poetarum Lesbiorum Fragmenta.* Oxford: Clarendon Press.
Maass, M. 1972. *Die Prohedrie des Dionysustheaters in Athen.* München: Beck.
McAlister, S. 1996. *Dreams and Suicide. The Greek Novel from Antiquity to the Byzantine Empire.* London & New York: Routledge.
Macready, S. & Thompson, F.H. (eds.) 1987. *Roman Architecture in the Greek World.* London: Society of Antiquaries of London.
McCredie, J.R. et al. (eds.) 1992. *The Rotunda of Arsinoe (Samothrace 7).* Princeton: Princeton University Press.
McDonald, W.A. & Rapp Jr., G.R. (eds.) 1972. *The Minnesota Messenia Expedition: Reconstructing a Bronze Age Regional Environment.* Minneapolis: The University of Minnesota Press.
MacMullen, R. 1966. *Enemies of the Roman Order: Treason, Unrest and Alienation in the Empire.* Cambridge, MA: Harvard University Press.

MacMullen, R. 1974. *Roman Social Relations 50 BC to AD 284*. New Haven: Yale University Press.
Magie, D. 1950. *Roman Rule in Asia Minor*. 2 vols. Princeton: Princeton University Press.
Mahar, C., Harker, R. & Wilkes, C. 1990. 'The basic theoretical position', in: Harker, Mahar & Wilkes (eds.), 1-25.
Manganaro, G. 1962. 'Graffiti e iscrizioni funerarie della Sicilia Orientale', *Helikon* 2, 485-501.
Manganaro, G. 1993. 'Greco nei *pagi* e latino nelle città della Sicilia 'romana' tra I e VI sec. d.C.', in: Calbi et al (eds.), 543-94.
Mason, H.J. 1974. *Greek Terms for Roman Institutions: A Lexicon and Analysis*, (American Studies in Papyrology 13). Toronto: Hakkert.
Masters J. 1992. *Poetry and Civil War in Lucan's Bellum Civile*. Cambridge: Cambridge University Press.
Matthews, V.J. 1996. *Antimachus of Colophon. Text and Commentary*, (Mnemosyne Suppl. 155.). Leiden & New York: Brill.
Maull, I. 1955. 'Hadrians Jagddenkmal', *Jahreshefte der Österreicher Archäologischen Institut Wien* 42, 53-67.
Mavrojannis, T. 1995. 'Apollo Delio, Atene e Augusto', *Ostraka* 4, 85-102.
Mazzoli, G. 1970. *Seneca e la poesia*. Milano: Ceschina.
Mee, C.B. et al. 1991. 'Rural settlement change in the Methana peninsula, Greece', in: Barker & Lloyd (eds.), 223-32.
Mee, C.B. et al. 1997. 'Catalogue of sites', in: Mee & Forbes (eds.), 118-210.
Mee, C.B. & Forbes, H.A. (eds.) 1997. *A Rough and Rocky Place. The Landscape and Settlement History of the Methana Peninsula, Greece*, (Liverpool Monographs in Archaeology and Oriental Studies). Liverpool: Liverpool University Press.
Meeks, W. 1983. *The First Urban Christians: The Social World of the Apostle Paul*. New Haven: Yale University Press.
Meister, K. 1967. 'Die Tugenden der Römer', in: Oppermann (ed.), 1-22.
Meister, K. 1994. 'La storiografia: Flavio Giuseppe, Appiano, Arriano, Cassio Dione', in: Cambiano, Canfora & Lanza (eds.), 117-47.
Melber, J. 1887. 'Prefatio', *Polyaeni Strategematon libri octo*. Lipsiae: B.G. Teubneri, 5-31.
Mellor, R. 1975. *ΘΕΑ ΡΩΜΗ The Worship of the Goddess Roma in the Greek World*, (Hypomnemata 42). Göttingen.
Mendels, D. 1998. *Identity, Religion and Historiography. Studies in Hellenistic History*, (Journal for the Study of Pseudepigrapha Supplement Series 24). Sheffield.
Metzler, J., Millett, M., Roymans, N., & Slofstra, J. (eds.) 1997. *Integration in the Early Roman West*. Luxemburg: Musée National d'Histoire et d'Art.
Meyer, B.F. and Sanders, E.P. (eds.) 1982. *Self-Definition in the Greco-Roman World*. Vol. 3 of *Jewish and Christian Self-Definition*. Philadelphia: Fortress Press.
Millar, F. 1965. 'Epictetus and the imperial court', *Journal of Roman Studies* 55, 140-48.
Millar, F. 1984. 'State and subject: the impact of monarchy', in: Millar & Segal (eds.), 37-60.

Millar, F. 1987. 'Empire, community and culture in the Roman Near East: Greeks, Syrians, Jews and Arabs', *Journal of Jewish Studies* 38, 143-64.

Millar, F. 1993. *The Roman Near East 31 BC – AD 337*. Cambridge, Mass. & London: Harvard University Press.

Millar, F. 1997. 'Porphyry: Ethnicity, Language and Alien Wisdom', in: J. Barnes & M. Griffin (eds.), *Philosophia Togata* II, Oxford: Clarendon Press, 241-62.

Millar, F. & Segal, E. (eds.) 1984. *Caesar Augustus. Seven Aspects*. Oxford: Clarendon Press.

Miller, F.J. 1960-5. *Seneca's Tragedies* I. London: Heinemann; Cambridge, Massachusetts: Harvard University Press.

Moles, J.L. 1978. 'The Career and Conversion of Dio Chrysostom', *Journal of Hellenic Studies* 98, 79-100.

Moles, J.L. 1983. 'Dio Chrysostom: Exile, Tarsus, Nero and Domitian', *Liverpool Classical Monthly* 8, 130-4.

Moles, J.L. 1992. 'Review of P.A. Stadter, *Plutarch's Pericles*', *Classical Review* 106, 289-94.

Moles, J.L. 1995. 'Dio Chrysostom, Greece, and Rome', in: Innes et al. (eds.), 177-92.

Moore, T.J. 1989. *Artistry and Ideology: Livy's Vocabulary of Virtue*. Frankfurt am Main: Athenäum Verlag

Moreschini, C. 1994. 'Elio Aristide tra retorica e filosofia', in: *ANRW* II.34.2, 1234-47.

Moretti, L. 1981. 'Iscrizioni di Tespie della prima età imperiale', *Athenaeum* n.s. 59, 71-77.

Moricca, U. 1915. 'Le fonti della *Fedra* di Seneca', *Studi italiani di filologia classica* 21, 158-224.

Mossman, J. 1991. 'Plutarch's Use of Statues', in: Flower & Toher (eds.), 99-119.

Mossman, J.M. (ed.) 1997. *Plutarch and his intellectual world*. London: Duckworth in association with the Classical Press of Wales.

Nash, E. 1969. *Pictorial Dictionary of Ancient Rome* I, (rev. ed.). London.

Nauck, A. 1889. *Tragicorum Graecorum Fragmenta*. Lipsiae: in Aedibus B.G. Teubneri.

Neils, J. (ed.) 1996. *Worshipping Athena. Panathenaia and Parthenon*. Madison: University of Wisconsin Press.

Nevett, L.C. 1995. 'Gender Relations in the Classical Greek Household', *Annual of the British School at Athens* 90, 363-81.

Nevett, L.C. 1999. *House and Society in the Ancient Greek World*. Cambridge: Cambridge University Press.

Nicosia, S. 1979. *Elio Aristide nell'Asclepieo di Pergamo e la retorica recuperata*. Palermo: Università di Palermo, Istituto di filologia greca.

Nollé, J. 1986. 'Pamphylische Studien', *Chiron* 16, 199-212.

Nollé, J., 1990. 'Side. Zur Geschichte einer kleinasiatischen Stadt in der römischen Kaiserzeit im Spiegel ihrer Münzen', *Antike Welt* 21,4, 244-65.

Oliver, J.H. 1983. *The Civic Tradition and Roman Athens*. Baltimore: Johns Hopkins University Press.

Oppermann, H. (ed.) 1967. *Römische Wertbegriffe*. Darmstadt: Wissenschaftliche Buchgesellschaft.

Orsi, P. 1918. 'Gli scavi intorno a l'Athenaion di Siracusa', *Monumenti antichi pubblicati dall'Accademia dei Lincei* 25, 353-754.

Pace, B. 1949. *Arte e civiltà della Sicilia antica* 4. Roma – Napoli – Città di Castello: S. A. Editrice Dante Alighieri.

Page, D.L. 1981. *Further Greek Epigrams.* Cambridge: Cambridge University Press.

Palm, J. 1959. 'Rom, Römertum, und Imperium in der griechischen Literatur der Kaiserzeit', *Acta Reg. Societatis Humaniorum Litterarum Lundensis* 57.

Papakostou, L. 1980. Ὁδὸς Νικήτα 9-13 καὶ Καρατζᾶ. Πάτρα. ΣΤ Ἐφορεία Προϊστορικῶν καὶ κλασικῶν ἀρχαιοτήτων', *Ἀρχαιολογικὸν Δελτίον* 35, *Χρονικά* Β1, 191.

Papastolou, I.A. 1980. 'Πάτρα. Ὁδὸς Κανακάρη 205 καὶ 207. ΣΤ Ἐφορεία Προϊστορικῶν καὶ κλασικῶν ἀρχαιοτήτων', *Ἀρχαιολογικὸν Δελτίον* 35, *Χρονικά* Β1, 182.

Payne, M. 1984. *Aretas Eneken: Honors to Romans and Italians in Greece from 260 to 27 BC.* Michigan State, dissertation.

Pekáry, T. 1972. 'Das Grab des Pompeius', *Bonner Historia Augusta Colloquia* 1970, 195-8.

Pelling, C. (ed.) 1990. *Characterization and Individuality in Greek Literature.* Oxford: Oxford University Press.

Pelling, C.B.R. 1988. *Plutarch, Life of Antony,* (Cambridge Greek and Latin Classics). Cambridge: Cambridge University Press.

Pelling, C.B.R. 1995a. 'The Moralism of Plutarch's Lives', in: C. Pelling, H. Hines & D. Innes (eds.), *Ethics and Rhetoric.* Oxford: Clarendon Press, 205-20.

Pelling, C.B.R. 1995b. 'Plutarch and Roman politics', in: B. Scardigli (ed.), *Essays on Plutarch's Lives,* Oxford, 319-56 (reprinted from *Past Perspectives: Studies in Greek and Roman Historical Writing.* Cambridge: Cambridge University Press, 1986, 159-87).

Penella, R.J. 1989. *The Letters of Apollonius of Tyana.* Leiden: Brill.

Penttinen, A. 1996. 'The Classical and Hellenistic periods', in: Wells (ed.) 1996, 285-342.

Pernot, L. 1981. *Les Discours siciliens d'Aelius Aristide. Étude littéraire et paléographique, édition et traduction,* New York: Arno Press.

Pernot, L. 1993. 'Platon contre Platon: le problème de la rhétorique dans les *Discours platoniciens* d'Aelius Aristide', in: M. Dixsaut (ed.), *Contre Platon I: Le platonisme dévoilé.* Paris: Vrin, 315-38.

Petropoulos, M. & Rizakis, A.D. 1994. 'Settlement patterns and landscape in the coastal areas of Patras. Preliminary report', *Journal of Roman Archaeology* 7, 183-207.

Pflaum, H. 1960-61. *Les carrières procuratoriennes equestres.* Paris: librairie orientaliste Paul Geuthner.

Pithou, P. 1590. *Epigrammata et poemata vetera ex codicibus et lapidibus collecta,* 1. Paris: N. Gillius.

Plassart, A. 1916. 'Fouilles de Délos', *Bulletin de Correspondence Héllenique* 40, 145-256.

Plassart, A. 1926. 'Fouilles de Thespies et de l'Hieron des Muses d'Hélicon', *Bulletin de Correspondence Hellénique* 50, 383-462.

Pomeroy, S. 1994. *Xenophon Oeconomicus.* Oxford: Clarendon Press.

Porter, J. E. 1992. *Audience and Rhetoric: An Archaeological Composition of the Discourse Community.* Englewood Cliffs, NJ: Prentice Hall.

Pretagostini, R. (ed.) 1993. *Tradizione e innovazione nella cultura greca da Omero all' età ellenistica. Scritti in onore di Bruno Gentili*. Roma: gruppo editoriale internazionale.

Price, S.R.F. 1984. *Rituals and Power. The Roman Imperial Cult in Asia Minor*. Cambridge: Cambridge University Press.

Puech, B. 1992. 'Prosopographie des amis de Plutarque', in: *ANRW* II.33.6: 4831-93.

Raaflaub, K.A. & Toher, M. (eds.) 1990. *Between Republic and Empire: Interpretations of Augustus and his Principate*. Berkeley: University of California Press.

Raaflaub, K.A. & Samons II, L.J. 1990. 'Opposition to Augustus', in: Raaflaub & Toher (eds.), 417-54.

Radt, S. 1977. *Tragicorum Graecorum Fragmenta*, IV. Göttingen: Vandenhoeck and Ruprecht.

Ramage, E. 1987. *The Nature and Purpose of Augustus' 'Res Gestae'*. Wiesbaden: Franz Steiner Verlag.

Ramsay, W.M. 1895-97. *The Cities and Bishoprics of Phrygia*. Oxford: Oxford University Press.

Raubitschek, A.E. 1945. 'Hadrian as the son of Zeus Eleutherios', *American Journal of Archaeology* 49, 128-33.

Rawson, B. & Weaver, P. (eds.) 1997. *The Roman Family in Italy*. Oxford: Clarendon Press.

Rawson, E. 1989. 'Roman rulers and the Philosophic Adviser', in: M. Griffin & J. Barnes (eds.), *Philosophia Togata* I. Oxford: Clarendon Press, 233-57.

Reardon, B.P. 1971. *Courants littéraires grecs des IIe et IIIe siècles après J.-C*. Paris: Les Belles Lettres.

Reardon, B.P. (ed.) 1989. *Collected ancient Greek novels*. Berkeley, Los Angeles: University of California Press.

Reggi, G. (ed.) 1993. *Storici latini e greci di età imperiale. Atti del corso d'aggiornamento per docenti di latino e greco del Canton Ticino, Lugano 17-18-19 ottobre 1990*. Lugano: EUSI (Edizioni universitarie della Svizzera italiana).

Rich, J.W. 1990. *Cassius Dio. The Augustan Settlement (Roman History 53-55.9)*. Warminster: Aris & Phillips.

Richardson, jr. L. 1992. *A New Topographical Dictionary of Ancient Rome*. Baltimore and London: Johns Hopkins University Press.

Richlin, A. 1992. 'Reading Ovid's rapes', in: *Pornography and Representation in Greece and Rome*, A. Richlin (ed.). Oxford: Oxford University Press, 158-79.

Rigsby, K. 1985. 'On the highpriest of Egypt', *Bulletin of the American Society of papyrologists* 22, 279-89.

Robert, L. 1948. *Hellenica* 6. Limoges: A. Bontemps.

Robert, L. 1978. 'Hadrien Zeus Kynégésios', *Bulletin de Correspondence Hellénique* 102, 437-52.

Robert, L. 1987. *Documents de l'Asie Mineure. Bibliothèque des Écoles Francaises d'Athènes et de Rome*, 239bis. Paris: École francaise d'Athènes. Dépositaire: de Boccard.

Robertson, N. 1996. 'Athena's Shrines and Festivals', in: Neils (ed.).

Robinson, D.M. 1929-1952. *Excavations at Olynthus*. Volumes 1-14. Baltimore: Johns Hopkins Press.

Rolfe, J.C. 1913. *Suetonius* I, (Loeb Classical Library). Cambridge, Mass.: Harvard University Press.

Roman, D. & Y. 1994. *Rome, l'identité romaine et la culture hellénistique (218-31 av. J.-C.)*. Paris: Sedes.

Romer, F.E. 1978. 'A Numismatic date for the Departure of C. Caesar', *Transactions of the American Philological Association* 108, 187-202.

Roos, A.G. 1912. *Studia Arrianea*. Leipzig: B.G. Teubner.

Roux, G. 1965. 'Pausanias, le 'Contre Aristogiton' et les énigmes de Marmaria à Delphes', *Revue des études anciennes* 67, 37-53.

Roux, G. 1992. 'Structure and style of the Rotunda of Arsinoe', in: McCredie et al. (eds.), 92-230.

le Roy, C. 1977. 'Pausanias à Marmaria', *Bulletin de correspondance hellénique, suppl.* 4, 247-71.

Runnels, C.N. & Munn, M.H. 1994. 'A register of sites', in: Jameson, Runnels & van Andel (eds.), 415-538.

Russell, D.A. 1972. *Plutarch*. London: Duckworth.

Russell, D.A. 1973. *Plutarch Classical Life and Letters*. London: Duckworth.

Russell, D.A. & Wilson, N.G. (eds. and trans.) 1981. *Menander Rhetor*. Oxford: Oxford University Press.

Russell, D.A. 1983. *Greek Declamation*. Cambridge: Cambridge University Press.

Russell, D.A. (ed.) 1990a. *Antonine Literature*. Oxford: Clarendon Press.

Russell, D.A. 1990b. '*Ethos* in Oratory and Rhetoric', in: Pelling 1990 (ed.), 197-212.

Russell, D.A. (ed.) 1992. *Dio Chrysostom: Orations VII, XII, and XXXVI*. Cambridge: Cambridge University Press.

Russell, D.A. 1993. *Plutarch: Selected Essays*. Oxford: Oxford University Press.

Sajdak, O. 1914-15. 'Spór o Hadryanowa zegnanie ze swiatem', *Eos* 20, 147-148.

Sandy, G. 1997. *The Greek World of Apuleius: Apuleius and the Second Sophistic*. Leiden: Brill.

Schachter, A. 1986. 'Cults of Boeotia 2', *Bulletin of the Institute of Classical Studies. Supplement* 38.2.

Schalit, A. 1969. *Herodes: der Mann und sein Werk*. Berlin: De Gruyter.

Schürer, E., Vermes, G. & Millar, F. 1973. *The History of the Jewish People in the Age of Jesus Christ* I. Edinburgh: T. & T. Clark Ltd.

Schürer, E., Vermes, G. & Millar, F. 1979. *The History of the Jewish People in the Age of Jesus Christ* II. Edinburgh: T. & T. Clark Ltd.

Schiavo, D. (ed.) 1756. *Memorie per servire alla storia letteraria di Sicilia* 1. Palermo.

Schizzerotto, G. 1968. 'Uguccione e l'epigrafe per il cavallo di Adriano', *Maia* 20, 276-83.

Schmalz, G.C.R. 1996. 'Athens, Augustus, and the settlement of 21 BC', *Greek, Roman and Byzantine Studies* 37, 381-98.

Schmitz, T. 1997. *Bildung und Macht. Zur sozialen und politischen Funktion der zweiten Sophistik in der griechischen Welt der Kaiserzeit*. München: C.H. Beck.

Schwartz, D.R. 1990. *Agrippa I: The Last King of Judaea*. Tübingen: Mohr.

Schwartz, S. 1995. 'Language, power and identity in ancient Palestine', *Past and Present* 148, 3-47.
Scullard, H.H. 1959. *From the Gracchi to Nero*. New York: Methuen.
Segal, C.1986. *Language and Desire in Seneca's Phaedra*. Princeton: Princeton University Press.
Settis, S. (ed.) 1998. *I Greci. Storia Cultura Arte Societá* 2. *Una storia greca* III. *Trasformazioni*. Torino: Einaudi.
Sgarlata, M. 1993. [1996]. *La raccolta epigrafica e l'epistolario archeologico di Cesare Gaetani conte della Torre*, (Seia 10). Palermo: Università degli studi di Palermo.
Sheppard, A.A.R. 1982. 'A Dissident in Tarsus? (Dio Chrysostom, Or. 66)', *Liverpool Classical Monthly* 7, 149-50.
Shear, T.L. 1930. *Corinth* V: *The Roman Villa*. Cambridge Mass.: Harvard University Press.
Shear, T.L. 1933. 'Excavations in the Athenian Agora. The Sculpture', *Hesperia* 2, 178-83.
Shear, T.L. Jr. 1981. 'Athens: from city-state to provincial town', *Hesperia* 50, 356-77.
Shipley, G. 1996. 'Archaeological sites in Laconia and the Thyreatis', in: Cavanagh et al. (eds.), 263-313.
Shotter, D. 1992. *Tiberius Caesar*. London: Routledge.
Silvagni, A. 1950. 'Iscrizioni cristiane di Siracusa', *Rivista di archeologia cristiana* 26, 221-22.
Simpson, C.J. 1977. 'The date of the dedication of the Temple of Mars Ultor', *Journal of Roman Studies* 67, 91-94.
Sinn, F. 1987. *Stadtrömische Marmorurnen*, (Beiträge zur Erschließung hellenistischer und kaiserzeitlicher Skulptur und Architektur 8). Mainz am Rhein: Philipp von Zabern.
Sjöqvist, E. 1954. 'Kaisareion. A study of architectural iconography', *Opuscula Romana* 1, 86-108.
Sjöqvist, E. 1962. 'Excavations at Morgantina 1961', *American Journal of Archaeology* 66, 135-43.
Sjöqvist, E. 1964. 'Excavations at Morgantina 1963', *American Journal of Archaeology* 68, 137-47.
Small, A. (ed.) 1996. 'Subject and ruler: the cult of the ruling power in classical antiquity', *Papers Presented at a Conference held at the University of Alberta on April 13-15, 1994 to Celebrate the 65th Anniversary of Duncan Fishwick*, (Journal of Roman Studies Supplementary Series 17). Ann Arbor.
Sohlberg, D. 1972. 'Aelius Aristides und Diogenes von Babylon. Zur Geschichte des rednerischen Ideals', *Museum Helveticum* 29, 177-200 and 256-77.
Solin, H. 1971. *Beiträge zur Kenntnis der griechischen Personennamen in Rom* 1, (Commentationes humanarum litterarum 48). Helsinki: Societas scientiarum Fennica.
Spawforth, A.J.S and Walker, S. 1985. 'The world of the Panhellenion. I. Athens and Eleusis', *Journal of Roman Studies* 75, 78-104.

Spawforth, A.J.S and Walker, S. 1986. 'The world of the Panhellenion. II. Three Dorian cities', *Journal of Roman Studies* 76, 88-105.

Spawforth, A.J.S. 1989. 'Agonistic festivals in Roman Greece', in: Walker & Cameron (eds.), 193-97.

Spawforth, A. 1994. 'Symbol of unity? The Persian-wars tradition in the Roman empire', in: Hornblower, 231-47.

Spawforth, A. 1997. 'The early reception of the imperial cult in Athens: problems and ambiguities', in: Hoff & Rotroff (eds.), 183-201.

Sperling, J.W. 1973. *Thera and Therasia*. Athens: Centre of Ekistics.

Spyropoulos, Th. 1980. 'Σπάρτη: οἰκόπεδο Σάλαρη-Κεφαλόπουλου', *Ἀρχαιολογικὸν Δελτίον* 35, Χρονικά Β1, 136.

Spyropoulos, T. 1983. 'Γύθειο: ὁδὸς Διροῦ καὶ Ἀρχαίου Θεάτρου οἰκόπεδο κυρ. Λιβιεράκου. Ε Ἐφορεία Προιστορικῶν καὶ κλασικῶν Ἀρχαιοτήτων', *Ἀρχαιολογικὸν Δελτίον* 38, Χρονικά Β1, 94-97.

Stadter, P.A. 1965. *Plutarch's Historical Methods; An Analysis of the* Mulierum Virtutes. Cambridge, Mass.: Harvard University Press.

Stadter, P.A., 1980. *Arrian of Nicomedia*. Chapel Hill: the University of North Carolina Press.

Stadter, P.A. 1996. 'Anecdotes and the thematic structure of Plutarchean biography', in: J.A. Fernández Delgado & F. Pordomingo Pardo (eds.), *Estudios sobre Plutarco: Aspectos formales*. Madrid: Ediciones Clásicas, 291-303.

Stadter, P. A. 2000. 'The rhetoric of virtue in Plutarch's *Lives*', in: *Rhetorical Theory and Praxis in Plutarch, Acts of the IV. International Congress, International Plutarch Society, Leuven, Belgium, July 3-6, 1996*. Leuven: Peeters, 493-510.

Stein, A. 1990. *Studies in Greek and Latin Inscriptions on the Palestinian Coinage under the Principate*, diss. Tel-Aviv.

Steinmetz, P. 1989. 'Lyrische Dichtung im 2. Jahrhundert n.Chr.', in: *ANRW* II.33.1, 259-302.

Stern, M. 1974. *Greek and Latin Authors on Jews and Judaism* I, Jerusalem: The Israel Academy of Sciences and Humanities.

Stevenson, G.H. 1939. *Roman Provincial Administration*. Oxford: Oxford University Press.

Stewart, A. 1990. *Greek Sculpture. An Exploration*. Yale: Yale University Press.

Stillwell, R. 1961. 'Excavations at Morgantina (Serra Orlando) 1960. Preliminary Report V', *American Journal of Archaeology* 65, 277-81.

Stillwell, R. 1963. 'Excavations at Morgantina 1962', *American Journal of Archaeology* 67, 163-71.

Strobel von, K. 1994. 'Zeitgeschichte unter den Antoninen: Die Historiker des Partherkrieges des Lucius Verus', in: *ANRW* II.34.2, 1315-60.

Sturgeon, M. 1977. 'The reliefs on the Theater of Dionysus in Athens', *American Journal of Archaeology* 81, 31-53.

Swain, S. 1995. 'Hellenic culture and the Roman heroes of Plutarch', in: B. Scardigli (ed.), *Essays on Plutarch's Lives*. Oxford: Clarendon Press, 229-64 (reprinted from *Journal of Hellenic Studies* 110 (1990) 126-45).

Swain, S. 1996. *Hellenism and Empire. Language, Classicism and Power in the Greek World AD 50 -250*. Oxford: Clarendon Press.
Syme, R. 1939. *The Roman Revolution*. Oxford: Clarendon Press.
Syme, R. 1958. *Tacitus*. Oxford: Clarendon Press.
Syme, R. 1968. 'The Ummidii', *Historia* 17, 72-105.
Syme, R. 1978. *History in Ovid*. Oxford: Oxford University Press.
Syme, R. 1982. 'The career of Arrian', *Harvard Studies in Classical Philology* 86, 181-211.
Syme, R. 1984. 'The crisis of 2 BC', in: A.R. Birley (ed.), *Roman Papers* 3. Oxford: Clarendon Press, 912-936.
Taliaferro Boatwright, M. 1983. 'Further thoughts on Hadrianic Athens', *Hesperia* 52, 173-76.
Tarrant, R.J.1995. 'Greek and Roman in Seneca's tragedies', *Harvard Studies in Classical Philology* 97, 215-30.
Thompson, H.A. 1966. 'The Annex to the Stoa of Zeus in the Athenian Agora', *Hesperia* 35, 171-87.
Thompson, H.A., 1987. 'The impact of Roman architects and architecture on Athens: 170 BC-AD 170', in: Macready & Thompson (eds.), 1-17.
Thompson, H.A. & Wycherley, R.E., 1972. *Excavations in the Athenian Agora Volume XIV: The History Shape and Uses of an Ancient City Centre*. Princeton: American School of Classical Studies at Athens.
Thompson, J.B. 1991. 'Editor's introduction', in: P. Bourdieu, *Language and Symbolic Power*, Edited and introduced by John B. Thompson. Cambridge: Polity Press, 1-31.
Tobin, J. 1991. *The Monuments of Herodes Atticus* (diss. University of Pennsylvania). Ann Arbor, Michigan: University Microfilms International.
Tod, M.N. 1951. 'Laudatory epithets in Greek epitaphs', *Annual of the British School at Athens* 46, 182-90.
Too, Y.L. 1995. *The Rhetoric of Identity in Isocrates. Text, Power, Pedagogy.* Cambridge: Cambridge University Press.
Tovar, A. 1971. 'Un nuevo epigrama griego de Córdoba. Arriano de Nicomedia, proconsul de Betica?' in: Laín Entralgo (ed.), 401-12.
Travlos, J. 1971. *Pictorial Dictionary of Ancient Athens*. London: Thames and Hudson.
Travlos, J. 1980. *Pictorial Dictionary of Ancient Athens*. (reprint). New York: Hacker Art Books.
Tsakirgis, B. 1988. *The Domestic Architecture of Morgantina in the Hellenistic and Roman Periods*, Doctoral thesis, Ann Arbor, University Microfilms International.
Tsakirgis, B. 1995. 'Morgantina: a Greek town in central Sicily', in: Fischer-Hansen (ed.), 123-47.
Turner, E.G. 1954. 'Tiberius Julius Alexander', *Journal of Roman Studies* 44, 61-64.
Tzavella-Evjen, H. 1985. 'Circular buildings and the sanctuaries of Apollo Hylates at Paphos and Kourion', in Πρακτικὰ τοῦ δευτέρου διεθνοῦς κυπριακοῦ συνεδρίου. Nicosia, 311-15.
Van Bremen, R. 1996. *The Limits of Participation: Women and Civic Life in the Greek East in the Hellenistic and Roman periods*. Amsterdam: Gieben.

Van der Stockt, L. 1987. 'Plutarch's Use of Literature: Sources and Citations in the Quaestiones Romanae', *Ancient Society* 18, 281-92.
Veblen, T.B. 1899. *The Theory of the Leisure Class*. New York: Macmillan.
Vickers, B. 1989². *In Defence of Rhetoric*. Oxford: Clarendon Press.
Vince, J.H. 1935. *Demosthenes* III, (Loeb Classical Library). Cambridge, Mass.: Harvard University Press.
Vinchesi, M. 1988. 'L'epitafio di Adriano per il cavallo Boristene (*CE* 1522 Bücheler)', in: *Disiecti membra poetae* 3, 180-188.
Walker, S. 1983. 'Women and housing in Classical Greece', in: A. Cameron & A. Kuhrt (eds.), *Images of Women in Classical Antiquity*. London: Croom Helm, 81-91.
Walker, S. & Cameron, A. (eds.) 1989. 'The Greek renaissance in the Roman empire', *Papers from the Tenth British Museum Classical Colloquium*, (Bulletin Suppl. 55). London: Institute of Classical Studies, University of London.
Walker, S. 1997. 'Athens under Augustus', in: Hoff & Rotroff (eds.), 67-80.
Wallace-Hadrill, A. 1994. *Houses and Society in Pompeii and Herculaneum*. Princeton: Princeton University Press.
Wallace-Hadrill, A. 1997. 'Rethinking the Roman atrium house', in: Laurence & Wallace-Hadrill (eds.), 219-40.
Wardman, A. 1974. *Plutarch's Lives*. London: Elek.
Wardy, R. 1996. *The Birth of Rhetoric. Gorgias, Plato and their Successors*. London/New York: Routledge.
Waterfield, R. 1992. *Plutarch: Essays*. London: Penguin.
Waterfield, R. 1998. *Plutarch: Greek Lives*. Oxford: Oxford University Press.
Weber, W. 1907. *Untersuchungen zur Geschichte des Kaisers Hadrianus*. Leipzig: B.G. Teubner (repr. 1973. Hildesheim & New York: G.Olms).
Welles, C.B. 1962. 'Hellenistic Tarsus', *Mélanges de l'Université Saint Joseph* 38, 41-75.
Wells, B. 1996. *The Berbati-Limnes Archaeological Survey 1988-1990*, (Acta Instituti Atheniensis Regni Sueciae 4° 44). Jonsered: Åström.
West, M.L. 1971. *Iambi et Elegi Graeci*. Oxford: Clarendon Press.
Wheeler, A.L. 1924. *Ovid. Tristia. Ex Ponto*, (Loeb Classical Library). Cambridge, Mass.: Harvard University Press.
Wheeler, E.L. 1984. 'Sophistic interpretations and Greek treaties', *Greek, Roman and Byzantine Studies* 25, 253-74.
Wheeler, E.L. 1988. 'Stratagem and vocabulary of military trickery', *Mnemosyne Supplementum* 108. Leiden: Brill.
Wheeler, E.L. & Krentz, P. 1994. 'Introduction', *Polyaenus. Stratagems of War*. Chicago, IL: Ares Publishers.
Wiegand, T. & Schraeder, H. 1904. *Priene: Ergebnisse der Ausgrabungen und Untersuchungen in den Jahren 1895-1898*. Berlin: Georg Reimer.
Wight Duff, J. 1909. *A Literary History of Rome*. London & Leipzig: T. Fisher Unwin.
Wight Duff, J. 1927. *A Literary History of Rome in the Silver Age*. London: Ernest Benn Limited.
Wilamowitz-Moellendorff, U. von 1925. 'Der Rhetor Aristeides', *Sitzungsberichte der preussischen Akademie der Wissenschaften* 1925, 333-53.

Willers, D. 1990. *Hadrians panhellenisches Programm. Archäologische Beiträge zur Neugestaltung Athens durch Hadrian*, (Beiheft zur Halbjahresschrift Antike Kunst 16). Basel: Vereinigung der Freunde antiker Kunst.

Wilson, R.J.A. 1990. *Sicily under the Roman Empire: The Archaeology of a Roman Province. 36 BC-AD 353.* Warminster: Aris and Phillips.

Winter, D. G. 1973. *The Power Motive.* New York: Free Press.

Wiseman, T. 1995. *Remus, a Roman Myth.* Cambridge: Cambridge University Press.

Wissmann, J. 1999. 'Zur Reception des "Protagoras-Mythos" durch Aelius Aristides', *Philologus* 143, 135-47.

Wörrle, M. 1988. *Stadt und und Fest im Kaiserzeitlichen Kleinasien*, (Vestigia 39). München: C.H. Beck.

Woolf, G. 1997. 'The formation of Roman provincial cultures', in: Metzler et al. (eds.), 9-18.

Worthington, Ian. (ed.) 1994. *Persuasion: Greek Rhetoric in Action.* London: Routledge.

Wright, J.C. et al. 1990. 'The Nemea Valley Archaeological Project: a preliminary report', *Hesperia* 59, 579-659.

Yegül, F.K. 1982. 'A study in architectural iconography. *Kaisersaal* and the Imperial Cult', *The Art Bulletin* 64, 7-31.

Zanker, P. 1990. *Power of Images in the Age of Augustus.* Michigan: University of Michigan Press.

Notes on Contributors

Karin Blomqvist, Dr.Phil., is Assistant Professor of Greek at the Department of Classics, Lund University.

Ewen Bowie has been Praelector in Classics at Corpus Christi College, Oxford, since 1965. From 1968-96 he was C.U.F. Lecturer in Greek and Latin Languages and Literature at Oxford University, and since 1996 he has been a Reader in Classical Languages and Literature.

Victor Castellani is Associate Professor of Classics and Humanities at the Department of Languages and Literatures, University of Denver. He has a B.A. in Greek and Latin from Fordham University (1968), and a Ph.D. in Classics from Princeton University (1971) with a dissertation on 'House and Home in Euripides'.

Paolo Desideri is Professor of Roman History at University of Florence since 1980. He is currently a member of the scientific committee which cooperates with S. Settis in the editing of *I Greci. Storia cultura arte società* to be published by Einaudi, Torino.

Jaap-Jan Flinterman, Ph.D. from the University of Nijmegen (1993), is Lecturer in Ancient History at the Vrije Universiteit in Amsterdam.

Renée Forsell, B.A., doctorate student in Classical Archaeology and Ancient History at the Department of Classics at Lund University.

Joseph Geiger, B.A. in History and Latin and M.A. in Classics from the Hebrew University of Jerusalem (1964 and 1967), D.Phil. Oxford University (1971), is Shalom Horowitz Professor of Classics at the Hebrew University of Jerusalem.

Jakob Munk Højte, Ph.D. in Classical Archaeology from the University of Aarhus (2001).

Arja Karivieri, Lic.Phil. from Åbo Akademi, Finland (1994), Ph.D. from the University of Turku, Finland (1997). Research associate in the Swedish Institute at Athens.

Kalle Korhonen, M.A. in Classics from the University of Helsinki (1995), is currently working on an edition of the Greek and Latin inscriptions in the city of Catania (Italy), which will be published in collaboration with Giovanni Salmeri (University of Pisa) in 2002.

R. Anthony Kugler, B.A. from Amherst College (1992), Ph.D. in classics from Brown University in Providence, Rhode Island (1999). Is currently working with Rosalie F. Baker and Charles F. Baker III on a compendium of Greek culture to be published by Oxford University Press.

Sophie Lalanne, Ph.D. in rites of passage in Greek novels. Assistant Professor at the University of Paris I Panthéon-Sorbonne lecturing in Greek history, especially Hellenism in the Roman Empire. Member of the research group, 'Phéacie', devoted to studying the cultural practices of ancient Greek and Roman society.

Anne Malling Eriksen is a doctoral student in the History of Ideas at the University of Aarhus, and was an associate member of Corpus Christi College, Oxford (1999).

Lisa Nevett, B.A. in Classics, M.Phil. in Archaeology, Ph.D. in Classical Archaeology – all from the University of Cambridge. Lecturer in Classical Studies, The Open University.

Erik Nis Ostenfeld, Dr.Phil., M.Litt. Oxon, is Associate Professor at the Department of Greek and Latin, University of Aarhus. Publications include: *Forms, Matter and Mind. Three Strands in Plato's Metaphysics* (The Hague: Nijhoff 1982), *Essays on Plato's Republic* (editor) (Aarhus: Aarhus University Press 1998).

Luigi Senzasono, B.A. in Greek Literature from the State University of Milan (1955), B.A. in History of Ancient Philosophy from the State University of Rome (1981), Ph.D. in History of Ancient Philosophy from the University of Naples 'Federico II' (1986-87).

Philip A. Stadter, Ph.D. from Harvard University (1963), is Falk Professor in the Humanities and Professor of Classics at the University of North Carolina at Chapel Hill, U.S.A.

Frances B. Titchener, B.A. in Classics from the University of Houston (1980), M.A. and Ph.D. in Greek from the University of Texas, Austin (1981 and 1988). Associate Professor of History and Classics at Utah State University, and editor of *Ploutarchos*, the Journal of the International Plutarch Society.

Helène Whittaker von Hofsten, M.A. from the University of Bergen (1983), Dr. philos. University of Tromsø (1996). Senior Lecturer in Greek and Latin Studies at the University of Tromsø.

Anthon Xenophontov, Ph.D. student, researcher, Lecturer in Greek Studies at the Russian Christian Institute, Saint Petersburg, Russia.

Index Rerum

Achaea, 55, 59, 61, 139, 181
Acropolis, 25-28, 30-32, 34-36, 42, 47, 49
acrostichs, 187-188
agonistic festivals, 41
Agora, Athenian, 36, 49, 51, 88
Agora, Roman, 32-34
Agrigento, 92-94
Amphiaraios, 55
anacreontics, 174
andron, 83
anti-Roman sentiment, 31, 32
antistrophe, 103
Ara Pacis, 34
Aramaic, 233-35, 239, 242
Arch of Hadrian, 40, 49-50
archiereus, 188
archon eponymos, 43
Areopagos, 88-89
Argolid region, 64-68
aristophaneans, 174, 182
Armenians, 237
Athens, 25-27, 29-33, 35, 40-46, 48-51, 60-61, 88-89, 139, 181, 187-88, 198, 201, 205, 238
atrium, 84, 91-95
Attic dialect, 234
atticism, 199, 203
audience for Plutarch's *Lives*, 123
Battle of Actium, 27-28, 31
bear hunt of Hadrian, 181
Berbati Valley, 66
bilingualism, 59-60, 70-71, 179, 233, 238-39
Boeotia, 65
Byzantium, 221
Caesarea, 240
catachannae, 176, 178-79, 185
Catacomb of Marcia, 73, 75

Catania, 71-72
central court, 83-89, 94
Chaeronea, 131, 136, 138-39, 141
choliambics, 184
Christian inscriptions, 73-74
Christianity, 138, 242
chryselephantine statues, 26, 41
Cimitero Maggiore, 73
citizenship, Roman, 222, 230, 235-38
Civil War, Roman, 112
Classical Period, 84, 88, 95
clementia, 113-14
client-kings, 237
colonialism, 167
conscientia, 114
conspicuous consumption, 203
conspicuous leisure, 203-4
dating of inscriptions, 71, 76
daughters, 143-44, 149
declaimers, 202
declamatory, 199
dedicatory inscriptions, 25-26, 30, 33-34, 55, 189,
Delos, 59, 61, 88
Delphi, 42, 61, 139
de-romanization, 149, 161
divine inspiration, 158, 160
divine will, 156
Egyptians, 235-36, 241
elegiacs, 174
Eleusinian Mysteries, 40, 41
elite, Greek, 61, 64, 67-68, 159, 170, 191, 199, 203, 205-6, 225-26
elite, Roman, 123, 188
epigrams, 73, 172, 174, 176, 180, 182, 185, 189, 191
epigraphic formula, 59, 71, 76
epitaphs, see funerary inscriptions

Erechteion, 26, 47
erotic poems, 177
fables, 158, 160, 162, 169-70
fides, 112-13, 116
funerary inscriptions/ epitaphs/ sepulchral inscriptions, 70-77, 92, 174, 177, 182-84, 233
generalship, 112-13, 213-14
geography, 218-19
gloria, 114, 119
Golden Age, 111
graffiti, 74-75
Greek, *passim*
Hadrianoutherae, 181
Hebrew, 235, 239
Hellenistic kings, 55-56, 58-62
Hellenistic Period, 27, 36, 65-68, 82-85, 88, 95
Hellenistic poetry, 102-4, 174, 189
hendecasyllables, 105, 174, 180
hexameters, 181
historia, 218
historians, 217, 221, 224, 241
historiography, 216, 218-19, 220-21
history, contemporary, 217-19, 221, 224
honorary statues, 55, 58, 61
honorific titles, 55, 59
House of Dionysus, 90, 91
House of the Official, 86-87
households, Greek, 81, 83-85
houses, classical, 82
houses, fourth century, 84
humanitas, 113-14, 222
iambic meters, 182
identity, 220, 222-24, 235-36, 238, 240, 242
Idumaean, 236, 238, 242
imperial cult, 26, 33-34, 40, 42
imperial favor, 168
Imperial Period, 70-72, 74, 216-17, 234, 240
impluvium, 84, 89, 91, 94
individual, the, 112, 120
Jerusalem, 242
Jewish War, 240

Jews, 233, 235-39, 241-42
job-seeker, 212, 214
jokes, in rhetoric, 159-60
Judaism, 236, 242
Juliopolis, 165, 166
Kassope, 84, 86, 88
Keos, 65, 67
Kos, 95
Late Antiquity, 202
Late Republic, 58-59, 92, 112, 179, 225, 240
legal speeches, 82
Library of Hadrian, 41
literacy, 76
literary tastes of Hadrian, 172, 185
macabre, the, 229-30
Macedonia, 212-14
macrostructural level, 101, 104-5, 107
Mallus, 163-64, 166-67
marital love, 226
matrona, 142, 144, 153
Messina, 71-72
Methana, 66-68
microstructural level, 101-2, 104-5
Mithridatic War, 60-61, 147
moderatio, 113-14
Morgantina, 85, 88
mos maiorum, 112-13, 116
mothers, 143-44, 146, 154
Mysia, 181
Nabataean, 236, 238-39
Naples, 71
Nemea, 65
Nisibis, 183-84
novels, Greek, 225-28, 230-31
novels, Latin, 228, 230
Olympia, 26, 47-48, 61
Olympieian, 41, 188
omens, 31, 157, 159-60
onomastics, 75
orations, 156
orations, Platonic, of Aristides, 198-200, 204
orators, 198-99, 201-3, 206

oratory, 198, 200-5
Oropos, 55, 57
Palestine, 233, 240
Panhellenic Union, 40-42, 188
Pantheon of Athens, 41
Parthenon, 25, 41, 47, 48
Parthians/Persians, 35-36, 140, 179, 183-84, 213-14, 237, 241
Pater Patriae, 115
patronage, Roman, 58, 213
Peloponnese, 68
Peloponnesian War, 205
Pergamum, 198
Phoenicians, 233-35
pietas, 112-13, 116, 118
Platonic *polis*, 35
poetry, Greek, 101,103, 107-8
polis-religion, 35
Pompeii, 92-95
Pontifex Maximus, 33-35
pottery, 66
population decrease, 65-66
propaganda, Roman, 35-36, 40, 43
proxeny status, 55, 58
quies provinciae, 166-68
rebuilding of Athens, 40
Republican Period, 30, 61-62, 72
rhetor, 212
rite of passage, 226-28
Roman authority, in Tarsus, 165-66
Romanization, 76, 95-96, 225-26, 230, 237-38
Romans, *passim*
Rome, *passim*
S. Maria Gesú, 73, 77
Sabine Women, 149
satirical poems, 177

scaenae frons (of the Theatre of Dionysus), 40, 43, 51
Second Sophistic, 198-99, 204, 212
Senate, 112, 222
sepulchral inscriptions, see funerary inscriptionss
Sicily, 72, 85, 92, 199
Side, 42
Silver Age, 111
Social War, 22
soldiers, 112-19, 131, 242
sophists, 159, 199, 203-5
spectacular, the, 228-30
state cult, 26
statue bases, 55-56, 58-59, 61-62, 172
stoicism, 200
suicide, 227
Syracuse, 70-72, 74-77
Syrians, 233-35, 238, 240-42
Tarsus, 156, 158-62, 164, 166-70, 235
Theatre of Dionysus, 33-34, 43, 47
theory of practice, 204
Thespiae, 180-81, 188
tholos, 26
thorybos, 161
tragedy, Roman, 229
urban poor, 138
values, Roman, 112, 117
Vigna Cassia, 70, 73-75
Villa Landolina, 70, 75-77
virtue, 112, 117, 120, 200
virtus, 111-12, 114, 116, 118-19, 151
wives, 143-44, 146, 149
women, 81, 83, 95, 102, 142, 149, 151, 155, 26
youth education, 225

Index Nominum

Achilles Tatius, 225, 228, 230
Adams, A., 49,
Admetus, 103
Aemilia, 147
Aemilius Paullus, 148
Aeneas, 116
Agrippa I, 238
Alexander the Great, 36
Alexander, son of King Herod, 238
Alexander, Ti. Julius, 235-36
Allison, P., 92-93,
Amazaspus, 183-84, 189
Ammianus Marcellinus, 234
Anderson, G., 137, 141 n.3
Anthia, 227-29
Antimachus, 173-74, 176-77, 183-84
Antinous, 41, 181, 183
Antistia, 147
Antonius (Mark Antony), 27, 30-32, 124, 143, 148, 237
Aphrodite, 36, 101, 105-6, 227
Apollo, 26, 103-4
Apollonius Rhodius, 104-7
Appian, 175-76, 217-19
Apuleius, 177, 225-27
Arafat, K.W., 41-42, 49
Archilochus, 174
Ariadne, 44-47
Aristides, 198-202, 204-6, 221
Aristobulus, son of King Herod, 238
Arrian, 179, 189-91, 217, 219
Arrius Antoninus, 184
Artemis, 189-90
Asinius Pollio, 238
Athena Parthenos, 48
Athena, 30-32, 35, 41-42, 47, 51, 104
Augustus, 25, 27-36, 40, 51, 55, 58-61, 70, 111-12, 131, 174, 238
Aurelia, 145
Aurelius, Marcus, 213, 219, 240
Babatha, 239
Baldassari, P., 27, 32, 37 n.22, 38 n.35
Basileus, 44
Basilinna, 44
Behr, C. A., 199, 200, 202, 207 n.2 n.3, n.6, 208 n.15, 209 n.32
Bejarano, V., 196 n.61
Benario, H.W., 121 n.10
Bennett, J. 135 n.49
Bernabò Brea, L. 76
Bernhardy, 176, 193 n.24
Birley, A.R., 52 n.13, 185, 191 n.1, 192 n.6, 193 n.25, 194 n.32, n.33, 196 n.61, n.68, 197 n.80
Boatwright, M.T., 193 n.22
Borsari, S., 76-77
Borysthenes, horse of Hadrian, 181, 183
Bosworth, A.B., 189-90
Boulanger, A., 206 n.1
Boulogne, J., 142
Bourdieu, P., 204, 210 n.48, n.50, n.52
Bowersock, G., 30, 34-35, 38 n.32, 215 n.14
Bowie, E., 220
Boyle, A.J., 108 n.1
Bruneau, P., 88
Brutus, 145-46
Büchner, K., 120 n.2
Bühler, W., 176
Caecilia (mother of Lucullus), 144
Caecilia Metella, 147
Caesar, 34, 113, 115-19, 145-46
Caligula, 60, 23
Callimachus, 179

Callirhoë, 227-28
Calpurnia, 146
Cameron, A., 185, 192 n.6, 195 n.56, 196 n.61
Carandini, A., 45
Cassius Dio, 27, 30-32, 173-74, 176, 181, 217, 219-20, 239
Castellani, V., 95
Cato the Censor, 112, 143, 147, 172, 223
Cato the Younger, 145, 148
Catullus, 141, 179
Chamonard, J., 88-90
Charicleia, 227
Chariton, 225, 228-30
Chloë, 227
Cicero, 111-12, 127, 137, 144-45, 147-48, 172, 218, 222-23
Claudia Appia, 147
Claudius, 40, 238-39
Cleopatra, 27, 31, 143, 149
Clinton, K., 52 n.4
Clodia, 147
Cohen, S.J.D., 246 n.50
Cohoon, J.W., 170 n.7, n.14
Coriolanus, 149, 152-54
Cornelia (wife of Pompey), 147
Cornelia, mother of the Gracchi, 129, 144
Cornelius Nepos, 81-82, 139
Croesus, 127-28
Crosby, 170 n.7, n.14
Cupid, 102, 105-7, 227
Curtius, L., 120 n.2
de Blois, L., 134 n.43
Deissmann, A., 244 n.15
Demeter, 43, 45
Demosthenes, 126-27, 137
Despoine, A., 53 n.42
Diana, 104
Dickmann, J., 93
Dio Chrysostom, 156-64, 166-70
Diogenes Laertius, 234
Dionysius of Halicarnassus, 149-54, 221-22

Dionysus Eleutherios, 43
Dionysus, 27, 31, 40, 42-48, 51, 90, 108
Domitian, 128, 131, 138-39, 173-74
Dontas, G., 41
Due, O. S., 122 n.23
Ebbinghaus, S. 194 n.39
Eisenhut, W., 120 n.2
Eros, 102, 104, 106-7, 181, 188
Etienne, R., 97 n.7
Euripides, 102
Europa, 103
Fanon, F., 170
Fantham, E., 120 n.1
Favorinus, 179
Fein, S., 191 n.1, 192 n.13, 193 n.25, 194 n.33, 195 n.48,
Ferrua, A., 76, 78 n.8, n.13, n.21, 79 n.39,
Finley, M., 203
Florus, 178-79, 239
Frisk, H., 108 n.2
Fronto, 176-77, 179
Fulcinia, 144
Fulvia, 143, 148
Gabrici, E., 92
Gaetani, C., 78 n.9
Gaius Caesar (adoptive son of Augustus), 35
Gamberale, L., 194 n.40, 195 n.48
Gardner, E.A., 92
Geagan, D., 43
George, M., 95
Germanicus, 172
Giomini, R., 109 n.3
Gleason, M., 204
Gracchi, the brothers, 123, 129-32, 144, 147
Graindor, P., 26-27, 34,
Grimal, P., 109 n.8
Hadavas, C.T., 134 n.25
Hadrian, 40-51, 65, 138-40, 172-79, 182-85, 187-91
Haeberlin, C., 187
Heliodorus, 225, 228-30, 234

Hellegouarc'h, J., 120 n.2
Helvia, 144
Heraclides, 202-3
Hermes, 204
Herod the Great, 236-37, 240
Herodes Atticus, 49
Herodian, 217, 220
Hersilia, 149-51
Hesiod, 101
Hestia, 34-35
Hoff, M., 27, 31, 32
Hollegaard Olsen, C., 92
Homer, 101, 103-5, 143, 173, 175-76, 231
Horace, 111, 141
Hortensius, 148
Hubbel, H.M., 208 n.18
Hänlein-Schäfer, H., 27, 37 n.3
Höghammar, K., 95, 97 n.10
Højte, J. Munk, 95
Iphigeneia, 227
Isocrates, 200-1
Jameson, M.H., 66
Jeremiah, 161
Jesus, 234
Johnson, W.R., 122 n.30
Jones, C.P., 133 n.14, n.17, 134 n.31, 138, 192 n.5
Jones, R.P., 92
Josephus, 235, 237, 239-42
Julia (daughter of Augustus), 34-35
Julia (daughter of Caesar), 147, 149
Julia (mother of Marc Antony), 145
Julian, 172
Julius Vestinus, 185, 187-91
Jupiter, 103
Juvenal, 137-38, 179, 236
Kaimio, J., 79 n.31
Karadimas, D., 206 n.1, 208 n.18, 209 n.32
Kent, J.P.C., 121 n.10
Korhonen, K., 92
Kreeb, M., 89-91
Kunst, K., 109 n.8

Laurence, R., 94
Le Corsu, F., 142
Leigh, M., 122 n.23
Leopardi, Giacomo, 217-18, 224
Leucippe, 227, 229
Licinia, 147
Lightfoot, J.L., 192 n.13
Livia (mother of Cato), 145, 147
Livia Augusta, 34, 35
Livy, 111, 113-14, 116, 150-53
Longus, 225, 227, 229-30
Lucan, 111, 115-19
Lucullus, 144, 14
Mai, A., 193 n.25
Manganaro, G., 76
Marcia, 148
Marcius Philippus, 148
Marius, 144, 147
Mark Antony, see Antonius
Mars Ultor, 35
Martial, 141
Masters, J., 122 n.23
Mazzoli, G., 109 n.5, n.7
Meister, K., 120 n.2
Meleager of Gadara, 233-34
Mellor, R., 29, 34
Mendels D., 244 n.15
Menemachus, 125-26, 130
Menippus of Gadara, 234
Miller, F.J., 110 n.20
Mommsen, T., 184
Moore, T.J., 120 n.6, 121 n.16
Mucia, 147
Maass, M., 43, 52 n.31
Nero, 43, 65, 115, 131, 139, 148, 188
Nerva, 131
Nevett, L., 96 n.1
Octavia, 148, 149
Octavian, 27-29
Orioli, F., 193 n.25
Orsi, P., 77 n.3, 78 n.21
Otho, 148
Ovid, 35, 141

Pace, B., 79 n.36
Page, D.L., 173, 191 n.1, 192 n.13
Pammenes, 26, 33
Pancrates, 173, 181
Parthenius of Nicaea, 174-75
Paul the Apostle, 26, 235, 237
Pausanias, 25-26, 36, 40-41, 46, 68
Payne, M., 55
Pelling, C.B.R., 134 n.43, 135 n.50, 140
Pernot, L., 206 n.1, 209 n.37
Pflaum, H., 187
Phaedra, 102
Pheidias, 41
Philo, 238
Philopoemen, 218
Philostratus, 159, 202-3, 205, 234
Pithou, P., 182
Plassart, A., 88
Plato, 35, 127, 131, 198, 200-1, 204-5
Pliny the Younger, 165-66, 174, 179
Plutarch, 30, 40, 49, 51, 81-82, 106, 123-32, 136-43, 145-53, 155, 173, 217, 220-23
Pollianus, 175
Polyaenus, 212-14
Polybius, 221
Pomeroy, S., 82
Pompeius Falco, 176-77
Pompey, 147-48, 175-76, 233
Pompilius, Numa, 146
Poppaea, 148
Porcia, 146
Price, S.R.F., 37, n.16
Psyche, 226-27
Publicola, 128, 152
Quintilian, 173
Raubitscheck, A.E., 52 n.17
Rawson, B., 134 n.35
Reardon, B.P., 210 n.42
Regilla, 49, 50
Rhea (mother of Sertorius), 144
Robert, L., 181
Robertson, N., 38 n.22

Roma, 25-26, 29-30, 32-36
Romulus, 40, 51, 112, 124, 149-50
Runnels, C.N., 66
Russell, D.A., 207 n.10
Sabina, 44-46
Sabine Women, 149-51
Sajdak, O., 196 n.61
Sappho, 103, 105, 143, 179
Schmitz, T., 204, 207 n.10,
Schwartz, D.R., 243 n.1, 245 n.35
Seneca, 101-4, 106, 108, 113, 229
Septimius Severus, 202, 220
Sertorius, 144
Servilia, 145, 147
Shakespeare, 146
Shear, T.L. Sr., 51
Silvagni, A., 76
Sinn, F., 78 n.18,
Sjöqvist, E., 86
Socrates, 127, 198, 201
Sohlberg, D., 199, 201, 206 n.1, 207 n.6, 208 n.20
Solon, 127-28
Sophocles, 106-8
Sosius Senecio, 123, 125, 132, 136, 140
Spawforth, A.J.S., 39 n.59, 41
Stadter, P.A., 135 n.50, 142,
Stein, A., 245 n.43
Stewart, A., 39 n.63
Stillwell, R., 86
Sturgeon, M., 48, 53 n.42
Suetonius, 31, 111, 174, 175
Sulla, 29, 147, 148
Swain, S., 124-25, 128, 132 n.8, n.9, n.13, 133 n.14, 134 n.40, 136, 203, 206, 207 n.8 n.9, 208 n.18, 210 n.47
Syme, R., 35, 120 n.6, 132 n.9
Tacitus, 111, 216, 236
Tarrant, R.J., 110 n.19
Tatia, 146
Terentia, 147
Thackeray, 245 n.47
Themistocles, 206

Theseus, 40, 42, 45-47, 49-51
Thompson, H.A., 51, 88
Tiberius, 61, 111-15, 117, 119, 172, 175
Trajan, 48, 131-32, 136, 140, 165-66, 172, 179, 181, 183-84, 190-91
Travlos, J., 27
Tsakirgis, B., 85-86
Tullia, 149
Tyche, 45-47
Uranus, 101
Valeria, 152-53
Veblen, T., 203-4
Velleius Paterculus, 111, 113-15, 117, 119-20
Venus, 36, 101, 227
Vespasian, 139
Vesta, 26, 34
Veturia, 153
Vickers, B., 207 n.1
Victoria, 51, 113,
Virgil, 111, 116, 141
Vitruvius, 81-82, 91
Volumnia, 152-54
Vulcacia Terrentia, 73
Walker, S., 39 n.59, 41, 82
Wallace-Hadrill, A., 92, 97 n.7,
Wardy, R., 207 n.1
Whycherley, 88
Wilamowitz-Moellendorf, U. von, 209 n.25
Williams, F., 192 n.6
Wilson, R.J.A., 77 n.1, 92
Wiseman, T., 121 n.8
Woolf, G., 96
Wyss, T., 192 n.6
Xenophon of Ephesus, 225, 228, 230
Yadin, P., 239
Yegül, F., 43
Yun Lee Too, 201
Zanker, P., 35, 121 n.9
Zeus Eleutherios, 42, 51
Zeus Kasius, 179, 184, 190
Zeus Polieus, 25-26, 30
Zeus, 33, 35, 40-43, 47-49, 51, 103, 106, 187, 189, 204

Index locorum

Ammianus Marcellinus
31.16.9: 234

Anacreon
13 (5) (Gentili): 109 n.7

Anthologia Palatina
5.160: 233
6.332: 179-80, 194 n.36
7.352: 192 n.19
7.377: 175
7.417: 233-34
7.419.7-8: 233
7.674: 175, 192 n.19
9.17: 191 n.1
9.137: 177-78
9.387: 191 n.1
11.130: 175, 192 n.17
15.25: 185-86, 196 n.62

Apollonius Rhodius
3.112-66: 104-5
3.278-84: 105
3. 286-96: 105
3.297: 109 n.2

Apollonius of Tyana
Ep.
11: 240

Appian
BC
2.86: 176, 192 n.20
Hist. Rom.
Prooem.15: 219

Apuleius
Apol.
11: 177, 194 n.30
Met.
4.24: 226
4.29-30: 227
4.32-6.24: 227

Archilochus
48 (West): 102

Aristides
Or.
2.35: 207 n.6
2.61-72: 207 n.6
2.149-56: 207 n.6
2.302-5: 208 n.19
2.362-437: 201-2
2.382: 200, 208 n.23
2.394-9: 204
2.397: 204, 210 n.58
2.429ff.: 199-211
2.429-33: 200-1
2.430: 201, 209 n.24
2.450: 208 n.19
3.347: 206
3.430.9-18 (Dindorf): 209 n.34
3.645-58: 205
3.677: 208 n.19
23.4: 209 n.36
26.63: 221-22
26.96: 205

Aristotle
Rhet.
1409A28-35: 110 n.18

Arrian
Cyn.
34-5.1: 190

Augustus
Res Ges.
1.1: 120 n.8
7: 34

Babylonian Talmud
bBerakhot
16b: 244 n.15
bTaanit
12a: 244 n.15

Cassius Dio
47.31: 157
50.8.6: 31
51.20.6-7: 27
54.3.4-7: 32
54.6.1-5: 32
54.7.3: 30
54.7.6:32
60.8.2: 239
68.5.4: 131
69.3.1: 174
69:4.6: 173
69.10.2: 181-82, 195 n.53
69.11.1: 176, 193 n.20
72.36: 219-20
73.23: 220

Chariton
Call.
1.1.2: 228

Cicero
Leg.
  2.5: 223

Cornelius Nepos
Prooem.
  6-7: 81

Demosthenes
  22.13: 36

Dio Chrysostom
  32.1: 159, 170 n.5
  32.4: 159, 170 n.5
  32.12: 158-59
  32.24: 161-62
  34: 156-71
  34.5: 159
  34.5-6: 157-58
  34.6: 162, 169
  34.10-11: 163
  34.12-13: 163-64
  34.23: 157, 170 n.2
  34.25: 168
  34.45: 171 n.14
  34.46: 167
  34.48: 168

Diogenes Laertius
  6.99: 234

Dionysius of Halicarnassus
Ant. Rom.
  2.16: 149
  2.35: 149
  2.45: 150
  8.39: 152
  8.51: 152
  8.54: 153

Euripides
Alc.
  8: 103

  570-77: 103
Hipp.
  1-6: 106
  347-8: 102
  415: 101
  522: 101, 108 n.1
  530-4: 106
  535-64: 108

FGrH
  150 FF30-48: 219
  199 F1: 243 n.11

Fronto
  1.141.3 (Haines): 176, 193 n.25
  2.102.2 (Haines): 177, 194 n.27

Heliodorus
Aeth.
  1.2.1-2: 228
  10.41.3: 234

Herodian
  1.1.5: 220
  1.2.5: 220

Hesiod
Th.
  131: 101
  188-98: 101
  440: 101
Op.
  618: 101
  722: 108 n.2

Homer
Il.
  3.156-60: 109 n.7
  5.837-9: 104
  6.161: 105
  16.748: 101

Inscriptions and related
AE 1977
  204: 80 n. 48
Bodl. Grabianus
  30.f.33: 176, 193 n.23
Bühler 1978
  55-60: 176, 193 n.23
CIL I^2
  692: 59
CIL X
  7082: 72
  7010: 72
  7129: 72
  7181: 80 n.54
  8314: 72, 78 n.18
  8315: 72
CIL XII
  1122: 181-82
IG II^2
  3173: 25
  3250: 35-36
  3286: 43
  3287: 43
  3311: 42
  3312: 42
  3314: 42
  3322: 42
  5034: 33
  5035 III 253-H II c: 43, 52
  5097: 34
  5114: 33
  5185 A (III 401): 49
  5185 B (III 402): 49
IG VII
  1828: 180-81
IG XIV
  34: 71-2, 78 n.9
  45: 73, 78 n. 21
  116: 78 n.8
  177: 78 n.8
  1085: 187
  1089: 174, 192 n.13

1097.8: 176-77, 193 n.26
2139: 183

IGR III
   209: 43

EE
   8.694: 72

IEphesos
   1539: 172, 191 n.2

NSc 1893
   298 n. 76: 77

NSc 1895
   492 n. 185: 77

NSc 1901
   344: 72

NSc 1907
   777 n.43: 76

NSc 1912
   299(i): 72

NSc 1915
   203(ii): 72
   206: 72

NSc 1920
   317 fig. 10: 72

NSc 1947
   189-91nn. 1-6 and 9: 75

SEG XXVI
   1215: 189

Isocrates
Antid.
   30: 201
   277: 208 n.19

Josephus
AJ
   14.403: 236
   15.342-3: 238
   15.373: 237
   17.320: 240
   20.169: 235, 243 n.13
   20.100: 236

BJ
   1.1-17: 241
   1.181: 136
   1.282: 237
   1.284: 237
   1.360: 244 n.25
   2.97: 240
   2.308: 239
   4.13: 242
   4.37-8: 242

Juvenal
   1.130: 236
   3.1-3: 137

Livy
   1.11-13: 150
   2.40: 153

Lucan
   4.490-1: 122 n.28
   4.502-6: 116-17
   5.262-7: 118
   5.274-7: 119
   5.284-5: 119
   5.289-90: 115
   5.310-11: 119
   5.340-43: 115-16
   5.360-4: 119
   5.385-6: 118
   7.257-8: 122 n.29
   7.454-9: 118
   7.760-7: 117

Macrobius
   2.4.11: 238

Mimnermus
   1.3 (West): 105-6

Moschus
   2.93-100: 103-4
   2. 115: 104

New Testament
Acta
   21.37-39: 235
   22.3: 235
   22.25-28: 235

2 Cor.
   11.22: 235, 243 n.15

Mt.
   15.22: 234

Phil.
   3.5: 235, 243 n.15

Ro.
   11.1: 235, 243 n.15

OGIS
   414: 238

Old Testament and Apocrypha
Jer.
   11.18: 161, 170 n.8

1 Macc.
   8.18: 241

2 Macc.
   4.13: 241
   6.8: 241
   11.2: 141
   13.2: 241
   14.38: 241

Ovid
Ars Am.
   I.177-82: 35

PLF
   31.10: 105-6
   130.2: 102

PLM
   4.102: 191 n.1

Pausanias
    2.34.1: 68
    5.20.9-10: 26
    6.24.10: 26

Philo
In Flacc.
    39: 238, 245 n.34

Philostratus
VS
    480-1: 159
    570f.: 202
    614: 203
    622f.: 202
    628: 234

Plato
Ap.
    31c-d: 201
Ep.
    7: 127
Grg.
    521d: 201
Leg.
    745b: 35
    821d: 35
Phaedr.
    255D8-E1: 109 n.3
Plt.
    259a-b: 201
Prt.
    320c-23a: 204
Symp.
    180C6ff.: 109 n.3

Pliny the Younger
Ep. Tra.
    10.33-4: 171 n.9
    10.77: 165-66
    10.78: 165-66
    10.117: 171 n.12

Plutarch
Mor.
  Amat.
    760d: 106
  An. an Corp. Aff.
    501e-502a: 218
  Conjug. Praec.
    140d: 82
    145b: 81-2
  Cons. ad Ux.
    609c-d: 82
  De Pyth. Or.
    408b-c: 218
  De Tranq. Anim.
    469d: 125
    470c: 124
    470f: 125
    471e: 125
    474c: 125
  Praec. Ger. Rep.
    798b: 125, 126
    798c: 126
    798f: 134 n.39
    813e: 125
    813f: 126
    814 a-c: 223
    814d-e: 133 n.16, 139, 141 n.5
    816a: 135 n.47
    816c: 131
    825c-d: 133 n.19
  Rom. Apoph.
    207f: 30
Vit.
  Aem.
    1.5: 218
  Alex.
    5.7-8.5: 127
  Ant.
    4.7-9: 124
  Caes.
    7: 145
    14: 148

  Cat. Mai.
    8: 143
    17: 143
    20: 143
    24: 143
  Cat. Min.
    25: 148
    30: 148
    52: 148
  Cic.
    1: 144
    20: 148
  Comp. Sol.-Publ.
    1-4: 128
  Cor.
    4: 154-55
    33-4: 154
  Dem.
    1-3: 136-37
    1.3: 126
    3.4: 127
  Galba
    1.6.9: 131
    1.8: 130
  Luc.
    1: 144
  Lyc.
    31.1-3: 127
  Mar.
    45.12: 125
    46.2: 125
  Nic.
    1.1: 139
  Per.
    4-6: 127
    12.6: 135 n.45
  Pomp.
    24.11-13: 132 n.10
    44: 148
  Publ.
    10: 128
    15.3-6: 128
  Rom.
    13: 124

14: 151
19: 151
Sert.
  2: 144
Sol.
  27.2-4: 128
Ti. Gracch.
  1-3: 129
  7,3-10.6: 129
  7.7: 132
  11.4: 129, 134 n.36
  12.6-17.5: 129-30
Tim.
  36.3: 173

Pseudo-Plutarch
Consol. ad Apoll.
  9.106b: 175

Polyaenus
Strat.
  1.1: 214
  1.8-12: 214
  1.13: 213
  7. Pref.: 214
  7.41: 214

Polybius
  27.15.4-5: 238

Porphyrius
Chr.
  frg.28: 235

Quintilian
  10.1.53: 173, 192 n.6

SHA
Hadr.
  15.13: 179
  16.2: 176, 193 n.24
  16.3-4: 177-78, 194 n.33
  16.6: 172
  25.9: 184-85, 196 n.61

Seneca
Ep.
  49.5: 109 n.5
Phaed.
  274-375: 102-10

Sophocles
Ant.
  781-800: 107

Suetonius
Aug.
  85: 173-74
  92: 31

Tib.
  59.1: 112

TGF
  p. 917: 106
  p. 329: 106

Tacitus
Ann.
  15.28: 236
Hist.
  1.11.1: 136

Theocritus
  7.96: 102

Velleius Paterculus
  2.91.2: 32
  2.114.1-2: 114-15
  2.114.3: 115
  2.115.5: 113-14

Vitruvius
De Arch.
  6.7.: 81, 91

Xenophon of Ephesus
Eph.
  1.2.5-8: 228